/ PUBLIC LIBRARIES

The Au Pair and Nanny's Guide

TO WORKING ABROAD

Susan Griffith & Sharon Legg

Published by Vacation Work, 9 Park End Street, Oxford

First published 1989

Second edition 1993

Third edition 1997

*The Au Pair & Nanny's Guide
to Working Abroad*

by Susan Griffith & Sharon Legg

Copyright @ Vacation-Work 1997

ISBN 1 85458 169 4 (hardback)
ISBN 1 85458 168 6 (softback)

No part of this publication may be reproduced or transmitted
in any form or by any means without the prior
written permission of the publisher

Publicity: Roger Musker

Cover Design by
Miller Craig & Cocking Design Partnership

Illustrations by John Taylor & Lorraine White

Imageset and Printed by **Unwin Brothers Ltd,** Old Woking, Surrey

Contents

PART I INTRODUCTION

INTRODUCTION   **8**
   Au Pairs, Nannies and Mother's Helps   8
   Origins of the Au Pair System   10
   Who is Eligible? — Male Au Pairs — North American Applicants — What Families are looking for   10
   Motives for Working with Children   16
   Deciding to Go — Where should you go?   17
   Red Tape — Regulations   19
   Training and Experience — NNEB — Other Qualifications   21
   Duties, Rewards & Risks   25

FINDING A JOB   **29**
   Agencies — Pros and Cons — Choosing an Agency — Agency Procedures   29
   Advertisements — *The Lady* — Other Publications   35
   Word of Mouth   38
   Job-hunting Abroad   38
   Interviews — Preparing for the Interview —Conducting Yourself at Interview   38

PREPARATION   **41**
   Contracts — Nannies — Au Pairs   42
   Health and Insurance   43
   Travel   46
   What to Take — Money —Packing   47
   While You're Waiting — Keeping in Touch —Last Minute Panics   49

PROBLEMS AND HOW TO COPE   **51**
   Initial Traumas — Breaking the Ice — Your First Day — Coping with the Previous Nanny — Winning the Children Over — Culture Shock — Homesickness   51
   Problems with Children — Resentment in Children — Crying — Disobedience — Discipline — Tantrums — Eating Problems — Food Allergies — Sleeping and Dreaming — Toilet Training — Bedwetting   57
   Problems with Parents – Pay and Time Off — Requesting a Pay Rise — Interference with your Social Life — Unrealistic Expectations — Maternal Resentment and Jealousy —Employee Resentment —Conflict over Discipline —Flirtatious Fathers — Marital Problems   66
   Coping with a New Arrival   74

LEISURE TIME AND DEPARTURE 79
  Creating a Social Life — Meeting Other Au Pairs/Nannies — Meeting
  Expatriates — Meeting the Locals 79
  Learning a Language — Preparation — Language Courses Abroad 82
  Time Off — Your First Day Off — Excursions and Activities —
  Departure 83

PART II COUNTRY BY COUNTRY GUIDE

Australasia	90	Italy	134
Austria	94	Netherlands	141
Belgium & Luxembourg	98	Scandinavia	145
Canada	102	Spain & Portugal	150
France	107	Switzerland	157
Germany	116	Turkey	161
Greece	122	United Kingdom	163
Ireland	128	USA	170
Israel	130	Rest of the World	180

PART III DIRECTORY OF AGENCIES 183

PART IV APPENDICES

Appendix 1 — SAFETY IN THE HOME 291
  Suffocation — Poisoning — Burns — Other Dangers 291
  First Aid — Asthma — Bites — Burns and Scalds — Choking - Concussion
  — Cuts and Bruises — Dislocation — Drowning — Emergency Procedures/
  Resuscitation — Fits — Foreign Bodies — Fractures — Hysteria — Insect
  Stings — Nose Bleeds — Poisoning — Splinters — Sprains —
  Suffocation 292
Appendix 2 — CHILDHOOD AILMENTS 298
  General Ailments — Chicken Pox — Colds — Constipation — Coughs and
  Sore Throats — Croup — Diarrhoea — Earache — Eczema — Head-lice —
  Stomach Pains — Teething or Toothache — Vomiting 298
  General Care During Sickness 301
Appendix 3 — COOKING FOR CHILDREN 303
Appendix 4 — FUN AND GAMES 313
Appendix 5 — EMBASSIES/CONSULATES
              in London and Washington 318
Appendix 6 — CURRENCY CONVERSION CHART 319

Preface

The term au pair was coined exactly a century ago in 1897. Roughly translated 'on equal terms,' it was originally used on the continent to describe an exchange of English lessons for French or German ones. Early on, however, the emphasis shifted to become a work-for-keep arrangement which included domestic duties and childcare. In practice, the relationship between au pair and host family nowadays is seldom one of equality but still has the potential for bringing enormous rewards.

Au pairing and nannying abroad can be a wonderful experience: you get to travel, to experience family life in a foreign environment and, assuming you find sympathetic hosts, to learn the language and experience a foreign culture. You'll learn a great deal about children and their upbringing, which will stand you in good stead if you start a family (or put you off the idea forever!)

The image of the starched nanny wheeling an enormous perambulator has been replaced by a more informal yet professional employee. Increasingly it is the norm rather than the exception for mothers to combine a career with having a family, and one of the ways of making this possible is to have a live-in child-carer. Teachers, social workers, musicians and journalists need an au pair or nanny just as often as movie stars, merchant bankers and members of the Royal Family.

The demand for live-in helpers is enormous and increasing all the time, not only in Britain and Europe but in North America and Australasia. This, combined with the comparative ease with which au pairs can get official permission to work, makes working with families one of the easiest ways of arranging to live and work abroad.

Yet in some ways the arrangement is a minefield, in which the potential for disaster is as great as the potential for success. Family placements are to some extent a gamble (on both sides), especially for au pairs who normally commit themselves to living for some months with people they have not had a change to meet. The many ways of reducing the risks are rehearsed in the pages which follow. A well-informed au pair or nanny has a much better chance of claiming her (or his) rights as well as fulfilling her responsibilities.

This book will help you to decide whether the demanding life of an au pair or nanny is for you. It offers advice on choosing the destination which will suit you best, and draws upon the experiences of many others to help you overcome domestic difficulties and make the most of your stay. In short, *The Au Pair & Nanny's Guide to Working Abroad* aims to maximize your chances of being a nanny or au pair on equal terms.

Susan Griffith
May 1997

Acknowledgments

This new revised edition of *The Au Pair & Nanny's Guide to Working Abroad* would not have been possible without the assistance of the many women — and a handful of men — who shared with us their experiences as live-in childcarers. The authors wish to express their gratitude to all those who enlivened our task with their vivid descriptions of their charges, whether beastly or angelic, and of their employers from Islington to Istanbul. As well as all the people who helped with the two previous editions, some of whose names appear throughout these pages, we would like to thank those who have made contributions since the last edition:

Helen Aspinall, Zoë Bremer, Ilke Cave, Laurence Chérifat, Angie Copley, Iain Croker, Shreen Imam, Embré Joubert, Maree Lakey, Camilla Lambert, Corinne Larrieu, Michelle Lindsay, Joanne Moscrop, Camilla Preeston, K. Rounce, Julia Stanton, Matt Tomlinson, Bianca Tonkin, Mig Urquhart, L. E. Wallace and Jill Weseman.

Also, Sharon Legg would like to thank the families for whom she enjoyed working: the Wolf family, the O'Hallorans and *la famille* Decoster.

Finally, our thanks are due to Dr. Philippa Swan for checking the medical accuracy of the text.

The author and publishers have every reason to believe in the accuracy of the information given in this book and the authenticity and correct practices of all organisations, companies, agencies etc. mentioned: however, situations may change and telephone numbers, visa requirements, exchange rates etc. can alter, and readers are strongly advised to check facts and credentials for themselves. Readers are invited to write to the authors c/o Vacation Work, 9 Park End Street, Oxford OX1 1HJ, with any new stories of their experiences; those whose contributions are used will be sent a free copy of the next edition.

PART I

Au Pairs, Nannies & Mothers' Helps

Working with Children
Deciding to Go
Finding a Job
Preparation
Problems and How to Cope
Leisure Time & Departure

Introduction

AU PAIRS, NANNIES AND MOTHER'S HELPS

The terms au pair, mother's help and nanny are often applied rather loosely, so it is worth spending some time clarifying the varying roles. All are primarily live-in jobs, concerned with tending to the needs of children, contributing to their emotional and mental development and imposing discipline when necessary.

Nannies are usually thought of as having some formal training, in particular the NNEB (National Nursery Examination Board) certificate. There are however 'nanny' positions open to women who have no paper qualifications but who have substantial experience of working with children. Nannies have sole charge of the children and are responsible for chores directly relating to them. They usually live in and command a full-time salary, since they will be on duty around the clock except on one or two days off per week. Daily nannying (i.e. live-out) is also a possibility after you have gained considerable experience. Salaries vary enormously at this senior level but are seldom less than £120 per week (or the equivalent abroad), and occasionally stretch up to £300; the average is £150.

Mother's helps will sometimes have sole charge but more usually will work alongside the parents, usually the mother. They will assist wherever necessary and be expected to perform a variety of tasks, not only related to the children but also to the household generally, including housework and/or cooking. They may be paid on a par with a trained nanny, but usually get less; £70-£100 per week is the standard range. The hours are normally eight hours a day, five and a half or six days a week plus several evenings of babysitting.

Au pairs are in a different category, though many of their duties overlap with those of a mother's help. The official purpose of the arrangement is to provide single women and men aged 18-27 with the chance to study a foreign language and culture while living as part of a family. Technically that means it is not possible to be an au pair in your own country or in one whose language you share, though there are exceptions, as in the case of the Au Pair in America scheme which is open only to English-speakers. Au pairs are meant to work for no more than 25 hours a week over five days, plus two evenings of babysitting, and get pocket money of not less than £35 a week in most countries. Unlike nannies and mother's helps, au pairs do not sign a contract since the arrangement is an informal one. Au pairs should be treated more like family members than employees. An au pair has much less responsibility for the welfare of the children than does a nanny, and is not normally expected to take sole charge of a young child.

Holiday au pairs usually work from July to September and accompany the family on their holidays. Since the children are out of school, there may be less free time than during the academic year and often no chance to study a language. Otherwise the same rules should apply as for ordinary au pairing.

These are in broad outline the kinds of live-in childcare positions with which this book is concerned. The kinds of arrangement into which families and live-in helpers settle are in fact infinite, and many of the guidelines and definitions set out in the pages which follow are open to interpretation and subject to all kinds of permutation. Two common variations are the demi pair and au pair plus. The **demi pair** works a maximum of three hours a day, plus some babysitting, in exchange for £20-£25 a week. The **au pair plus** merges with the mother's help since she is often required by households with two working parents who are away from home the whole day but she usually gets paid less than a mother's help because she may not have had much childcare experience. The average weekly pay in this case is £45-£50.

All of these definitions can very easily become blurred, for example a number of jobs advertised as nannying positions are really mother's help jobs in disguise, i.e. there is more housekeeping than would normally be involved in a nannying job. A classic example of the casualness with which these terms are confused appeared in the press coverage of the tragic death of a nine-month old baby in Boston in the care of the British au pair Louise Woodward in 1997. The term nanny was frequently used, whereas the accused 18 year old was a participant on one of the au pair programmes to the USA. She was unqualified and inexperienced and arguably should not have been permitted to take sole charge of a baby.

To simplify matters, the term 'au pair' is used most often throughout, since this book is aimed primarily at those who want to go abroad to work. But much of what is said about au pairing is equally relevant to nannying either in the UK or abroad.

ORIGINS OF THE AU PAIR SYSTEM

The first recorded use of the word 'au pair', which means literally 'on equal terms' in French, is in 1897 in the *Girl's Own Paper*. It refers to English girls teaching their language in France in exchange for lessons in French. But soon the emphasis altered, and caring for children became the central duty of au pairs rather than teaching. Since then a great deal of grandiloquent prose and highflown sentiments have been spouted on the subject of au pairing, describing it as the ideal way to experience a foreign culture from the inside, learn a language, etc. You would almost think that the only motive which families have in taking on an au pair is to help her appreciate their culture and learn their language. In fact it is usually a case of a harassed mother looking for a cheap home help. Between these two contradictory viewpoints, however, there is plenty of scope for successful and satisfying employer/employee relationships from which both parties benefit in the ways that are intended by the system.

The high moral line on au pairing, which views it as a road to self-improvement, is not a recent import. On the continent the system has its origins in Switzerland at the end of the last century when, for the first time, large numbers of single young women were moving away from home to take up jobs in the cities. The church and other groups who saw themselves as moral guardians anticipated that a decline in morals would accompany this independence, so they encouraged young women to live and work in families, not only for the sake of their morals, but so that they could acquire useful household skills. The language learning element came a little later, since German-speaking Swiss girls would be placed in French-speaking households, where they could learn Switzerland's second language.

The UK began au pair exchanges with Switzerland in the early 1920s, then with Austria in 1930. After World War II the number of participating countries and au pairs rose dramatically, so that today there are hundreds of thousands of au pairs in Europe. It is estimated that there are over 20,000 in Greater London alone. Although it began as a peculiarly European notion, it has been taken up in the USA as well and, more recently, in Australia. It is a concept which, although old-fashioned in many ways, is capable of shifting and adapting to modern times and of reflecting the attitudes of contemporary society.

WHO IS ELIGIBLE?

The greatest attraction of looking after children for many is that it is one of the easiest ways to fix up work abroad, since the demand is so great. It has been estimated that about half of all women with children in industrialised nations work full or part time. Often the qualifications for being hired by these working mothers are minimal and it is not unusual for young women aged barely 18 who have never worked and who have no experience with children beyond occasional babysitting to be successfully placed in a foreign household. Although agencies and families almost always state that they *prefer* au pair candidates to have had some practical experience of looking after children, most are prepared to consider anyone with a genuine liking for children, a positive attitude towards domesticity and a reasonably mature character. Most will require at least one reference which simply testifies to your reliability and common sense.

The second great advantage of au pairing over other jobs abroad, is that often it is easier to make your status legal. Work permits are notoriously difficult to get for 'proper jobs' in most countries of the world, but often exceptions are made for live-in help (see the section on *Red Tape* below).

The minimum age can be a stumblingblock for some school leavers who are not yet 18. The majority of agencies prefer not to accept applications from candidates younger than 18, as the Australian Camilla Preeston (resident in Hong Kong) discovered:

> *I had decided even before I had finished school that I would take a year off between school and university, and au pairing seemed like the perfect way to do this. Being seventeen and a half made things much more difficult in the beginning though. I sent off endless letters to agencies in Britain and overseas but most flatly replied that I was too young, though a couple said that they would try anyway. I eventually had success with a Canadian agency who were happy to help me find a job in France. The reason they didn't turn me away may have been because the fee they levy is paid upfront before a family is found (though they claim to have placed all applicants to date). By the time they had found me a family in Calais, four months of my year off had already gone by and I was almost ready to give up. I immediately accepted the offer, perhaps a little hastily. However, had I refused it, I might not have found another family willing to accept me due to my age, and it was the first family offer I had received in the four months I had been trying.*

Obviously Camilla's youth did not prevent her from coping with what turned out to be a difficult situation, where she was expected to accept a lot of responsibility for the children (including a newborn baby) and the running of the household, while the mother was away for five days and two nights a week.

Male Applicants

One very important category of applicant will not find the job hunt at all easy. Despite the progress made over the past couple of decades in trying to dismantle sexist stereotypes, it is still very difficult for men to arrange family placements. For once, the employment situation is reversed; normally it is women who must prove that they are better than men when competing for the same kind of job. But just to gain equal footing in childcare, men must have excellent references and plenty of experience. Many agencies refuse point-blank to register men simply because they are so rarely asked by families to supply a male au pair or nanny that it is not worth their while to process applications from males. According to a recent press article, one experienced male nanny was turned down by 59 agencies before he was taken on and placed by a Surrey agency. In conservative societies abroad, the situation is even worse, as the owner of Hilma's Agency in Israel describes:

> *It is almost impossible for males here. We had one, many years ago, who was a big success (he was great, in size as well as character), the family not very conventional and it was just fantastic. Years later he came to Israel and introduced us to his fiancée and again later he came with his wife and children. Most families do not want to think even about having a male. They tell you, 'What would the neighbours think?' or 'I could never ask him to do my laundry'.*

Before February 1993, males were prohibited by law from becoming au pairs in the UK, even though this contravened EU Equal Treatment Directives. Due to heavy lobbying by youth exchange organisations, equal rights campaigners and Euro-MPs, the legislation was changed so that the definition of au pair in

Britain no longer specifies gender, only age and nationality. A high percentage of au pair applications from Central Europe (mainly Hungary, Czech Republic and Slovakia) is now from males, and some agencies specialising in placing East European au pairs with British families aim to place about 10% males.

Hello! I'm the new au pair

But no legislation can dismantle prejudice overnight. Men who reply to au pair/nanny adverts are often met with bemusement and, in some cases, hostility. Even broad-minded parents, who buy the sort of children's books which show fathers ironing and cooking, are often unreceptive to the idea of a male au pair. High profile cases of paedophiles working in children's homes have frightened many potential employers. Male applicants must be prepared to be asked outright by agencies and at interviews with parents whether they are gay or child molesters. Such assumptions are very discouraging in these supposedly enlightened times.

So rare and exotic a breed are male nannies that they are likely to become featured in newspaper articles. An article in the *Sunday Times* entitled 'Male nannies taking over in the nursery' turned out to be about the same individual as one on the same subject which appeared in the *Daily Telegraph* two and a half years later. Simon Willis, an Australian, encountered incredulity when he tried to get a job looking after children in London. He was asked by the woman who had placed the advertisement on a notice board at London University whether he was replying on behalf of his girlfriend. He had to employ all his male wiles and powers of persuasion just to arrange an interview. But he did get the job and the little girl instantly adored him.

But the situation is very slowly improving. Colleges offering the NNEB course report that they are receiving a few applications from men whereas a few years ago they received none at all. Even the exclusive Norland College in Berkshire has interviewed male applicants. Male au pairs are not so uncommon in some countries, including France where Ian Croker au paired for a year:

As a male au pair, I accept that I may be a rarity though the picture is not quite as gloomy as many men think. Certainly in France, there are quite a few male au pairs (four in my village near Fontainebleau alone). In my experience the boys tend to get placed in families with a lot of energetic children or families that have had problems with a high turnover of au pairs. My agency claims that the boys they have placed have had fewer problems with homesickness and therefore more staying power. Parents are increasingly aware of the benefits of having a boy, and many feel that their children are safer when out with a guy, especially in the city. Two friends of mine (both guys) are also au pairs and none of us has ever experienced any ribbing from our family or friends. There certainly are narrow-minded people around, and I was rejected by several families purely on grounds of gender. But then applicants are turned down all the time because of their colour, religion or just on the grounds of their passport photo.

The best chance which young men have of fixing up a live-in position is to emphasise their willingness to teach the children English. Persistent sexism means that any men who do manage to find a family willing to take them on will probably find that they are not expected to do those domestic chores which their female counterparts would unthinkingly be given. Instead they will be sent to the local park with the kids and a football. Steve Ducker had a marvellous time in Rome. His duties extended no further than coaching the 12-year-old boy in English after school and amusing him by taking him on little expeditions. In exchange for this he had a luxurious flat to himself and had plenty of free time in which to explore Rome and environs.

North American Applicants

Many North Americans are eager to learn the language and absorb the culture of European countries, and indeed some do become au pairs, though the term is not widely known in the US and Canada. The red tape is more difficult for them than for au pairs from European countries, however they are rarely prohibited from spending six months or a year working with families.

The following agencies with entries in the Directory at the end of this book all have au pair programmes in Europe for Americans:

Accord Cultural Exchange, 750 La Playa, San Francisco, CA 94121 (415-386-6203/fax 415-386-0240). Au pairs sent to France, Germany, Spain, Austria and Italy. Fee for year-long placement is $1,800; summer placement fee is $750.

Alliances Abroad, 2830 Alameda, San Francisco, CA 94103 (fax 415-621-1609; e-mail AllianceA@aol.com). Au pairs placed in Austria, France, Spain, Germany, Finland, Italy, Netherlands, Switzerland, Ireland, England and Canada. Fee is $700.

American Institute for Foreign Study, 102 Greenwich Ave, Greenwich, CT

06830 (1-800-727-AIFS/727-2437; e-mail: info @aifs.org,www.aifs.org). Au pair and study placements in France (Riviera and Paris), Spain (Granada) and Germany (Cologne). Fee of $2,795 for one semester (including flight), $4,295 for one academic year.

Au Pair in Europe, PO Box 68056 Blakely Postal Outlet, Hamilton, Ontario, Canada L8M 3M7 (905-545-6305/fax 905-544-4121). Au pairs placed in 18 countries including most western European countries plus Australia and Bermuda. Registration fee is charged. Enquiries to the Directors, Corinne and John Prince.

AuPair Homestay, World Learning Inc, 1015 15th St NW, Suite 750, Washington, DC 20005 (202-408-5380/fax 202-408-5397). Sends au pairs of both sexes to Britain, France, Germany, Iceland, Finland, Netherlands, Norway, Switzerland and Argentina for 3-12 months. Programme fee is $775 which includes programme support throughout.

If something goes wrong report it at once

InterExchange Inc., 161 Sixth Avenue, New York, NY 10013 (212-924-0446/fax 212-924-0575. Small number of au pairs aged 18-25 sent to Austria, Finland, Netherlands, Italy, Norway and Spain. Enquiries to Casey Slamin.

WISE (Worldwide Internships & Service Education), 303 South Craig St, Suite 202, Pittsburgh, PA 15213 (412-681-8120/fax 412-681-8187). Au pairs placed in Finland, France, Netherlands, Switzerland and Germany. Fee is $600. Enquiries to the Administrator, Linda Greenberg.

The British Home Office does not allow Americans to become au pairs in Britain on the principle that they share a common language. But there are ways around this for students who are eligible to apply for a 'blue card' from the Council on International Educational Exchange in New York (see chapter on Britain).

What families are looking for

An experienced au pair-cum-nanny claimed that to do the job well you need a 'sense of humour, the patience of a saint, a liking for children and the ability to leap over toy buildings in a single bound'. A love of children is an obvious prerequisite, and will cover up a multitude of sins. But other qualities which parents are looking for include a mature attitude to assuming responsibility. All parents want to feel confident about leaving their children in the care of another person, so they are looking for someone who is sensible, trustworthy, able to assume control, and who will report major mishaps as appropriate.

Families want somebody reliable who will drive carefully, remember to lock up and who will not invite guests indiscriminately into the home. They also expect to be able to trust you, not only with their valuables but with money for shopping, children's treats, etc. Any accidental damage in the home should immediately be admitted and an offer to replace it tendered. Most agencies will have encouraged families to take out liability insurance on their au pair or nanny's behalf which should cover major problems.

A cheerful disposition is greatly valued in family situations. All parents want a warm, healthy atmosphere in their homes, and are disconcerted by girls who are moody or volatile. A calm approach to life in general and little disasters in particular is what is called for. Live-in helpers who are reduced to hysteria by the sight of a spider or the squeak of a mouse won't do their charges any good.

Personal hygiene is just as important as making sure the children are kept clean and tidy. Parents resent it if you don't clean up after yourself, even if it is in your own room or on your day off, though none is likely to go as far as the wife of the Israeli Prime Minister Benjamin Netanyahu who was reputed to make her nanny wash her hands up to 300 times a day.

A large number of agencies and families absolutely prohibit smoking among their staff. If you are a smoker but serious about nannying, you might want to consider giving up. It is no good pretending that you never touch cigarettes when you obviously do. Even if you manage to bluff your way into a job, you will be climbing the walls once you start and are not able to smoke freely. If you try to do so secretly, there'll be all sorts of tell-tale signs. Non-smokers have very sensitive noses.

All children have a tendency to be early risers so it helps if you are too. If you are a night hawk by nature, you will have to exercise self-discipline and resign yourself to reorganising your habits and your social life.

MOTIVES FOR WORKING WITH CHILDREN

For many, a childcare job is simply an easy transition to the world of work and a way of acquiring a higher standard of living than is normally possible in one's early working years. In addition to your own room, you may have your own TV, the use of a car, and the chance to accompany the family on exotic holidays. There will be no need to worry about organising or paying for transport to work, finding accommodation and all the other headaches normally associated with starting a job in a new place.

In addition to the worthy goals of learning a language and experiencing a foreign culture, many people simply want to see the world and can't afford a straight holiday. Jane Newel was a trained nanny with two years residential experience in Britain when she noticed an advertisement in a national newspaper for an experienced nanny to care for a three-year-old girl:

It was January when I saw the job advertised and I was immediately interested because it involved a lot of travel. The winter blues were getting to me since I was extremely fed up with the British climate and longed for some sunshine.

Others are less concerned about the climate and are trying to escape from a difficult or boring situation at home. Pam Bain was a nurse who, at the age of 22, decided to become a mother's help in Paris.

I was engaged to be married at the time the job was offered, but I jumped at the chance because I felt uncertain about marriage and needed some time alone to think.

It can also be a very good way for young women to assert their independence from over-protective parents. Some au pairs learn to appreciate their own families more after intimate acquaintance with another family.

DECIDING TO GO

Some questions that you should be asking yourself when trying to decide whether or not to pursue the idea of working for a family abroad should be answered at a very early stage. You will probably be asked many of these questions on an agency questionnaire, so it is worth thinking them through ahead of time.

How much do you like kids? Jessie Lane, who spent an enjoyable three months au pairing in France, makes this point:

Before you go, ask yourself, do I really love children? If you can tolerate all their moods, good and bad, their rudeness, not to mention spite, then you will be all right.

If you have had very little exposure to young children, try to arrange some since you may discover that you lack the appropriate quantities of patience to take charge of them for an extended period. If you do have experience of children you might give some thought to what age group you most enjoy. Nannies often have a favourite age, though every stage brings its own pleasures and problems. For example, babies can be carted around on private errands and you may find that they adapt to you more quickly than older children. But you might also find their dependence restricting and miss not being able to hold a conversation. A job as an au pair with school age children (except in the summer holidays) allows much of the day free. The more flexible you can be the better; you don't want to limit your choices too much, for this will make it harder to find a suitable job.

How much are you prepared to put up with? Could you cope with a major loss of privacy? Au pairs are occasionally made to share a bedroom with the children, which can be a shock to anyone who is not used to sharing. How much do you value your free time? In theory au pairs work no more than five hours a day, whereas a mother's help position is more like a full-time job.

What kind of lifestyle are you seeking? If you have visions of working for a celebrity family, living in the lap of luxury in some sunny part of the world, you are almost certainly going to be disappointed. And even if such a situation did materialise the reality might not match the anticipation. Rich and celebrated families can be very demanding, and you may have to work extremely hard for your material perks, with little free time to enjoy them. Furthermore you are more likely to be treated like a servant than a family member. It all depends on the situation and on your own individual goals and aspirations.

Where should you go?

After you have sorted out the general issues, you can then concentrate on particulars, such as which country to work in. Assuming you have no predisposition to a certain country or language, it might be helpful to read through the country chapters in order to decide on a destination. In these chapters, we indulge in gross generalisations such as German standards of cleanliness are exceedingly high, American children are spoiled or British families tend to protect their privacy to the point of excluding their au pairs. Of course there are slovenly Germans, model American children and gregarious Brits. But we have made an attempt to provide something of the flavour of working in families around the world.

If you know someone who has visited or (preferably) lived in the country which interests you, try to find out from them what it is like, encouraging them to be as candid as possible in order to balance the inevitably rosy view conveyed in the tourist office literature (though of course this should be consulted too). Best of all of course is to meet someone who has worked in a family situation in that country. Experiences differ radically. Some say that Mediterranean people tend to be more demanding of their home helps, whereas others think that conditions are less favourable in northern Europe where you are more likely to be given heavy housework and not encouraged to engage in the relatively enjoyable task of speaking English to the children.

You will next have to establish whether or not it is feasible for you to work in your chosen country. As you will see from the country-by-country section of this book, certain countries require visas or work permits which may be difficult or time-consuming to obtain. Make enquiries of the agencies and of the appropriate embassy before you proceed.

Are you confident enough to commit yourself to go to a country far away or would you prefer to retain the possibility of getting home quickly if necessary?

What length of contract are you seeking? Except in the case of summer placements, most families expect you to stay at least six months, and contracts for the academic year (normally September to July) are also very common.

Do you satisfy the age requirements? Many agencies and families will not accept anyone less than eighteen (sometimes nineteen). A few countries like Belgium, the UK, Italy and Spain, allow seventeen year old au pairs, though they will often have to provide parental authorisation. Some countries are reluctant to supply temporary work permits to people over a certain age, for example working holiday visas for Australia are normally given to people 26 or under.

How good is your knowledge of the relevant language? How much interest or aptitude do you have for learning it? Could you cope in a situation where you were reduced largely to sign language?

Can you afford the travel expenses? Bear in mind that it is a condition of entry to some countries that you have a return ticket in your possession so make sure you can afford this.

Assuming you won't have much say in where exactly you are placed, are you willing to adapt to a lifestyle which may be completely unfamiliar to you, for example if you are from a big city how would you fare in a remote rural setting and vice versa?

How many children are you prepared to care for? You will not be paid five times as much for looking after five children instead of one, so you have to ask yourself whether or not you would be happy living with a large family. Very large families are a rarity these days, of course, and it is unusual to have more than two or three charges. You should also consider whether or not you are prepared to work for a pregnant mother. The new arrival could bring a drastic change in the work load, especially if the mother plans to return to work shortly afterwards. Also your relationship with the other children may become more vexed, if they become jealous of their new sibling.

Not all families who require nannies are harmoniously united. In fact, there is an increasing demand for home-helps as more and more marriages disintegrate. Would you be prepared to work for a one-parent family? This might involve greater responsibility for you, but you might be compensated for this by higher wages and more autonomy.

Are you prepared to work alongside the mother? If you enjoy taking on full responsibility and prefer to work alone, then obviously a sole-charge position is the best for you. It can be very trying to work with a mother, especially if you have very different views on how children should be raised. Too late Pam Bain realised how spoiled she had been by having been independent in her previous job:

> As a nurse, I had been used to my own routine and being left to get on with the job, so I found it difficult working so closely with the mother. It was hard to know when she wanted me around and when she didn't. She also seemed quite jealous of my relationship with the baby and that made things pretty strained between us at times.

On the other hand there is a certain advantage in being able to share the running of the home and to know that you are not completely alone if a crisis develops.

RED TAPE

The majority of countries in which au pairs wish to work are members of the European Union, i.e. the UK, Ireland, France, Germany, Netherlands, Belgium, Luxembourg, Austria, Denmark, Italy, Greece, Spain, Portugal, Finland and Sweden. Within the EU the red tape is minimal for all nationals of member states who wish to work, whether as au pairs, nannies, or in any capacity. Anyone intending to work should have a ten-year passport, which in Britain costs £18 for 32 pages and £27 for 48 pages. If you arrive in an EU country with the intention of working or staying longer than three months, you should apply for a residence permit at the local town hall or police station before the three months is up. To obtain a residence permit, you have to show adequate means of support, which should present no problems for au pairs.

In theory there is also free reciprocity of labour within the European Economic Area (EEA) which encompasses those Western European countries which have decided to stay outside the Union, viz. Norway, Iceland and Liechtenstein. Switzerland has obtained an exemption to the free reciprocity of labour and has its own rules for au pairs (see chapter). Outside Europe, legislation varies from country to country. Israel, Turkey, Canada, the United States and Australia all offer possibilities for au pairs, mother's helps and nannies. Although the red tape in North America is considerable, thousands of people do cross the Atlantic to work with families. The restrictions and procedures for obtaining the appropriate documentation are provided in each of the country chapters. Similarly there are schemes for Americans and Canadians to become au pairs in Europe (see previous section *Who is Eligible*).

Whereas au pairs can benefit from sympathetic legislation in many countries which exempt them from work permit requirements and taxation, nannies and mother's helps may find that they encounter more difficulties over the formalities. Full-time nannying is usually considered a 'proper job' which means that the normal immigration rules for foreign workers are invoked. For example, the rules recently changed in Britain, so that au pairs plus (i.e. those working virtually full-time) must now be EU nationals, whereas au pairs can be from a longer list of European countries (see chapter on the UK).

The usual practice is for the employer to apply to his or her local employment authority for permission to hire an alien. The family may have to prove that no national is available or qualified to undertake the job and that an earnest attempt has been made to fill the job with a local. Then the nanny must apply to the relevant embassy in her home country. It is most unusual to be allowed to apply for a work permit after arrival, though this rule does differ and the embassy literature should always be consulted.

This whole process is long-winded (usually taking several months) with no guarantee of success and is normally only worthwhile in highly paid permanent jobs. Since the line between au pairs, mother's helps and nannies is a woolly one, it may be possible for you to arrange a job appropriate to your qualifications without becoming too entangled in red tape.

Regulations

The Council of Europe based in Strasbourg drafted a European Agreement on Au Pair Placements in 1979, which is no longer in print. It sets out the rules which in an ideal world would govern all au pair placements. Nine countries have signed the agreement though only Denmark, France, Italy, Norway and Spain have ratified it, which is to say passed legislation which can enforce it. Britain is one of the countries which has refused to ratify it, giving as its reason the following:

> *The United Kingdom has not signed that agreement because of concern that it would require a binding contract between the au pair and the receiving family which would conflict with the traditional informal arrangements and shift the emphasis from an opportunity to learn English and something on the way of life here as a member of a family to actual employment. There would also be the question of policing the arrangements and the considerable resources this would involve.*

The terms of the agreement are as follows:
(1) An au pair placement consists of a temporary family stay during which young foreigners can perfect their knowledge of the language and culture of the host country.
(2) Au pair placements can be extended for up to a maximum of two years.
(3) The au pair should be between the ages of 17 and 30 (though individual countries are permitted to specify different minimum and maximum ages).
(4) The au pair must have a medical certificate signed by a doctor within the past three months, stating that the candidate is in good health.
(5) The rights and duties of the au pair and of the host family should be set out in a contract or any written agreement before the au pair leaves the country of residence.
(6) The agreement should indicate to what extent the au pair will participate in the life of the host family and guarantee a certain level of independence and privacy.
(7) The au pair should receive all meals and a private room.
(8) Enough free time should be allowed for the au pair to attend a language course, to benefit from the cultural opportunities of the country and to attend religious services if she so wishes. She must have at least one day off per week, of which at least one per month should be a Sunday.
(9) The au pair should be expected to work no more than five hours per day, excluding meal times.
(10) In countries in which there is no official mechanism for providing social security the host family is responsible for obtaining private health and accident insurance for the au pair.
(11) The au pair arrangement should be terminated with no less than two weeks' notice on either side.

These are no more than guidelines but, viewed as guidelines, they are useful. There are of course numerous cases of abuse, for example families neglect to arrange insurance or they ask their au pair to look after the children all day, instead of just for five hours. But at least the official criteria provide a basis for discussion between families and helpers.

Certain members of the European Parliament keep lobbying for the recognition of the status of au pairs, and for the outstanding member states to ratify this agreement. They also want the status of au pairs to be defined, and generally accepted standards of living and working conditions and educational and social security provisions to be set out. It calls for the setting up of state advisory and information structures for the benefit of au pairs and host families, one of whose functions would be to register au pair agencies and language schools.

One important step forward in the late 1990s is the establishment of several specialist regulatory associations for au pair agencies. The International Au Pair Association (IAPA) has as one of its goals to lobby governments to better regulate au pair agencies, for example by introducing a licensing scheme. The Association has established a Code of Conduct among its members to promote professionalism in a field which is sometimes associated with abuses and exploitation. Agencies can become members only after demonstrating their credentials over at least two years of operation, though it should be noted that standards of quality are not uniform among members. The IAPA also issues a Code of Conduct for au pairs and host families. The official address of the IAPA is c/o FIYTO (Federation of International Youth Tourism Organisations), Bredgade 25 H, 1260 Copenhagen K (tel 33 33 96 00/fax 33 93 96 76).

IFAA
International Fellowship of Au pair Agencies

- Professional Code of Practice for all members
- Independent Advice, Families and Au Pairs
- Telephone and fax advice for members
- Assistance for New Agencies in the UK and Overseas
- List of Agencies available upon request

- Information seeking service
- Certificate of membership
- Mediation service
- Regular updates on au pair guidelines and nationalities available to the au pair programme
- Only £100 per year membership fee (UK)
- Only £100 per year membership fee (Other)

For more information or advice please contact:

Claudine on Telephone/Fax: +44(0)1273 887431

Another association which is attempting to establish international standards for au pair agencies is the International Fellowship of Au Pair Agencies (IFAA) whose Director is Claudine Simpson: 48 Milton Drive, Southwick, West Sussex BN42 4NE (tel/fax 01273 887431). It was founded in 1995 in response to the abolition of the requirement for au pair and nanny agencies to be licensed by the Department of Employment. At the time of writing the IFAA had 18 members, mostly in the UK. The IFAA gives its member agencies information on how to advertise free of charge in Hungary, the Czech Republic, Italy and Belgium as well as in the UK.

But there are still a great many privately run agencies which are not members of any regulating body. Some are excellent, providing a service equal to or better than the established agencies brandishing the logo of an international association. Others are not. It will be a long time before au pairs will be protected by formal legislation in whatever country they choose to work.

TRAINING AND EXPERIENCE

Women who are considering childcare as a career should investigate enrolling in a suitable training course. Although a paper qualification is not a prerequisite for employment as a nanny, increasingly it helps candidates in the job hunt (as well as in doing the job).

The range of childcare courses available is diverse. Many courses are provided locally to trainees through colleges of further education and will require attendance in day or block release format. Alternatively there are open learning courses available through some colleges and independent organisations where trainees can pursue the Childcare National Vocational Qualification (NVQ) which uses the experience gained in the workplace (including private employers) supported by portfolios produced by trainees in their free time. These courses will require on-site assessment visits to verify the trainee's competence.

Examples of organisations which oversee NVQs at levels 2 and 3 are Springboard Bromley at Bromley College, Rookery Lane, Bromley, Kent BR2 8HE (0181-462 1222) and Lucy Clayton Courses, 4 Cornwall Gardens, London SW7 4AJ (0171-581 0024). A one-term intensive nursery training course at the latter institute costs £1,100 while a four-week summer course costs £440. They also offer the new one-year Certificate in Child Care and Education validated by CACHE (see below) at a cost of £1,000 and a one-week babysitting course for £175. The nanny agency *Pat-a-Cake* supplies an intensive training course for

---

SPRINGBOARD BROMLEY
Training Opportunities Training Solutions

Do you need a Child Care Qualification?

CHILD CARE & EDUCATION N.V.Q. LEVEL 2 & 3

- Open learning
- Full or part time
- Assessor training
- TDLB Awards (incl. D32/33/34)

Contact Maxine or Margaret on 0181 462-1222
(-0094 fax) to discuss your Personal Training Plan.
Financially assisted places available, phone for details.

girls wishing to travel abroad which includes a first aid and childcare certificate.

NNEB

The Rolls Royce of qualifications is the NNEB, which stands for National Nursery Examination Board. The Board was replaced a couple of years ago by CACHE (Council for Awards in Children's Care and Education), though the Diploma in Nursery Nursing retains the prestigious name NNEB. It is the most widely recognised qualification and is taught as a two-year diploma course at hundreds of local authority colleges and several private ones throughout Britain. CACHE can send you a list of centres offering the diploma; write to CACHE at 8 Chequer St, St. Albans, Herts. AL1 3XZ; 01727 847636/Publications Department: 01727 810818). Many courses are over-subscribed, so early application is advised.

Three private residential nanny colleges offering the NNEB Diploma course in England are:

Norland College, Denford Park, Hungerford, Berks. RG17 0PQ. Tel: 01488 682252.
Chiltern Nursery Training College, 16 Peppard Road, Caversham, Berks. RG4 8LA. Tel: 0118-947 1847.
Princess Christian College, 26 Wilbraham Road, Fallowfield, Manchester M14 6JX. Tel: 0161-224 4560.

All three colleges charge very high fees (e.g. upwards of £10,000); write for their prospectuses if interested.

CACHE also administers other childcare qualifications such as the CCE Certificate (Child Care and Education), ADCE (Advanced Diploma in Child Care and Education) and also NVQs.

Other Qualifications

Anyone considering enrolling in a childcare course should make sure that the qualification for which they intend to study will be respected by potential employers and agencies. Other diplomas such as those granted by BTEC and City & Guilds are not as widely recognised as the NNEB though their proponents maintain that they are demanding courses.

BTEC (Business & Technology Education Council, Central House, Upper Woburn Place, London WC1H 0HH; 0171-413 8400) offers a National Certificate and Diploma in Childhood Studies (Nursery Nursing). The Certificate course lasts one year (full-time) and is aimed at candidates with some experience whereas the Diploma lasts two years and is for school leavers with at least four GCSEs (minimum grade C). Fact Sheet (code Z-081-0) on Nursery Nursing National Programmes can be requested from SPS, BTEC Orders Department, Airfield Industrial Estate, Warboys, Huntingdon, Cambs. PE17 2SH. BTEC qualifications are available through about 200 colleges and are free to most students. Part-time fees are normally paid by the students employer.

The *NAMCW* (National Association of Maternal and Child Welfare, 40/42 Osnaburgh St, London NW1 3ND; 0171-383 4117) offers a one-year Certificate and two-year Diploma. These courses are available at some sixth form colleges and through employment training schemes. One well established provider of the NAMCW course is Isle College, Ramnoth Road, Wisbech, Cambridgeshire PE13 0HY. The work covered in the one-year full-time course prepares candidates to be assessed for an NVQ Level 2 in Child Care and Education if they wish.

Some other childcare training centres include:

Early Years Training, 42 Wibury Villas, Hove BN3 6GD. Tel: 01273 778775.

London Nursery Training College — 0171-372 3079. Offers childcare courses by correspondence.

Riverside Centre, Minton Lane, North Shields NE29 6DQ. Tel: 0191-200 5200.

Smart's Training, 20A St. James's Road, Kingston-upon-Thames. Tel: 0181-541 1384. 5 centres (London, Croydon, Heathrow, Kingston and Finchley) where Saturday sessions are organised for full-time childcarers wishing to obtain an NVQ in Childcare.

Surrey College School of Child Care, Administration Centre, Abbot House, Sydenham Road, Guildford, Surrey GU1 4RL. Tel: 01483 300057/565887.

City & Guilds (1 Giltspur St, London EC1A 9DD; 0171-294 2468) is the primary body for vocational assessment in the UK, including in the field of Health and Social Care. Of primary interest are the categories Child Care & Education, Child Care and Caring for Children (0-7).

There has been a boom in nanny schools in Australia. One of the best known is the Pam Arnold Centre (163 Halifax St, Adelaide, SA 5000; 08-8223 2502) which offers the Nationally Accredited Diploma in Child Care and Nanny Training full-time, part-time and by correspondence, and offers a placement service afterwards. They have a ten-week Au Pair course integrated in their two-year Diploma. Two alternatives in Australia are the Susan Rogan Nanny School in Melbourne (03-9670 2744/9670 9672) and the Dial-an-Angel Academy of Childcare in Canberra (36–38 Botany St, Phillip, ACT 2606; 282 7733).

Many successful nannies have landed high-paying jobs, including jobs with royalty, without the benefit of formal qualifications. Several agencies place inexperienced girls in homes in Britain as 'trainee nannies' at a fairly low wage, so that they can build up the necessary experience and references to move to more senior positions.

Wider experience of working with children than is possible when working in one family can be gained from working in nurseries, day care centres or looking after children for a tour operator. Increasingly nannies and kids' reps are employed by major UK tour companies to look after their clients' children, for example Cosmos Holidays (17 Homesdale Road, Bromley, Kent BR2 9LX; fax 0181-466 0802), Airtours (01706 909027) and Thomson Holidays (Greater London House, Hampstead Road, London NW1 7SD; 0171-387 9321). Camping tour operators like Eurocamp (PO Box 170, Liverpool L70 1ES) and Canvas Holidays (12 Abbey Park Place, Dunfermline, Fife KY12 7PD) hire young women (preferably with a childcare qualification) for their holiday centres on the Continent. Mark Warner (George House, 61-65 Kensington Church St, London W8 4BA) recruit a large number of child carers for their Mediterranean Watersports Clubs. Nannies must be qualified (NNEB, NVQ or equivalent). Often ski tour operators such as Simply Ski (Chiswick Gate, 598-608 Chiswick High Road, London W4 5RT) and Inghams/Bladon Lines (56-58 Putney High St, London SW15 1SF) offer childcare facilities to clients which are staffed by nannies.

Mark Warner

MEDITERRANEAN WATERSPORTS CLUBS

Seasonal Work April-October

We are looking for outgoing, conscientious and hardworking nannies to work in our exclusive Beachclub Hotels in Corsica, Italy, Sardinia, Greece and Turkey. Applicants must be NNEB/NVQ or equivalent qualified. We employ Nannies, Heads of Department and Childcare Managers.

Benefits Include

Childcare opportunities

- Wages from £45 per week
- Full board
- Medical insurance
- Travel expenses
- Use of watersports facilities
- Possibility of working in similar positions in Winter in the Alps

If you wish to be part of a successful team and would enjoy the challenge of a summer in the Mediterranean, please contact the Resorts Recruitment Manager, Mark Warner, George House, 61-65 Kensington Church Street, London W8 4BA. Telephone 0171 393 3179 (24 hour line).

We also have a varied number of Winter jobs in the Alps from November to May.

SUMMER IN THE MED

DUTIES

Au pairing and nannying can incorporate any number of duties beyond caring for children. It is worth emphasising that the job is often very demanding. Try not to have unrealistic expectations and never be seduced into thinking that you are on holiday. You will no doubt have opportunities that might not have come your way had you stayed at home, but first and foremost you are abroad to work.

Your primary duties will revolve around the children. Try to find out ahead of time what ages they are and, if you are inexperienced, read a childcare manual such as one by Miriam Stoppard or Penelope Leach.

Most families will expect you not only to keep their children's rooms tidy, but also to do some light housework. 'Light housework' is notoriously open to interpretation, however, so do be careful that you are not exploited. It is usual to be asked to dust, vacuum, wash dishes and keep the children's rooms clean.

It would be surprising not to be responsible for the children's clothes, though you should not be expected to do any hand washing. The vast majority of families who hire live-in helpers own a washing machine and usually a dryer, which should cut down the time taken to do this chore and on any ironing you may be expected to do.

Normally you will be expected to prepare the children's meals. You might even be required to cook for the adult members of the household sometimes, so be honest about how good you are at cooking and how much (or little) you enjoy it.

The amount of shopping you will be required to do varies considerably from family to family. Some will expect you merely to pick up a few items at the local grocery store while others will make you responsible for the entire food budget. Usually, the parents will go on a major shopping expedition once a week and leave you to purchase any extras that may be needed.

Candidates with driving licences are at a distinct advantage when applying for jobs since many parents will want you to ferry their children to school, to the doctor/dentist/dance class, etc. Not all parents are willing to lend their au pair or nanny a car, but if they do require you to drive, they will usually allow you to use the car to take the children out for day trips, or even allow you to borrow the car for your own private use during your free time. Always be scrupulous about paying for your own petrol, unless you have come to some arrangement. (The arrangement was not very satisfactory in Annie Stevens' case in Brussels where she was allowed to borrow the family's Mini but was charged a mileage rate which she calculated was exactly twice the cost of petrol.)

Some families in Europe prefer foreign nannies or au pairs so that they can assist the children with another language. Your task will be made a lot easier if the children share their parents' ideas about the benefits of language learning, not to mention have a certain aptitude. It may be a case of giving a scheduled lesson once a day or simply chatting to them in English or reading them stories. Maree Lakey, an Australian au pair in Austria, found this language-teaching aspect of her job more problematic than she had expected:

> I am basically there to help the four children aged 11-17 with their English learning, although this is not necessarily always easy. On the whole they have little desire to learn and see their lessons with me as more of a chore than anything else, but I guess that's not so unusual. I've found out how hard it is to try to speak correct English with them and to explain grammar rules which I have forgotten. It's also a bit difficult sometimes as my Australian English often differs from what the children have to learn. The children are of course not sympathetic to my difficulties, insisting that I should be infallible, being a native speaker.

REWARDS

If the arrangement works, it can be absolutely great. Emma Colgan says that her year off between school and university as an au pair in Hamburg was possibly the best thing that she ever did and she would recommend it to anyone and everyone:

> I was very lucky in that I lived with a lovely family who really treated me as a member of the family (in fact they spoilt me rotten on occasion). I was included in family celebrations, outings and dinner parties, and was taken on holiday with them. If I was not going out in the evenings I was always welcome to sit with them, talking for hours or watching a good film over a bottle of wine. They were incredibly generous and kind, giving me extra money for school books, socialising, etc. They said to me over and over again, 'Our house is your house'. They trusted me implicitly and because they treated me so well, I naturally wanted to work hard for them.

Emma is probably right when she goes on to say that her situation was an exceptional one. Few au pairs have the good fortune to work for such ideal employers. In fact Emma didn't think of them as employers, but rather as her 'German parents'. She now considers them friends and keeps in touch with them regularly.

Even if your host family isn't quite as generous and as easy-going as Emma's you will almost certainly improve your knowledge of a foreign language. This is valuable not only for modern language students. Helen McMillan had planned to study for a degree in languages but was anxious to spend some time travelling before she settled down to university life, so she accepted a six-month contract as an au pair in Italy, which she greatly enjoyed:

> *All that sunshine and good life went to my head, and I found I couldn't face three more years of poverty as a student. My Italian was so good by then that I decided to skip further study and went to work for an Italian firm instead. I now travel all over Europe on business trips (and incidentally keep in touch with the family I worked for). When I think about it, that au pair position changed the entire course of my life.*

Whereas some use their new-found facility with a foreign language to decide their future course or career, others take up a professional rather than a casual interest in childcare. There is a host of related careers, from teaching to running your own au pair agency which might develop from a successful stint as an au pair.

Almost all au pairs claim that the principal benefit of their experience (whether or not their relationship with their families was successful) is that they gain confidence in themselves. Susie Walton is one of the many who says that she came back from her year abroad (in her case the American Midwest) a changed person, much more assertive and confident about doing things on her own. It also helped her to get on better with people. Often a year of au pairing or nannying abroad teaches you to make friends quickly, which is surely a life-enhancing skill.

RISKS

The relationship of au pair to family is not like the usual employer/employee relationship; in fact the terminology sometimes used is 'hosts', 'hospitality' and 'guests', which is to view the arrangement in somewhat more idealistic terms than the reality will support. To be treated as a member of the family is splendid in theory, however it means that the success of the arrangement depends more than usual on whether or not individuals hit it off, so there is always an element of risk when living in a family of strangers. Some girls are decidedly opposed to the idea of being treated as a member of the family, since it means that they may not have fixed hours and duties. The families that throw up their hands in horror at the mention of a contract or the notion of being business-like about the arrangement are often the ones who expect you to be on call around the clock.

Few au pair experiences are an unmitigated success, and there is almost always an admixture of misery to a greater or lesser degree. Some randomly selected articles published in newspapers and magazines over the past few years are variously entitled 'Au Pairs - Look Before You Leave', 'Perils and the Au Pair Girl' and 'Sun, Seas and Servitude'.

Homesickness is the most common problem and is probably unavoidable at the beginning of your sojourn abroad. You will feel yourself to be a million miles away from friends, family and a comfortable routine. But even after you settle into the life of your host family, loneliness can persist if you don't take positive steps to create a social life (see the section on *Leisure Time* below). Much depends on your own attitude, as Pam Bain admits, after recounting how unhappy she was in Paris:

> *I look back now and think that perhaps if I'd been in a more optimistic frame of mind, I might have tried harder to enjoy myself. I didn't feel much like socialising so I didn't make friends and, personally, I was glad to get back home.*

The relationship between parents (especially the mother) and au pair is a very difficult one. In many situations you are neither employee (with fixed hours and duties) nor friend (with the trust and affection which friends bestow on one another). If the relationship does not work out, it can lead to downright disaster. Few situations contain more potential for misery. Plenty of employed people are unhappy with their jobs and seek the consolation of family, friends and a social life. Others are lonely or unhappy at home but enjoy the atmosphere of their workplace. But in a family placement, the two categories merge and an unhappy situation can be very difficult to escape from. Frances Thirlway, who was made miserable by the thoughtlessness of her employers in Munich, recalls how she used to retreat to the local library just to be out of summoning distance. She thinks that she read through the whole of German literature that year. And when the family took a holiday in the south of France, Frances would wander off into the hills with a book, which was a form of hiding from the family. It is possible to spend your free time less solitarily than Frances did. Annie Stevens, who disliked her employers in Belgium, signed up for French classes where she found a Chilean boyfriend, and Nicola Wenban spent all her free time in Vienna at a much more congenial home where an English friend was au pairing.

Even if you are treated well by your family, another common cause of complaint is the loss of independence noted above. Janet Renard, an American student who au paired in Sicily, thinks that the younger you are (preferably between 18 and 21) the easier it is to adapt to a family situation in which a great deal must be shared, including your time. Once you have tasted the independence of having your own flat, it is difficult to give up that freedom. But if you are fresh from school, you may appreciate the security and familiar pattern of family life.

There is another risk which a few veteran nannies have mentioned, which is that their experiences have put them completely off the idea of having their own children. Others of course came away with an opposite attitude, since they are eager to put into practice what they have learned and to avoid the parental mistakes to which they have been exposed.

Finding a job

The prospects for finding a childcare job abroad, even for the unqualified, are very good. British nannies have a worldwide reputation for being the best and in some countries (Canada or the United States for example) it is a status symbol to hire someone with a British accent. As an increasing number of mothers pursue their careers and the divorce rate rises, there is more demand for all kinds of live-in helpers. There are three main ways of finding a nannying position abroad; these are through (1) agencies, (2) advertisements and (3) word of mouth.

AGENCIES

The primary role of au pair, nanny and domestic agencies is to introduce prospective au pairs/nannies to suitable families. Introduction is not quite the right concept in the case of foreign placements, since the matching of families with au pairs is usually done on paper. Agents act as clearinghouses for various application forms and try to satisfy the requirements of families with the applicants registered with them. If a Spanish family wants a Roman Catholic, English-speaking dog-loving, non-smoking au pair with a driving licence, then the agent will do her best — the vast majority of agencies are run by women — to find a suitable candidate. Some agencies go to great lengths to match you with the right family, since it is in their business interest to satisfy their clients with an acceptable commodity, you.

Unlike the kind of temporary employment agency which acts as your employer, au pair agencies are never more than referral services. If you have a contract, it will be with the family not the agency, though they may facilitate drawing up a contract for you if you wish.

Wanted: Roman Catholic English Speaking Dog-loving Non-Smoking Au Pair with Driving Licence

Pros and Cons

Using an agency is usually the easiest way of finding work, though certainly not guaranteed to be trouble-free. Angie Copley is just one satisfied customer who was favourably impressed with the ease of fixing up a job abroad:

> After passing a BTEC National in Social Caring, I decided I would go to Italy for a year and work as a nanny. I found the address of the Au Pairs Italy agency in your book and wrote to them. Before I knew it, they had found me a family in Sardinia. I couldn't believe that it was so easy. All I had to do was pay for a flight out there and that was that.

Many agencies fulfil a variety of functions in addition to mere placement, such as advising on visas, insurance and cheap travel. One of their most valuable services is that many have corresponding agents abroad who can (in theory) act as neutral intermediaries in the event of incompatibility between you and your family or in cases of exploitation. Most of them promise to try to find a different family if a placement breaks down altogether. They can also advise on a host of topics such as how to apply for a residence permit or register with a local doctor. Many of them are also willing to put au pairs in the same vicinity in touch with one another; some even run social clubs themselves.

Judith Twycross's experience with a Sussex agency which arranged a placement in Seville worked out according to the text book:

> The main advantage of going through an agency was that I was given a choice of five or six families over a three-week period whom I could ring up and speak to myself or ask the Spanish agent to check various details. This was very important to me as I had certain specifications from which I was not prepared to waver, such as I wanted to have at least two set evenings off a week and all day Sunday. I also did not want babies under the age of two and I wanted to guarantee that I would be able to attend language classes.

The English-speaking agent in Madrid was very helpful when I was trying to choose a family. She rang twice to speak to me and the family during my first month to check everything was going well and to clear up any misunderstandings. She also arranged a meeting between me and another au pair working in Seville which made the task of settling in and developing a social life considerably easier.

In view of the fact that most agencies earn their money from charging clients (i.e. families), and not charging the au pair/nanny at all, this must be one of the few spheres where it is possible to get something for nothing. However, set alongside the advantages of using an agency, there are inevitable drawbacks. Once you have lodged an application the uncertainty can be irritating or even nerve-racking. You may hear nothing for weeks or even months, particularly if you choose to apply direct to an agency abroad, and then suddenly the offer of a family may come through which you are obliged to accept or reject immediately, and quite often for an almost immediate starting date. It is a good idea not to assume too much, and to keep in close communication with the agency to check on the progress of your application.

Do not have inflated expectations of what your agency is capable of achieving. The mother of an 18 year old who registered with an agency in order to get a summer placement in Sweden was livid when she heard nothing for several weeks. No doubt this was not due to inefficiency but to the fact that no Swedish vacancies were available, although the agency was probably at fault for not explaining the difficulty to the applicant and her family. Eventually the application was withdrawn and the girl arranged an excellent job with a Swedish-speaking family through family friends.

Some au pairs have complained that if you go through an agency you are taking pot luck. Reputable agencies supposedly prevent problems; however in some cases they create them. They are at the mercy of the information their agents or the families abroad give them, and this can often by misleading, sometimes purposely so. In their enthusiasm for sewing up placements (and collecting their commission), a few agents stoop to unscrupulous practices. For example, you should probably give a wide berth to any agency which suggests you lie or exaggerate on your application form (e.g. that you speak the language, have more childcare experience than you actually have). Sally Stanley was told by her agent in London that the Spanish family to whom she was being sent would be having a holiday in Majorca at some point, though this was never even mentioned after she arrived. Meanwhile the agent (either in England or in Spain) had told the family that Sally was planning to stay for a whole year, although she had made it quite clear on her application form that she had to resume her studies in October. The agency had given her an urgent starting date which she scrambled to meet, only to find that her charges would be away on holiday for a further week. This series of fiascos is not typical but it is best to be sceptical about things you are told by your agency.

Such misunderstandings could perhaps have been avoided by direct communication between family and au pair. Most agencies do encourge as much of an exchange of information as possible between the two parties (if there is time and a common language) but it is still difficult to form a complete and accurate picture. Always make a point of obtaining the family's phone number from the agency and also the number of their agent abroad. A couple of long distance phone calls could clarify many things and put your mind at rest.

There are of course no reliable statistics on the number of agency placements which work out satisfactorily, but a few years ago the proprietor of one of the largest agencies in Britain estimated that only half of the placements she made worked out while the other half came unstuck.

Choosing an Agency

Just as the services on offer differ from agency to agency so does the fee structure. In general if the agent you contact is being paid directly by the family, you pay nothing. But if there is a mediating agent, usually in your home country, then a fee may well be payable. At present the maximum which can be charged by agencies in Britain for arranging placements abroad is $40 plus VAT, assuming they employ the services of a foreign agent. A few choose to charge less than the maximum, but the vast majority charge £47. This allowable maximum has remain unchanged for more than a decade and there are rumours that it will be raised in the near future, though by how much was not known.

The fee in the UK is payable only after you have been offered and accepted a placement. Because no money can be requested 'up-front,' many agencies complain that girls apply to a number of agencies and without fear of penalty wait for the most appealing offer, thereby putting agents to a lot of trouble for nothing and leading to bad feeling. In many cases the drop-out rate of applicants is between 50% and 75%, which is a discouraging statistic for agents. Most European agents are not bound by such restrictions and charge applicants quite steep fees (especially in France) which means that they take the applications they do receive seriously and try very hard to find a suitable placement.

It is possible in many cases for a British applicant to apply directly to an agent in Europe and thereby cut out the middle man/woman and save the £47 fee. Not all Continental agencies are willing to consider privately lodged applications, but most will. Make sure that the fee they charge local girls for sending them abroad will not be levied on you. For example the main agencies in Austria charge at least the equivalent of a week's pocket money. Applying directly may work out satisfactorily, but it might also result in a higher degree of insecurity for you while you wait to be offered a job. And of course you will incur some expense in postage, phoning and faxing.

With so much variation among agencies in what they offer and what they charge, it is a good idea to contact at least four agencies initially, in order to compare their services. To supplement the 235 agencies listed in the Directory section of this book, you can check the adverts in *The Lady* magazine (described below) where new agencies are likely to advertise. Alternatively check in your local Yellow Pages: the new heading 'Nanny and Childcare Agencies' makes it easier to locate relevant agencies than previously when they were included in the general heading 'Employment Agencies and Consultants'. Computer buffs can make use of the internet: a search of the word 'au pair' or 'nanny' will produce long lists of agency web sites.

Unless you have unusual requirements (e.g. you want to go to a family in Lappland), it is advisable to choose just one agency with whom to register. If you are unhappy with their service for any reason, you should contact them and tell them that you are going to apply to another one. Sharon Legg, one of the authors of this book, registered with several agencies at once and lived to regret it:

> I learned my lesson the hard way. While I was looking for work in France, I used three different agencies simultaneously and it all became extremely confusing. I was receiving phone calls from families and, because their English was often

poor and my French non-existent, I found it difficult to establish which agency they were connected with. It all became very awkward indeed and I upset a lot of people!

If you apply too widely, it can work to your disadvantage. One Italian agency refused to try to place one girls whose application she had received from six different agents.

In the first instance phone or write (enclosing a self-addressed stamped envelope), briefly describing any relevant experience you might have had, what kind of position you are seeking and requesting an application form and general information about the agency. You should be able to conclude a certain amount from the tone and style of the agency literature. On the one hand you may receive a glossy and professionally packaged dossier with detailed country-by-country information, on the other a badly photocopied application form with little background information. Amateurish presentation isn't necesarily a bad sign, since it probably indicates that the agency is a one-person operation which may even be run from a private home. Sometimes this means that you will get more personal service though they are unlikely to have as great a choice of client families.

Another thing to watch out for is whether regular office hours are maintained and whether personal visits are encouraged. It is unusual for interviews to be compulsory (unless you are going for full-time nanny jobs) however an informal meeting with the agency staff is a good idea if geographically feasible. A few agencies seem to operate with a telephone answering machine, which is not ideal if you have any questions or last-minute panics.

Obviously you want to choose a reputable agency. As mentioned earlier, employment agencies in the UK no longer have to be licensed by the Department of Employment, though even in the days when they were, there was little regulation. One sign of a reputable agency is whether or not it belongs to one of the associations, the IAPA or the IFAA, described above. A certain number of au pair and nanny agencies are members of the Federation of Recruitment and Employment Services (FRES), 36-38 Mortimer St, London W1N 7RB (0171-637 1288) which acts as the national trade association for employment agencies and seeks to uphold standards of conduct within the industry. FRES members tend to be at the elite end of the market. Send a large s.a.e to receive a list of about 40 au pair agencies which belong to the FRES.

The Roman Catholic organisation ACISJF (Association Catholique Internationale de Services pour la Jeunesse Féminine) provides an au pair placement service in most of the countries in which it operates. The London branch (see the International Catholic Society for Girls in the Directory) or the International Secretariat (37-39 rue de Vermont, PO Box 22, CH-1211 Geneva 20; 22-734 9685) can provide addresses. The YWCA in many cities runs an au pair referral service, though usually for people already in town.

If in any doubt about an agency, ask them to refer you to one or more au pairs on their books who may be willing to describe their experiences with the agency and (even more importantly in some cases) with their partner agency in your destination country. The services offered abroad differ drastically.

Agency Procedures

It is difficult to be specific about how far in advance of your proposed starting date it is wise to initiate your enquiries. The time taken depends on the country you want to work in, the number of client families your agency has at any one time, and your available starting date. The fax machine has transformed the process and instantaneous placement is possible if you happen to apply at a time when there are unfilled vacancies. Quick placement is seldom possible for summer assignments, for which most agencies insist on early application. Wendy Smith discovered this too late:

> *I applied around Easter to several au pair agencies for a summer position in France and heard nothing. I eventually telephoned them in early June and it would seem that I was already too late to find temporary employment.*

Apart from summer placements, the vast majority of au pair openings coincide with the academic year, lasting from September to June. The next most popular time for starting a job is January, since many jobs become vacant after Christmas.

The application form which all agencies will send you should be filled out meticulously. In all likelihood it will be the only information on which the matching with a family is based and making a good impression is of prime importance. There might also be a questionnaire which will help the agency to get to know your requirements in greater detail.

In addition, the application dossier which you are asked to submit usually includes one or more photos, at least two references (which in some cases is required by law), a declaration of good health signed by a doctor, and (quite often) a curriculum vitae and/or a handwritten letter addressed 'Dear Family' describing yourself and your reasons for wanting to work as an au pair.

The photo does not have to be a professional shot, but you should take care to project the right image. A head and shoulders photo, preferably with an engaging smile is best. Another good idea is to send a family shot, preferably with you cuddling a young cousin. Resist the temptation to send a party photo, in which the cocktail or pint of bitter you are clutching will probably create a negative impression no matter how flattering the photo may be. If you are in doubt, send along a selection from which the agency can choose.

References are not as important as they are in many other jobs, though of course the more glowing the better. The normal procedure is for you to collect them yourself rather than have them sent to the agency directly. It is advisable to send photocopies in case you need the originals again later. School or college-leavers will need to provide a reference from their head teacher (though a few agencies specify that they are not interested in academic references), plus one of a domestic nature. This might be from a mother whose children you regularly babysit, or perhaps from a holiday job which involved domestic chores.

The letter introducing yourself should mention where you were born and brought up, a description of your family and their interests, any travelling you have done either in an organised group or independently, what kind of schooling you have had and your attitude to it, any jobs, hobbies or ambitions and of course why and for how long you want to work abroad and why you think your personality is suitable.

The doctor's certificate can be a simple statement signed by a physician that you are 'mentally and physically fit for work abroad'. Most (but not all) GPs charge about £10 for this statement. Things get more complicated when the medical certificate is a requirement of the visa (see country chapters) and needs to be translated into the relevant language.

When corresponding with an agency, always remember to enclose a stamped addressed envelope. For the price of a stamp, they will conclude that you are a thoughtful and efficient person.

ADVERTISEMENTS

When you answer an advertisement and deal directly with prospective employers, matters are more in your own control than if you rely on the offices of an agency. You are free to make all your own arrangements, which some independent-minded people prefer. The advantage for families of relying on adverts rather than on agencies, is that they are spared any agency fee. The disadvantage for both parties is that if something should go drastically wrong, there is no one who can be asked to mediate.

When sending photos take care to project the right image

The Lady Magazine

The Lady is a weekly magazine founded in 1885 and published on Tuesdays which contains columns of advertisements for nannies and au pairs. Few magazines hold such a monopoly on their field of specialisation as *The Lady* does. Of the multitude of readers who invest 65 pence each week, the majority are not as interested in the editorial content (with articles on minor members of the Royal Family, on knitting, etc.) as in the pages of classified advertisements. Mig Urquhart read the magazine for the first time on the train to France when a friend showed it to her:

> I would never had considered au pair work; I'm not particularly keen on children and wasn't that good a cook. Then I saw The Lady. What a magazine! Or should I say what classifieds? How is it possible for so many people to need and be able to afford domestic help, even in a recession? And people still hire butlers! I was gobsmacked by the paper, but several positions caught my eye.

The individual jobs abroad, which are listed under the heading 'Overseas Domestic Situations Vacant', cover a tempting range of destinations from Cairo to Cologne, Vancouver to Vicenza though of course the majority are in France and Germany. There are of course even more jobs advertised in Britain under 'Situations Vacant Domestic'. The geographical breakdown of the 68 ads for posts abroad in a recent issue offered the following: 18 vacancies in France, 15 in Germany, 9 in Switzerland, 6 in Austria and Italy, 2 in Belgium, Denmark and Sweden, and 1 each in Spain, Israel, Norway, Netherlands, Turkey, Saudi Arabia and Mustique in the Caribbean. Dozens of agencies also advertise in the same pages. After scanning an issue or two you can decide whether to try an agency and/or make direct application to families (though in a few cases small adverts which look like private adverts are in fact placed by an agency to fill a specific vacancy).

Because *The Lady* is such a popular vehicle for finding live-in jobs, there is terrific competition. Literally hundreds of girls tend to apply for the same jobs and so, for many, a certain number of silent rejections is inevitable. Try to obtain a copy of the magazine as early as possible on the Tuesday of publication (most newsagents open about 6.30am) and set aside the rest of the day to scour the adverts and to apply for the jobs that interest you. If the advert contains a phone number, do call, because if you don't someone else will and they might get the job as a result. If the advert does not include a phone number, you could consider trying to obtain it from International Directory Enquiries (dial 153) and stand out from the crowd of applicants by ringing. Take into consideration different time zones. You don't want to contact a family at the crack of dawn or very late at night. Even if they are tolerant of the inconvenience on that occasion, your carelessness will not make a good impression.

It is a good idea to have copies of your cover-letter and CV already prepared as well as plenty of stamps, so that postal applications can be despatched without delay. The first few applications to arrive will probably receive the most detailed attention. Again, it is a good idea to send a stamped addressed envelope for the reply. Here is an example of a cover-letter:

Your Full Address
Your Telephone Number
Date.

Dear . . .
   I read your advertisement in The Lady magazine (or other) this morning with great interest, and now I am forwarding my curriculum vitae in the hope of being considered for the post. I hope you will find me a suitable applicant and I look forward to your reply.

Yours sincerely (or faithfully)

If the name of the prospective employer is known, address him/her by name and sign the letter 'Yours sincerely'; if you are replying to a box number and the name of the family is not included in the advertisement, address the letter 'Dear Family' and use 'Yours faithfully'. (In most cases it will be the lady of the house with whom you will initially be dealing, but there is no need to assume that at this stage.)

You should write the letter in your own handwriting (unless you are afflicted with an illegible or unattractive scrawl) to lend a personal touch. It is of course preferable to write to a foreign family in their own language. Some people, who have little or no knowledge of the language, are tempted to enlist the help of a linguistically talented friend or relative; however this is risky since it is bound to set up false expectations should you get the job, and so it is probably better to write in English.

Your CV (known as resumé in North America) should be typewritten and include all of the following: name and address, telephone number, date of birth, nationality, details of education and work experience (including babysitting), additional skills (e.g. swimming or first-aid) and hobbies. Don't list too many extracurricular interests or the family may wonder how on earth you ever fit work into your hectic schedule. If you drive, don't forget to mention it, and also let the family know if you are a non-smoker.

You can of course place your own advert, as Julie Richards did:

> I had difficulty in getting a job when I was at home in the UK, as I didn't have any experience or qualifications as a nanny. In the end I put an advert in The Lady, and had about 30 offers of jobs.

A sample advert might read: 'Au pair, age 20, seeks position with family abroad. One year's similar experience with good refs. Driver. Non-smoker. Enthusiastic and hard-working.' Unless you want to protect your privacy with a box number, you will get faster results and a better response by including a phone number.

Although the magazine is not widely distributed abroad, past advertisers have received replies from all over the world (including North America) to a single advert. *The Lady* can be contacted at 39-40 Bedford Street, London WC2E 9ER (0171-379 4717/fax 0171-836 3601). Any advert that private advertisers place must be sent in by post and prepaid; the first ten words cost £15.40, and each further five words or less £7.01, including VAT. If the advert is placed from outside Britain VAT at 17.5% is not payable. The text and payment must be received by the preceding Wednesday.

Other Publications

Also look out for the weekly magazine *Nursery World* with articles, adverts and listings of interest to nannies and mother's helps. It is published on Thursdays and costs £1.10. Subscription enquiries should be sent to *Nursery World*, Freepost WD29, London EC1B 1BY (0171-837 8515) while the general contact address is Lector Court, 151-153 Farringdon Road, London EC1R 3AD (0171-278 7669). As well as publicising job vacancies in nurseries, it has a large section called 'Jobs with Families' both in the UK and Overseas.

The national press sometimes publish advertisements for nannies, though the choice is not large. *Overseas Jobs Express* (Premier House, Shoreham Airport, Sussex BN43 5FF; 01273 440229) is a fortnightly newspaper which contains some adverts for nanny and au pair agencies; a 3-month subscription costs £18.95. For domestic positions in country areas, the *Horse & Hound* can be a useful source. Australians and New Zealanders in Britain often consult the adverts in *TNT* or *New Zealand News*, free magazines distributed in London and famed for their selection of advertised jobs.

You can try to obtain a newspaper from the country you plan to work in, though usually the delay involved ruins your chances of landing a specific job. Similarly, you can place your own advertisement in foreign publications either directly or through their UK-based agents. This will be expensive (estimated minimum £50) but might be worthwhile if you have your heart set on an unusual destination like Buenos Aires or Brunei or on countries to which access is difficult. Check addresses of overseas publications in *Willings Press Guide* in any library. Alternatively contact a media representative in your own country, e.g. Smyth International Media Representatives, 234 Aylmer Parade, London N2 0PQ.

Another newspaper which might be worth checking is *LOOT* (24-32 Kilburn High Road, London NW6 5TF; 0171-328 1771) which bills itself as 'London's noticeboard'. Among its many categories of classified ads (which are free to private advertisers) are 'Au Pair Jobs Offered/Wanted'. The paper is published daily Monday to Friday and costs £1.30. It is just one of many free newspapers worldwide in the Free Ads Paper International Association, usually printed on coloured newsprint. It is possible to advertise free of charge in any of these papers (from San Diego to Sofia, Rio to Ravenna) which are listed in each issue of *LOOT* with instructions for placing ads.

WORD OF MOUTH

Sometimes au pairs who have worked abroad are asked by their employers to find a replacement upon their return home. If you happen to have a friend or acquaintance working for a family overseas, and you are considering doing likewise, you might end up being the replacement. It can be a great advantage knowing your predecessor who can give you first-hand information about the parents' strengths and weaknesses as employers and about the children. On the other hand, if the job doesn't work out and you decide to leave prematurely, it could embarrass your friend.

Hannah Start suggests contacting English language schools in your home town to find a position. Professional people from abroad on short intensive language courses might well be looking for an au pair on whom to practise their English once they return home. Hannah fixed up a plum job in Paris this way.

JOB-HUNTING ABROAD

If you are already abroad, check the adverts in the local press, assuming you can read them or can find someone to translate them for you. It is worthwhile in many cases consulting any English language publications such as the *Greek Weekly News* or the *Anglo-Portuguese News;* these are mentioned whenever relevant in the country chapters. You can visit the offices of au pair agencies abroad who might be able to place applicants on the spot with little delay (see Directory for addresses).

Other ways of hearing about openings are to check notice boards at the local English-speaking churches or bookshops, in supermarkets (especially in resorts), and at the local university, to ask the headmistress of a junior school if she knows of any families looking for an au pair, to put up notices at playgroups, or visit a school at the end of the school day and chat with the mothers and au pairs who are there to collect their charges. Clinics, laundrettes, newsagents and second-hand children's clothes shops may also post relevant notices.

Sometimes foreign cultural organisations such as the Alliance Française, the Goethe Institut or the British Council can be helpful. If you sign up for a language course abroad or simply cultivate the company of the students, you'll probably get to know some au pairs and through them the names of families in need of home help.

The demand for live-in help and babysitters in ski resorts around the world is very strong. In some cases, there are even notices up in the local tourist office of ski resorts from Crans-Montana in Switzerland to Thredbo Australia asking for domestic and childcare help.

INTERVIEWS

Unless you apply for an au pair position once you are already abroad, you probably won't have an interview with the family nor with the agency except in special cases. This is not true however with nanny and mother's help jobs where, in most cases, the candidates will be interviewed by the agency, or by someone appointed by the employers.

Some foreign parents arrange an interview to coincide with a trip to Britain. You might meet one parent while on a business trip or the whole family on holiday. Occasionally the interviewing is left to the present or most recent nanny. It is very rare to be transported to the family home abroad for a meeting. They will often come to London rather than elsewhere in Britain so it is an advantage if you are prepared to travel up to the city if necessary. Travel expenses are not usually reimbursed, so some money should be set aside for this purpose.

Preparing for the Interview

The first thing you should do is prepare any questions you might want to ask the parents. Try to commit these to memory and introduce them into the conversation at appropriate intervals, rather than laboriously read them from a long list. The more enjoyable and interesting you can make the meeting, the better impression you will make. Some experienced nannies feel that it is as much a case of the nanny interviewing the family as the other way round.

If you lack practical experience, it might be an idea to read a reference book on childcare such as those by Miriam Stoppard or Penelope Leach, favoured childcare gurus. It is also worth looking at *Bringing Up a Family 0-9 Years* by Mary Batchelor, *Healthy Eating for your Child* by H. Bampfylde and J. Dickerson and even *Dr. Spock's Baby and Childcare Book* by Benjamin Spock. In Matt Tomlinson's view, this is especially important for males:

> *If you've never seriously looked after kids before, do your homework. Get loads of ideas on things to do and read a couple of books. Mothers are quite useful, if only so you can avoid the mistakes they've made! My mother was quite supportive, giving me lots of good advice and also a copy of Penelope Leach's seminal guide to raising small children, which I recommend strongly for anyone hoping to work with under 5s.*

It is very important to look presentable at any interview and nannies and au pairs are no exception. Avoid wearing jeans and sneakers even though this will probably by your 'uniform' once you start work. On the other hand, don't go to the interview dressed to kill. The parents will probably find it hard to envisage you cleaning up after the children and subconsciously dismiss you as unsuitable. Most families are looking for someone who projects herself as tidy and reliable. Try to present the balanced image of someone who is sensible but fun, polite but informal.

Sometimes you will meet the family at the office of the agency, but it is more common to meet them at a hotel or private house. If it's a place that is unfamiliar to you, allow yourself plenty of time to find it. If very long distances are involved and you have friends or relatives who live in the interview area, ask if you can stay with them the night before. It'll save you having to arrive at the interview looking creased and worn out from travelling.

Conducting Yourself at Interview

If the interview has been arranged for you by an agency, there will probably be other candidates present and you might not be seen straightaway. You can put this waiting period to good use, however, depending on the circumstances. The children might be there and if this is the case, you must try to familiarise yourself with them. It will give you an opportunity to determine whether or not you would enjoy being their nanny and, besides, you would be wise to show an interest in them. A candidate who ignores prospective charges will not be rated very highly. On the other hand do not gush all over them, since this is sure to alienate them. Do not underestimate the power which children wield. If they take a shine to you, the parents might hire you in spite of a lack of formal qualifications. Similarly, if you pay them little or no attention, they are unlikely to support you, and the parents will notice your lack of enthusiasm.

The same applies to the current nanny. If she is present make a point of chatting to her, for she is a wealth of information. Try to interpret her attitude towards the family, and take note of how they interact with her. Does she seem to enjoy working for them, and do the parents treat her in a friendly manner? The nanny might also be in a position to influence the parents' choice, so don't be lulled into a false sense of security. Keep the conversation fairly business-like and don't give anything away that could be interpreted as a negative trait later on.

If you are left in a room by yourself use the time to go over any points you plan to raise at the interview. You will probably start to feel particularly nervous at this time but try to relax by breathing deeply and reminding yourself that the parents are not professional interviewers and are probably dreading the ordeal as much as you are.

They will usually begin the interview by giving you more details of what the job involves. Try to leave with a clear idea of what will be expected of you. Ask what your day(s) off will be and how much you will be paid, remembering that wages vary considerably depending on the country and type of situation. Take note of any fringe benefits on offer (use of car, for example) since these might compensate for an otherwise low salary. Topics you might raise are what the children eat (i.e. how much cooking will be expected of you), their attitude to television and discipline generally. Don't forget to raise subjects such as pets. They can mean extra work for you, and if you have any animal allergies they could make your life a misery. If the children aren't present, ask to see photos of them. The parents will be pleased at your interest.

Remember to ask about the previous nannies, since the way the parents talk about their former employees could well be revealing. Barbara Henson, an American woman who decided to look for a nannying job after she arrived in London, found a job in Camberwell but realised too late that the family had had eight nannies in two years and her predecessor had attempted suicide. Also find out whether you will be living as part of the family or as a more formal employee. Try to discover whether they enforce strict rules (and will therefore back you if you punish the children) or allow their children a free rein.

Once questions on both sides have been answered, don't try to prolong your time with them unless otherwise invited to do so. It is likely they will be waiting to see other applicants so just shake their hands, smile brightly and thank them for their time.

If you come away from the interview feeling that you are interested in the job, take some notes on what has taken place. It's amazing how quickly important details can be forgotten, especially if you are being interviewed by more than one family within a short time. It's also a good idea to write a brief note to the parents, thanking them for their hospitality (most families will have provided some sort of refreshment at the interview), telling them how much you enjoyed meeting them (assuming that is true) and that you are enthusiastic about the job. Writing such a note may seem a little crawling, but it's proof of good manners, which might give you the edge over the competition. If you obtained the interview through an agency, you should phone them when you get home to tell them how you think it went, and whether or not you are interested.

Preparation

After you have secured a job, there may or may not be a waiting period during which you will have a chance to organise the practicalities of moving abroad and to prepare yourself in other ways. If you are going to a country which requires immigration procedures (e.g. Canada and Switzerland), you may find that you will have several months at your disposal. In addition to deciding what to take and which ticket to buy, you should think about health and travel insurance, necessary documents such as visas, and about having a contract drawn up.

The main association for nannies in Britain is the Professional Association of Nursery Nurses (2 St. James' Court, Friar Gate, Derby DE1 1BT; 01332 372337). PANN is an independent registered trade union for nannies. One of their briefs is to lobby for legislation which would require nannies to be professionally qualified and registered. Whereas childminders must be registered with their local authority and submit to a police check, there is absolutely no legal requirements for nannies. The Children Act of 1989 did introduce one change: that nannies who work for more than two families must register with the local authority, though the vast majority of nannies work for just one or two families. Potential problems are periodically highlighted by tragic incidents in which babies are abused or abducted by those caring for them.

An alternative organisation is the National Association of Nursery Nurses/ NANN, 17 Lamb Close, Garston, Watford, Herts. WD2 6TB (01923 893967).

CONTRACTS

Once you have received a job-offer and have decided to accept, what happens next? If you are dealing with an agency, the offer will probably come from them. If it comes direct from your future employer, you should inform the agency that an offer has been made and accepted, since they will want to collect their fee from the family. You should be totally honest with them at all times, as they have been instrumental in finding you a job and you may want to employ their services again.

Nannies

This is the point at which a formal contract or alternatively an informal agreement should be drawn up, either with the guidance of the agency or independently. In the UK, all employers are by law obliged to provide written Particulars of Employment within the first eight weeks of employment. This should set out clearly the extent of your duties and free time, the length of stay, wages and the amount of notice which must be given on either side, whether the family will pay for health insurance and what will happen in the event of sickness. If the family has had a bad experience with a nanny, they might want to list acceptable reasons for disciplinary measures (i.e. verbal warning in the first instance, written warning and finally dismissal) such as unsatisfactory dress standards, unreliable timekeeping, after-hours behaviour which might harm the reputation of the employer, etc. The reasons for immediate dismissal are usually theft and drunkenness.

If you are arranging a post independent of an agency, you might like to obtain a copy of a model contract of employment from PANN (contained in their Information Pack available for £3). If the contract is provided by your agency or employers, study the agreement carefully before signing, making sure they have remembered to append their signatures. Sign the original and take a photocopy before returning the original to them, accompanied by a less formal note.

Although contracts are mainly intended to benefit the employee and to safeguard her against exploitation, it is a legally binding document and, in extreme cases, its violation could result in a lawsuit for breach of contract. This however is very rare: although it is not uncommon for nannies to leave their employers without due notice, resulting lawsuits are almost unheard of. Leaving prematurely is not to be recommended, however, since the family will also sign in good faith, and the contract should be maintained by both parties until it is mutually desirable to terminate it. You will soon learn that it is necessary to be a little flexible. One of the main disadvantages of this kind of work is that you can't always clock off when you are expecting to. Rather than viewing this as a breach of contract, try to recall the times when you receive unexpected bonuses, for example when the mother decides to take the children out by herself one afternoon, thus leaving you with more free time than you had anticipated.

Au Pairs

Contracts are not very common in au pairing jobs. Initially, you usually receive only a letter of invitation from the family which may not specify hours, duties or pocket money. If there is time, you might wish to write to the family to ask them to provide a written agreement.

It is preferable to have something in writing in case of serious disagreement. If this is impossible, you should at least have a business-like discussion about these matters either on the telephone beforehand or in person once you arrive and make notes during or immediately afterwards (see the section on *Problems* below). Sometimes families are reluctant to put things in writing, since they want the arrangement to be entirely informal and flexible. You will have to use your judgment whether or not to insist on something in writing.

HEALTH AND INSURANCE

Some families pay for or contribute towards the cost of medical insurance and it is essential to find out well in advance whether your employers are prepared to do this. In some cases they are compelled by law to provide insurance, so check the country chapters in this book and with your agency. Even if you are allowed to participate in the national scheme of the country you are going to, you may find that there are important exclusion clauses such as dental treatment, non-emergency treatment, prescription drugs and so on.

No matter what country you are heading for, but especially if it is an EU country, you should obtain the Department of Health leaflet T5 *Health Advice for Travellers Anywhere in the World* available from post offices or by ringing the Health Literature Line 0800 555777.

If you are a national of a European Economic Area country (namely the UK, Ireland, Netherlands, Belgium, Luxembourg, Denmark, Germany, France, Italy, Spain, Portugal, Greece, Sweden, Finland, Iceland, Norway and Austria) and will be working in another EEA country, you will be covered by European Social Security Regulations. Advice and the leaflet SA29 *Your Social Security Insurance Benefits and Health Care Rights in the European Community and in Iceland, Liechtenstein and Norway* (dated April 1996) may be obtained from your local Department of Social Security or from the Overseas Contributions (EU) department of the Contributions Agency, International Services, DSS, Longbenton, Newcastle-upon-Tyne NE98 1YX (06451 54811).

All EEA nationals planning to go to another member state should be sure to acquire form E-111 (called the 'E-one-eleven') which is a certificate of entitlement to medical treatment in other member states. The application form is contained inside leaflet T5 mentioned above. Whereas ordinary tourists can apply at their local post office, people who are intending to work abroad should send the application to the Contributions Agency in Newcastle. Unfortunately they can take a long time to reply, so write off as early as possible. Take several photocopies of the certificate since in some countries you need to hand over a copy of the E-111 to any doctor or chemist with whom you deal.

The UK also has Social Security agreements with some other countries. If you are planning to work in any of the following countries, write for the appropriate leaflet from the Overseas Contributions section of the Contributions Agency: Australia, Barbados, Bermuda, Canada, Cyprus, Israel, Jamaica, Jersey & Guernsey, Malta, Mauritius, New Zealand, Philippines, Switzerland, Turkey, USA and republics of the former Yugoslavia.

Given the limitations of state-provided reciprocal cover, you may decide to take out comprehensive private cover which will cover extras like loss of baggage and, more importantly, emergency repatriation. The cost of bringing a person back to the UK from any overseas country in the event of illness or death can run to thousands of pounds. In all other countries not listed above comprehensive private medical insurance is essential. Advice can be sought from the Association of British Insurers (51 Gresham St, London EC2V 7HQ; 0171-600 3333) or simply ring several local companies to compare policies and premiums.

Medical insurance policies can be bought either as a package which will cover a wide range of risks, or selectively which permits you to choose the amount and type of cover you want. Make sure you don't under-insure yourself and remember that all policies contain exclusion clauses, which should be studied carefully. Your nanny agency might be able to advise on matters of insurance. One company which has a special policy for au pairs is Geoffrey Wallis Ltd. (11 World's End Lane, Green Street Green, Orpington, Kent BR6 6AW; 01689 860888) which charges £35 for three months of cover in Europe, £66 for nine months and £81 for a year.

A North American company which specialises in health insurance cover for Canadian students going abroad and for temporary stays in Canada is ETFS (10 Saint Mary St, Suite 505, Toronto, Canada M4Y 1P9).

Some companies to consider for long-term insurance cover abroad are:

Atlas Travel Insurance Services Ltd., 37 King's Exchange, Tileyard Road, London N7 9AH. Tel: 0171-609 5000.

Endsleigh Insurance, Endsleigh House, Ambrose Street, Cheltenham, Gloucestershire GL50 3NR. ISIS policy is frequently recommended by student and youth travel organisations. They have offices in most university towns both in Britain and Europe.

Europ-Assistance, 252 High St, Croydon, Surrey CR0 1NF. Tel 01444 442211. Voyager Travel policy covers periods of up to 18 months. Costs £236 for 12 months in Europe and £481 worldwide. The policy is invalidated if you return home during the period insured.

Our Way Travel Ltd., Foxbury House, Foxbury Road, Bromley, Kent BR1 4DG. Tel: 0181-313 3900.

TRAVEL INSURANCE
Don't go Uninsured!

Short & Long Term Cover
Business or Pleasure
Contact the Travel Insurance Specialists:

Foxbury House, Foxbury Road, Bromley, Kent BR1 4DG.
Tel: 0181-313 3900   Fax: 0181-313 3652

Travel Insurance Agency, 775B High Road, North Finchley, London N12 8JY. Tel: 0181-446 5414/5.

If you do have to make a claim, you may be unpleasantly surprised by the amount of the settlement eventually paid. Loss adjusters have ways of making calculations which prove that you are entitled to less than you would have believed possible. They are however less likely to be tight-fisted over well-documented medical claims.

National Contributions

In countries where no Social Security agreements exist, the leaflet NI38, *Social Security Abroad,* gives an outline of the National Insurance contributions and social security benefits in countries with no reciprocal agreement with the UK. If you work for an employer in another country you may be liable to contribute to that country's Social Security scheme; however if you become employed by a United Kingdom employer you may be required to pay UK National Insurance at the Class 1 rate during the first 52 weeks of employment abroad. Even if you are not obliged to pay, you may want to pay voluntary contributions (Class 3) so that you will still qualify for certain benefits upon your return to the UK. Leaflet NI208 gives the latest rates for contributions and is available at your local DSS. Should you decide to pay contributions while abroad, you can apply by using form CF83 on the last page of leaflet NI38. These contributions may be paid at regular intervals or, alternatively, in a lump sum.

Sharon Legg regretted not having taken these precautions:

While working abroad as an au pair, I was foolish enough not to consider medical insurance because I was confident that nothing serious would ever happen to me. On my last day, I was taken suddenly and seriously ill and required urgent medical attention. One is not paid very much as an au pair but luckily I had managed to put most of my earnings aside. In less than 24 hours, I had blown all my money on medical fees. Then, when I returned to Britain, I was refused sickness benefit on account of insufficient National Insurance contributions, since I hadn't paid while I was out of the country. I learnt my lesson the hard way, so leave nothing to chance.

As mentioned above, it may be the family's responsibility to make contributions on your behalf (as it is in the UK for employees earning more than £62 a week) however one cannot assume that the family will automatically abide by the regulations.

TRAVEL

Except in the case of highly prized professional nannies, you must pay for your own travel costs. Very occasionally a family will pay for your fare home if you have completed a one-year contract. There are exceptions, for example the Au Pair in America programme in which your flight is organised for you and paid for by the family. In a few cases, your placement agency may be able to offer advice on travel, but mostly you will have to sort out your own arrangements. You should shop around for the best bargain, remembering that it is preferable to pay extra for a confirmed reservation on the outward journey. Since the family will probably want to meet you at the airport if you are flying, last minute bargains and standby fares are not ideal. It is always better to have an open return ticket, so that you will feel more in control of the situation. Also, certain countries require a return or onward ticket as a condition of entry. To cover the contingencies of wanting to cut short or to extend your term of employment, it is not advisable to book a return date which cannot be altered without incurring great expense. Check the travel section of the country chapters for ideas and a rough guide to ticket prices.

For long haul flights, discounted tickets are available in plenty and there should never be any need to pay the official full fare. Previously the sale of these tickets was restricted to the original 'bucket shops', often seedy but usually reliable agencies. Now High Street travel agents such as Thomas Cook, Hogg Robinson and Pickfords are openly selling discounted tickets. This makes cheap air travel much more accessible for people living outside London. But the very lowest fares are still to be found in London bucket shops. They advertise in *TNT, Time Out* and the *Evening Standard*. You can also obtain the phone numbers of three or four agents who handle your destination from the

Air Travel Advisory Bureau (0171-636 5000). Phone a few outfits and pick the best price.

The principal agencies specialising in travel for students and budget travellers are:

Campus Travel, 52 Grosvenor Gardens, London SW1W 0AG. Tel: 0171-730 8111. Also 0161-273 1721 in Manchester, 0131-668 3303 in Scotland, 0117-929 2494 in Bristol. Britain's largest student and youth travel specialist with 44 branches in high streets, universities and YHA shops.

Council Travel, 28A Poland St, London W1V 3DB. Tel: 0171-287 3377 (Europe) and 0171-437 7767 (worldwide). Travel division of the Council on International Educational Exchange in New York which organises international work exchanges.

STA Travel, Priory House, 6 Wrights Lane, London W8 6FT. Tel: 0171-361 6161 (Europe), 0171-361 6262 (worldwide). Leading agency for independent and youth travel with more than 130 branches worldwide including the US.

Trailfinders Ltd., 42-50 Earls Court Road, London W8 6EJ. Tel: 0171-938 3366 (longhaul) and 0171-937 5400 (Europe and transatlantic).

Travel Bug, 597 Cheetham Hill Road, Manchester M8 6EJ. Tel: 0161-721 4000. London Office: 0171-835 2000.

Travel Cuts, 295a Regent St, London W1R 7YA. Tel: 0171-255 2082 (longhaul), 0171-637 3161 (North America) and 0171-255 1944 (Europe).

In the US, contact any Council Travel or STA office. If your dates are flexible, contact Air-Tech (584 Broadway, Suite 1007, New York, NY 10012; 212-219-7000) which fills last minute seat vacancies at very low prices, e.g. $169 one way from New York to Europe. Air-Tech has representatives in other US cities and also in Europe, i.e. Amsterdam (020-421 2738) and Prague (02-402 3853).

European railways offer good discounts to those under 26. Eurotrain (52 Grosvenor Gardens, London SW1; 0171-730 3402), Euro-Youth (0171-834 2345) and Wasteels Travel (0171- 834 7066) all offer reduced rate international rail tickets. The most comprehensive system of coach services is operated by Eurolines, a consortium of the largest coach operators in Europe including Britain's National Express. They will send a brochure of their destinations and prices if you ring 01582 404511.

If you suffer from travel sickness, try taking Stugeron tablets for sea and air travel. These seldom cause drowsiness so you should still be quite alert when you arrive. If sea sickness is a particular problem, tuck a small book (a passport will do) into the waistband of your skirt or trousers. Having something solid near one's stomach seems to help.

WHAT TO TAKE

Money

If at all possible try to save a certain amount of money so that you won't be financially dependent on the family if things don't work out. Bear in mind that you might not be paid for the first fortnight or month, so you will need some money to tide you over, preferably some in the local currency. The rest should be in travellers' cheques, which can be purchased from any bank and most building societies. Be sure to keep the serial numbers of the cheques separate from the cheques in case they are stolen. A credit card can also be a handy asset when you are abroad, unless you are given to improvidence.

48   *Preparation*

Packing

As the day of departure draws closer, you will need to sort out your wardrobe and select clothes that will be compatible with the climate you are going to. For hot countries take at least one pair of comfortable leather sandals or rubber flip-flops which will allow your feet to breathe. Natural fibre clothes, especially cotton, are much better in hot climates than synthetics for the same reason. Some light-weight, long-sleeved clothes would not go amiss to protect you from sunburn and insect bites. Remember too that in some countries standards of modesty are different from what you may be used to, so you should be prepared to abide by the laws and customs of your host country.

For cold climates pack thermal underwear, two pairs of gloves or mittens which can be worn together and a woolly hat. A lined coat and non-slip boots are also a must. If you don't already own suitable clothing, it is probably better to wait until you arrive, so you can buy things as you need them and won't have to lug them around with you.

Try not to overload yourself, since by the end of your contract you will have accumulated as much again. It will probably be a while before you establish a social life, so concentrate mainly on your working necessities. You can always get things sent out later by post, if your family and friends are obliging. Some nannies are happy to live in jeans, shorts and T-shirts, but you will have to adapt this according to your preference and that of your employers. Whatever you decide, try to look neat and presentable at all times.

In addition to local maps and a dictionary, you might want to take a fat

---

Tommee Tippee is the name you can trust for a full range of baby accessories to suit you, your budget and your lifestyle.

Britain's favourite baby brand means little ones and their nannies have more fun!

Widely available in many countries or through mail order. For details of how to order call the helpline free on **0500 979899** (UK only) or write to:

**The Consumer Helpline,
Jackel International,
Dudley Lane, Cramlington,
Northumberland NE23 7RH**

paperback to keep you company in your own language while you're finding your feet. If cooking will be among your duties, a copy of a basic cookery book could be invaluable; Mig Urquhart claims to owe a sizeable debt to the old edition of *Delia Smith's Complete Cookery Course*. Avoid taking electrical appliances to countries whose systems differ from Britain's. Although most of Europe is now on 220 volts alternating at 50 cycles per second as in Britain, the plugs are seldom compatible. The Standard North American voltage supply is 110, so Americans will have to buy a transformer as well as a plug adaptor if they decide to take a hair-dryer or some other appliance. These can be more easily found in Britain than in the US.

You might also want to pack a few small items of sentimental value which will help make your new room more familiar and homely. It is a good idea to buy each of the children a small gift to present to them upon arrival. These needn't be expensive; small souvenirs of your home town might suffice, and help to win them over initially. Toys and baby equipment made by Tommee Tippee are recommended.

WHILE YOU'RE WAITING

If there is a sizeable delay before you are due to set off, you can use the time to improve your knowledge of the language with teach-yourself tapes or even a short intensive language course. Check the facilities at your local library, since language tapes can be very expensive to buy. At the least invest in a good dictionary which will probably prove more useful than a phrase book.

You should also investigate the courses available near your new job, either by asking the family, the agency or some relevant organisation such as the Spanish or Italian Institute. Remember that most schools close down during the summer and, besides, many families will move to beach or mountain locations in the summer, far removed from any language institutes. Further information about language courses may be found in the chapter *Leisure Time* below.

Another way of putting your time to good use is to attend a first-aid course. All kinds of medical emergencies can occur with children which can be alarming unless you are prepared. Also consult the appendices on *Safety in the Home* and *First-Aid*, though reading is no substitute for practical demonstrations and participation.

Once you know exactly where you'll be living, you should do as much preparatory reading about the country you're destined for as you can. One of the most useful pieces of research you can do is to locate your new address on a detailed city map. It is also useful to have some notion of where key places and public transport routes are in relation to where you'll be living. You may be able to consult city maps at an Embassy reading room or a big public library. You might prefer to buy a map: Edward Stanford Ltd. (12-14 Long Acre, Covent Garden, London WC2) has as complete a selection of maps as any in the country.

Sharon has an unusual further suggestion for preparing yourself for departure:

> I always make a point of writing a letter to myself before the trip, and taking it with me to read in times of homesickness. It sounds very strange but it helps! In it I remind myself of all the reasons why I wanted to leave home (painting it as black as I possibly can!) and then I emphasise all the good things I hope to

achieve by working abroad. A little reminder goes a long way to renewing enthusiasm.

Keeping in Touch

In the interval before taking a job, it is important to keep the lines of communication open by dropping the family a line from time to time. You could begin by sending the children some postcards of Britain. After all, there's no need to wait until you arrive before starting to develop a relationship with them. Do not hesitate to use the telephone unless there are serious linguistic problems. This will save both parties needless anxiety that the other side has had a change of mind or heart.

Be very careful to make a detailed plan for meeting your employers, and also a contingency plan in case there are unexpected delays. If you have never met the family, ask for a photograph and an identifying feature (e.g. hat, umbrella, etc.) One agency suggests using brightly coloured luggage labels and sending an identical set to the family to bring with them to the airport. Pam Robb worried for the whole ten-hour flight to Western Canada how she would recognise the family, which turned out to have been quite unnecessary since Edmonton Airport is so small that by the time she cleared customs, the only person left around was the one who had come to meet her.

Last Minute Panics

Don't be surprised if you get cold feet as the time of departure approaches, especially during the last few days when your family and friends will make a fuss over you as they bid their farewells. Circumstances may have changed somewhat if there has been a considerable lapse of time between application and departure, but try not to change your mind, since a termination at this late stage is bound to cause a great deal of distress and aggravation. Your new family have put their trust in you and expect you to fulfil your part of the bargain. Unless you are sure you can cope with it, your nearest and dearest are best left at home once you have decided to leave the house. Tearful farewells from parents and friends (especially boyfriends) will just make you feel worse. Sometimes the lead-up to leaving is far harder than actually getting on the plane/boat/train. Once you're aboard, you will soon regain your initial excitement and enthusiasm for what lies ahead.

Problems and how to cope

This chapter may seem disproportionately and discouragingly long. In fact the whole book is peppered with stories which illustrate various kinds of problems and disasters great and small which can beset au pairs and nannies. After reading this you may be left with the impression that whoever thought up the idea of au pairing should have been locked away forever with a self-willed three-year-old given to tantrums. However we hope that by bringing out the full range of problems which can arise you may feel a little better prepared (whether psychologically or in practical terms) for the particular problems which you encounter.

INITIAL TRAUMAS

If you have already met the family at an interview, arriving should not be too traumatic since you will know roughly what to expect. However most au pairs and some mother's helps will be meeting the family for the first time at the airport or station in which case they should have detailed instructions about where to meet and how to recognise the family. It is important to consider your appearance when you arrive. Nobody expects you to look like a model from *Vogue,* but try to make an effort. Choose reasonably smart but comfortable clothes which won't look too crumpled after a journey. A subtle spray of perfume should make you feel fresher, especially if you have had to sleep in your clothes. Knowing you look as good as possible will promote a positive image and help boost your confidence.

Winning the Children Over

Breaking the Ice

Don't assume that the task of breaking the ice is solely the family's responsibility. People's personalities and cultural traits vary enormously and your new family may feel even more awkward and shy than you do. To overcome your own shyness, focus your attention on the children, especially if you don't feel at home with the language. No one will expect you to be a great conversationalist, but some attempts at general small talk (e.g. questions about their country) will not go amiss. You may want to draw some comparisons with your own country, without of course implying criticism of theirs. If the children are withdrawn at first, they will soon start to respond if you pay them enough attention.

No matter how tired you are when you first arrive, spend a little time socialising with the family before going off to your room. You will probably be given a tour of the house and be offered some refreshment. It would be unusual if you were expected to do any work on your first day but show your willingness to help even if you are very jet-lagged and ready to fall into bed. Families nearly always expect you to eat your first meal with them so you can get to know each other better. You should always offer to help clear the dishes before you take your leave for the night.

Providing you're not too exhausted, it's a good idea to unpack as soon as possible. A bare and unfamiliar room can be depressing to wake up to, so try to get it organised before you go to bed.

Your First Day

Your main objective on the first day is to gain some idea of the family's routine and try to slot yourself into it as smoothly as possible. Don't attempt to reorganise anything at this point, even if you think it would be beneficial to the family. You need to find your feet before adopting such responsibilities.

Here is a list of tasks to which you might give priority in the first few days:
(1) Make sure your new family knows the name, address and telephone number of your next of kin.
(2) Make a list of all the emergency telephone numbers and keep it handy.
(3) Locate the first-aid box, fuse-box, etc.
(4) Learn how to operate household appliances.
(5) Ask for a set of keys to the house. Find out where spare ones are kept, in case you find yourself locked out.
(6) Take note of any house rules.
(7) Establish when you can expect to be paid and how much you will have to pay in deductions (if applicable).
(8) Sort out which chores are to be allocated to you. You might find it useful to draw up some sort of rota for house duties so you can organise them and fit them in each week.
(9) Ask when your first day off will be, so you can plan accordingly, and have something to look forward to.

Coping with the Previous Nanny

Au pairs almost never overlap, however sometimes families will ask the nanny being replaced to stay on for a limited period to help make the transition a little smoother. This short period of overlap can either be a great help or an extra source of aggravation, depending on the circumstances and your point of view.

On the good side of the equation, the initial work load will be halved and you will be able to adjust gradually to the household responsibilities. The nanny will be able to give you lots of tips on the various quirks of each family member, and answer questions that you might not like to ask the parents at this stage. She will be able to introduce you to her friends and will have more time than the mother to show you around.

Unfortunately, the previous nanny can also be somewhat intimidating. She will seem much more capable and efficient than you, and your already fragile sense of confidence could totally disappear. The children will make it blatantly obvious that they would much rather have *her* than *you* and, understandably, this makes your task even more difficult. Try not to be overcome by your feelings of inadequacy and remember that it is only a matter of time before you become equally efficient and just as treasured by parents and children alike. Being new in any job is an uncomfortable feeling, and as a live-in helper, it is doubly hard because it is your home as well.

Even when your predecessor — either au pair or nanny — is no longer present, the family's fond memories of her can be enough to make you grind your teeth. They may, for example, refer to your room as 'Wendy's room' even though Wendy has been long gone. When you hear things like, 'Wendy did it this way' or 'Wendy never used to do that' it can be infuriating but it is something you just have to learn to live with. Try to be tolerant of this reaction in the children. We all feel suspicious of change and it is normal for them to miss someone who was such an important part of their world. The phase will pass as you learn how they prefer to have things done and the family becomes more used to your ways.

Winning the Children Over

In the beginning, the children may well have difficulty adjusting to you, and you will have to work quite hard to earn their trust and cooperation. This can be especially difficult because you have so many other practical problems to deal with, as well as adjustment worries of your own. The first few weeks are vital, however, in building a relationship with your charges since this could set the tone for the duration of your stay. Therefore you want to make sure that things get off to a good start.

Wendy never used to do that

One of the best things you can do is to be flexible and adapt as well as you can to the established routine. It will help the children feel more secure if you are consistent and continue the daily patterns they are used to. Obviously no one should expect you to be a clone of the previous live-in helper or the mother, but try not to impress your personality too forcefully at first.

If the children are being generally difficult, try to avoid confrontations as much as possible by making it fun for them to cooperate instead. For example, if they are deliberately dawdling over getting dressed in the mornings, try starting a race to see who finishes first, and reward the winner with a treat after breakfast. You could also pretend to be dependent on them. Make them feel important by saying how much you need their help to show you where everything is. Ask them to take *you* to school because you're frightened of getting lost (which may, indeed, be no exaggeration).

Should they be particularly nervous of new-comers and create a fuss every time you go near them, remember that they are not being deliberately bad-tempered but are probably feeling insecure. Try to be tolerant and don't force the issue. Subtly involve them in play by doing anything that will attract their attention. Perhaps you could start by making something out of modelling clay or Lego and as they become increasingly interested they will probably want to try it themselves. Before you know it, they'll be joining in and you'll be on your way to building a friendship as well as a Lego castle. It might take a lot of patience, but you will probably be rewarded for it eventually.

It may not be much fun for a vegetarian au pair working for a carnivorous family

Culture Shock

One of the hardest things you'll have to cope with in your first week is culture shock. This is bound to strike whenever anyone drastically changes his or her lifestyle and encounters unfamiliar attitudes, customs and even food. In some cases you may be faced with the truth of certain stereotypes, such as Spaniards are lax about punctuality or Germans obsessive about cleanliness. In other cases you may find the stereotypes upended (e.g. a punctilious Spaniard, a slapdash German, a standoffish American) and this can be even more disconcerting. If you're lucky the family will make allowances for your culture shock, though ultimately it is you who must do the adapting. If you are having real difficulties adapting to one aspect of your new life, it is better to mention it (tactfully of course) than to let it fester. It is hard enough to pick up signals of distress in your own culture, let alone across cultural barriers, so you should not expect your new employers to be mind-readers. Besides they will probably respect you for being forthright, even if they cannot immediately alter whatever is worrying you.

You might even discover that some of their strange ways are actually better than what you are used to. Yvonne Standard tried to be as flexible as possible when she worked for a family in the States:

> I was very unadventurous about food before I went but rather than make a scene by saying I didn't like something, I would try everything that was offered. I had my first taste of pasta and pizza in their home. I didn't know much about cooking before I went, but helped the wife in the kitchen a lot (she was a good cook) and I learned quite a bit.

Small children may not understand your need for privacy

The more you know about the family ahead of time, the easier it will be to cope with the shock of your new situation (and vice versa). If you are a vegetarian, a compulsive jogger or a transcendental meditator, it might be best to inform the family before you arrive and discover their attitude. Emma Colgan, who is a vegetarian, was treated with the greatest respect by her German family who forbade her from washing up the meat pans, whereas another vegetarian au pair went to another carnivorous family in Austria, and she had to work in a kitchen dangling with sausages and to prepare and cook the meat while herself living on ice cream.

One of the most difficult things to adjust to is a loss of privacy. In the vast majority of cases you will be given your own room, though there may be some pressure on you not to retire to it very often nor to close the door. Small children cannot be expected to understand your need for privacy especially if in their culture there is a stronger emphasis on the extended family and communal living. A few ground rules will have to be laid down and enforced as gently as possible. In a few cases you may be asked to share a room with one of the children. This should probably be resisted if at all possible though sharing with small infants who sleep through the night is usually not too troublesome. However it is a point that should always be established before you accept a job.

Homesickness

This can hit at any time throughout your trip, but it will probably be particularly acute during your settling-in period. You are bound to feel a little lost at first and think more fondly of your real home, so many miles away. Be prepared to find yourself gasping for some fish and chips, English bacon, Radio 4, your favourite TV programmes and newspapers (though the latter can usually be bought a day or two late in major European cities). These feelings are natural and you must try to understand them as something that will pass, rather than an indication that moving abroad was a big mistake.

Keeping busy is always a good way to keep worries at bay, so concentrate on establishing yourself in your new situation. Usually the job will occupy your time, though in a few cases au pairs have minimal duties and might find themselves with a great deal of time on their hands in which to mope. Turn to the chapter on *Leisure Time* for advice on how to build a social life and keep amused.

If your job consists mainly of caring for a young child and you are not accustomed to the need for constant vigilance, you may find yourself getting bored and missing the fun of your previously unencumbered life at home, as Janet Renard did in Sicily:

The baby was fine, but it's true that the exotic surroundings couldn't make up for the fact that baby care is monotonous.

If you find yourself becoming unduly depressed or bored, it is probably a good idea to express your feelings to your employers who may give you more free time in which to take advantage of your new setting and to help overcome your longings for home.

PROBLEMS WITH CHILDREN

Resentment in Children

It is quite common for a child left in the care of a full-time helper to feel resentful of his or her mother's absence. Unfortunately the child sometimes channels this resentment towards his au pair/nanny instead, and so reacts badly towards her or him. This is more common in the early stages when a new helper has taken over and a stable relationship with the child has not yet had a chance to develop. Children's sense of logic tells them that if they can drive the au pair away, then mummy will be restored to them. Of course, things aren't that simple, and it is very easy for a state of conflict to set in. Try not to take a child's reaction towards you as a personal affront. He or she would probably have reacted the same way to anyone in your shoes, and it is more your role in their life that they are rebelling against, rather than a person.

Camilla Preeston found her introduction to the children of the French couple with whom she planned to spend six months discouraging:

> When I arrived, I was made to feel very welcome, although I was exhausted from the 14-hour flight from my home in Hong Kong and the 6-hour time difference. Monsieur and Madame had prepared my room and Mme provided me with just about everything from a bathrobe to a toothbrush. She told me that she wanted me to be more of a big sister to the little girls (aged $2\frac{1}{2}$ and $3\frac{1}{2}$) than an au pair. However the next day, my first efforts with helping Mme were met with a slap on the face from the youngest girl. It was only natural of course for them to feel some resentment. Mme was preparing a thesis in medicine and couldn't afford to spend a great deal of time with her children, plus she was expecting a new baby. I found out that the girls had been looked after by other people almost since their birth, which might have explained their resentment.

When trying to cope with such resentment, encourage children to articulate their feelings by asking leading questions. Something like: 'I used to feel sad when my mummy went off to work/out for the day when I was a little girl.' Substitute whatever you think appropriate. Once you've confirmed the source of the resentment, you might try reasoning, assuming the child is old enough to understand. Justify the mother's absences. For example: Mummy goes to work to earn enough money so she can pay for the family's treats, such as holidays, etc. You could also mention that she went to great lengths to find someone like yourself to be her special assistant. Stress all the fun things you have planned and how you're looking forward to spending time with the children (even if they are being so unreasonable that you dread the very sight of them).

The next thing to do, is grit your teeth and summon up as much patience and tolerance as you can possibly muster. As the children learn to trust you, it won't be too long before your positive feelings towards them become genuine and mutual.

Crying

Obviously, it is less disquieting when older children cry because they can articulate their feelings through speech. Once you know what's wrong, you can deal with the matter appropriately. With babies, however, it's more complicated because crying is just about the only way they can communicate. There is nothing more alarming than a screaming baby when you can't discover what's wrong.

As you become more familiar with a child, you will begin to distinguish its needs according to the type of cry. For example, a cry of hunger will sound different from a cry that indicates tiredness. If you're not sure, though, it's better to work your way through a basic check-list. Check nappies to see if they need changing; if they don't, give the child something to drink, and if that fails try a bottle of feed. A cry of distress could indicate colic or teething (discussed later) or some other less obvious source of pain. For example, something sharp like a safety pin may be sticking into the child.

On the other hand, he could be just plain bored or lonely, in which case a back rub and a few soothing words would help, or play some music and dance with him in your arms. If you're trying to finish some chores, put the baby in a carrier and carry him around with you if he's not too heavy and do both at the same time. Alternatively, take him out for a walk.

There may be times when children are so over-tired that nothing you can do will placate them. This situation should be avoided in the first place if at all possible, by sticking to a regular sleep schedule. Put them gently to bed with some soothing music playing in their room and leave them to cry themselves to sleep. Check on them every ten minutes or so, just to be on the safe side. Crying sometimes makes babies thirsty, so you might need to offer them another drink. If a child continues to cry but you're sure that there's nothing seriously wrong, accept that you've done all you can and remove yourself to a distant part of the house, for your own sanity.

Children can play up a bit

Disobedience

When you first begin your job, chances are the children will 'play up' a bit. This is quite normal because they are testing you to see how far they can go. It is very important that you impose firm but fair limitations on their behaviour and be consistent in what you will and will not accept from them.

Suppose they continue to be uncooperative; what do you do? Well, there are times when a quick smack on the behind would seem to solve the immediate problem, but parents often disapprove so that might not be a viable alternative. In any case, smacking should be reserved for gross misdemeanours and should never be overly aggressive. Counting to ten before you take any action sometimes helps to get things into perspective first. Disagreeable small children can be banished to a corner of the room without anything to amuse them, which usually works in a surprisingly short period of time. Remember that young children have a different concept of time, and ten minutes can seem like an eternity to them, so don't overdo it.

With older children, threatening to cancel a planned event might be all you need to exert some control. Be prepared to carry out such threats, though, or the child will simply ignore what you say in future. Make sure the punishment is justified by the crime. You shouldn't be unfair about it or they will rebel against you constantly. For minor disobediences you could withhold part of their usual snack on that particular day, and for something more major you could cancel a trip to the swimming pool or a planned picnic. Don't make threats a habit, though, or they will become meaningless, and habitual shouting often goes unheeded. Ask yourself if what you're angry about is really worth all the aggravation, and save a stern tone of voice for when it's really needed.

Try to avoid using sweets as a way of manipulating your charges. No one respects bribery, and it can prove expensive as well as damaging to their teeth. Consider whether or not the children are getting enough positive attention from you. If being naughty is the only time you really communicate with them, the chances are they'll be continually uncooperative. To a child, negative attention is better than nothing. Use an award system instead. The more you praise a child for good behaviour, the more likely he is to reproduce it.

Discipline

This can be a very touchy subject, especially if your idea of discipline is vastly different from that of the parents. Discipline means teaching a child what is acceptable behaviour and what is not, but this is open to interpretation. What is naughty to you (such as failing to say 'please' and 'thank you') may be the norm in your new household. Occasionally you may find the reverse is true. If you are unclear about a discipline issue, you must discuss it with the parents since, once again, consistency is very important. Avoid disciplining the children when the mother is present and obviously in charge. Keep in the background and never interfere in an issue between parent and child.

Children feel much more secure when they are taught to live within certain boundaries. Try not to restrict the child unnecessarily, but do offer guidance and set an example. It is better to substitute requests for demands, but there will be times when a command is unavoidable, for example, to warn a child who is approaching danger. Save your 'Nos' for when it really matters and always explain your reasons why. 'Because I said so' is not good enough.

During your first week, it is perhaps better not to be too much of a disciplinarian. You don't want to alienate the children before you've even had a chance to settle in. Remember that your goal is to build a loving relationship, not terrify them. On the other hand, this doesn't mean that you should pander to them either. If you do, it will be much harder to establish your authority later on. Aim to strike a balance, exerting more influence as you settle in; this process usually takes place in the natural course of things in any case.

Children will be doubly receptive to discipline which is applied with sensible good humour and inventiveness so they do not perceive it as discipline at all. For example Sharon invented a game which she called 'Mr. Plaque' to encourage young children to clean their teeth. She would tell them that Mr. Plaque and his band of merry men were hiding between their teeth, hoping to damage them unless they were scrubbed away with a toothbrush. She would examine the inside of their mouths and say that she just saw Mr Plaque behind a tooth. They enjoyed chasing him with brushes so much that her problem was getting them to stop!

One difficult problem is whether or not to inflict corporal punishment for bad behaviour. Personal views and cultural traditions do vary but generally parents do not encourage their nannies and au pairs to smack their children.

Some find the idea anathema. When Frances Thirlway dropped a casual remark, little more than a jest, to her employer about some children needing a good hiding, the mother reared back in horror, and went around for weeks muttering darkly about what a monster of violence Frances must be. If the parents are set against physical punishment (or indeed if you are) you will have to substitute other ways of disciplining them.

Even if you are granted a free hand, spanking should be used only for extremities of naughtiness and as a last resort. Try to avoid carrying out such punishments in front of others. There is no need to inflict the additional burden of public humiliation upon a child.

A discussion of the problems which arise when there is a major discrepancy between your ideas of discipline and that of the parents follows in the section *Problems with Parents*.

Tantrums

Many childhood tantrums could be avoided if those in charge of them learnt to read the warning signs before they got out of hand. Allowing a child to become so tired or hungry that he ends up distraught, is poor planning and unnecessary. Also, if the au pair or nanny is inconsistent, conflict may arise over misunderstandings. For example, if a toddler is allowed to walk most days, he may well resent it if you suddenly insist he has to ride in the push-chair. Explain to him the reasons for your change of routine.

Sometimes, though, whatever you do, a tantrum ensues. This is especially common in the two to three year old age group when children are striving to exert their independence. Remember that the more attention you give them, the more you are indirectly rewarding them for undesirable behaviour. Stand firm and tell the child that if he or she wants your attention, they will have to stop the tantrum first. Say it once and then totally ignore them until they stop. This is much easier if you're at home than in a public place, where an unpleasant scene can be somewhat embarrassing. Try to deal with the problem as soon as you sense it arising. Don't wait until a child is already screaming and kicking on the floor before you act. If it does get to this stage, try whispering in their ear. Sometimes kids will stop screaming as curiosity gets the better of them and they decide to quieten down so they can hear what you have to say. If the child is so angry that he holds in his breath, splash his face with cold water, since the shock will force him to take in air.

If you are in the home, removing the child to a separate room may be an immediate solution. It gives you a chance to calm down and deprives the child of an audience. Alternatively, try distracting him by doing something unusual. Mimic his actions and stage your own tantrum. With any luck, you could both end up laughing.

Eating Problems

You should encourage your charge to stick to a routine of meals. If the children are used to snacking at liberty, they might whine a bit once you start imposing a meal system, but you must stick it out or you'll be preparing food constantly, half of which will go to waste. Children soon learn, and it is just as much for their convenience as for yours since once they start school, they won't be able to eat at will.

Try not to over-react if you're landed with a fussy eater. The angrier you get at meal times, the more power the child exerts over you, so it's best to ignore picky eating.

Sharon encountered a particularly worrying case:

I was once looking after a little boy of two who was a very fussy eater and I had a lot of trouble trying to persuade him to eat nutritious things. At one point, I was so worried that I took him to see a doctor who reassured me that it was just a phase and that the child would eventually start eating a more normal diet of his own accord. Sure enough, his eating gradually improved.

Have you ever noticed how, for example, when you've been eating a lot of sweet food in any one day, you suddenly develop a craving for something savoury? Well, I think it's nature's way of redressing the balance, and even children will automatically crave something their body lacks. Also, once I had the doctor's reassurance that there was nothing seriously wrong, I became much more relaxed at meal times and I think this attitude was communicated to my charge.

Make sure a poor eater comes to the table hungry. Perhaps it's better to eliminate snacks. Give small portions of food so he isn't overwhelmed by the task in front of him. Don't make an issue out of finishing everything on his plate; children know when they've had enough and you should respect this. Warn him that there'll be nothing more to eat until the next meal break. If he complains of hunger a short time later, then that's just too bad; make him wait.

The same applies to picky eaters. If children are deliberately playing with their food, put a reasonable time limit on meal times and then clear away whether they have finished or not. Don't force them to eat something they hate. Children do go through fads so continue to give balanced meals and let them select what they like. They will start to eat properly long before they are in danger of starving to death!

Food Allergies

Some foods, especially those with a lot of E-additives, have been shown to cause hyperactivity in some children. This can be a very disturbing condition whereby the child is very excitable, lacks concentration, appears to need very little sleep and can be very destructive. If you suspect that the child in your care is a sufferer, keep an eye on his diet which may give you a clue as to how to improve his behaviour. It has been found, for example, that some children respond badly to Tartrazine, an artificial dye used in certain orange drinks. If your charge behaves exceptionally badly after consuming a particular kind of food, there may be an allergy link. Try eliminating the suspect pabulum from their diet and observe any alteration in conduct. Obviously, if there is a dramatic improvement, the offending food should be avoided.

Research concerning a possible connection between diet and hyperactivity is far from conclusive, however, so it is best to seek medical advice when dealing with the problem. Indeed, what you consider to be hyperactive might actually be normal high spirits. If you have little or no previous experience of dealing with children, it can come as a shock to discover just how active and exhausting some of them can be. Giving them extra scope for letting off steam may be all that is required, so make sure your charges have plenty of opportunity for physical exercise.

Sleeping and Dreaming

If your charge usually has trouble getting off to sleep at nights, try taking him for a walk before bedtime. A relaxing bath usually helps. It's best to give the children some sort of notice that bedtime is approaching so that they don't suddenly have to disrupt their play. If they put up resistance, be firm with them and stick to a set routine. Give them their bath at the same time each evening and put them to bed straight afterwards. A bedtime story is an additional way of helping them to wind down. Avoid robust games or television programmes which will excite them, and choose a book that is calming rather than scary. Ask them if there is anything they need before they go to bed; it will save delaying tactics later on. They'll eventually adapt to, and respect, your rules. Allow older children to have a light on for a limited period of time, so they can read to themselves. Then be firm and consistent about switching the light off.

Babies sometimes confuse day with night. Try to prevent them from falling asleep before bedtime by stimulating them, otherwise you'll have problems getting them to sleep at the right time. The same applies to naps. If they are sleeping too long, gently wake them up. Give them their bottle in a dim light to help emphasise the closing in of the day and the approach of bedtime. Adding a little cereal to the final feed should abate hunger through the night.

If the parents are going out in the evening, it can be a little unsettling for the children if the departure coincides with their bedtime routine. Should this happen often, you would be justified in suggesting that they leave at a more convenient time whenever possible. After the children have already fallen asleep is ideal, but this isn't always practicable. Therefore, encourage the children to say goodbye to their parents so that they understand that you will be in charge for the evening. They'll probably make a fuss initially, but once the parents have gone, they usually settle down. Distracting them with something amusing should help.

A trick with toddlers is to spray a little perfume or put a dab of handcream on their hand and then tell them to sniff the scent until it's gone. The scent itself, combined with deep breaths should be enough to relax them so they fall asleep.

Fear of the dark is very common and you should be sympathetic. Leave the door open and the hall light on, and give the child a cuddly toy to hug. Try putting a radio in the room with the volume turned low. Nightmares can usually be dealt with by giving calm reassurances. Lying down with them until they go back to sleep is also very comforting, but time-consuming for you. If the bad dreams persist, and are particularly frightening for a child, they might warrant professional counselling. Sleepwalkers should be walked back to bed and precautions should be taken. For example, a gate across the top of the stairs and child-proof window catches, or bars on the windows. It is quite normal for children to sleepwalk occasionally because their minds are so active, but if you are concerned that there might be an underlying emotional problem, do seek professional advice.

Early risers can be deterred from disturbing the whole household by putting a collection of absorbing play-things beside the bed. Do this after the child is asleep, though, otherwise he'll be playing all night. Leaving out a covered bowl containing dry cereal or crackers will also stave off early morning hunger. Setting an alarm clock and telling older children not to disturb anyone before it rings will keep them in their rooms (you hope). Don't forget to show them how to switch it off.

Finally if you use an intercom which has a wire running from the child's room to the sitting room or kitchen so you can hear from a distance if they start crying, make sure you have the speaking and listening ends the right way round. One family we know were delighted at how soundly their child slept until they discovered that they had the device back to front so that the child could hear everything that was said downstairs but the parents could hear nothing from upstairs.

If you use an intercom make sure you have it the right way round

Toilet Training

Many children respond well to toilet training between the ages of eighteen months and two years. However, every child is different, so if you seem to be having problems, try stopping the training for a few weeks and then pick up where you left off.

Children learn mainly by imitation, so if you don't feel too inhibited, allow the toddler in the loo with you sometimes or rope in a compliant older brother or sister instead. Incorporate whatever language the family uses to describe the body's processes so the child becomes familiar with the terms with which he needs to express himself. Once you have gained some idea of your charge's habits, put him or her on the pot around that time. Providing some books or music can help amuse children while you are training them to sit in the bathroom. Turning on the taps or whistling may also encourage them to urinate. If you don't get the desired result, try not to be impatient. The more tension involved, the worse it will become.

Never punish your charge for 'accidents', since it is harmful to make a child feel guilty about an action he hasn't yet learned to control. Involve them instead in the cleaning-up process, for this will teach them responsibility. Letting them wear plastic pants instead of nappies around the house also encourages them to exert more control in the absence of a safety-net.

Above all, reward children for any successes because they will then be more inclined to repeat them. Praise them when they tell you that they want to 'go' — even if the cry comes too late. Emphasise in a calm but firm tone that next time he should tell you before instead of after.

Sometimes a child who is already trained will revert to soiling his pants again. This could be a sign of tension in his life. Perhaps he has just started playschool or there's a new baby in the family. It may be necessary to repeat part of the toilet training but if you relieve the cause of the anxiety, the problem should resolve itself.

Many children respond well to toilet training

Bedwetting

This is only to be expected if you are currently trying to toilet train a child, but sometimes older children can have difficulty as well. Again it may be a sign of tension: perhaps a change of schools has caused it, or even a change of au pair. Try to find the root cause and remedy it if you can. A little reassurance might be all that is needed. You should consult a doctor if bedwetting becomes a habit, because it can sometimes indicate an allergy to cow's milk or other problem.

If a child is prone to wet the bed, the first thing you should do is to protect the mattress by covering it with a plastic sheet; do it as unobtrusively as possible so as not to draw unnecessary attention to the problem, making the child feel guilty or ashamed. They might also become subconsciously aware that the bed is 'safe' and so exercise little control over their bladder muscles.

You could try restricting fluid intake shortly before bedtime, but if bedwetting is a real problem this will just reduce the amount of fluid passed. Besides, a child who is thirsty probably won't settle down to sleep. Taking him to the loo before you go to bed yourself might improve things. They will be half asleep, of course, but don't take over completely. By leading him through the motions they will learn the routine and begin to do it automatically. Pick them up out of bed and lead them by the hand to the toilet; don't carry them. You might have to do this regularly for a few nights before you meet with success. If a child's bed is still wet in the morning, get them to help you strip it and put the sheets in the washing machine. Teach them, in a kindly way, to take responsibility for their actions. Above all, reassure the child that he or she will grow out of it.

PROBLEMS WITH PARENTS

Even if you have sole charge or a liberal degree of autonomy, you are still answerable to the parents, and it is imperative that you maintain a good relationship with them. If the parents are agreeable but the children difficult, the work will be tolerable. It tends not to work the other way round, though. If you don't get on with the parents it can be utter misery and lead to your premature departure or dismissal. Sometimes there is a personality clash whereby it is no one person's fault but it just seems impossible to see eye to eye. If this situation cannot be resolved, it is better for all concerned if you look for another job. But before you consider such a drastic measure always discuss the problem with the parents. Many disagreements could be sorted out if only they were discussed long before they reached crisis proportions.

Pay and Time Off

Since both au pairing and nannying are often such flexible and informal jobs in comparison to, say, a secretary in a large firm, things can be a bit untidy when it comes to regular pay cheques and time off. Sometimes there is a genuine reason for such lapses. It is quite conceivable that a busy mother could forget pay-day once or twice and pay you late, and parents working shifts can sometimes become muddled over free time. How should you proceed, though, if this becomes a habit?

First of all, have a mutually arranged date so you know when to expect your wages and free time; otherwise *you* may become confused. If discrepancies arise, some sort of routine will make it easier to sort out. Being paid on the first day of every month, for example, is much better than a vague 'every few weeks'. If the parents are slap-dash about this, be firm. You've earned your money and you have a right to regular wages. Keep a note of when you are paid and how much, if it isn't always a fixed sum, for example, if the parents pay you to work an extra day instead of compensating for the time later on. You should ask in advance of a public holiday whether you will be compensated for it. If your pay-cheque is overdue, don't let it run to more than a week before reminding them. You may hate the thought of haggling over money, but once in a while it may be necessary to assert yourself. Don't delay until it gets out of hand; the bigger the sum grows, the harder it will be to ask for it and you'll only become resentful.

If you're having a hard time extracting your pay, an agency can come in very handy. It is useful to have an intermediary in these matters, and the agency staff will probably be more experienced and professional in dealing with such problems. Never ask an agency to sort out your trouble for you until you've tried talking over the discrepancy with the family first. Agencies should only be brought in as a last resort. Au pair and nannying positions are usually fairly easy to come by, so if your situation is intolerable, don't be afraid to look for another job. Estrangement for financial reasons, however, is very rare. Most families who hire help make sure that they can afford the salary.

Discrepancies over free time are more common because there are no hard and fast rules. Your job description should give you some guide as to how much free time you can expect but this is often implemented rather loosely. For example, you may find you are required to babysit a few evenings more than was originally agreed, but it is up to the individual to decide how much extra time she is prepared to give. As long as your cooperation is appreciated, it's worth being flexible over certain requests, e.g. staying in an extra evening or two in the week. Think of the opportunities you have to run personal errands when, in theory, you are supposed to be working for your employer. A formal company would never be that flexible.

By all means speak to the employers, if you feel your time is being taken advantage of. Just because the parents work shifts or go on business trips, there is no reason for you to miss out on entire days off. You will have to fit in with their schedule, of course, but you should still be compensated for any time owing to you.

If you have a hard time extracting your pay

Holiday time can be problematic, unless it has been discussed at the beginning. Sometimes families are reluctant to promise a holiday until they get to know and trust their live-in helper and want to reward her. In some countries (like Belgium and Switzerland) au pairs are entitled by law to paid holiday if they fulfil their six month or one year contract. In general, if you have worked for a family for a whole year, you should be given at least two weeks off with pay. Most parents give you the option of an independent vacation or one taken with the family. Consider the pros and cons carefully. Holidays with young children are seldom restful, and if it is a self-catering affair it will be even worse. There are advantages, however, since the holiday expenses will normally be paid for by your employers and the trip might be one you couldn't normally afford. Make sure you know in advance what your options are. Obviously, if the parents are paying for the holiday, it is only fair that you give them some assistance in return, but it would be very disappointing to work as normal, only to discover afterwards that it counted as your vacation.

If you feel strongly about having Christmas and Easter off, there's no harm in trying to arrange it with parents. Remember, though, that most families could do with your help on these occasions and you will probably have to compromise. If you get on well with the family, it can be a very enjoyable time to be with them, especially the children. Some families may prefer privacy at these times, in which case you should respect their wishes and find an alternative place to celebrate.

Requesting a Pay Rise

Only you can judge whether or not you are paid your worth, bearing in mind the fringe benefits you receive and the overall budget of the family concerned. However should a mother become pregnant while you are still in her employ (see below), you have the right to negotiate a pay rise if she expects you to be working for her after the baby is born. A new arrival can have a significant impact on your work load, especially if the mother plans to resume her career afterwards.

The best time to request a pay rise is when you can expect the least number of interruptions and the parents are at their most relaxed. If the request is denied, you must decide if you are willing to continue working there at the current rate. If a rise is agreed, establish exactly how much so you can decide if it is satisfactory.

It is worth mentioning here that few au pairs or nannies work in private families because of the money. There are some lucrative positions around, but generally girls offer their labour in exchange for experience and the pleasure involved in performing a worthwhile job with plenty of scope for enjoyment.

Interference with your Social Life

Decent families should understand that your life does not revolve exclusively around them. In other words, you are entitled to a social life. No one has the right to tell a fully grown woman what time she ought to come in at night, providing she isn't noisy when she returns and her job performance is not adversely affected by, for example, over-sleeping and/or a hangover. Nobody wants to leave their child in the care of someone who is only half-awake — or half-dead. If the parents complain about your late nights, ask yourself if they could be justified in doing so. This is one situation where it is frequently the au pair who is being inconsiderate.

Some families can be very awkward about allowing you to bring friends home. Sometimes this can be for security reasons; if their home harbours a lot of valuables, you can understand their concern about strangers entering their house. Use your discretion and always ask your employers for permission in advance of receiving guests. Throwing parties in the parents' absence is definitely out, unless they specifically invite you to do so. Having one or two friends over during your free time seems reasonable enough. After introducing them to your employers, it's best to entertain them in your own living quarters so that you don't impose on the family's privacy. Conducting a romance under these circumstances is more tricky, but if your family is reasonably hospitable, they may not mind. If you have permission to enjoy dinners *à deux* once the children are in bed, make a point of replacing the extra groceries which you have consumed. Your employers are responsible for feeding you only, not your circle of friends as well.

Even if your family is particularly liberal, most do not approve of their nanny's boyfriend spending the night in her room. Save your nocturnal activities for his apartment or somewhere other than your place of work. There should be no reason why you shouldn't sleep elsewhere on your nights off, providing this doesn't interfere with your work the next day.

Unrealistic Expectations

Au pairs and (occasionally) nannies are sometimes expected to do an unreasonable amount of work. While au pairs are supposed to be learning about the German/French/Italian way of life, they may end up learning only Frau Rottbleit's/Mme. Travailleur's/Senora Mostruoso's way of life or at least of housekeeping, with all its irrationalities and eccentricities.

If the employers are reasonable, you should be able to discuss what you consider to be an excessive burden of work. Many mothers unthinkingly pile on more duties when they see that their au pair or nanny is coping adequately with the present ones. The best line of argument in this case is that you feel you will be neglecting the children if you attempt too much cleaning and laundering.

A pair of German psychiatrists liked the lawn hoovered every day

Other employers are just plain neurotic and you may achieve nothing by complaining. For example the wealthy Italian family for whom Susie Walton worked made her do all the laundry, except the sheets, by hand since they didn't approve of washing machines. Frances Thirlway worked for a pair of German psychiatrists who, when on holiday in France, hoovered the garden patio daily and expected Frances to share their standards of cleanliness. Camilla Preeston's host mother in France expected her not only to do the washing and drying up but to disinfect the sink, brushes, sponges, tap and rubbish bin on every occasion. But this was only the beginning of the burdens placed on her just-turned-18 shoulders:

Mme decided she wasn't getting enough work done on her thesis (which she partly blamed on me, not the fact that instead of working she would do things such as wash the girls' dolls' clothes). So she decided to spend five days including two nights away from home. This change made a big difference to my working hours and I had sole charge of the three children for up to two days at a time. To help, Mme drew up a timetable for me, which started at 7am and ended at 8pm (which left no room for my French lessons). I had by this time taken almost full responsibility of the new baby, which to my surprise also meant on my days off on more than one occasion. Mme expected me to pick up the two girls from school by bus with the baby which wasn't too easy. Needless to say, I was very tired by the time I went to bed and even more so when the baby started teething and wouldn't sleep during the day.

Like most au pairs, Camilla found it very difficult to talk to her host about her hours and missed French lessons. Because she had only two months left to go, she decided that it wasn't worth the effort of arguing.

Maternal Resentment and Jealousy

When a mother works or has other obligations, she often doesn't spend as much time with her children as she would like. Hiring a home-help is one way of relieving the pressures on her, but for many women a degree of conflict remains. It is quite possible for a mother to resent your role in her child's life even though she has arranged things that way and is otherwise glad of your help. Problems such as these may be diminished by a little sensitivity on your part. When the mother arrives home and has had a chance to catch her breath, ask her whether or not she needs your help. This gives her the option of spending some time alone with her children. Natalia de Cuba adopted a technique which the mother greatly appreciated, of leaving detailed notes on the kids' behaviour, little successes, nightmares, etc.

You may find yourself beginning to occupy first place in the child's affections, which can create a very awkward situation. After working for a busy family in Rome for several months, Emily Hatchwell was appalled when the four-year-old girl rushed to her instead of to the mother when the two adults entered the room together. At that point she began purposely to distance herself from the little girl, and this strategy seemed to be effective.

Au pairs often have problems when they find themselves working alongside a mother who has quit a satisfying job to have children. Inevitably some of these mothers feel envious of their husbands who continue to enjoy the satisfaction of their careers, and they may channel their resentment towards the live-in helper. One of the first things that Carla Mitchell's employer in Paris did (a psychiatrist who was no longer practising) was to give her a book to read called *Mother's Day is Over,* a radical feminist argument that the impulses of motherhood are *not* universal to women. Carla found this quite disconcerting and rightly diagnosed deep unhappiness in her employer.

If you do end up working alongside the mother, it can be difficult to determine when your services are required and when they are not. Explain that you are going off to do some chores, but are available if she needs you to take over with the children. This way, you are not avoiding your duties, but at the same time you are leaving her in control.

Employee Resentment

One of the most galling problems that a few au pairs face is that they are treated not as a member of the family but as a servant, and this can lead to real bitterness. For example, the parents may fail to introduce their live-in helper to visiting friends and yet ask her to fetch or serve things. You have to get used to being invisible, which is hard on the ego. You have to be fairly lucky to find employers who will treat you as an equal but there is plenty of scope for decent treatment between these two.

A less predictable form of resentment can arise if you have grown extremely close to the children. Then, when the parents come home, the children abandon you and you suddenly feel superfluous. This is sometimes so blatant that it can become hurtful, and you resent the mother for taking over. Even though you recognise the rightness of the children preferring their parents, you may still find it difficult to remain detached.

There are occasions when you have had a particularly enjoyable day with your charge(s) and everything goes fine until the mother comes home. All hell seems to break loose, and you end up wishing she hadn't bothered to return. Once again, this is quite common behaviour. Children sometimes store up all their bad feelings so they can give vent to them when the parents return. Don't blame the mother or father for this reaction or feel guilty that it's somehow your fault. It may be that the children are subconsciously punishing their parents for having left them.

By contrast, it can sometimes seem as though the mother or father gets to do all the fun things with the children while all the hard work is left to you. You can perhaps console yourself that at least you may be helping to strike a blow for equality within marriage, since if you weren't there to do the drudgery, it would probably be the mother who would have to do most of the scivvying, leaving the father to adopt the role of kindly godfather. In any case, you too can participate in the fun. If you organise your chores properly, there should always be time for you to do enjoyable things with the children. Try taking the initiative and organise some outings of your own to the zoo, to exhibitions, or whatever you like. All work and no play will make you a dull (and resentful) person.

An unexpected source of resentment can develop once you start making friends with other nannies. You get a privileged insight into how other families operate and sometimes end up feeling that you have a raw deal. Au pairing and nannying positions do vary enormously and, chances are, there will always be someone with an apparently better job than you. Try to establish whether or not your envy is justified and then take steps to resolve it, if you can. Either accept what you have and appreciate it, or look for another job. Seething resentment is not a good atmosphere in which to raise children.

Conflict Over Discipline

If you and your employers have vastly different views on how to raise children, a great deal of bad feeling can result. Usually it is a case of the parents being more lenient with their offspring than the helper thinks is appropriate, leaving the au pair or nanny to suffer the consequences of the parents' indulgence. Once again, communicating your feelings as tactfully as you can and then compromising is the best policy, and you may even learn something from an exchange of ideas. British parents tend to be stricter with their children than many other nationalities and you may come to appreciate the advantage of a more relaxed approach to child-rearing. It is important to remain open-minded about attitudes that are different from the experiences of your own upbringing. This was a bitter lesson that Maree Lakey from Australia had to learn when she au paired for a wealthy family in Germany:

> *I come from a very modest background and was shocked at the amount of toys, clothes and other possessions which the children had. I witnessed with disbelief how the children were 'disciplined' by the parents. If something didn't quite go their own way, they would fly into a screaming rage. The mother, who was also extremely excitable, would yell back at the children at first. She would however never stick to her guns; instead she would eventually back down and the children would later receive some sort of present to 'make everything good again'. My attempts at discipline would most likely end in the children going to the mother or grandmother, who would promptly disregard what I had tried to enforce and give them what they wanted. I could never compete with this. It was an impossible situation. Once I was totally fed up and uncharacteristically voiced my disapproval. My outburst was met with shock and a quick assurance from the mother that of course the children must obey my decisions as much as those from the parents. These were empty words and so I just had to accept the situation.*

If you do think that some basic change in routine would benefit family relations or the behaviour of the children, you should consider trying to discuss the possibility with the family, employing all your skills of diplomacy. In some cases you will find the parents more than willing to take advice from their live-in helper, if they have come to respect her judgment and native good sense. For example a 20 year old Irish woman, who got on famously with her sophisticated New England employers, noticed that the little boy was becoming increasingly spoilt. She identified the source of the problem as the parents' tendency to lavish too much attention on him whenever they were together. Maeve advised the mother to ignore the boy for half an hour on her return from work and then play with him. Not only did the mother take the advice but the boy became much easier to handle and better behaved almost immediately. So it is possible to make some useful contributions.

Sometimes the parents are unwilling or unable to see your point of view in which case you are bound to accept their way of doing things. They are, after all, paying for a service, and in this respect it is you who must be more flexible. Au pairs have far less responsibility than nannies for the discipline of children, but in both cases there is a limit to what you can achieve or how much you can interfere. Some au pairs, like Jessie Lane, think that it is a waste of energy trying to inculcate any manners or habits which have not been taught by the parents:

> *The bringing up of a child is up to the parents and don't forget it. I am sure that had I let the children have their own way, I would have got on a lot better and had a much nicer time.*

This is of course much easier said than done, and the compulsion to correct bad manners or reprimand selfish and rude behaviour can be irresistible.

If you spend most of your time clenching your teeth and seething with silent fury it is best to look for another job. Unfortunately it is often not until you live with a family that such problems come to light.

Flirtatious Fathers

The *idea* that fathers regularly make passes at their au pair or nanny is far more prevalent than the reality. Often the father is quite a remote figure and most are far too sensible or preoccupied to consider such an affair. It would be naïve to assume, however, that such events never occur, so how do you cope if it happens to you? It is simple common sense to distance yourself as soon as you sense danger. Different cultures can have conflicting views on such matters, and this can sometimes lead to misunderstandings. When in doubt, however, trust your instincts and leave the room. If he persists, communicate in no uncertain terms that you are not interested. If that doesn't do any good, threaten to tell his wife. If it becomes necessary to carry out your threat, be prepared for dismissal. If things have progressed to that stage, it's probably time to leave in any case. No job is so good that it's worth putting up with harrassment. If the attraction is mutual, you should do your best to discourage the feelings. You are there to benefit the family, not to destroy it.

One prospective au pair heading off to Paris was so worried about this problem that she chose a single parent family which seemed to offer ideal conditions. Not long after her arrival she discovered that the woman who was her employer (whose profession had been described as 'stylist' on the forms) was a pornographer. This combined with the fact that the boy was a complete brat brought her to such a low ebb that she burst into tears one evening, whereupon the employer began stroking her hair. She left the next day.

The idea that fathers regularly make passes at the au pair or nanny is more prevalent than the reality.

Marital Problems

With marital breakdown at an all-time high around the world, you may find yourself working in an atmosphere of tension and unhappiness. Any marriage problems are unlikely to be evident to you until you are actually in their midst.

This of course puts pressures on the children who will sense the strain and fear the disintegration of their family.

The extent of such a problem depends on the personalities and actions of the people involved and is, therefore, largely out of your control. You are not a marriage guidance counsellor, so refuse to be drawn into any marital disputes. Remain as impartial as possible, even though your loyalties may lie more with one parent than the other, and concentrate on the children. They will need a great deal of affection, encouragement and distraction during such turbulent times. Matt Tomlinson enjoyed his life with a young French family so much that he continued to visit them on return trips to France, and he was sorry to learn that they were divorcing. His advice is to try and keep the children out of it and be your usual self, since they will need something solid more than ever.

If you are working for a family in which the parents are already divorced, the situation is bound to have affected the children to some degree. The apparent loss of a mother or father causes them to feel bereft and insecure. Male au pairs or nannies can be of help in redressing the balance in cases where the father has left the family and it is a great shame that this option is so rarely available.

COPING WITH A NEW ARRIVAL

The arrival of a new-born baby in the family will generate much joy and excitement, but it will also mean more work for you and bring its own unique set of problems.

One of the first things to consider when a mother informs you of her pregnancy is whether or not you will still be working for her by the time the baby is born. If your contract is due to expire shortly before or after the birth and you have no plans to extend it, remind your employer of your proposed leaving date. This should give her plenty of time to arrange for someone to replace you before the birth.

During the pregnancy, be prepared for mood swings, exhaustion and complaints from the mother. She may be feeling resentful that her body is no longer her own and she can't do everything she was used to doing. If the au pair is the only person around, she will bear the brunt of the moaning.

Naturally, a new infant adds considerably to the workload. Even if the mother looks after the baby, you will be left with other tasks which were previously shared. Prior to the baby's arrival you should establish if a maternity nurse will be hired, and what new duties will ensue. Consider, for example, the increase in laundry and your possible involvement in night feeds. Make sure you fully understand what will be expected of you.

Telling the Children

Usually it is the mother who will announce the imminent birth to her children, so do not broach the subject first without her consent. Nine months can seem like a very long time to little children so it is best not to relay the news too early in the pregnancy. When this time has come, be prepared to answer any questions they might ask you.

In the meantime there are some practical things you can do to help prepare them. Talk about the baby, emphasising how tiny and vulnerable he or she will be, and how you need the children to help you look after the new little one. Encourage them to mix with infants so they learn what to expect. Above all, reassure them that affection does not come in limited supplies and they will be loved just as much as their new brother or sister.

Generally speaking children are greatly interested in the prospect of a new arrival and thrive on the general air of expectation and excitement. When the baby is born they should be encouraged to handle him or her and play their part in the new regime so that some of the glamour of the event rubs off on them. Children's natural curiosity means they are likely to be very keen on all the details surrounding and following the birth.

Explaining the Facts of Life

You'll never have a more natural opportunity to explain the facts of life than when there is a pregnancy in the family. The mother might prefer to deal with this subject herself, however, so you should first establish how involved she wants you to be, if at all.

If the parents wish to handle the matter by themselves, and your charge is asking you awkward questions, reply in a casual tone of voice that you do not know the answer but suggest he asks his mum or dad. Nannies more than au pairs, usually find that their involvement in the child's sex education is expected. If you are given this responsibility, don't introduce the subject yourself but wait until your charge takes the initiative. Answer the questions only when he or she poses them and reply in language appropriate to the child's age. If a child is old enough to ask the question, he is old enough to receive a reply.

The most common question children will ask is, where do babies come from? Don't elaborate unnecessarily by bombarding them with too much information. A simple explanation that babies grow in their mummy's tummy should suffice for the time being. The mother will probably allow her children to feel the baby kicking inside her. Should your charges ask how the baby got there, just tell them that he grew from a tiny seed that was planted inside his mother.

Older children may require more advanced explanations depending upon the knowledge they have already acquired to date. Keep your answers direct and uncomplicated, and try not to be unnaturally solemn. This can add tension to what should be a relaxed discussion. A humorous picture book on the subject is Babette Cole's *Mummy Laid an Egg!* aimed at 6-8 year olds.

When the mother is in hospital

Unless a relative comes to help out while the mother is in hospital, this could be an exceptionally busy time if you are not used to sole charge. You might have to curtail your evening social life for a while, leaving the father free to visit his wife. It would be nice if you offered to work your days off during the mother's absence, especially if the father is struggling to cope alone. Suggest taking some extra time off in a month or so instead, once the baby has arrived and a new routine has been established. Your thoughtfulness will be appreciated and you will have the opportunity to take a mini-holiday later on.

Providing the parents have no objections, take the children to visit their mother. This will reassure them that they have not been abandoned, and help to familiarise them with the new baby.

Coping with the Mother

The first few weeks after giving birth and returning home can be a particularly difficult time for a mother, even if she has been through it all before. She may be prone to mood swings as a result of hormonal changes in her body, and suffer from fatigue. You should encourage her to rest as much as possible, offering to take over the care of the infant when necessary. Avoid interfering and dominating the proceedings, however. The mother will want some time alone to enjoy her new child, so concentrate more on the other children and on keeping the house running smoothly. For the first couple of weeks you may have to adopt chores, such as grocery shopping, that were not previously your responsibility.

Post-natal irritability or tearfulness can be difficult to understand, but try to be tolerant, sympathetic, and offer support and reassurance whenever needed. If you are used to sole charge, it will take time to adapt to your new supporting role.

Jealousy

By encouraging the children to help with the baby you will avoid the risk of their feeling disgruntled by the appearance of the new brother or sister. You cannot entirely make up for this, but spending as much time as possible with the older children will further help to alleviate their insecurity. Try also to plan more activities than you normally would and grant new privileges, emphasising that it's because they are so grown up now that they have a younger brother or sister. For example, if parents are in agreement, you could extend bedtime by fifteen minutes.

Listen to any outbursts from the older children and reassure them that you understand. Tell them a story about how you felt towards your own baby brother. Be watchful for acts of aggression towards the baby but make allowances for any mild acts of jealousy since drawing attention to them could make things worse.

Feeding

Not all women are able to breast-feed and if the mother chooses to return to work shortly after the birth, you will have to take over feeding by bottle.

Fresh milk should not be used for new-borns because of its high sodium and phosphate content. Commercial feeds are suitable and can be bought either in powder or liquid form. Make the formula up exactly as directed by the manufacturer. If you make it too concentrated, you will over-load the baby's kidneys.

It is essential that all bottle equipment is washed and sterilised before use. You can do this by soaking the bottles and teats, etc. in boiling water for five minutes and then leaving them to drain under a cover. This method will cause more wear and tear, however, and there is an easier way of doing things. It is possible to buy a special tank which you fill with a hypochlorite solution. All feeding equipment can be sterilised in that, until it is needed again. Do not prepare and keep feeds warm for any length of time because milk is a culture medium for bacteria. The bottles can be made up twenty-four hours in advance, however, and stored in the fridge. Throw away any left-over milk once it has been heated.

Warm up the bottle just before a feed by standing it in a jug of hot water.

Microwaves can also be used though it is difficult to obtain a balanced temperature. It is very easy to overheat the formula and then you will be left with a hungry baby screaming for his dinner while you frantically try to cool the bottle under running water. Always test the feed on the back of your hand or your wrist before giving it to the child, to make sure it is tepid and not too hot. If the formula becomes cold during feeding, re-heat it. Babies seem to prefer heated liquid, probably because breast milk is warm.

The teat hole should be big enough to allow a regular flow of milk. Too little and the baby will become frustrated; too big and he will take too much, possibly causing him to choke. To make the teat bigger, pierce with a sterilised needle. Ideally, it should take about fifteen minutes to complete a feed. Bottle-fed babies tend to suffer more from wind, so you should stop half-way through to burp him. If the baby gulps his milk, give him one or two tablespoons of cooled boiled water, just before his feed. It will take the edge off his appetite and he will drink more slowly. Babies like a drink of warm unsweetened boiled water anyway, so give him a few sips from time to time as part of his routine.

Mealtimes should take place in a quiet, relaxing atmosphere if at all possible. Place a bib around the baby's neck, prop him up into a half-sitting position and hold him close against your breast while feeding him his bottle. It helps if you are free to concentrate on your new charge, giving him plenty of eye contact.

This can be difficult if you have other children to care for too, so get them fed and settled with some amusement first. If meal times clash, give the older child a small snack to stave off his hunger.

Most babies need feeding every three hours but some more frequently. Don't try to force a child to finish his bottle. Just note how much he has drunk and he will probably make up for it later in the day.

Nappy Rash

This is caused by bacteria from the baby's stools which breaks down his urine into ammonia, and burns the skin. The bacteria thrives in alkaline conditions which is why bottle-fed babies tend to suffer from it more. (The stools of breast-fed babies are more acidic.)

To avoid nappy rash as much as possible, change the baby frequently. Disposable nappies are easier but more expensive. Cloth nappies should be soaked and washed thoroughly to remove the ammonia. Avoid using plastic pants as these keep the urine close to the skin and will aggravate the rash. Air the baby's bottom regularly. Let him lie face-down on an old blanket to protect the carpet.

If a baby does get nappy rash, stop washing the baby's bottom with soap and water which will dry the skin and exacerbate the rash. Use a liquid cream instead, such as baby lotion. Make sure he is dried well after a bath; this can be done most efficiently with a hair dryer on a warm (not hot) setting. Apply a thick barrier cream to his bottom, such as zinc oxide or petroleum jelly, before securing a clean nappy.

Seek medical advice if the rash seem particularly inflamed and persistent.

Colic

Young babies up to the age of three months are sometimes afflicted with colic, which causes acute spasms of pain in the intestines. The child doesn't just cry, he screams, becomes red in the face, clenches his fists and draws both his legs up towards his stomach. Gripe water is a traditional remedy for this, but its effectiveness is unproven and, besides, you may have trouble obtaining it abroad. Warm drinks of boiled water can be given instead and encourage the child to burp by patting his back vigorously. Applying a warm (not hot) covered hot water bottle to his abdomen may also offer relief.

Stimulating the New-born

Babies are far more intelligent than they are sometimes given credit for, and they should not be ignored once their basic needs have been tended. Give the baby plenty of cuddles and spend some time singing or talking to him. It won't be long before he or she responds to your facial expressions.

New-born babies cannot focus their eyes on objects further away than one foot, so when amusing him don't hold the playthings too far away. Make his room as colourful as possible. You could begin by decorating his nursery wall with the parents' congratulation cards, providing they have given you permission to do so. Put bright transfers on the inside of his crib and hang a musical mobile over the side. It's a good idea to hang a second one over his change table to amuse him while changing his nappy. Putting a mirror on the wall beside him will also provide some entertainment.

Take your young charge for walks in his pram so he gets plenty of air and comes into contact with stimuli outside his home. It is very useful to double up on baby supplies for outings. This enables you to have a permanently packed bag ready for impromptu excursions except for the addition of a few last-minute articles. The following check-list might prove helpful: nappies, plastic bags for used nappies, safety pins for cloth nappies, spare set of clothes, baby wipes/cotton wool/tissues/toilet paper, plastic sheet for changing (washable wallpaper works just as well), baby lotion, barrier cream, talc, bottle and teat, formula, bib, playthings. Remember to replace all the non-perishables when you return, in preparation for the next outing.

Leisure time and departure

CREATING A SOCIAL LIFE

Building a social life from scratch is hard enough at any time but becomes even more difficult in an alien tongue and culture. Unless you are exceptionally lucky and find yourself content to socialise with your host family, you will have to take positive steps to meet people and participate in activities outside the confines of your employers' home. This may require uncharacteristically extrovert behaviour for you, but overcoming initial inhibitions almost always pays worthwhile dividends. There is no substitute for a friend when you are feeling low. Even an acquaintance (preferably one who speaks your language fluently) can go a long way to relieve some of the loneliness and isolation.

Meeting Other Au Pairs/Nannies

Working for a family can get very claustrophobic and it is most important to make friends of your own away from the home. When work, children or parents are getting you down, it is essential to have someone else you can have a good moan with and so keep a sense of proportion about the usual stresses and strains of family life.

Don't wait until your first day off to begin the search for companions. Ask your employers to introduce you to other households who hire live-in helpers. Most will be more than willing to oblige if they know any, since it is in their best interests for you to be happy and to settle. You may be surprised at the number of foreign young people in your vicinity doing just what you are doing: for instance in a small village 80km south-west of Paris, Jessie Lane encountered no less than 17 English or English-speaking au pairs. Other au pairs can provide an important support network since you will be faced with similar problems.

Look out for other au pairs or nannies at parks, recreation centres, playschools, etc. and while collecting the children from school. Many Mothers and Toddlers Groups (especially in parts of London) would be more accurately called 'Nannies and Toddlers'.

One of the great advantages of using agencies for placements abroad is that they are usually able to provide a list of a few au pairs in your destination neighbourhood, though it will be up to you to make contact. Some corresponding agents abroad arrange coffee mornings especially for new arrivals, as well as follow-up social events, some of which may be open to anyone and publicised in the local English language press. The ratio of women to men is usually chronically unbalanced as Nicola Wenban found in Vienna where there was one male au pair and hundreds of women.

Some au pairs have shown initiative in making contact with other au pairs. Leeson Clifton, who came from Canada to be a mother's help in Britain, placed an advertisement in the local paper for an au pair get-together which was a great success. Natasha Fox kept a record of the adverts she had noticed in magazines for live-in jobs in Helsinki and contacted the addresses after arrival. Making the first move to contact strangers can be a bit nerve-racking, but you would have to be very unlucky to meet with a lukewarm response to such an overture.

Meeting Expatriates

If there is a shortage of congenial au pairs or nannies in your vicinity or if you are tired of conversations about nappy rash and children's diets, you might well benefit from the company of your fellow countrymen to combat loneliness or homesickness. The local English language bookshop might prove a useful source of information about forthcoming events for English speakers, as will any newspapers or magazines published in English such as the *Bulletin* in Brussels or the *Athens News* in Greece. Seek out the overseas student club if there is a university nearby. Even the least devout of au pairs have found English-speaking churches to be useful for arranging social functions and offering advice. If there is a bar in town which models itself on a British or Irish pub, you will no doubt find a few die-hards drinking Guinness, who might be more than willing to befriend you.

The most obvious way to meet other foreigners is to enrol straightaway in a language course or perhaps classes in art and civilisation (see the section

Learning a Language below). Even if you are not particularly serious about pursuing language studies, language classes are the ideal place to form vital social contacts. You can also join other clubs or classes aimed at residents abroad. During Emma Colgan's very successful year as an au pair in Germany, she joined the English amateur dramatics group called the Hamburg Players:

> Admittedly this did not benefit my German at all, but I enjoyed myself and made very good friends, especially with a girl my age who still visits me in England.

Meeting the Locals

Meeting the local residents may prove more difficult, though circumstances vary enormously according to whether you live in a small village or a big city, with a gregarious family or a socially isolated one, and so on. If you don't spend all your free time moping at home, you are bound to strike up conversations with the locals, whether in cafés, on buses or in shops. Admittedly these seldom go past a superficial acquaintance, but they still serve the purpose of making you feel a little more integrated in the community.

Annabel Roberts enjoyed her stay in Germany but reported:

> I didn't meet any young Germans. Most of us au pairs found that they only held an interest in you as foreigners, and when the novelty wore off they lost interest. This seems harsh, but all the girls I spoke to agreed.

Annabel goes on to recommend taking a supplementary job if possible, such as private tutoring in English, to meet the locals. Her 'pupil' often invited her out with a group of friends.

Again students will probably be more socially flexible than others and it is worth investigating the bars and cafés around the local university or polytechnic. If you have a particular hobby, sport or interest, find out if there is a local club where you will meet like-minded people; join local ramblers, jazz buffs, Amnesty International, etc. You only have to become friendly with one other person to open up new social horizons if you are invited to meet their friends and family.

Australian Mary Scollen, working as a mother's help in England, asked a young London policeman directions to Carnaby Street, got chatting, exchanged telephone numbers and finished up going out on a date with him a few days later.

LEARNING A LANGUAGE

Until you feel reasonably comfortable in the language, you will not only find it difficult to meet the local people, but you will not enjoy simple tasks like shopping or answering the telephone. It is surprising how quickly you will acquire a certain facility if you have a basic grounding and if you have to survive in the language. Au pairs consistently report that when forced to speak daily in a foreign language, they learn more in a month than during years of study at school.

Au pairs are in fact less prone to complain that communication with their family is impossible than that their employers insist on speaking English, thereby preventing them from improving their own fluency in the local language. On the other hand, people who have no knowledge of foreign languages would be unwise to fix up a job with a non-English speaking family.

Preparation

If you intend to go abroad and have never studied the language, you should consider enrolling before departure in a part-time or short intensive language course at a local college of further education or following a self-study programme with books and tapes. There are a great many teach-yourself courses on the market though they are expensive and you might prefer to make use of a local library.

Perhaps a more enjoyable way of learning a language before being thrust into a monolingual domestic situation is to speak it with some natives. Several agencies arrange exchanges or paying guest stays on the continent. Try the En Famille Agency (The Old Stables, 60b Maltravers Street, Arundel, West Sussex BN18 9BG) which specialises in France and charges an agency fee of £55. Alternatively the Experiment in International Living (287 Worcester Road, Malvern, Worcs. WR14 1AB; 01684 562577) arranges homestays of up to 4 weeks in 30 countries. A homestay might provide a good opportunity to sound out prospects for returning as an au pair or mother's help at some future date.

The Central Bureau for Educational Visits & Exchanges (10 Spring Gardens, London SW1A 2BN) publishes a book *Study Holidays* (£7.95 including postage) which provides information on language courses throughout Europe.

No matter what your level of proficiency, a good dictionary will prove an invaluable ally, so be sure to pack one.

Language Courses Abroad

In some countries, such as Switzerland and to some extent France, the au pair visa is contingent on enrolling in formal lessons. But whatever the rules and whatever your standard, it is a very good idea to sign up for a course, if only for the social advantages.

It should be easy to find out about local courses from your agency, your family, the tourist office or even just the Yellow Pages. Fees vary wildly, but state-funded courses are invariably cheaper than commercial ones. In some countries, it is customary for the family to pay part or all of the fees (as in Sweden), though this is usually at the discretion of the employers.

Jessie Lane was determined to learn French so tried not to spend all her spare time with her fellow au pairs and faithfully attended classes at a local college, which helped her come to terms with the grammar with which she had always had a problem.

> A big consideration before going abroad (assuming there will be other English speakers there) is to make up your mind whether you are going to have a good time or to learn the language.

Obviously it is possible to combine these by following a prescribed course where your knowledge of the language is sure to improve, as will your social life.

Lessons are not of course essential to learning a language, especially if you speak no English with the children you are looking after; but they always help. In some cases it can also provide an actual qualification. Emma Colgan found that it was helpful in her situation when returning to England (to pursue a university course in international business and German) clutching some sort of exam certificate as concrete proof to the folks back home that she hadn't spent the whole time changing nappies and sipping German lager.

Problems

Some au pair positions are as far from a form of study as it is possible to be. Improving your knowledge of the language may be difficult or impossible for any number of reasons: because you have too little free time or are worked so hard that you are too shattered to use your leisure time to study, because the language classes are inaccessible (financially or literally) or closed (as is usually the case during the summer vacation), because the family insists that you speak English to them and their chidlren, and so on. If the latter is the case, discuss your dilemma with the parents and try to find a compromise whereby you speak English at certain times and their language at others. Speaking with children can be one of the best (and least embarrassing) ways to improve your vocabulary and pronuncation, since your little charges won't hesitate to correct you when you make a mistake while reading their favourite stories.

If your family isn't cooperative, you will either have to exert a lot of self-discipline (i.e. study from books and force yourself to speak to native speakers outside the home whenever you can), or find another family where it will be easier to make progress. If your primary aim is not being achieved, you will only become increasingly resentful and disappointed unless you take action.

TIME OFF

Au pairs and nannies find a thousand ways to spend their afternoons, days, or weekends off. The key is to get out of the house, and so avoid the possibility of being called upon. The value of using your spare time to attend language classes has already been stressed. But you will also want to explore your new environment either by yourself or with a new-found friend. Daytime excursions on your own (to parks, museums, galleries, shops, etc.) will probably be more enjoyable than venturing out alone in the evenings.

Your First Day Off

On your days off you will want to explore further afield, but don't get too carried away with sightseeing plans at the beginning. There will be plenty of time for that later on, and many chores may require urgent attention first, for example, opening a bank account, visiting your agency, etc. Perhaps this will also be your only chance to investigate and then enrol in classes or get in touch with any contacts you have been urged to look up by the folks back home. It is also an idea to locate the British Consulate (if you are living in a city) and ask them what services they provide for British residents either on a day-to-day basis or in an emergency.

On your first night out, do not alarm your new employers by returning at an ungodly hour and try to be especially quiet. As they get to know and trust you, their anxiety should fade away on this score, though you should be aware that some families impose a curfew especially during the week, partly out of concern for their young au pair's safety.

Excursions and Activities

Your location will to a large extent dictate your range of amusements. Those who are lucky enough to be within easy reach of Rome or Paris will never exhaust the beautiful and interesting places. But people on a German army base or in a small industrial town in northern Spain may have more difficulty. If you know you are going to be some distance from a major centre, consider acquiring a vehicle of some kind, whether a bicycle, moped or even car. A lack of transport may not be the only impediment to organising excursions, if you find yourself working for an over-protective family who disapprove of too much independence (see *Problem Parents: Interference with your Social Life*).

Even if you find yourself a long way from a wide range of entertainments, it is possible to have an enjoyable time abroad. One outlet is sport. Lucy Sumner was lucky enough to fix up an au pairing job in the small alpine resort of Monêtier-les-Bains in France and used her free time in the obvious way. Not only did she take up skiing for its own sake, but she found it an excellent way to meet both residents and tourists. But this doesn't always work. Irene Platt thought that a good way to meet the locals in her small French town was to join the tennis club, but was dismayed to have her application turned down on the grounds that she would be there for too brief a time.

Holidays

Although you probably won't get paid enough to contemplate a holiday on the grand scale, make an effort to organise at least one complete break away from your place of temporary residence. Even a couple of days by the seaside or visiting a tourist attraction in the region can revitalise your interest in being abroad and provide a refreshing break from routine. If you stay in a youth hostel, you'll see new faces and hear new viewpoints on the culture in which you have been immersed. And if nothing else, it will give you a chance to mingle with your peers instead of children.

Holidays with the family can be a real perk, and some lucky au pairs find themselves spending weeks aboard the family yacht or at a mountain lodge. One of the highlights of Natalia de Cuba's experience of au pairing in France was the week which was spent at the family's country house in the south of France; part of the reason for the success was that the family was very relaxed when freed from schoolwork and business'.

But be careful to distinguish ahead of time between your holiday time and theirs, since you will probably end up working much harder than usual when the children are out of school and demanding more attention (see the section *Problem Parents: Pay and Time Off*).

In each of the country chapters which follow, an attempt has been made to suggest specific ideas for using your leisure time and to pass on tips from au pairs and nannies who have discovered all sorts of diversions.

Use of a Car

Many families, especially in country areas, will allow their au pair or nanny to use a car in the evenings or during their time off. This is a privilege and should be seen as such. You will already be using the car as part of your work, for shopping or taking the children out so you will have checked that the insurance covers you as an additional driver. If you are using a family car for your own purposes you should return it with the same amount of petrol in the tank as when you borrowed it and be particularly careful to drive sensibly and not drink. If something goes wrong report it at once.

DEPARTURE

Giving Notice

Once your contract is drawing to an end and you know you will not be extending it, or if your circumstances have changed and you wish to leave earlier than expected, try to give the family as much notice as possible. This will give the parents time to find a suitable replacement, and the children time to adjust to the idea that you will no longer be living with them.

Avoid leaving impetuously during the heat of an argument. It would be a shame to undo all the good work you've invested in building up a decent relationship with your employers, and it isn't very fair to the children who will be affected by your sudden departure. If you want to terminate your contract, it shouldn't be done suddenly and on bad terms. Bid the children farewell in as friendly a manner as possible, even if it isn't from the heart. It can be awkward, working your notice if things are difficult between you, and in many cases the employers will insist that you leave straightaway. But if they don't, stick it out for the sake of the children. Any unexpected disruption in their home-life is bound to have an upsetting effect on them, and children's feelings should not be hurt unnecessarily. If you cannot avoid leaving under a cloud just pack your things quietly, say goodbye to the children and leave.

Similarly, moonlight flits are undesirable. At least have the courtesy to tell your employers that you wish to leave, face to face. The worst thing about slipping away without a word of warning (apart from being sneaky) is that you deny the children an opportunity to say goodbye to you. This is especially cruel if you have been with them long enough to develop a trusting relationship. If you don't bid them a formal farewell, they will probably go on expecting your imminent return.

Throwing parties in the parents' absence is definitely out

Preparing the Children

If your contract has been a successful one, your charges will have grown to love you (although they may have strange ways of showing it sometimes!), depend on you and generally regard you as one of the family. Therefore, when the time comes for you to leave, it can be quite traumatic for them even if they've always been told that you won't be their nanny forever. Six months or longer may seem like a lifetime to children and they will have forgotten that your stay was always going to be temporary.

Bed-time is not a good time to break the news because they may lie awake worrying about your departure. Fears always seem much worse at night when one is tired and surrounded by darkness. On the other hand, don't be surprised if they greet your news with little concern or curiosity. Not all children express their feelings in obvious ways. They may become clingier than normal, calling for you in the night or misbehave more than usual. Try to read the signs with tolerance and answer them with reassurance. Tell them stories about your family and describe your home in detail, if you haven't already done so. It helps if they have some idea of where you're going and that you can be contacted by phone or letter. This is especially important since you will probably be moving out of visiting range. If so, try to send postcards from your new abode to let them know that they aren't forgotten. Above all, reassure them at every opportunity that you will still love them, even though they will no longer be in your care.

Children have an uncanny knack for becoming particularly endearing during your last week; or perhaps it's because you interpret their behaviour more positively now that you know your time together is coming to an end. Either way, it is very flattering if your charges are averse to your being replaced and make it plain that they would prefer you to stay. Don't encourage any last-minute acts of devotion towards you, however, in preference to the new nanny. Of course the children will miss you, and you them, but it is your duty to help make the transition as smooth as possible. Tell the children all about her and display her in a good light, so they have a positive image of her. This will help them to adjust once she takes over.

Meeting the New Nanny

It's quite common to be introduced to the new nanny and be asked to show her the ropes before you leave. This is better for the children because it gives both parties a chance to adapt to each other before the new girl's contract formally begins. Try to help her as much as possible because the more quickly she settles in, the better it will be for the family.

Tell her all about the children's routine and maybe make a few notes if you think it might help her. If you're very public-spirited, you can leave notes on evening entertainments, libraries, etc. and draw a few maps so the new au pair or nanny will have some idea of where the shops, children's school and local park are. Show her how to use the household equipment but try not to bombard her with too much detail. Avoid gossiping about your employers. Let the girl form her own impressions, just as you did. When you live with a family, they allow you a privileged insight into their intimate lives, and you should treat this with respect and confidentiality.

Encourage her to take the lead with the children, while you drop into the background as much as possible. If she considers it necessary to discipline them in your presence (or if she fails to discipline them when you think it is called for), it can be tempting to interfere if you think she's handling the situation badly. Bite your tongue. She's in charge now and you must allow her to get on with it. NEVER criticise her in front of the children, thereby undermining her authority, since this can lead to problems. If you want to give her the benefit of your experience, do so in private. Concentrate on the household chores, leaving her with the children as much as possible.

Farewell

Saying good-bye can be very sad and very difficult, but it doesn't mean the end of the relationship. Many au pairs and nannies remain in close contact with the families they have worked for, receiving photos and keeping up-to-date with their news. You may be sent drawings at Christmas, gifts on your birthday, Valentine cards in February and through this correspondence, you can follow the children's development, albeit from a distance.

PART II

Country by Country Guide

Rules & Regulations
Advantages & Disadvantages
Specialist Agencies

Australasia	Israel
Austria	Italy
Belgium & Luxembourg	Netherlands
Canada	Scandinavia
France	Spain & Portugal
Germany	Switzerland
Great Britain	Turkey
Greece	USA
Ireland	Rest of the World

Each chapter contains a section on the visa regulations, health and insurance, the advantages and disadvantages of working in that particular country, how to fix up a job either through an agency or independently, general points about what to do in your leisure time and a list of the agencies which deal with that country. Agencies which are italicised in the text are included in the Directory at the end of the book.

Australasia

AUSTRALIA

Australia and to a much lesser extent New Zealand are increasingly promising destinations for people interested in doing some childcare work. As always, visas pose the worst problem. The main loophole is the working holiday visa valid for one year. Young people of certain nationalities (British, Irish, Canadian and Dutch) who wish to organise a working holiday in Australia whether as a mother's help or anything else (fruit picker, typist, etc.) should apply to their local Australian consulate for a working holiday visa. These visas are available to people aged 18-25 (and very occasionally 25-29) who can prove that they have sufficient savings (minimum of £2,000) and that they wish to work only to fund a holiday. Americans interested in au pairing should enquire of *Alliances Abroad* in San Francisco whose recent literature referred to an Australian programme.

The concept of au pairing is not foreign to Australians and several agencies include the word in their names, for example *Au Pair Australia* south of Sydney, *The Au Pair Connection* in the northern suburbs of Sydney and the *Australian Nanny & Au Pair Connection* in Melbourne. These agencies are familiar with the working holiday programme and are prepared to try to place foreign au pairs in families for periods of less than three months (to satisfy the terms of the visa). Holiday positions for the summer (December-February) and for the ski season (July-August) are available. Many agencies are able to offer a choice of posts at short notice. When Julia Stanton from Harrow left one job after a week of working, because of the long hours (very little time off between rising at 7am to walk the dog and 8.30pm when the children went to bed), Rosemary McCormack of the agency Australian Nanny & Au Pair Connection found her a much more suitable job the same day.

The introductory letter from the Au Pair Connection gives a flavour of working as an au pair in Australia:

> We have helped hundreds of girls to find work in Sydney, the Blue Mountains, the Gold Coast of Queensland, Brisbane and country areas. You do not need experience, only the love of children. It is certainly an excellent way of working and living here as well as gaining a better understanding of our culture. As an au pair you will be working an average of 25-40 hours per week. In most cases weekends are free to discover Sydney and meet with friends. You can become part of the family, sharing in outings and family life, or choose to have independent activities in your time off. Most families have the luxuries of swimming pools and/or tennis courts, and sometimes they allow use of the family car.

Finding a Job

A handful of European agencies have links with Australian agencies, including *Quick Help* and *Elizabeth Elder* in the UK and *Travel Active Programmes* in the Netherlands.

Two other agencies which might be worth trying are Busy Lizzie International Nanny Service (7 Berkley Ave, Everard Park, South Australia 5035) and Nannies Abroad (4 Charles St., South Melbourne, VIC 3205; 3-9645 9222/fax: 3-9686 0243) which, despite its name, places foreign au pairs in Australia as well as sending Australian nannies abroad.

Nanny agencies are normally interested in longer term prospects. In addition to *Dial-an-Angel* and *International Nannies Services* listed in the Directory, the partner agencies of *Family First International* in Guildford Surrey could be tried in Sydney (12/162 Kurruba Road, Neutral Bay, NSW 2089), Brisbane (338 Given Terrace, Paddington, Brisbane, QLD 4064), Perth (Nanny Bureau International, 8/24 St. Quentin Avenue, PO Box 407, Claremont, WA 6010) and Melbourne (21 Bradford Avenue, Greenvale, VIC 3059). Most belong to the AANA (Australian Association of Nanny Agencies).

The primary activity of many nanny agencies in Australia is to place Australian au pairs in the USA (since they are now entitled to participate in the US-approved au pair programme) and nannies and mother's helps in the UK, since Australian women are popular as child-carers in London and elsewhere. Leads on jobs in Australia might be available from London agencies which specialise in placing Australian and New Zealand nannies in Britain; check ads in the free London weekly magazine *TNT* and agencies with Antipodean links like *Bligh Appointments* and Koala Nannies (22 Craven Terrace, London W2 3QH). Bligh is one of the most important general employment agencies in Australia, with offices in most Australian cities; if in Australia ring their Sydney office for nanny leads (9th Floor, 428 George St; 02-9235 3699). *Occasional & Permanent* also has an office in Australia. The New Zealand agency Nannies Abroad International (36 Sylvan Ave, Northcote, Auckland) is also concerned mainly with outgoing placements rather than incoming ones.

The long-established *Dial-an-Angel* agency has numerous offices around Australia and can be contacted on the following phone numbers: Newcastle NSW (049-293 065), Wollongong NSW (042-272 611), Penrith NSW (047-22 3355), Canberra (06-282 7733), Brisbane (07-3878 1077), Queensland Gold Coast (07-5591 8891), Sunshine Coast (07-5479 3973), Melbourne (03-9525 9261), Adelaide (08-8267 3700) and Perth (09-328 3336). It covers all the types of childcare vacancies from au pairs to experienced housekeepers. Other agencies can be found in the *Yellow Pages* for the major cities under the heading 'Domestic Services'.

Most nanny agencies in Australia will expect to interview applicants and check their references before placement, so there is not much point in contacting them before arrival. Au pair agencies by contrast may be able to fix up a family placement for candidates who apply by post.

Posts are also advertised in daily papers, particularly the *Sydney Morning Herald* and Melbourne *Age*. Check the Monday Job Market of the *Herald* under the 'Situations Vacant — Domestic and Rural' column. In fact almost all the jobs listed are in the city rather than the country. As in America, a driving licence is not only a valuable asset but virtually essential to getting a job.

Working in Australia: Pros and Cons

The standard wage for a 30-hour-a-week au pair job is $120-$150 a week, while nannies and mother's helps (between whom there is no real distinction in Australia and New Zealand) normally earn A$250 or more. According to one agency, there is an acute shortage of au pairs between April and August when some families will pay above the standard rate. The hourly rate for casual nannies is about $10 an hour, more for well qualified staff.

Non English-speaking au pairs can be directed to local language schools according to their first language, since there is excellent provision for English teaching throughout the country. A few European agencies run programmes for students which combine language study and living in with a family (for example *3 Esse* in Italy).

Rowena Caverly was very pleased with the help which Dial-an-Angel gave her in finding a nannying job:

> As someone who finds crowded hostel life a bit wearing, nannying provided me with both a roof and a job. I first approached Dial-an-Angel in Melbourne. Since I was on a working holiday visa, I knew I would only be in Melbourne for a couple of months and that seemed acceptable. It is best to offer the agency an honest time limit. It took a few weeks to get a job offer; although their books were full, many families required a minimum of six months. I took on a live-in job with a part South African part Canadian family which was originally for six days but I stayed a month. I remained in touch with people I had met at the hostel and made a few of them green with my tales of regular meals, constant hot water and access to a car. A temporary joy for sure.
>
> Months and many miles later, I arrived in Brisbane with only a month of working time left to offer. I approached the local branch of Dial-an-Angel and was in luck. The Melbourne office sent a glowing reference (thank God) and there were some short-term and one-day jobs available.

Most agree that Australians are excellent employers and Australia a wonderful country in which to spend some time in a family, including Matt Tomlinson who found that there were a few Australians willing to go against tradition and entrust their children to a young man while on ski holidays:

> One of the nicest things about nannying in Australia, you tend to get treated as an equal by the parents, whereas barmen, waiters and ski lift operators do not. If I hadn't had to go back for my final year at university I would probably be a very well paid nanny in Melbourne by now.
>
> The Aussies are still quite blinkered about male nannies, though. On a couple of occasions I was asked outright whether I was a child molester. I found the only solution was to stay very cool and not take it personally. I got references from a few of my most regular clients.

This didn't prevent him from taking charge of a small nanny agency in the ski resort of Mount Buller in Victoria:

> The work was a bit irregular but when it was busy, the money was good ($500 a week) which gave me enough for my lift pass and snowboard gear. Being a nanny was a real laugh. It was being paid quite a lot of money to sledge, build snowmen, snowball, eat crisps and build dens. Sure, I had my fair share of monsters, but as I rarely had the same children for more than a few days there was always light at the end of the tunnel.

An interesting angle for those with childcare experience and basic skiing is the Ski Kindergarten. In Buller they take 3-6 year olds but most of the other resorts have a creche too.

Directory References

For agencies based in Australia, see: **Au Pair Australia** (NSW South Coast), **Au Pair Connection** (North Sydney), **Australian Nanny & Au Pair Connection** (Melbourne), **Dial-an-Angel** (Sydney, Brisbane and interstate), **International**

Nannies Services (Melbourne) and **Stablemate Equestrian Staff Agency** (outer Sydney).

For agencies in Britain which deal with Australia and occasionally New Zealand, see: Academy Au Pair & Nanny Agency, Delaney, Edgware, Elizabeth Elder, Lucy Locketts, Nannies Now, Occasional & Permanent, Pat-a-Cake, Quick Help and Sonia Brooke Placement Agency.

Other agencies abroad which send au pairs to Australia/New Zealand include:
Canada: Au Pair in Europe, Paragon Personnel
France: Butterfly et Papillon
Germany: Rodata
Greece: Galentina's
Ireland: Langtrain International
Israel: Hilma's
Italy: 3 Esse, L'Aquilone, ARCE
Netherlands: Activity International, Travel Active
Spain: Intercambio 66, Interclass

ASIA

Hong Kong

While Chinese families normally employ Cantonese speakers as babysitters and nannies, the large British and expatriate community often prefers English speakers to look after their precious offspring. Hiring a British nanny has become more problematic since June 1997 when Hong Kong ceased to be a colony of the United Kingdom and became part of China. It was not known at the time of writing how much impact the change would have on the employment market, but it seems likely that the chances of finding work as a nanny in Hong Kong will be reduced.

In the past, Hong Kong was reputed to be an excellent place to work as part of a household since most families employed at least one *amah*, usually a Filipina, to wash, iron, cook, etc. Several years ago, Rowena Caverly was assigned her first job by a Hong Kong agency within three days. She had a variety of one-off jobs and did some basic home pre-school teaching. Babysitters are especially sought after between December and February, the busiest time in the Hong Kong social calendar with Christmas and two New Years. Rowena describes her experiences in Hong Kong:

> *I worked for many different nationalities including Danish, Australian, Japanese, American and British. Hong Kong life is fast-paced and all the children seemed to have a multitude of activities and interests. As it is a small island, I often bumped into last week's charges whilst looking after this week's. I made the mistake on one occasion of offering to help the amah but the household work is their job and some take offers of assistance as an insult to their abilities. A lesson learnt.*

Apart from Hong Kong, the Far East affords few opportunities. The traffic in mother's helps is in the opposite direction, with many Oriental women aspiring to work in Western households. Although there is plenty of wealth in Japan, virtually no Japanese families have foreign staff to care for their children since this is not part of Japanese culture. Few middle-class Japanese women go out to work and therefore the majority stay at home to look after the children and the household themselves. Of course there are plenty of Western families

94 Country Guide

posted to Japan who may be looking for a nanny. Contact one of the nanny agencies which operate worldwide (listed just after Country chapters).

Austria

The Regulations

At the time of writing, Austria had been a full member of the European Union for more than two years. This has made the red tape easier for au pairs from the EU than it once was but harder for non-Europeans. Officially au pairs from outside the EU must obtain both a work and residence permit *(Beschäftigungsbewilligung)*. Although this can be applied for inside Austria, the process is so expensive and time-consuming that almost no one attempts it.

If a host family wants to try to obtain a *Beschäftigungsbewilligung* for their non-EU au pair, they should apply to the local employment office (*Landesarbeitsamt*). Before the permit can be approved, the authorities must see an agreement or contract (signed by the employer, the au pair and the agency) and proof that health and accident insurance cover has been obtained by the au pair. The agency should help with this process and tell the au pair where to take the documents to be stamped (for a fee).

Maree Lakey from Australia, who went from Germany to Austria to au pair in the autumn of 1996, was told by her Austrian au pair agency that she had no chance of obtaining the permit. She therefore took their advice and registered officially as a guest, which seems to be the norm in Vienna:

I simply did as most au pairs do, which was to de-register myself after the first three months, which was for me at Christmas time when I left the country to visit friends in Germany. After my return in January, I registered again, and after completing another three months the same procedure again. The only problem was that by chance the Vienna city authorities failed to receive my de-registration papers in December, which meant that I received a very nasty letter in February which told me I had overstayed. That was cleared up but it gave me a shock as I had heard of other Australians who had been deported. I never heard of anyone who went through the official procedure of applying for a work permit.

Health and Insurance

Au pairs pay no tax and cannot contribute to the state-run health and social security scheme. EU nationals should be sure to take an E-111 to Austria. They must take the E-111 to the Gebietskrankenkasse (regional health insurance office) where they will be given more forms allowing them to register with a doctor. In Vienna the Gebietskrankenkasse is at Wienerbergstrasse 15-19, 1100 Vienna; there are also provincial offices in the Tyrol, Carinthia, etc. If you wish to supplement the basic health cover provided by the E-111, the au pair agencies in Austria can recommend suitable private policies.

Working in Austria: Pros and Cons

Austria, together with Switzerland, was one of the first countries to host au pairs so there is a well-developed tradition. Well-established and respectable agencies between them place over 1,000 au pairs in Austria each year. Most of the families live in the cities of Vienna, Salzburg and Linz, where there are enough other au pairs to reduce any feelings of isolation. The agencies will try to place friends who apply together near one another. This is usually possible for the standard stay of September to June, but less easy for summer placements. Many Austrian families visit the Alps during the summer and this can provide a good opportunity to see some of the most scenic areas in Europe.

The cost of becoming an au pair is high in Austria: the agency fees are around AS800, while the recommended insurance costs AS2,000-AS2,500 for six months. The minimum pocket money of AS700-750 per week has not risen for about five years, though some families now offer AS800 +. The weekly pay should be specified on the *Beschäftigungbewilligung*. Au pairs plus normally earn from about AS1,000 a week. Furthermore Austria has a high cost of living and so it is essential to take some money with you for travel and emergencies. Since the family must sign an undertaking that you will leave Austria at the end of your contract, you are supposed to show that you have enough money for a return ticket.

Austrians are reputed to be exacting employers, though it is impossible to generalise. Writing from Austria in 1997, Maree Lakey cheerfully reported that she had enjoyed the first three months of her placement, despite the four teenage children's unwillingness to knuckle down to English conversation lessons with her (as agreed) and the substantial amount of housework. However her host mother treated her with respect which in Maree's view makes all the difference. Many Austrian families speak little English, so a grounding in German will make your stay much more tolerable.

The agencies offer a back-up service and will try to find you another family if things don't work out. They even extend their advisory services to au pairs who have not arranged their families through the agency. Nicola Wenban's relations with her Viennese employers deteriorated over the first few months until she was barely on speaking terms with them and was pointedly excluded from any family treats. She found the level of ingratitude for all her hard work and extra hours breathtaking and finally she gave her week's notice. She then went to her agency *(Auslands-Sozialdienst)* and poured out her tale of woe; they were very attentive and sympathetic and immediately offered to find her another family. But by then she was so fed up that she was longing to go home to England, and regretted that she had not gone to the agency much earlier. They asked her to fill out an assessment form, which she was delighted to do in the hope of preventing other girls from going through what she had.

Fixing up a Job

The two mainstream agencies in Austria are *Auslands-Sozialdienst* (the Austrian branch of the International Catholic organization ACISFJ) and *Okista* (the Austrian Committee for International Educational Exchange). The third agent listed *Irmhild Spitzer* in Linz acts independently and works with many agents worldwide. All are accustomed to dealing with direct applications from foreigners. The two Vienna agencies combine forces rather than act in competition and run an au pair club and provide many other services between them. Maree Lakey took advantage of a trip to Salzburg as part of the social programme organised by Auslands-Sozialdienst, which proved a good starting point for her to form some contacts.

Their requirements are not very strenuous and many inexperienced 18-year-olds are placed. The agencies can take a long time to reply to correspondence as Ann Derry found:

> I arranged an au pair position with a family near Salzburg through the agency Okista. Arranging things was hectic enough and the agency took a long time to reply to my initial application, and things only started moving after a continuous string of phone calls to Vienna. In the end I heard from them just two weeks before I was set to go.

Okista and Auslands-Sozialdienst charge a fee which is equivalent to about a week's pocket money. Irmhild Spitzer charges a hefty AS1,800 for a year long placement (and AS1,080 for a summer placement). The fee must be paid up front, though it will be returned if the agencies are unable to find a suitable placement (more likely in the case of summer stays). If you have reservations about the first family to which they send you, do not accept; you are entitled to consider up to three families before deciding.

Of course it is always possible to bypass the services of an agency, either by relying on adverts in the *Lady* or after you arrive, which is what Ann Derry did when she grew dissatisfied with her Okista placement:

> After three months I moved to another family, where things were much better. There was a lot more work, but the atmosphere was so nice that I didn't mind. To find this second job, I didn't use the agency. The 'au-pair grapevine' is very efficient, and when you start asking around, it is amazing how many people know families that need help.

If you want to make contacts who might know of families looking for an au pair, one suggestion is to try the English Church in Vienna on Jauresgasse. Ask if you can attend one of the vicar's weekly get-togethers where you may even get a free meal. Among the church stalwarts several are very familiar with the problems faced by au pairs and, according to Nicola Wenban, are full of advice.

Many possibilities for seasonal au pairing also exist in the mountain resorts of the Tyrol, especially during the winter. Tour operators like Crystal Holidays (The Courtyard, Arlington Road, Surbiton, Surrey; 0181-241 5128) hire nannies to work in various alpine resorts. Family positions can also be arranged privately as Camilla Lambert did:

> I was offered a job as an au pair with a family whose father coaches the Austrian ski team and needs extra help during the winter when he is away. This offer was in response to a small ad I had placed in the Tiroler Tageszeitung newspaper. This is the best way to find any kind of job in and around Innsbruck.

Leisure Time

The au pair club in Vienna is quite active though, predictably, it is not the place to meet the opposite sex. One au pair reported that when she attended, there was only one male, a Frenchman, who was invariably mobbed by all the French girls. The club organises theatre trips and excursions such as day trips to Salzburg and ski weekends, though these are often outside the budgets of au pairs. There are also parties (especially around Christmas), craft days and special masses, and meetings for girls in the provinces.

There is an International Student Club at Vienna University (Schottengasse

1) which au pairs are encouraged to join, with a bar, TV room and common room with foreign language newspapers. Nicola Wenban and her friend Laura attended one of the Club's discos and were disappointed to find the room full of middle-aged men from the Middle East. Some of the club's other activities sound more promising, such as an evening with a Cuban theme, discussion groups, etc.

Maree Lakey decided to take the initiative in building a social life after she had been in Vienna a short time:

> I was a very lonely person for the first six weeks in Vienna, until I placed a contact notice on the billboard of the British Bookshop in Vienna. This was a great idea and I got a number of calls, especially from Austrians which was a bonus as I would never have met any Austrians otherwise. It is so true that the Viennese are hard to make friends with, so I was lucky to have found some exceptions. The only trouble with such a contact notice was the unwelcome phone calls I received from a few annoying males, but the children in my family handled this problem quite well when they answered the phone. My social life was at its best during my last two months in Vienna in 1997 after I met another Aussie au pair at the agency's meeting (we are a rare breed!) and the two of us became regulars at one of the Irish pubs in the city. It didn't take us long to become part of a group mainly consisting of British blokes and we enjoyed many an amusing evening. I really hated to have to leave.

Language classes are held at the universities in Vienna, Salzburg, Innsbruck, Graz and Linz as well as various institutes such as the non-profit Internationales Kultur-Institut (IKI) and Goethe Institute in Vienna. Also the folk high schools or *Volkshochschulen* offer German classes throughout Austria. Most courses start either in September/October or January/February and fees start at around AS2,000 per term, rising to more than AS5,000 depending on how many hours you wish to study. Nicola Wenban was pleased with the IKI course in Vienna (Opernring 7; 56 73 21) both for the standard of German teaching and for the social contact. She attended five hours of classes on two evenings a week. The only drawback which Nicola could identify in IKI is that it is very popular with au pairs (especially Swedes) whose common language is English so they had to make a conscious effort to practise their German whenever they were together.

Some au pairs have found that it is not as easy to make friends with Austrians as it is with foreigners in Vienna. The Viennese can give the impression of being aloof and image-conscious, even snooty, though they are probably just reserved like the British. Nightlife is expensive and Nicola found that the only nightclubs she could afford were frequented by 'wolf gangs' (men on the prowl).

A quite different form of entertainment can be enjoyed at the Vienna State Opera. Comparatively cheap standing room tickets are sold two or three hours before a performance, though you have to queue to get these.

Outside sophisticated Vienna, people will be friendlier. In the villages the people show a keen interest in any foreigners who choose to come and live in their tight-knit communities; in fact you may receive more attention from the young men of the village than you want.

Travel

Fares to Vienna haven't increased significantly in recent years. A high season return on Austrian Airlines at the time of writing was £149, with restrictions (the cheapest returns may have a three-month maximum validity). The cost of a one-way ticket is about the same as a cheap return. Try the Anglo-Austrian

Society (0171-222 0366) for information on regular flights on Austrian Airlines, British Airways and Lauda Air.

Okista operates as a youth travel bureau as well as an au pair agency and can arrange cheap flights from Vienna. Okista has branch offices in Graz, Innsbruck, Linz and Salzburg. The Eurotrain fare for under 26s to Vienna is £132 one way, £262 return. The under 26 coach fares quoted by Eurolines to Vienna are £64 single, £99 return, departing in September.

If you arrange to have time off for a holiday or at the end of your stint as an au pair, you might consider travelling east of Austria into Hungary, which is adjacent and still exceedingly cheap. Weekends in Budapest are entirely feasible. If you are on a tight budget and have some time, don't buy a through ticket to Budapest. It is cheaper to buy one to Hegyeshalom just across the border and then buy a local onward ticket. A more romantic way to make the trip is by boat along the Danube which takes five hours.

Directory References

For agencies based in Austria, see: **Auslands Sozialdienst** (Vienna), **Okista** (Vienna) and **Irmhild Spitzer** (Linz).

For agencies in Britain which deal with Austria, see: Abbey Au Pairs, Academy Au Pair & Nanny Agency, Bloomsbury Bureau, Bunters Agency, Childcare International, Edgware, Euro Employment Centre, Family Match, Helping Hands (Essex), Hyde Park International, International Catholic Society for Girls, Jolaine, London Agency, Mondial, Nanny & Au Pair Connection, People & Places, Quick Help, Solihull, Students Abroad, Universal Care, UK & Overseas.

Other agencies abroad which send au pairs to Austria include:
Australia: Australian Nanny & Au Pair Connection
Belgium: Services de la Jeunesse Feminine, Stufam
Canada: Au Pair in Europe
France: Accueil International, Au Pair Service, Euro Pair Services, Institut d'Echanges Franco-Europeens, Inter-Séjours
Greece: Au Pair Activities
Hungary: Avalon '92
Ireland: Au Pair Bureau of Ireland, Careers Information Services, Limerick, Job Options Bureau, Langtrain International
Italy: A. C. Link, L'Aquilone, ARCE, Soggiorni All'Estero per la Gioventù
South Africa: All Aboard
Spain: Agencia Intercambios, Interclass
Switzerland: Pro Filia, Swiss-O-Pair
USA: Accord Cultural Exchange, InterExchange, WISE

Belgium & Luxembourg

The Regulations

All nationalities can become au pairs in Belgium though, as usual, it is much more straightforward for EEA nationals. The usual rules apply: EU nationals arriving in Belgium intending to stay for a period of three months or more should register within eight days at the local Town Hall where the *administration communale* (usually located in the Town Hall) will issue either a temporary *certificat d'immatriculation* valid for three months or the one year certificate of registration (*certificat d'inscription au registre des étrangers* — CIRE).

Non-EU citizens will have to obtain an authorisation of provisional sojourn from the Belgian Embassy in their home country before arriving in Belgium. Their contract with their host family must be approved by the *administration communale* before a one year 'B' work permit can be granted by the regional Office National de l'Emploi (ORBEM in Greater Brussels, FOREM in French-speaking Belgium or VDAB in Flemish-speaking Belgium). To qualify, a document proving that the applicant has a working knowledge of either French or Dutch must be submitted or, alternatively, proof that he or she has registered in a language course in Belgium. Those who apply for an extension or want to change employers may find that the authorities check to make sure that these au pairs have been attending language classes for at least ten hours a week.

Luxembourg has ratified the European Agreement on Au Pair Placements, with the result that au pairs in Luxembourg must submit four copies of an 'Accord Placement Au Pair' to the Administration de l'Emploi (38a rue Philippe II, 3rd Floor, L-2340 Luxembourg; 352-47 68 55) before they can have their status regularised. The Accord amounts to a contract and must set out in detail the conditions of work and be signed by both the employer and the au pair. In the case of non-EU nationals, the Accord must be obtained before entry to the country. The Embassy in London (27 Wilton Crescent, London SW1X 8SD; 0171-235 6961) issues a leaflet called 'Au Pair Jobs in Luxembourg'.

Health and Insurance

According to Belgian law, au pairs must be insured against accidents and illness either by possessing an E-111 (which will cover only 75% of the cost of treatment and medicines) or by inclusion in their host family's insurance policy. Most families will obtain insurance from the local *Mutualité/Ziekenfonds* office rather than purchase a more expensive private policy. But there can be long delays while this is being processed, so it is imperative to arrive with an E-111 or your own travel insurance to cover you for the first few months.

Employing families in Luxembourg are obliged to register their au pairs with the social security system. After arrival, the employer should go to the Caisse Nationale d'Assurance-Maladie des Ouvriers (125 route d'Esch, L-1471 Luxembourg or a local branch) to fill out a *declaration d'entrée*.

Working in Belgium: Pros and Cons

Belgium is a country which is often ignored. Sandwiched between France and the Netherlands, its population can be broadly divided between the French-speaking people of Wallonia in the south and those who speak Flemish (which is almost identical to Dutch) in the north. Of course the large number of multinational companies, attracted by the presence of the European Commission, creates a huge and fluctuating demand for live-in childcare, though it must be said that nursery provision is so good in the major cities that many families opt for creches rather than nannies or au pairs.

Most au pairs who want to learn French think only of going to France, rather than to a French-speaking family in Belgium. The French-speaking Belgians (known as Walloons) live mainly in the south of the country. The Belgian authorities take the language learning aspect of au pairing seriously and there are plenty of courses available (for monolingual Belgians as well as for foreigners). Like the Dutch, many Belgians have a good grasp of English and you may find that the locals with whom you come into contact as well as your employers will prefer to practise their English on you rather than have your French practised on them.

There is a strong demand for qualified nannies which several agencies cater for such as *Nannies Incorporated*. The other main cities in Belgium where there is a reasonable demand for au pairs include Antwerp, Ghent and Ostend which are primarily Dutch speaking cities but with some French families as well. Among expatriates in Brussels, English may well be the working language of the household.

It is difficult to generalise about working conditions in Belgium, but on the whole the culture shock should not be too great. The monthly rate of pocket money for au pairs is BF10,000-BF15,000 whereas mother's helps should receive up to BF18,000. Au pairs are entitled to one week's paid holiday after six months work. Summer au pairs can sometimes be placed, though as is the case throughout Europe, it is necessary to apply early for these posts, by the middle of May at the latest.

If Belgium is often neglected, Luxembourg is overlooked completely. Yet it is an independent country with a steady demand for live-in childcare. The main language is Luxemburgish but both German and French are spoken and understood by virtually everyone.

Fixing up a Job

Quite a few agencies in the UK and continental Europe (with the exception of France) deal with Belgium, usually concentrating on French-speaking families. There are also several agencies in Belgium which you can approach independently: *Windrose, Stufam* and *Services de la Jeunesse Feminine* (the Belgian branch of ACISJF/In Via). The norm is for agencies to charge applicants who apply directly rather than through an agency in their own country an administrative fee starting at BF1,000 and rising to BF2,000 in the case of Windrose.

Experienced mother's helps and nannies looking for work in Belgium should contact *Nannies Incorporated* (with offices in London, Brussels and Paris) or *Irish Nanny Services* in Dublin.

Most Belgian cities are so accessible from southern England that families advertising in the *Lady* or elsewhere may well arrange an expenses-paid interview with you, possibly in a Channel port. Despite having no relevant experience beyond having led a girl guide group, Annie Stevens was invited by a family who were resident in Brussels to an interview in Calais, where she could meet the children before accepting the job.

If you are already in Belgium, check the adverts in *The Bulletin,* the English-language magazine catering for the expatriate community in Belgium which is published each Thursday (at a cost of BF85). There are usually several adverts for au pairs and other live-in help in each issue, however the majority of these are in English-speaking families. One Brussels agency seen advertising their childcare services in a recent issue was Baby Kid Sitting (tel: 2-524 17 07). The free weekly newspaper *Vlan* is an effective advertising medium for prospective au pairs under the heading *Gens de Maison*. The daily *Le Soir* is also worth consulting for au pair jobs.

Agency placements in Luxembourg are rare. Most positions are found through advertisements in *The Lady* or in the papers, including the English language *Luxembourg News* (25 rue Philippe II, L-2340 Luxembourg; 47 00 53). Luxembourg Accueil Information (10 Bisserwee, L-1238 Luxembourg-Grund; 24 17 17) is a centre for new arrivals and residents. They provide a range of services including keeping files of families looking for au pairs and of young European women looking for au pair placements and also publishing a magazine three times a year which carries relevant classified adverts. One possible contact from whom recent confirmation was not received is Europair a.s.b.l., 14 rue de Luxembourg, L-8077 Bertrange (352-31 93 14). The youth and student office Centre Information Jeunes (CIJ, 76 Boulevard de la Pétrusse, L-2320 Luxembourg; 40 55 50/fax 40 55 56) can sometimes assist prospective au pairs and after placement can advise on the formalities. The national employment service (Administration de l'Emploi, address above) may have leads on au pair, mother's help and nanny positions.

Leisure Time

Even in larger Belgian cities, au pairs find it easier to meet the locals than in, say, Paris or Vienna. Annie Stevens found Belgians warm and generous to strangers, which compensated a good deal for her unhappy employment situation. Public transport is on the whole good, even to the suburbs, though suburban services tend to finish about 10pm.

If you are in Brussels and want to meet more English-speaking people, check the listings in *The Bulletin* for entertainments and meetings, as well as the adverts for pubs and discos frequented by the English-speaking community. The *Bulletin's* publishers bring out a Supplement called *Newcomer: An Introduction to Life in Belgium* in spring and autumn which can be picked up free from the office (Ackroyd Publications, 329 Avenue Molière, 1180 Brussels). Although it is aimed at the affluent expatriate market, it contains some useful information such as a list of English-language bookshops, social clubs, children's library (which you are more likely to visit in working hours than in your leisure time) as well as sections called 'Getting to Grips with the Red Tape' and 'Job-Seekers' Guide'.

There are many French and some Dutch courses from which to choose, some of which are listed in *Newcomer* (though with no indication of fees). Another source of advice on courses as well as other services is Brussels Welcome Open Door (rue de Tabora 6, 1000 Brussels; 2-511 81 78) which is a Catholic information office for all new arrivals (open10am-6pm, closed Sundays). The National Youth Information Centre (CNIJ) is a non-profit making organisation which coordinates ten youth information offices in French-speaking Belgium which can give advice on leisure, youth rights, study and accommodation. A leaflet listing addresses is available from CNIJ at Impasse des Capucins 2 bte. 8, 5000 Namur (81-22 08 72). Their *Guide for Young Visitors in Belgium* is now available only on the internet (http://www.inforjeunes.be).

Travel

Any travel agents can inform you of the sailings to Ostend or Zeebrugge from Dover or Ramsgate and sell you a ticket. The under-26 fare on both the train and coach from London is about £27 one way, £39 return.

In Belgium two recommended agencies for youth travel are ACOTRA World (rue de la Madeleine 51, 1000 Brussels) and Connections (19-21 rue de Midi, 1000 Brussels).

Directory References

For agencies based in Belgium, see: **Nannies Incorporated** (Brussels), **Services de la Jeunesse Feminine** (Brussels), **Stufam** (Wemmel) and **Windrose** (Brussels).

For agencies in Britain which deal with Belgium and occasionally Luxembourg, see: Acadcmy Au Pair & Nanny Agency, Au Pair Agency (Edgware), Au Pairs Echange, A.Z.E., Bunters Agency, Childcare International, Edgware, Euro Pair, Family Match, Hyde Park International, Helping Hands (Essex), International Catholic Society for Girls, Jolaine, Mum's the Word, Nanny & Au Pair Connection, PEC, Problems Unlimited, Solihull, Students Abroad, Tarooki, UK & Overseas, Universal Care

Other agencies abroad which send au pairs to Belgium are:
Austria: Auslands-Sozialdienst
Canada: Au Pair in Europe
Czech Republic: Au Pair International CZ, Student Agency
Germany: APSI, IN VIA
Greece: Au Pair Activities
Hungary: Avalon '92
Ireland: Au Pair Bureau of Ireland, Dublin School of English, Irish Nanny Services, Job Options Bureau, Langtrain International, Swan Training Institute
Italy: L'Aquilone
Slovakia: Agentúra Nomati
South Africa: All Aboard, Au Pair Discover C.C.
Spain: Interclass
Sweden: IRCA

Canada

The Regulations

The current regulations governing domestic employment in Canada date from March 1994. Write to the Immigration Section of the Canadian High Commission and request a copy of the brochure 'The Live-in Caregiver Program' which contains a sample contract. Prospective nannies must meet three basic criteria. They must have sufficient ability in English or French to be able to communicate effectively in an unsupervised setting. They must have successfully completed a course of study which is equivalent to completion of Canadian secondary school (normally five GCSEs). Finally, they must have sufficient formal training or sufficient relevant work experience. Formal training means they must have successfully completed a relevant course of at least six months duration comprising full-time classroom study. Relevant work experience means at least one year of full-time paid employment including at least six months of continuous employment with one employer, in the childcare field, within the previous three years. Note that the training need not have been consecutive and may include courses taken at school though it must include first aid and CPR.

Once you have been matched with a family, probably via an agency in Europe or Canada, you will be sent details of the family and an offer of employment validated by the employer's local Canada Employment Centre. A copy of this will also be sent to the Canadian High Commission and you will be contacted by them, usually within a few weeks with instructions on how to submit your application by post though in a few cases, applicants are called to the High Commission for interview. The fee for processing applications is C$150.

When your application has been approved, you will be sent instructions about the compulsory medical examination. You cannot choose just any doctor but must go to one of the private doctors specified by the High Commission; depending on where you live, there may be no choice. This will incur a further expense of about £100. The examination is very thorough including blood tests and chest X-ray so there is not much point in applying unless you are in excellent health. Once the certificate of good health has been sent to the High Commission, you should receive the work permit within a month.

This means that the whole process takes on average three to four months. (The processing time is usually four months in France.) Because there can be unexpected delays, it is unwise to buy a ticket with fixed dates before you receive the permit. Kathryn Halliwell, who was applying from New Zealand, made this mistake:

The red tape was supposed to take no more than six weeks. In actual fact I had to pay for a private courier service to get my passport and work permit back from the Canadian Consulate in Sydney in time to catch my flight. This was after repeated phone calls to Sydney to remind them that I existed.

In the long waiting period, you should keep in touch with your host family and try to learn as much about them as possible. You might also want to take driving lessons, since being able to drive is almost as essential a skill in Canada as it is in the US. If you have a British licence already, it is advisable to purchase an International Driving Permit from the AA or RAC.

The employment authorisation will be valid for one employer, though it can be changed within Canada as long as your subsequent job is as a live-in childcarer. If you leave your job prematurely on good grounds, you should be eligible for unemployment benefit while you look for another job, since you will have been paying into the scheme. The authorisation can be renewed within Canada for a further year (again for a fee). After completing two years, you are eligible to apply for an open work permit (one which allows you to take any job in Canada) and eventually landed immigrant status, i.e. permanent residence.

Although the regulations as stated are not significantly more stringent than they were four years ago, it seems that the red tape has become so difficult that a number of agencies have stopped trying to place nannies in Canada, including the specialist agency Childcare in Canada. In 1997 the director Gillian Jones wrote, 'The Canadian Immigration authorities have made it very difficult for families to sponsor overseas, and we have virtually no jobs.' Nannies who would like to pursue this might still try to contact Childcare in Canada, 40 Kingsley Court, Welwyn Garden City, Herts. AL7 4HZ (0171-391001).

Health and Insurance

Eventually you will become eligible to participate in the subsidised or free healthcare scheme which operates in your province. For example the British Columbia Medical Plan and OHIP (the Ontario Health Insurance Plan) cost about $40 a month. In some cases you are eligible as soon as you arrive; however there is usually a time lag of up to 90 days when it is a good idea to have private cover. If you fail to fix up something ahead of time and there is going to be a period when you will ot have any cover, you can buy emergency cover by the day. ETFS (10 Saint Mary St, Suite 505, Toronto, Ontario M4Y 1P9; 1-800-267-8834/416-413-7674) sells a 'Visitors to Canada' policy which costs $2 a day and Blue Cross also offer daily cover; pick up an application form in any drug store. These may work out cheaper than taking out a short term travel insurance policy before you leave home, but will cover only medical emergencies.

Working in Canada: Pros and Cons

Far more people dream of living and working in Canada, whether temporarily or permanently, than can ever fulfil their dreams. In reaction to the high levels of immigration in the 1960s and a worrying rate of unemployment, the Canadian government has actively promoted a 'Canada-only' policy when it comes to employment. Working for families is one of the few exceptions and provides one of the most straightforward ways of acquiring the chance to live in Canada. Some estimates indicate that as many as half of foreign nannies apply for residency at the end of two years.

There is a great demand for British nannies among the professional classes, particularly in Toronto, Vancouver and Calgary. Bear in mind that these are vast sprawling cities and you might find yourself living an hour's commute from downtown. Many such families are so affluent that extra incentives, such as free air fares, may be offered to nannies with special skills or experience. Your living quarters are usually spacious and comfortable and you will probably enjoy a relatively high standard of living. Like American employers, Canadians are usually very friendly and open and unhierarchical with their live-in staff. Carol Dredge was a 19-year-old secretary when she decided to go to Canada for a year:

I was bored and desperately needed a change. When I met the family, we just sort of clicked and quickly became more like friends than employers. The parents were very easy-going and informal though the children were a bit spoilt. Really it was one of the best years of my life.

With any luck you should be able to develop a relaxed relationship with them, as with the children. There are very few cases of nannies breaking their one-year contract due to a failure to get on with their families, which must be a good sign. Another nanny confirms that employers take a laid-back attitude provided you can cultivate a good relationship with the children:

It was probably my childcaring experience and love of kids that got me the job: I am a rotten cook and a fairly pedestrian housekeeper, but the family put up with all that because the kids liked me. The job wasn't bad; when the kids were at school, I had hours to myself to potter round, do some cleaning and prepare dinner. More often than not, I read or watched TV waiting for the kids to come home at 3.30pm.

Many of the expectations will be similar to those encountered in the US; for example there is a very strong preference for non-smokers, swimmers and car drivers. A large proportion of Canadian families own (or rent on an annual basis) a lakeside or mountain holiday home, usually referred to in Canada as a 'summer cottage'. One ex-nanny described her spare time, 'hiking, water-skiing, cycling, ice skating and skiing — Canada is made for the outdoors lover.'

Working as a nanny in Canada has more status attached to it than au pairing in Europe, and the conditions of work reflect this. The federal government sets out guidelines for hours, time off, salary and deductions which most families and all agencies in Canada abide by. As of 1997, the minimum hourly wage was between $5 and $7 depending on province. For example most nannies working in Ontario earn the minimum wage of $6.85 for the first 44 hours, more if they have an NNEB. From this, allowable deductions for food, accommodation, income tax (some of which may be reclaimed when you leave Canada), unemployment insurance and pension reduce the gross salary by nearly a half. The net salary of a nanny in Canada is usually between $700 and $900 per month which, considering the cost of living in Canada, is not an unreasonable wage and allows some nannies to save. The current salary for a nanny in Alberta is $1,080 from which compulsory deductions for income tax, unemployment insurance and pension contributions are made as well as up to $300 a month for room and board. The net wage is similar in British Columbia, i.e. $160 per week.

These salaries are based on a 44 hour week. If you do extra babysitting you should be paid as overtime, possibly time and a half. The offer of employment which you and your employer signed at an early stage of the recruiting procedure, normally serves as a contract setting out hours and duties. Most of the families who employ nannies comprise two working parents, so you normally have sole charge during the day and weekends off. There is usually a reasonable amount of flexibility about how you handle the children and what you do in your time off. You are entitled to two weeks paid holiday a year.

There are fewer jobs available for British nannies in Montreal or other French-speaking areas, since Québecois agencies and families tend to look to France for their live-in helpers, for example to the *Association Nationale Franco-Quebecoise*. However there are pockets of French-speakers throughout Canada, and it is a good idea to ascertain the language of the household before accepting a family. This is something which Pam Robb signally failed to do:

> *Just prior to Christmas, a family in Edmonton offered me a position since their previous nanny had left suddenly and they needed a replacement immediately. During my first evening I was to discover a very important fact which had not been evident from our correspondence: French was the dominant language spoken in their house. The twin girls of 4 years spoke only in French; luckily 8-year old Oren spoke English, French and Hebrew. That first week was tough with Rachel, Naomi and me struggling to understand each other. (The twins learnt English quicker than I learnt French!) Joining the family in the living room in the evenings was difficult, since the time was spent trying to make conversation in French, listening to the stereo in French, or listening to Mr. Kaufman play his guitar... often in French!*

Pam obviously was landed with an atypical Canadian family. Not only were they French-speaking and strict observers of the dietary rules of Judaism (something else of which Pam had not been forewarned), but they disapproved of television and didn't own one.

Fixing up a Job

Fewer agencies in Britain are prepared to try to place nannies in Canada than was the case a few years ago. One agency that you might try is the *Janet White Agency* (run by Janet White, herself a Canadian). Most agencies in

Canada accept direct applications, though it is probably more reassuring to have an agent in your home country to consult when you are going through the visa application, especially since most UK and European agencies offer their services to applicants free of charge.

It is possible to arrange a job on your own via contacts or advertisements. Pam Robb found her job in Edmonton by answering an ad in *The Lady*. Advertised jobs are likely to be in smaller towns where agencies are less accessible. Probably any employer advertising in *The Lady* will have had a British nanny before and should therefore know the immigration ropes.

Many domestic jobs are advertised in Canadian papers as Miss T. Lye from Malaysia discovered when she was in Toronto:

> After looking through the classifieds in the Toronto Star, the main tabloid, I called up several numbers for nannying. Most were unwilling to employ me without papers, but I found one job nannying and housekeeping for a good wage. As I didn't pay taxes or rent, my wage allowed me to save a considerable amount of money.

The *Vancouver Sun* also has a classification 'Domestic & Daycare Jobs' as does the *Province* the other main Vancouver paper.

Leisure Time

Once you get on the nanny circuit you should have no trouble building up a social life. Most agencies in the major cities are active in running a social programme for nannies working in Toronto. In some cases an agency newsletter informs nannies of upcoming events (e.g. skiing trips, new arrivals' tea parties, etc.) and also advises on practical matters such as how to obtain a provincial driving licence (which is compulsory after residing in the province of Ontario for three months), recipes popular with Canadian children, etc. Local community centres sometimes organise regular coffee mornings for nannies and their charges.

Even without the help of a local agency, you will eventually bump into other nannies from a range of countries (especially the Philippines) and other expatriate Britons. One nanny who arranged her job independently felt lonely and cut off until she met another nanny. This came about when she boarded a city bus and the driver introduced them.

According to government guidelines, all nannies must get a minimum of two weeks of paid holiday a year plus $1\frac{1}{2}$ or 2 days off a week (quite often on weekends), plus statutory holidays. This allows a reasonable amount of time for seeing some of the country and perhaps taking up a new sport such as skiing or skating.

Most nannies want to cross the border into the US at some point and it is worth obtaining a US visa before leaving home. Although British tourists no longer need a visa for a short holiday in the States, Britons working in North America and crossing from Canada would be well advised to have one in their passport to avoid complications.

Travel

A sample return fare between London and Toronto in September might be £259 though lower off-season fares are also advertised. Airport taxes (of about £25 in total will have to be added to the fare. The Canadian student travel organisation Travel Cuts has an office in London which is worth trying (295a Regent Street, London W1R 7YA; 0171-637 3161).

If you can't afford the flight, ask your agency about the possibility of borrowing the sum from your future employers, and repaying it out of your first few months' salary.

Directory References

For agencies based in Canada, see: **Calgary Nannies** (Calgary, Alberta), **Mary Poppins Nannies** (Oakville, Ontario), **Q.C. Personnel** (London, Ontario) and **Paragon Personnel** (Burnaby, British Columbia)

For nanny agencies in Britain which deal with Canada see: Academy Au Pair & Nanny Agency, Childcare International, Janet White, Park Lane Nannies, Sinclairs and Students Abroad

Other agencies abroad which send nannies to Canada are:

Australia: Australian Nanny & Au Pair Connection, Dial-an-Angel
Austria: Auslands-Sozialdienst, Okista, Irmhild Spitzer
Belgium: Services de la Jeunesse Feminine
Czech Republic: Au Pair International CZ
France: Association Nationale Franco-Quebecoise, Euro Pair Services, France Au Pair, Inter-Séjours
Germany: AU-PAIR e.V.
Greece: Galentina's
Ireland: Job Options Bureau, Langtrain International
Italy: 3 Esse
Netherlands: Travel Active
Slovakia: Agentúra Nomati
Sweden: IRCA
Switzerland: Freundinnen Junger Madchen

France

The Regulations

As in all other member states, EU nationals are permitted to stay in France for up to three months without obtaining a residence permit *(carte de séjour)*. Once you have a job as a *stagiaire aide-familiale*, the preferred designation for au pair, meaning 'trainee home help,' you should apply for a *carte de séjour* at the local police station *(préfecture)* or town hall *(mairie)*. Take your passport, four photos and some proof of your local address (e.g. letter from your host family). The list of requested documents differs from place to place and in some cases you will be asked to show an officially translated and authenticated copy of your birth certificate, which must show your parents' names. Au pairs are considered students in France so you will be asked for a certificate of education (in French) and proof of the language course in which you have enrolled. Details of the procedures are available from the Recruitment Advisor or Consul-Adjoint at the French Consulate in London (Service Social, Bureau

Emploi Formation, PO Box 520, 21 Cromwell Road, London SW7 2EN; 0171-836 2026/2033; fax 0171-838 2018). If already in France, any of the six British Consulates in France should be able to advise.

By law au pairs coming to France from outside the EU must be women or men aged between 18 and 30, have some knowledge of French and have pre-registered in a language course in France which entitles them to obtain a student visa before arrival. Non-EU au pairs with student visas should apply for the *carte de séjour* within eight days of arrival in France. (This does not apply in the case of summer stays.)

There is a special scheme by which American students with a working knowledge of French (normally a minimum of two years' study at university) are allowed to work in France for up to three months at any time of the year. This scheme is administered by the Council on International Educational Exchange (205 East 42nd St, New York, NY10017; 1-888-COUNCIL). Eligible Americans already in France may apply to the Council office in Paris (1 Place de l'Odéon, Paris 75006; 1-44 41 74 69) which provides a lot of support to programme participants. Americans can request the information sheet *Employment in France for Students* from the Embassy's French Cultural Services (972 5th Avenue, New York, NY 10021; 212-439-1400).

Americans and other non-Europeans in Paris regularly fix up informal au pair positions via notice boards and the grapevine. Despite the absence of residence and work permits and a contract, the arrangement seems to work out in most cases. Beth Mayer describes her situation compared to a British friend:

I have lived here with no papers with no problems for over a year. They never stamped my passport when I entered the country nor when I travelled in Europe. They don't seem to care that I'm here, but unfortunately the case is different for Africans and many other foreigners — maybe even for a black American. It's the way things are here.

Health and Insurance

By law, French families are supposed to make social security payments to the local URSSAF office on behalf of their au pairs staying longer than three months. EU nationals should rely on the E-111 perhaps topped up by private insurance for the first three months. Most agencies urge their families to register the au pair immediately, though they cannot enforce this. Payments are high (nearly half the pocket money in some cases), and therefore families have been known to shirk their responsibility. Make sure you know what the situation is before you find yourself incurring medical costs as Alexandra Wheeler did, and had to pay £300 herself. Because her status wasn't regularised, she couldn't obtain a *carte de séjour* so eventually changed to a job where she was registered and did obtain a five-year *carte de séjour*. If you are going to France for a summer placement, it is better to rely on private insurance or the E-111.

Even if your family does pay contributions to cover illness and accident you are still responsible for obtaining third party or 'civil liability' insurance *(l'assurance responsabilité civile)*. In some cases agencies will organise this on your behalf or offer a supplementary insurance policy at a reasonable price. It is worthwhile getting maximum cover in France since the procedures for reclaiming health costs, even with an E-111, are time-consuming and result in reimbursement of only 70% of costs.

Information is available from the local Caisse Primaire d'Assurance Maladie which in Paris is at 173-5 rue de Bercy, 75586 Paris (1-43 46 12 53). If you need medical care, be sure to go to a *médecin conventionné*, i.e. one whose fees are in accordance with the state insurance authorities, and make sure you get a receipt *(feuille de soins)* which should enable you to apply for reimbursement later.

Working in France: Pros and Cons

The demand for foreign au pairs in France is almost as great as it is in Britain and ever-rising, according to the agencies. Some complain that supply does not meet demand. Looking after children does not confer much status, at least according to Miss Laurence Chérifat who set up her own agency, *Programme Au Pair in England*, after a successful stint as an au pair herself and after coming to the conclusion that reliable and efficient agencies in France are a rare commodity:

> *In France there are no qualifications equivalent to the British ones like NNEB and NAMCW. Many people here think that when you look after children, you do it because you cannot find a better job. I hope things will change because being a nanny or mother's help is a real and exciting job.*

One advantage for prospective au pairs who do not have a whole year to spare or simply want a taste of the French way of life, is that summer placements are very common, some for as short a period as four weeks. Au pair jobs for the winter season are also possible to come by. Lucy Sumner looked after the children of a hotel-owning family from December to May in Monetier-les-Bains near the Italian border:

> *My job involved two hours cleaning the family apartment and baby-sitting from 5pm until M. and Mme. returned from the hotel which they ran ... often after midnight. In addition to free afternoons, I was entitled to 1½ days off which they scrupulously adhered to, and so I had plenty of time for skiing. As I was willing to make the effort, I soon got to know the locals and became completely absorbed in the village life. I thoroughly enjoyed every aspect of my time in France.*

French people are less often bilingual than Germans or Scandinavians (which may or may not prove that they are as culturally chauvinist as they are often reputed to be) so, unless your French is good, you will feel excluded, especially at the beginning of your stay. In any case a basic knowledge of French is usually essential for agency placements of any duration in France, even if you bypass the formalities which require you to prove that you have already been studying French. On the other hand, many au pairs eager to improve their French are frustrated in their attempts as Natalia de Cuba was:

> *I found that the French I learned with the kids was limited to 'Stop' and 'Come here' and 'What are you doing?' while the mother was fluent in English. I learned a great deal more with friends I met outside work.*

Inevitably some families expect too much work from their au pairs, but (statistically-speaking) the French do not seem to be as demanding as some other nationalities and are less interfering in how the children are treated and the housework done. If your charges are of school age, you may find that they won't have many idle hours for you to fill since the French educational system keeps them occupied with their studies for much of the time (though in some regions school children have Wednesdays off for extra-curricular activities, when they may well be your sole responsibility).

Although many urban French families live in rented flats, au pairs are normally given their own room. It is common, especially in Paris, to be given the garret room, formerly the maid's quarters (called *une chambre de bonne*) with a washbasin and perhaps a hotplate. This arrangement suits many au pairs since it provides a certain level of privacy. Parisian families do not have a reputation for being generous with domestic facilities as Kathryn Kleypas discovered:

> They did not let me use the washing machine or telephone in their Paris home. The lack of a handy telephone was a great inconvenience to me and sometimes made me miss out on impromptu social events because my friends in Paris were not able to get in touch with me. And when San Francisco had the earthquake, I had to keep trying to get in touch with my family by pay phone.

In fact a more serious drawback for Kathryn was that 'the parents were very very reserved and had a hard time communicating things to me; I was often expected to guess what they might be trying to say'.

Despite problems, the joys of living in Paris for a time need not be extolled here. With luck your employers will allow you to take the children (especially if they are under school age) on excursions to the Eiffel Tower, the Georges Pompidou Centre, the Musée d'Orsay, the Luxembourg Gardens (where you will find au pairs of every nationality walking the children) and so on. One problem often encountered by au pairs hoping to experience Paris is that they find themselves living in a distant suburb. Quite a few foreigners are too hasty in arranging what seems at the outset a cushy number and only gradually realise how little they enjoy the company of children and how isolated they are. At least with a *carte orange* (see *Leisure Time* below), trips into central Paris are cheap, if time-consuming. Unless you actively like small children, it might be better to look for a free room in exchange for minimal babysitting (e.g. 12 hours a week).

Matt Tomlinson went into his au pair job in the country near Paris with his eyes open:

> I'd heard too many horror stories from overworked and underpaid au pair friends to be careless, so chose quite carefully from the people who replied to my notice on the upstairs notice board of the British Church (just off the rue de Faubourg St Honoré). My employers were really laid back, in their mid-20s so more like living with an older brother and sister. The little boy was just over two whilst the little girl was three months old, and they were both completely adorable. On the whole it was great fun. Baking chocolate brownies, playing football and finger-painting may not be everybody's idea of a good time but there are certainly worse ways to earn a living (and learn French at the same time).

Although it is still more difficult for men than women to find au pair placements, France seems to be streets ahead of Britain in this respect, as Iain Croker reports:

> I have had a thoroughly rewarding and enjoyable year as an au pair in France — so much so that I'm going back again in September for another year. Certainly in France there are quite a few male au pairs — four in my village near Fontainebleau alone. In my experience the boys tend to get placed in families with a lot of energetic children or families that have traditionally had a large turn-over of au pairs. After a year in the sticks with four kids I feel I have proved myself and my agency have offered me one of their best placements in Paris, one child and my own apartment. By the way, my agency (Soames International) is great.

The pocket money for au pairs in France is linked to the legal minimum wage known as SMIC *(salaire minimum interprofessionel de croissance)* which is about 35FF per hour. The monthly pocket money is currently 1,600FF a month, 1,700FF in Paris (paid at the end of the month). The standard working week consists of 5½ hours per day Monday to Saturday, with variations of course, as reported by Tracie Sheehan (who nevertheless greatly enjoyed her job near Geneva):

> *The law stating that an au pair should not work more than 5½ hours a day definitely does not apply to me, or for that matter any of my au pair friends. My day is usually 8.30am to 7.30pm, though I only mind one little boy who goes to school, so I always have my afternoons free. But the housework is not too taxing and when the weekend comes the mother (a single parent) literally forbids me even to clear up after breakfast. She takes a genuine interest in my life here and in Ireland and includes me on any family outings. I have been very lucky. I know one au pair who has to mind five kids, do all the cooking and only gets Sunday afternoons off. She is treated like a servant by the kids, and the parents are not very family-like towards her.*

As usual it is impossible to generalise about the kind of treatment you can expect.

For girls who want to concentrate on their studies and not commit themselves to a full au pair workload, there are positions available for demi pairs. In exchange for 12 hours of work per week, demi pairs receive room and board but no pocket money. Babysitting in Paris pays about 30-35FF an hour for looking after one child, more if there are several children. Au pairs plus should earn 2,200FF per month and nannies 4,000-5,000FF.

Fixing up a Job

Au pairing has always been a favoured way for young women to learn French and, increasingly, for young men too. Dozens of agencies in all European countries can arrange placements and many specialise in France (see end of this chapter). About 20 agencies in France are included in the Directory of Agencies, most of them long established.

Almost every agency listed in this book makes placements in France, and you may want to compare the services offered by several. In the case of France you do not save money by applying directly to a French agency since the fees they charge applicants are nearly as high as the fees they charge families, usually at least 700FF and up to 1,000FF. Since many of them purport to be non-profit cultural exchange organisations, this is a little hard to fathom, but that is the situation. The fee for summer placements is usually only slightly lower than for longer term placements.

Although the majority of agencies are based in Paris or its suburbs, there are plenty of important agencies in the provinces such as *Butterfly et Papillon* in Annecy, Association Famille Jeunesse in Nice (4 rue Massena, 06000 Nice; 4-93 82 28 22), *Contacts* in Tours and *SILC* in Angoulême. The first three are members of IAPA.

The nomenclature of the agencies can be confusing in some cases since many go by similar-sounding acronyms, for example *AFJE* (Accueil Familial des Jeunes), *APEC* (Association pour la Promotion des Echanges Culturels) and *L'ARCHE*. If you have a specific destination in mind contact the nearest bureau, though most do not confine themselves to the local area. There seems to be a shortage of agencies in northern France i.e. Normandy and Brittany.

North Americans can fix up au pair placements directly with a French agency, bearing in mind that the high placement fees must be paid in advance and that in some cases very little information about the family is available at the time the fee must be paid. Americans who wish to study at the Sorbonne or other institutes may wish to keep down the cost by combining study with au pairing. US organisations like *Accord Cultural Exchange* and *Alliances Abroad* offer combined study-work programmes.

BUTTERFLY ET PAPILLON
5 avenue de Genève
74000 **ANNECY - FRANCE**

"Au Pair & Nanny Agency"
(also "language school" & "students exchange programmes for individual or groups")

- Nannies, Au pair : **all year and summer placements** in the region of the **French Alps**.
- Aged between : **18 and 25** (au pairs) / 30 (nannies)
- Pocket money au pair : **1600 FF/month**
- Child care experience and **level of French** required
- Having **3 months (min.) to 18 months (max.)** to spend in France

Contact persons : Veronica & Pascale
Tel n°: **33 - 4 50 46 08 33** or **33 - 4 50 67 01 33**
Fax n° : 33 - 4 50 67 03 51

Almost all agencies require a medical certificate and a basic knowledge of French, though the latter requirement is flexible. Agencies will try to accommodate applicants with a weak knowledge of French by placing them in bilingual families, families with infants, or ones where mainly cleaning is needed. Requirements vary; for example, some will place applicants aged between 25 and 30 while others confine their placements to younger candidates. The deadline for summer placements is usually the end of March, though some agencies accept applications for summer jobs until early May. The preferred summer period lasts from the end of June to the middle of September. For shorter summer placements, au pairs are often given no more than a couple of days notice of their destination. August is the month for holidays throughout France, so there are some short-term placements for the month, usually in the country or by the sea.

It is also possible to fix up an au pair job through an agency on the spot, though not during the summer months (when au pair agency employees, like everyone else, take holiday). *AFJE* says that they can generally place a girl in central Paris within a fortnight of arrival, and will help her find affordable accommodation while she is waiting. Being on location while your agency is trying to place you has the usual advantage that you can meet the parents and children before committing yourself to a job with them. If you are considering this method, ascertain from your agency before travelling to France how prompt placement normally is, since it may be difficult part-way through a term.

Qualified nannies can often find resort jobs via ski tour operators in the UK such as Simply Ski (Chiswick Gate, 598-608 Chiswick High Road, London W4 5RT) and Powder Byrne International (4 Alice Court, 116 Putney Bridge Road, London SW15 2NQ). It is possible to find an au pair job in a ski resort on-the-spot, though if you don't succeed straightaway, you will find the cost of living very high. Matt Tomlinson noticed a range of possibilities in Courchevel:

> *The standard deal for nannies seems to be flight, uniform, board and lodging, skipass, skipack and 500FF a week. For that you work six days with maybe a couple of evenings of babysitting. You don't get to ski all that much, but most do it for the ambience and camaraderie. An NNEB and some experience seems to be a standard requirement, but I was offered a job on the basis of experience, references and, surprisingly enough, being a guy. It seems that positive male role models to take the little lads snowballing and sledging are quite sought after. I met quite a few people who had been hired mid-season as there is a fair amount of turnover. One girl rang up the operator on spec and was on a plane 36 hours later.*

A high proportion of advertisements in *The Lady* are in France. Although Mig Urquhart had not intended to take up au pairing, she could not resist the range of possibilities which her first reading of the *Lady* magazine on a train to France opened up for her:

> *Several jobs caught my eye and I applied for one that suggested more cleaning and cooking than looking after kids (since I'm not particularly keen on children). I got the job because I phoned up a week after writing and caught Jenny unawares. The phone number wasn't in the ad. I got it from directory enquiries. She had received about 30 letters and decided not to hire anyone because she couldn't choose between them. I must have sounded OK on the phone and, because I was able to get to the house easily, we met and she decided to take me on.*

In Paris various notice boards *(panneaux)* are famous sources of live-in jobs. Natalia de Cuba arrived in Paris penniless in January after travelling around Europe for several months. She jotted down a few telephone numbers at the American Church (where there was a huge crowd) and by that evening she had the keys to her own 'cute little box room with a distant view of the Eiffel Tower'.

The American Church at 65 Quai d'Orsay (tel 1-47 05 07 99; métro Invalides) is the mecca for people of all nationalities looking for live-in jobs as au pairs, cleaners or English tutors. The notices posted upstairs are the official ones, issued every day, and mainly for au pair jobs and accommodation. The downstairs board is more chaotic and it will take about half an hour to rummage through all the notices. It does no harm to put your own notice up here, since it's free. This worked for Matt Tomlinson, as mentioned above.

The Centre d'Information et de Documentation Jeunesse (CIDJ) near métro Bir Hakeim in Paris (101 Quai Branly, 75740 Paris; tel 1-44 49 12 00) has a notice board carrying lots of studenty-type jobs including au pairing. Furthermore the Paris CIDJ issues several relevant leaflets. For a catalogue of *fiches* (leaflets) by post, including one on the regulations affecting foreign students in France, send four international reply coupons to the above address. Most *fiches* cost 10FF if picked up in person or 20FF if requested by post. There are 32 regional CIJs throughout France which also carry notices or au pair jobs, as do Centres Régional des Oeuvres Universitaires et Scolaires (CROUS) in French university towns.

Other notice boards in Paris include the one at the American Cathedral (23 ave. George V) and the two British churches, St. Georges at 7 rue August Vacquerie in the 16th *arrondissement* and St. Michaels at 5 rue d'Aguesseau in the 8th. The British Council at 9-11 rue de Constantine has a notice board with some live-in jobs though security is tight and you should go dressed as smartly as possible. Julian Peachey got a job looking after a little French boy this way and Arthur Solovev from Russia arranged a job with a Franco-American family picking up the boys from school. He was not at all sorry that the family was more American than French since he had the impression that French children are more remote than the fun-loving 'gangsters' he had to look after.

Although the notice board at the Alliance Française (101 Boulevard Raspail; métro Notre Dame des Champs) is for the use of registered students of French, you may be able to persuade a student to look at the adverts for you, many of which are exchanges of room for some babysitting. The notice board is in the annex around the corner at 34 rue de Fleurus.

Most of the above expat meeting places distribute the free English language newsletter *France-USA Contacts* or *FUSAC* which comes out every other Wednesday. It comprises mainly classified adverts which are best followed up on the day the paper appears, and carries a number for au pair agencies, mostly just giving a phone number. It is even possible to place adverts in this paper before your arrival in France. An advert in *FUSAC* costs 125FF for 25 words, and can be sent to 3 rue Larochelle, 75014 Paris or in the US to France-Contacts, 48 West 12th St, GO, New York, NY 10011-8369. For $15 they will post a notice for you at the FUSAC Ad Center before you arrive in Paris.

Long-stay expatriates favour the western suburbs of Louveciennes, Bougival, Chatou, Croissy, Marly-le-Roi, Le Pecq and St. German-en-Laye. Therefore these areas have a demand for English-speaking live-in staff, so it might be worth putting up a notice on a local supermarket (e.g. Prisunic) or English-language bookshop notice board.

You can also introduce yourself at one of the many creches or *garderies d'enfants* in the cities, where you will meet au pairs, nannies and mothers, all of whom may have some suggestions for fixing up a job with a family. If you want to meet parents, you could start by doing occasional babysitting; see the CIDJ leaflet *Garde d'enfants* or check the Yellow Pages.

Leisure Time

Complaints that the French are a snobbish, contemptuous and untrustworthy race usually emanate from Britons who go to France with negative preconceptions and who stay for a short time. The experience of au pairs usually contradicts these clichés and most return from their sojourn in France filled with admiration for the French way of life. One of the most basic differences is the reverence with which the dinner table is regarded, resulting not just in a higher standard of cuisine but in transforming it into a social centre. French families will linger round the table for hours of conversation and wine, and au pairs are nearly always included in the conviviality.

If you want the companionship of other foreigners, it is easy enough to find them at your language school, working as au pairs in your neighbourhood, strolling round the Luxembourg Gardens and so on. Alexandra Wheeler found friends in Paris through all these avenues as well as looking up former penpals, students who had been to Britain on school exchanges, etc. Irish pubs are a good place to meet other young English-speakers. In Paris try Dicey Riley's (5 rue Montorgueil) or Johnny's (55 rue Montmartre).

As usual it is easier to make friends in smaller towns. Tracie Sheehan's positive experiences in the affluent town of Annemasse (10km from Geneva) provide a useful antidote to the clichés:

There are many au pairs in the area, though all my friends are local. It appears that English-speaking people (especially female!) are objects of fascination here, so a good way to make introductions is to grab an amiable looking person and ask for directions, e.g. to the tourist office or simply proclaim extreme loneliness and invite them to go for coffee. Actually people here have been so nice to me that it's like being in Ireland.

To get the most out of Paris, a *carte orange* is essential. In many cases the family will provide one, but if not you should invest in one (at a cost of about 275FF). This monthly transport ticket gives unlimited travel on public transport (métro, bus and R.E.R.) within a specified zone of greater Paris, and is much better value than buying a *carnet* (booklet) of tickets, which in turn is much cheaper than buying tickets singly. Be careful not to buy the *carte orange* towards the end of the month since the validity lasts for a calendar month only. Similarly the weekly ticket lasts from Monday to Sunday midnight.

Most au pairs sign up for a language course if only to make friends. Unfortunately many are expensive. Prices outside Paris are somewhat cheaper, but the very cheapest ones may conflict with working hours. Beth Mayer arrived speaking only a few words of French and urgently wanted to sign up for a French course. She searched for an inexpensive school, and found that most prices started at the same monthly fee as au pairs earn in pocket money (for 2½ hours of lessons a day). Eventually she found a great school (which didn't ask to see a visa or any papers) for 350FF per month for a class every day (9-10.45am or 11am-12.45pm). There is a beginner's level and two levels above that. The name is ASSOFAC Centre Social in the 20th *arrondissement* (93 rue Alexandre Dumas, 75020 Paris; 1-43 70 38 35). She met people from all around the world in her classes, from Iraq to Vietnam.

It is more usual for au pairs to attend classes only two or three times a week. The CIDJ (address above) publishes a leaflet *Cours de Français pour Etrangers* which is a useful starting place. The Service Cultural section of the French Consulate in London and New York will also send information, though this tends to be about full-time intensive courses.

Here is a list of some well known courses in Paris:

Alliance Francaise: 101 Boulevard Raspail, 75006 Paris
Institut Catholique: 21 rue d'Assas, 75006 Paris
France-Langues: 2 rue de Sfax, 75006 Paris
Institut Parisien: 87 boulevard de Grenelle, 75015 Paris
Institut de Langue Francaise: 15 rue Ars'ene-Houssaye, 75008 Paris
Université Sorbonne: 47 rue des Ecoles, 75008 Paris

Depending on your location, you might want to investigate others. If you are not specifically interested in studying the French language, you might want to consider the courses on French art and civilisation offered by the Sorbonne, which are popular with foreigners residing in Paris.

Although you can make preliminary enquiries by post, most schools will expect you to register in person and in many cases pay the full fee in advance. If you cannot afford to register in a course, it is possible to become an *auditeur/auditrice libre* at any French university which can be a most enjoyable way to learn something that interests you and to meet local students. But it won't help you if course registration is a requirement for your visa.

As has been mentioned, language courses are not available during the summer, and in fact the au pair's leisure time dwindles radically when accompanying a family on vacation. Several agencies warn that it is impossible to distinguish between work and leisure during the summer.

Older au pairs and mother's helps with a university education often supplement their pocket money by doing occasional English language tutoring fixed up locally (through notice boards or contacts of your family).

Travel

Fares to Paris are very competitive at the time of writing due to the cost cutting of the ferry companies to compete with the direct rail service through the tunnel. Several coaches depart from London Victoria daily bound for Paris, charging less than £30. Nouvelles Frontières, a French company with a branch in London at 2-3 Woodstock St. London W1R 1HE (0171-629 7772) which offer an open return to Paris on British Midlands for £78. This company has many branches in France which sell one way tickets Paris to London (in Paris phone 41 41 58 58).

In France the equivalent of the Young Person's Rail Card is called the Carrissimo, available to anyone under 26 years old from French railways (SCNF) and applicable to all routes except Paris suburban lines (RER). The Carrissimo card offers half-price fares on many journeys or a 20% discount on others depending on the time of travel. Details are available from the Rail Shop in London on 0990-300 003.

Directory References

For agencies based in France, see: **Accueil Familial des Jeunes Etrangers** (Paris), **Accueil Franco-Nordique** (Paris), **Accueil International** (St. Germain en Laye), **Alliance Culturelle Internationale** (Nice), **APEC** (St. Cloud), **l'ARCHE** (Paris), **Au Pair Service** (Frêne), **Butterfly et Papillon** (Annecy), **Euro Pair Services** (Paris), **France Au Pair** (Saint-Palais-sur-Mer), **Contacts** (Tours), **Goelangues** (Paris), **Good Morning Europe** (Paris), **Inter-Séjours** (Paris), **Nannies Incorporated** (Paris), **Relations Internationales** (Paris), **SILC** (Angoulême) and **Soames** (Fontainebleau).

Almost all au pair agencies in Britain and Western Europe make placements in France. Here are some UK agencies which specialise in France: Au Pair Agency Bournemouth, Au Pair Connections, Au Pairs Echange, BELAF and Norfolk Care Search (including to Corsica).

All the US au pair placement organisations send au pairs to France: Accord Cultural Exchange, Alliances Abroad, AuPair Homestay and WISE.

Germany

The Regulations

As an EU country, Germany is a straightforward destination for European au pairs, males as well as females, who flock there in their thousands every year to gain fluency in the second most popular language on the continent. Furthermore, au pairing is a possibility for young people of all nationalities who wish to improve their German, and formalities are minimal for Americans. The age limits for au pairs in Germany are 18 and 24 (though older candidates from the EU can be placed, up to 27 or 30). It is a general requirement that au pairs have some knowledge of German, though exceptions are made in the case of native English speakers.

All au pairs must register within a week of arrival with the local authority (*Einwohnermeldeamt*), taking with them four photos and a letter from the host family. After having done this it is possible to apply for a residence permit (*Aufenthaltsgenehmigung*) from the aliens' authority (*Ausländerbehorde/ Ausländeramt*) probably located in the *Rathaus* or the *Kreisverwaltungsreferat* (Area Administration Centre). For EU nationals, the *Aufenthaltsgenehmigung* will be valid for an initial three months and extendable for the duration of the au pair stay.

Prospective au pairs from outside the EEA and the US must apply for a special visa before leaving their home country, since it cannot be issued after arrival. They must submit to the German Consulate an invitation letter including written confirmation that the host family will pay for a medical check-up on arrival. Processing will take two to three months, so candidates who wish to work for the normal stint of an academic year should apply by the preceding May. The paperwork is so extensive, that agencies normally stipulate that au pairs requiring a visa stay for a minimum of ten months. Maree Lakey found the process fairly nerve racking when she applied for the visa in Melbourne Australia:

> *Despite applying three months in advance, the visa didn't come through until a few days before I was due to fly, and only then because I phoned my host mother in Germany and asked her to enquire personally from her end. The Consulate told me they assumed the delay was due to the large number of applications in Frankfurt. The initial visa needed to be extended after three months, which involved an enormous amount of paper work and legwork on my part. On the whole I feel very envious of my many Australian friends who have a British passport and have no such restrictions with regards to travel and working overseas.*

On arrival, non-EU citizens will be issued with the key document, the *Aufenthaltserlaubnis* (residence permit). This will be extended for up to a year, provided the mandatory medical certificate (*Gesundheitszeugnis*) has been obtained from the local health department (*Gesundheitsamt*). This costs approximately DM30 which the family undertakes to pay. A work permit (*Arbeitserlaubnis*) will also have to be obtained from the local labour exchange (*Arbeitsamt*).

German bureaucracy is notorious, so be prepared to surrender your passport for extended periods and to queue for permits during limited opening hours.

Health and Insurance

Although only non-EU au pairs have to obtain a *Gesundheitszeugnis*, the German agencies insist that all applicants provide a medical certificate translated into German before arrival.

It is compulsory for families to insure their au pairs against accident and illness. Existing conditions cannot be treated under this policy, nor can certain dental problems, so au pairs from the EU should obtain an E-111 from the DSS and follow the instructions about registering with the local sickness insurance office (*Allgemeine Ortskrankenkassen* or AOK) upon arrival. The AOK will issue a *Krankenschein* (certificate of eligibility for free treatment) and a list of doctors and dentists who practise within the scheme. If you require hospitalisation, you must get the permission of the AOK first (except in an extreme emergency).

Working in Germany: Pros and Cons

Au pair placements in Germany normally follow the European Agreement on Au Pair Employment, so any exploitation which au pairs encounter should be reported to the relevant agency. On the other hand, most au pairs in Germany find that expectations are high and there is little tolerance for idleness. Au pairs whose primary intention is to learn German sometimes get a nasty shock when their host family sets out their schedule of tasks, so if possible check on this before accepting a post. Maree Lakey from Australia regretted that she had not stood up for herself more vigorously:

> I was all too willing to make my job in Frankfurt work, and basically that meant that when the mother said 'jump', I nodded obediently and asked 'how high?' She realised this of course and took full advantage. The notion that au pairs work an average of 5 hours a day, 30 hours a week with 2 evenings of babysitting is a total farce. I never heard of anyone who stuck by these guidelines. On the whole I was working double this amount.

The monthly pocket money for an au pair in Germany is about DM400. Most families pay for a monthly travel pass (to allow you to attend language classes) and a few pay your fare home if you stay for the promised period of nine or ten months. In return they will expect hard work which usually involves more housework than au pairs normally do, as Maree Lakey found in 1996 when she wrote to describe her year as an au pair in Frankfurt:

> I found that Germans do indeed seem to be obsessed with cleanliness, something which made my duties as an au pair often very hard. I also found that from first impressions Germans seem to be unfriendly and arrogant, however once you get to know them and are a guest in their home, they can be the most wonderful and generous people. The Germans I met were sincerely impressed by my willingness to learn their language and at the same time genuinely curious about life in Australia, my home country.

The stereotype of the obsessive cleanliness of the Germans also held true in Frances Thirlway's experience. Her Munich employer took such exception to the way Frances did the ironing and other chores that she would take over the job herself, leaving Frances to look after the baby (which defeated the purpose of the mother's having given up her job to stay at home).

Although the extra perks are not as generous as in neighbouring Switzerland, it is customary to be given a paid fortnight's holiday after six months of work.

Munich, Hamburg and Berlin are among the most popular destinations, though the main placement organisations have offices throughout the country including the eastern *Lander* (for example *IN VIA* has offices in Magdeburg, Leipzig, Rostock and others in the former East Germany). They will try to accommodate any geographical preferences you might have, though there are still far fewer opportunities in the east than the west part of Germany.

The vast majority of available jobs are for the duration of the school year. The school terms differ between northern and southern Germany, which will affect the starting dates of most jobs. Northern school children return to school in mid-August and carry on till late May, while southern schools do not resume classes until late September and disband at the end of June. Summer placements are very uncommon in Germany. The only agency which claims to be able to make more than a handful of summer placements is *EuroPractica*. Also the German YMCA (see entry for *VIJ*) says that it will try to place university students with good German in summer posts, but demand is low.

A basic knowledge of German is a requirement for most placements. Without any grounding in the language, it will be easier to find a job with a service family, who often provide generous terms of employment, e.g. paid travel, German lessons, etc. After qualifying as an NNEB nanny, Carol Rowan arranged a job at a US base at Metz near the French border. She stayed several years, moving easily between families (once by putting up a notice in the base post office). When she decided it was time to leave Germany, she found work with an American family who were planning to return to the States, and she accompanied them. A nanny recruitment agency for American service families in Germany was recently advertising in *LOOT*: Nanny Service, PO Box 1747, D-67606 Kaiserslautern; tel 631-950173.

In addition to the language requirements, proof that the applicant has a basic knowledge of housekeeping is also often requested. Fortunately a letter from your mother will suffice (and most mothers are prepared to perjure themselves in such a cause).

You should be prepared for a certain amount of culture shock if you work in a German family. For example, manners may be more formal than those to which you are accustomed, as Emma Colgan found:

The northern Germans are actually very formal and at first I was always forgetting to stand up when someone entered the room, or I used 'Du' instead of 'Sie'. I also had to get used to the continual shaking of hands.

In fact Prussian stiffness is mostly a thing of the past and your chances of being placed with a welcoming and fair-minded family are as good in Germany as anywhere else.

Fixing up a Job

Commercial au pair agencies have been allowed to operate in Germany since 1991 so the Zentralstelle für Arbeitsvermittlung in Frankfurt is no longer involved. Continuing restrictions mean that none is allowed to charge a placement fee, though all request international reply coupons. Of the agencies with branches throughout the country, the two principal ones both have church affiliations: IN VIA to the Catholic church and VIJ to the Evangelical Lutheran Synod:

In Via, Ludwigstr. 36, Postfach 420, 79004 Freiburg. The long-established non-profit Roman Catholic agency whose full title is Katholische Mädchensozialarbeit, Deutscher Verband e.V. Has branches throughout Germany and one in England (*German Catholic Social Centre*) and one in Paris (Foyer Porta, 14 Pierre Demours, 75017 Paris; 1-45 72 18 66). The Munich office is particularly keen to attract au pairs: In Via, Schellingstrasse 47-49, 80799 Munich (89-28 28 24).

Verein für Internationale Jugendarbeit, Wesselstrasse 8, 53113 Bonn (0228-69 89 52). The German YWCA has 25 offices in Germany and one in London (39 Craven Road, London W2 3BX; 0171-723 0216).

Anyone in Britain who is contemplating a stint of au pairing in Germany might in the first instance contact the *German Catholic Social Centre* (In Via's representative) or the Verein office, both of which are in London. They can forward all the bumph and application forms to you. If you are still undecided you are welcome to drop in to discuss possibilities and to meet German au pairs in London.

RODATA GMBH – AU PAIR VERMITTLUNG

GIESSENBACHSTR. 16   D-83022 ROSENHEIM   TEL. 08031 38162   FAX 08031-33369

RODATA AU PAIR – Au Pairs aus allen Ländern nach Bayern/Deutschland

RODATA AU PAIR – nur sorgfältig ausgesuchte Familien

RODATA AU PAIR – die zuverlässige Vermittlung durch Lehrkräfte

RODATA GMBH – AU PAIR VERMITTLUNG

GIESSENBACHSTR. 16   D-83022 ROSENHEIM   TEL. 08031-38162   FAX 08031-33369

The other main agencies in Germany include *AU-PAIR e.V., Au Pair in Germany, Au Pair Service International (APSI), EuroPractica* and *Rodata*, all of which have entries in the Directory. Another possibility is the Au Pair Service, Im Brunnengarten 14, 78256 Steisslingen.

While it is possible for Americans to be placed directly through the German agencies, many prefer to go through a mediating agency in the US (see list at end of this chapter). The average programme fee is $725. *WISE* in cooperation with *Au Pair in Germany* offers American au pairs a DM100 bonus on arrival since they are in such demand. *Alliances Abroad* in San Francisco not only places straight au pairs but also language tutors. Participants receive room and board with a family in exchange for tutoring them in English for 10-12 hours a week for between one and three months. The placement fee is $1,200 for one month, $1,450 for two and $1,700 for three months.

It is also possible to find a job independently through advertisements, notice boards and so on. The Saturday edition of *Suddeutscher Zeitung* carries plenty of adverts, though many are aimed at German girls to work for families abroad. If you are looking for a job on an American base, get hold of the *Stars and Stripes*. Ana Maria Güemes got her job as a mother's help in Biebesheim this way.

Leisure Time

One of the great bonuses for au pairs in Germany is the opportunity to attend subsidised classes at the *Volkshochschulen* (VHS) which exist in nearly every town of the republic. In addition to offering 'German for Foreigners', they offer a range of evening classes in drama, handicrafts, sport, languages and so on. Most bookshops sell the prospectus of courses available, though you can make direct enquiries if you prefer. Terms begin in September and January, though you can usually join at any time.

Emma Colgan was delighted with the *Volkshochschule* which she attended in Hamburg twice a week:

> Our class resembled a United Nations meeting with representatives from Iran, Libya, Turkey, France, Spain, Denmark, Israel, Thailand, etc. The lessons were naturally conducted in German and helped me to maintain my written German. At the end of the course in May, I sat the Mittelstufe Prüfung II as set by the Goethe Institute and passed with 'gut'. Unfortunately nobody seems to have heard of this exam in England.

Nevertheless Emma was pleased with her own achievement. It is not necessary to study for a qualification since the *Volkshochschulen* courses are primarily designed for enjoyment.

Serious language students might prefer to register in the German classes conducted on most university campuses. These usually get underway in October and April. Private language schools also proliferate and some offer special discounts for au pairs. Some au pair contracts require the family to pay for all study expenses. It might be worth noting that the purest German is spoken in the north, but even if you are living in Bavaria where there is a pronounced accent, the teaching will be of standard German.

Both VIJ and In Via will advise their members on clubs and social events. In major centres they have their own au pair clubs which organise outings, concert trips, etc. Au Pair in Germany (part of GIJK) organises cultural events for au pairs throughout the country. Once your German is proficient, you can join any neighbourhood class or club to meet the local people. Despite the difficulty of following instructions in aerobic exercises in German, Emma Colgan found the classes fun.

Despite the difficulties Maree Lakey had with rude and hostile behaviour from her 5 and 11 year old charges and the huge burden of housework she was assigned, she found many compensations in her extracurricular life:

> My language skills did improve, with relatively little effort and through language classes I not only gained a certificate to testify to my ability but made many friends who helped make life a little easier. I was disappointed to find the nightlife in Frankfurt not terribly appealing: techno-music dominated the discos and over-friendly unsavoury characters crowded the pubs. My favourite pastime was going to the cinema with my Swedish pal; we saw about 60 films over the course of the year, both in German and English. Frankfurt has many cultural outlets such as concerts and opera, however these were out of my budget.
>
> Making friends with the locals was of course quite difficult. I found that with a bit of luck and effort I was able to strike up conversations with neighbours, people in the park or in shops, all of which helped me gain a sense of belonging in the community. Sometimes a simple conversation resulted in a dinner invitation or outing which I really enjoyed. I took full advantage of the fact that everybody seemed to be interested in meeting an Australian. As a bonus I met my current boyfriend in Germany, who was previously my penfriend for some years.

Travel

The cost of flights compares favourably with the train to major cities in central and southern Germany. For any flight to Germany it is worth contacting the German Travel Centre, 403 Rayners Lane, Pinner, Middlesex HA5 5ER (0181-429 2900) who were offering open returns on British Airways or Lufthansa to Munich for about £160. Cities in northern Germany like Aachen and Düsseldorf can be reached more cheaply by train or coach.

Directory References

For au pair agencies based in Germany, see: **APSI** (Erligheim), **AU-PAIR** e.V. (Landsberg am Lech), **Au Pair in Germany/GIJK** (Bonn), **Au Pair Service International** (Constance), **EuroPractica** e.V. (Essen), **IN VIA** (Freiburg and throughout Germany) and **Rodata** (Rosenheim).

For agencies in the UK which deal with Germany, see: Abbey Au Pairs, Academy Au Pair & Nanny Agency, Anglo Pair, Au Pair Agency (Edgware), Au Pair International (London), Au Pair International (Uckfield), Au Pairs of Surrey, A.Z.E., Bloomsbury Bureau, Bluebell, Bunters Agency, Childcare International, Delaney, Edgware, Euro Employment Centre, Euro Pair, Family Match, German Catholic Society for Girls (specialises in Germany), Helping Hand Agency, Helping Hands (Essex), Helping Hands (Hants), Home From Home, Homelife, Hyde Park International, International Catholic Society for Girls, Janet White, Jolaine, Johnson's Au Pairs, London Agency, Mum's Army, Nannies Now, North South, Pat-a-Cake (specialises in Germany), People & Places, Quick Help, Solihull, Students Abroad, Tarooki, Top Notch Nanny Agency, UK & Overseas (specialises in Germany), Universal Care, VIJ (specialises in Germany).

Other agencies abroad which send au pairs to Germany are:
Australia: Au Pair Australia
Belgium: Services de la Jeunesse Feminine, Stufam
Canada: Au Pair in Europe
Croatia: Glogovic
Czech Republic: Au Pair International CZ, Student Agency
France: Accueil Familial des Jeunes Etrangers, Accueil International, Alliance Culturelle Internationale, l'ARCHE, Au Pair Service, Butterfly et Papillon, Euro Pair Services, France Au Pair, Goelangues, Good Morning Europe, Institut d'Echanges Franco-Europeens, Inter-Séjours, Relations Internationales, SILC, Soames
Greece: Au Pair Activities
Hungary: Avalon '92
Ireland: Au Pair Bureau of Ireland, Careers Information Service (Limerick), Dublin School of English, Irish Nanny Services, Job Options Bureau, Langtrain International, Swan Training Institute
Israel: Hilma's
Italy: A. C. Link, L'Aquilone, ARCE, Learn & Travel, Soggiorni All'Estero per la Gioventù
Slovakia: Agentúra Nomati, SAPA
South Africa: All Aboard, Au Pair Discover C.C.
Spain: Agencia Intercambios Culturales, Centros Europeos Galve, Intercambio 66, Interclass
Switzerland: Agenzia Inter-Au Pair, Heli Grandjean, Pro Filia, Swiss-O-Pair
Turkey: Dogan
USA: Accord Cultural Exchange, Alliances Abroad, AuPair Homestay, WISE

Greece

Regulations

Residence permits should be applied for by anyone intending to stay in

Greece for longer than three months. To get a residence permit in Greece, take your passport, proof of support (which normally consists of a contract or letter from your host family) and a medical certificate to the local police station or, in Athens, to an office of the Aliens Department *(Grafeio Tmimatos Allodapon)*, e.g. 173 Alexandras Avenue (1-641 1746). The bureaucratic procedures are still fairly sluggish and frustrating and some au pairs have opted for renewing their three-month tourist visa when it is due to expire by popping over a border and re-entering on another tourist visa.

Non-EU nationals who find employment are supposed to have a 'letter of hire' sent to them in their home countries. Although there is a chance that an English-speaking nanny with qualifications and experience from North America, Australia or South Africa might be granted a permit, in reality most work without a residence permit. In its desire to conform to EU policies, the Greek government has increased the fines for illegal workers, though live-in child-carers are unlikely to be traced. So much of the work undertaken in Greece (including by Greeks) is done 'black', many long-stay foreigners encounter few problems.

Detailed information sheets on the procedures for EU nationals intending to work in Greece and on the social security system can be requested from the Labour Counsellor, Embassy of Greece, 1a Holland Park, London W11 3TP (0171-221 6774). Unfortunately there is no separate leaflet for au pairs.

Health and Insurance

Au pairs from the EU should register with IKA, the Greek social insurance fund, to enable them to get free medical treatment and prescriptions at 25% of the cost. Take your E-111 to the IKA office (in Athens the address is 8 Ayiou Constantinou Street) to obtain a list of participating doctors who treat IKA patients free of charge. Anyone staying for more than four months should have medical and accident insurance paid for by their family, though this should be checked.

It is no longer obligatory to have a health certificate issued by a Greek hospital in order to apply for a residence permit. If you do have to get one locally to fulfil the red tape requirements, the health check may not be very thorough, as described by Jain Cook, who has been living in Patras for several years:

A few days after having your chest X-rayed, you go along to a dingy office where they don't even look at the X-ray but throw it on the floor and scribble on a piece of paper — that's your health certificate. Depending on their mood, they might also require a blood test (for HIV and venereal disease) and even a stool test.

Working in Greece: Pros and Cons

Anyone who has had a holiday in Greece or even just ogled the brochures might want to consider living with a Greek family for an extended stay. Yet working hours in Greek families tend to be much longer than in other countries and you may have only one full day off a week in which it will be difficult to do much touring or sightseeing. Yet Greeks are proud of their country and understand that their au pairs will want to use their time off to travel, and some will be flexible enough to allow for several days to be taken off in a row.

There is relatively little demand for 30-hour-a-week au pairs. Since very few people want to learn modern Greek, au pairing (strictly speaking) is rare. The majority of positions are for women who are willing to work long hours, up to 60 hours a week. The line between au pairs and mother's helps is more blurred in Greece than elsewhere, and mother's help positions are sometimes available to people without a background in childcare but with an outgoing personality, self-confidence and a willingness to devote virtually all their time to working for the family. Most Greek children do not go to bed before 10pm, so evening work is commonplace.

The average rate of pocket money for a 30-hour-a-week au pair is 13,000 drachmas, though most families pay more and expect far longer hours (at least 50 a week plus babysitting, sometimes averaging four evenings a week) and pay 24,000 drachmas a week. Qualified nannies command monthly salaries of up to 250,000 drachmas. You can expect to be paid at the end of each week, at least one week in arrears. If you leave after less than four weeks or without giving the agreed one or two weeks' notice, you are likely to forfeit at least one week's wages. On the other hand if you complete a year's contract, there is a chance that the family will pay your return airfare.

Family placements are usually for six to twelve months, though summer positions are available, preferably from the second week of June to the second week of September. Hours are especially long in the summer, of course, when children are out of school. The two main centres for jobs are Athens and Thessaloniki, both of which are so hot in the summer that many families repair to an island or mountain retreat. Yacht trips for summer au pairs are not unusual, though the cramped conditions (which often involve sharing sleeping quarters with the children) detract somewhat from the romance. Many families insist that their summer au pairs be able to swim.

As is true throughout the Mediterranean, extended families in Greece are closely knit and will often warmly welcome a foreign girl into their family circle. This has potential disadvantages, especially for those who value their privacy. The cultural difference between British reserve and Greek gregariousness can be charming when you are on holiday, but more problematic when you are living in a family. It is not uncommon to be expected to share a room. Even if you have a room to yourself, both the children and parents are likely to disregard the door as a barrier. Claire Robson found herself having to resist night after night invitations to join the family in front of the television which was of course all Greek to her. There is also a tendency to assume that your property is communal; teenage girls are apparently very partial to any cassettes or cosmetics you might own; the latter are very expensive in Greece.

A minority of Greek women work and so in many cases, mother's helps work alongside the lady of the house. It is not unusual for fathers to remain working in the cities while their families escape to cooler altitudes, and the motivation of some Greek women for requesting a summer au pair is for companionship. This can be a little wearing unless the mother's English is good. Vivienne Wood had a wonderful two months working for a family comprising an American mother, Greek father and bilingual children, and found not only could she enjoy the company of the family more since they all spoke English, but she didn't have to work as hard either. If the family does not speak good English, the language barrier is extreme.

Anyone who has spent time in Greece and noticed the outside steps being scrubbed daily may have inferred that standards of cleanliness are high in Greece, and a lot of housework including cooking may be expected of a mother's help. On the other hand many Greek families employ cleaning staff too. Personal hygiene is of paramount importance and you may have to adjust your habits accordingly. Because such a high percentage of Greek adults smoke, there is a higher level of tolerance of the smoking nanny in Greece than elsewhere, though naturally non-smokers are always preferred.

Greeks are almost idolatrous when it comes to their children and so you may often encounter the spoiled brat phenomenon. In the words of one agency, many have been largely raised by a 'dotting grandmama'. It is customary to be asked to provide English tuition for the children, since speaking English is a skill greatly prized in Greece. This can usually be done on a completely informal basis. In fact informality is a key to successful au pairing in Greece where rules are less important than personal rapport.

The restrictions on the au pair's freedom imposed in conservative countries like Greece are illustrated in this extract from a Greek family's letter of introduction to their new au pair from Finland:

> *Another very important matter I should mention is that the activities of the au pair in her free time and personal life have to comply with the rules and principles of the house. This mainly refers to being careful which places one visits and the quality of people one keeps company with. The au pair should not drink or smoke and the time of return at night should be not later than 2am.*

Fixing up a Job

Only a small number of British agencies arrange jobs in Greece and none of the American ones. Perhaps because Greeks are not famed for their promptness and efficiency, links between overseas agencies and Greece are not as strong as with some other countries and certainly the choice of families on the books of some British agencies is not very extensive. This means that delays in placing people can be substantial, especially those without childcare experience.

A relatively new agency has received a great deal of praise from partner agencies and au pairs it has placed. *Au Pair Activities* with an office in the suburb of Nea Smyrni (accessible from Syntagma Square on trolley bus route 10) accepts postal applications from young European and American women and also can place candidates after arrival in Athens. The agency is run by Popy Raekou and her mother who charge no fee. They distribute occasional newsletters, arrange social gatherings for their au pairs and provide a friendly and personal service to au pairs including in a crisis.

The well-established *Galentina's European Childcare Consultancy* keeps detailed dossiers on vacancies, most of which are for a year, providing

---

Galentinas European
Nannies, Au Pairs & Mother's Helps
P.O. Box 51181, T.K.145.10 Kifissia
Athens, Greece
Tel/Fax: (301) 808.1005   e-mail: mskiniti@groovy.gr

Screened families – Airport Pickup – Arrival
Orientation – 24hr Agency Support – Counselling
"Change your life, with the Greek experience"

information about the children and the household, e.g. 'single ship-owning mother travels a lot' or 'summer on islands and yacht'. They can send a detailed booklet describing the agency and the duties expected of their staff which they urge prospective candidates to read very carefully, to avoid misunderstandings later.

Primarily a hostel for women, the YWCA at 11 Amerikis (1-362 6180) runs an occasional referral and placement service for young women looking for work in the greater Athens area, as well as offering adult education courses in modern Greek, dance, Greek handicrafts, etc., which provide a good chance to meet people and make friends.

It is sometimes worth checking the Situations Vacant column of the English daily *Athens News* (3 Christou Lada, 10237 Athens; 1-333 3404) and the newer *Greek Weekly News* (Averof 15, Polytechniou, 10433 Athens; 1-825 0848). Adverts are mostly for live-in jobs in private households, and range from the distinctly dodgy to the legitimate. Vaughan Temby was sorry he replied to an ad and landed himself with a 'hideous valet/houseboy job' from which he fled after only two days. You could also try placing your own advertisement in the column 'Lessons' or 'Situations Wanted'. The advertising rate at both papers is dr 2,000 for 15 or 20 words.

Mig Urquhart arrived in Athens on a Friday in September, got the *Athens News* on Saturday, had an interview on Sunday and started a live-in job a week later, even though she had hoped to avoid that option. Live-in jobs of course cut out the hassle and cost of finding accommodation. Although Mig liked the children and the father well enough, she didn't enjoy being treated more like a servant than a member of the family by the mother. The last straw was being told she was hanging up socks on the washing line the wrong way and being faced with piles and piles of ironing so she too quit.

Julie Richards had registered with several British agencies who came up with nothing. She decided to go to Athens in any case and was offered five jobs in the first few days. The main advantage of waiting until you get to Greece is that you can meet your prospective family first. When considering live-in jobs, take your time and thereby you will be adapting to the Greek pace of life. Try to visit the family, drink coffee with them and bargain amiably about wages, duties and time off.

Leisure Time

Greek society is still very conservative and, as throughout the Mediterranean, a wild social life is not really a possibility and the life can be restrictive. Although public transport is excellent during the day, services are severely curtailed in the evenings making late night socialising difficult as well as unpopular with families. Certainly it will be very unlike holidaying on the Greek islands, where topless sunbathing and discos are the norm.

Girls will be expected to join in most family events such as trips to the taverna (which normally include the children) or to festivals at the local Greek Orthodox church (for which modest attire is needed). Cinema is popular in Greece and most films are subtitled rather than dubbed into Greek.

The rich Athens suburbs of Kifissia and Politia are full of families who hire au pairs so if you happen to find a job there, it should be easy to make friends. The suburbs of Pangrati and Filothei are also well-heeled enough to support a large au pair community, as is the more central suburb of Kolonaki.

The Mediterranean sun makes up for many drawbacks, though be sure to take plenty of cold weather clothes if you are going to spend the winter there.

Greek hospitality is justly famed and if you have a chance to explore the countryside on your own you will be offered food and invited into people's homes. Although *kafeneions* (cafés) are a decidedly male preserve, women visitors seldom experience any hostility. They may even be bought a drink.

If you do want to learn Greek, the state offers free language courses in some places. In Athens, you can investigate the courses offered by the Foreign Language Preparatory School at Athens University. Most courses start in October and finish before the summer. The American Hellenic Union in Athens offers affordable morning language courses which some au pairs join.

Travel

The cheapest way to get to Athens is by coach. For example Olympic Bus Ltd (0171-837 9141) runs a weekly service in the summer which costs £60 one way (£120 return). The trip takes three days and three nights. You will see cheap flights advertised for less than £150 return, though these are charters which restrict you to one, two, three or four week visits. Ask travel agents about an open standby return on British Airways or Olympic Airways. It is advisable to have a return ticket (preferably with a return which can be changed or refunded if your plans change) since it is difficult to obtain cheap fares to London from Greece.

Travel within Greece is relatively cheap (particularly the ferries) so it should be possible to see some of the country with the money you save from your family placement. On the other hand, girls who have long working weeks may find themselves envying the thousands of free spirits who converge on Greece every year simply to travel.

Directory References

For agencies based in Greece, see **Au Pair Activities** (Athens) and **Galentina's** (Athens).

For au pair agencies in Britain which deal with Greece, see: Angels International, Au Pair International (Stockport), Au Pair International (Uckfield), Bloomsbury Bureau, Edgware, Euro Employment Centre, Homelife, Jolaine, Lucy Locketts, Nanny & Au Pair Connection, Solihull, Students Abroad, UK & Overseas

Other agencies abroad which send au pairs to Greece are:
Austria: Auslands-Sozialdienst
Canada: Au Pair in Europe
Denmark: Exis
France: Au Pair Service, Euro Pair Services, France Au Pair, Relations Internationales
Germany: APSI, Rodata
Italy: L'Aquilone
South Africa: All Aboard

Ireland

The Regulations

The Republic of Ireland is a member of the EU and so no work permit is needed by EU nationals. British citizens do not even require a passport. Au pairing in the Irish Republic for young women from the Continent is broadly similar to the situation in the United Kingdom. Although some agencies claim to be able and willing to place all nationalities, in practice most placements are of European nationals who come to Ireland to learn English. Those intending to stay for more than three months should apply for a residence permit; enquire at the police station. The language learning requirement is enforced more seriously in Ireland than in Britain and visa extensions will normally be given only after a certificate of attendance at a language course is submitted. All language schools in Ireland are private, but fees are somewhat lower than in Britain.

American, Canadian, Australian and New Zealand students who would like to consider working as nannies in Ireland are eligible to apply for an 'Exchange Visitor Program Work Permit' valid for up to four months at any time of the year. Participants must be students between the ages of 18 and 30 and have the equivalent of about £500 available to fund themselves while looking for work. Once in Ireland, the Union of Students in Ireland Travel Service (USIT) will advise on job opportunities (19 Aston Quay, O'Connell Bridge, Dublin 2; 1-677 8117), though they do not normally deal with live-in childcare jobs. The Work in Ireland programme is administered by Council in the US (205 E 42nd St, New York, NY 10017) and the Canadian Universities Travel Service Ltd. (Travel CUTS) in Canada.

The employment service of Ireland is FAS (Foras Aiscanna Saothair) with about 70 offices throughout the country which EU nationals may consult. A list of licensed employment agencies, including a few which deal with home placements, can be obtained from the Department of Enterprise & Employment (Davitt House, Adelaide Road, Dublin 2).

Mig Urquhart ended up staying in Dublin for two years and says that the FAS is very useful if only because you can use their phones to follow up leads. She also found the Dublin Corporation Youth & Community Information Centre in Sackville Place off O'Connell St (run by the library service) helpful for consulting the papers. Finally she took advantage of the cheap CV service for the unemployed offered by the Trade Union Trust (Solidarity Trust Resource Centre, 48 Fleet St, Dublin 2).

Health and Insurance

An E-111 form brought by EU nationals is especially useful in Ireland. It enables holders to apply for a medical card which gives entitlement not only to free health care but also dental treatment at appointed clinics. As in Britain, Irish families do not make national insurance contributions for au pairs, so non-EU residents should consider making private provision.

Fixing up a Job

Several of the au pair placement services in Ireland included in this book are offshoots of English-teaching centres in Dublin as is evident from their names: for example *Dublin School of English, Langtrain, Language Centre of Ireland* and the *Linguaviva Centre.* These schools are only secondarily au pair referral services, run for the benefit of students enrolled in their own English courses. By contrast, the *Au Pair Bureau of Ireland* and *Job Options Bureau* in Cork are primarily au pair placement agencies, which can place au pairs in families all over Ireland.

Au pairs who are placed through the Dublin agencies are normally obliged to study at the associated school. The Language Centre requires au pairs to attend its twelve-week course (at present IR£231 for five hours a week), while the Linguaviva Centre offers reasonably priced month-long courses. These courses tend to be exam-oriented with a wide range of options available, from Cambridge certificate to commercial English. Most are open to full-time foreign language students as well as au pairs (who must necessarily study part-time) and so most run a lively programme of discos, outings and other social events.

The preferred minimum stay is six months, and summer stays are comparatively rare. The recommended pocket money is on a par with that in Britain, IR£40 a week for 30-35 hours of duties. There is also a strong demand for au pairs plus willing to work 40 + hours a week, and their weekly wage is about IR£50. One important difference between Irish and English agencies is that the ones in Dublin charge a placement fee to incoming au pairs, normally IR£50-£100, though this may be waived in the case of girls applying through a European agent or if they are already in Ireland. Experienced nannies placed through agencies ike *Irish Nanny Services* and *Job Options* are paid from IR£100 a week.

Many European young people are more drawn to Ireland than England as a venue for learning English because of the reputation of the Irish for being hospitable and family-oriented (not to mention Roman Catholic which is a factor for many girls from Spain, etc.). Although the general standard of living in Ireland may be lower than many young people from the Continent are used to, the kind of families who employ au pairs normally live in just as much comfort or even luxury as anywhere.

Directory References

For agencies based in Ireland, see: **Au Pair Bureau of Ireland, Dublin School of English** and **Irish Nanny Services** (all in Dublin), **Job Options Bureau** (Cork), **Langtrain International, Language Centre of Ireland, Linguaviva Centre** and **Swan Training Institute** (all in Dublin).

Other agencies abroad which send au pairs to Ireland are:
Austria: Auslands Sozialdienst
Belgium: Stufam
Czech Republic: Au Pair International CZ
France: Accueil Familial des Jeunes Etrangers, Accueil International, Au Pair Service, Euro Pair Services, France Au Pair, Goelangues, Institut d'Echanges Franco-Europeens, Inter-Séjours, Relations Internationales, SILC, Soames
Germany: APSI, AU-PAIR e.V., IN VIA, Rodata
Italy: L'Aquilone, ARCE, Learn & Travel, Soggiorni All'Estero per la Gioventù
Slovakia: Agentúra Nomati
South Africa: Au Pair Discover C.C.

Spain: Agencia Intercambios Culturales, Centros Europeos Galve, Intercambio 66, Interclass
Sweden: IRCA
Switzerland: Pro Filia

Israel

The Regulations

Like most countries, Israel officially insists that anyone in employment must obtain a work permit. Although not officially exempt, au pairs almost never obtain a work permit (unless they happen to be the Prime Minister's Dutch au pair who hit the headlines in 1997 for being unceremoniously removed from her post after allegedly burning the soup). One of the requirements would be that you commit yourself to stay one to two years. Thus virtually all au pairs are working illegally in Israel on tourist visas, though no one seems to care. The established agencies are pushing to alter this situation.

When you arrive in Israel, be prepared for a potentially gruelling interview at immigration, when you may be asked to show an outbound air ticket and/or enough funds to support yourself. Even if you have a pre-arranged family placement, request a tourist visa at immigration control which will be valid for three months. When asked to give your contact address in Israel, write down a youth hostel or hotel. If you do give the name of your host family, you should claim that they are friends who have invited you to stay as their guest. The tourist visa can be renewed either by applying to the Ministry of the Interior with 'proof' that you are doing something worthwhile (like studying Judaism or Hebrew, or doing voluntary work). Others who want to stay longer in Israel take a trip to Jordan, Cyprus or Egypt and get a new tourist visa on re-crossing the border.

Rising unemployment and inflation are causing the government to scrutinise its regulations more closely, which recently resulted in a pledge to reduce the number of illegal foreign workers. The targeted workers are mainly from Romania, Thailand, Turkey and the Philippines, so this is unlikely to affect live-in childcarers, and the agencies continue to welcome all nationalities as au pairs, mother's helps and nannies.

Health and Insurance

A comprehensive private insurance policy is essential, since Israel has no reciprocal arrangements with Britain or the US. The au pair agencies in Israel will insist that you have full medical and accident cover before they will place you. For the purposes of travel insurance, Israel counts as Europe since it borders the Mediterranean. If you wait until you arrive, you should be able to insure yourself against accident and medical expenses for $1-$1.50 a day, which must be renewed every couple of months.

Families may ask prospective employees to show a medical certificate which indicates that they are free of HIV and hepatitis.

Working in Israel: Pros and Cons

On the plus side, there are plenty of Israeli families, especially in Tel Aviv, Jerusalem and Haifa, eager to employ mother's helps, even those who lack experience but are prepared to work very long hours, typically 8½-9 a day. On the negative side, many stories circulate of exploitation and ill-treatment of live-in helpers.

A considerable amount of housework will be expected of a mother's help, especially if she happens to be around in the period leading up to Passover in April, when practising Jews like to have their houses immaculate. In addition to the daily routine, you can be asked to do up to four evenings of babysitting per week. Nanny/mother's helps should receive a day and a half off per week, though these may not be consecutive.

In return for all this hard work, wages are moderately high. Those who stay for an entire year have a chance of having their fare home paid by the family as well as a fortnight's paid holiday. In some cases (and the number is decreasing), families will give their employee a week's holiday after six months work. The standard starting wage is the shekel equivalent of US$650-700 a month. (It is customary to quote wages in dollars to protect foreign workers against galloping inflation.) These wages compare favourably with wages earned by young people working on moshavim (collective farms); volunteers doing strenuous agricultural work ten hours a day are often paid no more than $350 monthly, out of which they must also pay for their food.

Summer placements in families are not too difficult to arrange, though Israel can be exceedingly hot in the summer. The hottest part of the country is the Red Sea resort of Eilat which is much less crowded in the summer than in the winter. During its busy season there is a strong demand for au pairs; a few vacancies are advertised in the newspaper but most are filled by word of mouth. If you are lucky, you might find yourself looking after one child on the beach all day. Eilat is also a very popular harbour for yachtsmen and women who sometimes need someone on board to look after their children. According to Catherine Young, some jobs found on-the-spot are for periods as short as a fortnight or a month, but you will probably have to hang around for a while before you hear of such an opportunity. Vacancies are sometimes posted on the gates to the Marina, but mostly they are filled by word of mouth. In fact it pays to check notice boards wherever you are, including in hostels.

In some cases culture shock can be compounded by a language barrier as Helen Aspinall found in her first live-in post in Israel which lasted nine months:

> *I worked from 6.45am to anything from 4pm (rare) to 8-9pm (normal). I had to clean all the house, do all the laundry and ironing, cook for the two little girls and entertain them. The girls spoke only Hebrew so out of desperation and necessity I began to attempt to learn the language from whatever source was available: radio, TV, friends, the children, a phrasebook, etc. I was expected to teach these two averagely-able little madams to converse in the Queen's English. This never happened of course as I had 101 other things to see to. For all this I was paid $550 and, regrettably, had no contract. The family treated me as an employee; the wife clearly expected me to be Julie Andrews and Mrs. Doubtfire rolled into one.*

In Helen's next job, she earned $700 for 40 hours of work per week rather than 60, but best of all she found herself in a warm busy family.

Another variant on au pairing is looking after children on a kibbutz. In the early days of the kibbutz movement, most children lived in a communal house

Country Guide

rather than with their parents. Although this practice is no longer carried out, foreign volunteers on a kibbutz are sometimes assigned the task of looking after children during the day. Anyone interested in working on a kibbutz should contact Kibbutz Representatives, 1A Accommodation Road, London NW11 8ED (0181-458 9235); or in the US, the Kibbutz Program Center (110 East 59th St, 4th Floor, New York, NY 10022).

Fixing up a Job

Live-in childcare is absolutely booming and any plausible candidate will have no trouble finding a job. Agencies place a range of nationalities from Colombian to Zimbabwean as well as European, American and Australian. Ads appear constantly in papers like the *Jerusalem Post*, though note that many adverts which sound attractive are placed by agencies who, when you ring, say that the advertised job has been taken but they have others on their books. Bianca Tonkin from Cornwall was placed with a wonderful family and offers this piece of advice:

> There are a lot of jobs here and so you really can pick your job. Once you know that a family wants you, you can afford to lay down the rules yourself regarding hours, money and days off, since it's hard to find an au pair. I must get asked twice a week in my neighbourhood of Ra'anana if I have a friend who wants a job.

It is a good idea to meet several families if possible and choose the one with

---

THE FRIENDLIEST FAMILIES
THE BEST CONDITIONS
THE AGENCY WITH A
CONCERN FOR AU PAIRS

If you would like to go abroad (for a minimum of half a year), love the sun and a warm climate, wish to experience a different culture (a bit Middle-Eastern though predominantly Western), perhaps desire to learn a different language and in addition want to earn well, then do come to Israel through our Agency. We choose our families carefully and will guide you through your stay here.

Hilma's Au Pair Intermediary
5 MOHLIVER ST., RISHON-LEZION
MAILING ADDRESS:
P.O. BOX 91 RISHON-LEZION 75100 ISRAEL
PHONE 972-3-9659937 FAX 972-3-9500577
E-MAIL: HILMAS.NETVISION.NET.IL

whom you feel most comfortable. You should be prepared to learn how to keep a kosher kitchen.

One agency has been recommended time after time by au pairs who have been placed by it. By all accounts, Mrs. Hilma Shmoshkovitz's agency, *Hilma's Au Pair Intermediary* offers an excellent service which includes allowing au pairs a chance to consider different job offers before deciding. The care with which she follows up her au pairs is praised, for example she sends out information before major Jewish festivals to explain what is involved or required and she also sends a reminder to the employing families of their au pairs' birthdays. Many of her satisfied au pairs appreciate that she is a European woman (originally from the Netherlands), sympathetic to their concerns. After being disappointed by several agencies, Miss L. E. Wallace was delighted to find Hilma:

Some of the families here in Israel tend to be very assertive about what they require and expect. Girls I have spoken to say that households can be very hectic and boisterous, and the children given a lot more freedom and so can be difficult to cope with. It is difficult for some girls to stand up to the family in discussions about working conditions, etc. This is why the agent has to be aware of the situation and prepared to deal with it. All of these things are acknowledged and dealt with by Hilma.

More recently, 24 year old Helen Aspinall described Hilma as an 'enthusiastic, garrulous and caring woman who genuinely cares where she sends girls. If a job turns out not to be suitable, she immediately does something to rectify any problems'.

Another long established agency is *Au Pair International* run by Mrs. Veronica Grosbard in a suburb of Tel Aviv. Like Hilma, she and her colleagues often have to pick up the pieces after girls have fled from unsuitable placements elsewhere, as happened to I. M. Mulkeen:

The family I had been sent to by another agency was a disastrous situation. Although I had au paired before, it was not what I expected. I was there to clean, and contact with the children was kept at a minimum. I totally recommend Au Pair International who sent me to my present family in Haifa which has proved a great success. I had a choice of several areas to go to. Each family had a file, a trial period and the agency provided telephone numbers to contact other au pairs. They are there to help all parties.

Anyone aged 20-35 with a nursing background, able to stay for at least a year, should contact the specialist agency run by S. Meiri (PO Box 8142, 52181 Ramat-gan). Nurses are in great demand in Israel to take care of elderly and handicapped people in their homes. Jobs are live-in, the salary is from $600 a month and work permits are available.

Very few British agencies send mother's helps to Israel, possibly because of an unwillingness to send Britons to such a troubled country. There are also some dubious agencies in Israel which travellers' hostels and other reliable sources warn against. If in any doubt about an agent's practices (e.g. inviting you to a home address for an interview), the best course of action is not to go unaccompanied, and to ask to be put in touch with au pairs who have been successfully placed.

One recourse for the nanny who feels herself to have been ill-treated, e.g. wages or passport withheld, can turn for assistance to the Ministry of Labor *(Sherut Ha'tasukah)* on 02-752405. Although they may be able to extract unpaid wages, etc., they will also ask you to leave Israel since you have been working without the proper authority.

Leisure Time

Israel is a fairly compact country with a great range of landscapes, from the mountains in the north which even have a few ski resorts to the Negev Desert in the south. Internal travel is very cheap, especially for those prepared to hitch-hike, a practice frowned on by some of the agencies. But it should be possible to do some sightseeing in your time off.

The families who employ home helps tend to be concentrated in a few prosperous suburbs (e.g. North Tel Aviv) and so you will usually meet up with your fellow au pairs locally. According to Bianca Tonkin, the au pair community is very close and shares all the gossip about dodgy agencies, bad families, etc.

Anyone who wants to study Hebrew seriously can do so at an Ulpan. Ulpan courses are run throughout the country, usually in conjunction with the Jewish Agency, to give students thinking of settling in Israel a working knowledge of Hebrew and an understanding of the Jewish way of life and history.

Travel

If travelling to Israel from Greece, investigate the cost of travelling on Poseidon Lines from Piraeus. An open return from London (valid for up to a year) on El Al Israel Airlines is approximately £239 for people under 26. Last minute one way fares are advertised for not much more than £100.

Directory References

For agencies based in Israel, see: **Au Pair International** (Bnei Brak, Tel Aviv) and **Hilma's Au Pair Intermediary** (Rishon le Zion, Tel Aviv).

For agencies in Britain which deal with Israel, see: Childcare International, Euro Employment Centre, Homelife and Students Abroad.

Other agencies abroad which send au pairs to Israel include:
Czech Republic: Au Pair International CZ
Ireland: Langtrain International
Slovakia: Agentúra Nomati

Italy

The Regulations

The rules for au pairs are confused in Italy and even agencies do not follow the letter of the law. In general au pairs are not eligible for work permits and must be covered by provisions for cultural exchange. In the main, au pairs from within the European Union simply register with the police within the first three days, where they will be given permission to stay for three months.

The 'Notes for British Citizens Wishing to Visit Italy' available from the Consular Section of the British Embassy in Rome (Via XX Settembre 80a, 00187 Rome) do not include any specific information for au pairs but they do outline the red tape requirements for all EU nationals wishing to work in Italy.

According to that information, those who arrive in Italy with the intention of working must apply to the police *(questura)* for a *Ricevuta di Segnalazione di Soggiorno* which allows them to stay for up to three months looking for work. Upon production of this document and a letter from an employer, they must go back to the police to obtain a residence permit — *Permesso di Soggiorno*. All working foreigners including au pairs should register at the local registry office *(Ufficio Anagrafe)*; in Rome the address of the Central Registry Office is Via Luigi Petroselli 50 (behind Piazza Venezia). This must be done before foreigners are allowed to do certain things, such as open a bank account.

Non-EEA nationals like American, Canadian, Australian and South African au pairs are not eligible for the *Permesso di Soggiorno*. They must arrive in Italy with a study or cultural exchange visa.

EU nationals who take jobs as summer au pairs need not worry about the *permesso* if they intend to stay less than three months. The only requirement for them is that they register within three days of arrival in the country, which is compulsory for all foreigners, including tourists who normally do it through their accommodation.

Health and Insurance

All the usual EU regulations for social security and health insurance apply to au pairs in Italy and EU nationals should be sure to take an E-111. This should be presented to the local Health Department (*Unità Sanitaria Locale* or USL) on arrival where you will be given a certificate of entitlement and a list of participating doctors and dentists. Au pairs from non-EU member states should take out private insurance since medical costs are very high in Italy. You can always purchase a policy after you arrive in the country, such as from any office of S.A.I., one of the major Italian insurance companies. Some agencies (such as Au Pairs Italy) offer an insurance policy specially drawn up for the agency's clients.

Some agencies warn that employing families may ask their au pair to be tested for HIV.

Working in Italy: Pros and Cons

Because Italian is such a beautiful and satisfying language, Italy is a popular destination for *alla pari,* also known in Italian as 'babysitters'. Even if you arrive without having studied much of the language — and this is quite common — you should be able to understand the basics after a relatively short stay. Italians are famous for their garrulousness, so your ear will soon become attuned, especially if you spend time with children of talking age. Italian family life is justly known for its closeness and vitality and many au pairs have greatly enjoyed their experiences.

If learning Italian is your main objective you may be disappointed to find that many Italians are eager to practise their English on you. Many also want to get their money's worth out of their English-speaking au pair by having her speak English to the children or even give unscheduled English lessons each day if the children are of school age (which may not be very popular with the children). For this reason there is a tendency for agencies to prefer well-spoken and educated girls, and some job descriptions specify girls from Southern England. This can of course provide useful teaching experience, especially if exaggerated later on a CV. What the expectations will be in this regard should be established in advance, especially if you are planning to pursue Italian studies at home.

Wages in Italy are about average for Europe, normally around 100,000 lire a week for au pair hours and 120,000-170,000 lire for full-time mother's help hours. There is also a strong demand for trained nannies and nanny/governesses. If you get on well with your employers, you may also find yourself the recipient of spontaneous acts of generosity in the form of gifts and treats.

As is true throughout the Mediterranean, children tend to be spoiled by their parents and other relations, so be prepared to cope with more wilful and attention-seeking behaviour than you may be used to. Dustie Hickey, who fixed up a job as a junior nanny in Rimini through a British agency, describes her charges:

A lot of the time the children (girls aged 6 and 8) I look after only want attention, and they do the strangest of things to get it. They don't show much respect for their parents because they more than often get their own way. If they are told off they become mad and hit their mother, which makes it difficult for me, as when I ask them to do something they ignore me. One minute they can be your best friend and the next they're trying to hit you!

But in general, Dustie had few complaints about her placement since she had a light work load (about five hours a day plus occasional babysitting), good pay and more days off than stipulated in her contract. On the other hand many families frequently bend the rules, for example by expecting the au pair/mother's help to supervise the children's evening meal on top of daytime duties. This can be a significant burden since Italian children almost never go to bed before adults. Joanne Moscrop from Grimsby found her two charges' schedule hard to cope with when she au paired in Milan:

Both the boys would sleep from around 3pm to 7pm when they would wake for their evening meal. Rather silly time for children to sleep in my opinion. Then the three year old began going to sleep later and waking at 8pm or 8.30pm so the children wouldn't go to sleep at night which caused tempers to rise.

Italy is not ideally suited to the shy and retiring. Some have found Italian behaviour too flamboyant for their taste, particularly in Southern Italy, and have (wrongly) assumed that a raised voice denotes real anger. It took Frances Thirlway a little while to get used to the flaming rows which occasionally engulfed her employers (usually ending in patently ridiculous accusations of infidelity). But she soon realised that this was the way they functioned and that the next day normality would be restored. At extended family gatherings in a Calabrian village, one or other member would often flounce out of the dining room after a shouting match, ostensibly in a rage, but really because they didn't fancy the next course; at least that was the conclusion Frances drew. In fact after a few months Frances felt so at home that she began to indulge in the odd bit of shouting herself. But not everyone will find it possible to adapt to behaviour which is so alien and unEnglish.

Away from the big cities it will be difficult to find people who speak much English, as Angie Copley found in Sardinia:

I thought it would be easy to learn the language, make friends, etc. but the first two months were the most difficult months of my life. Nobody spoke English in the town, and at times I felt very lonely and isolated. It was frustrating not to be able to make friends until I had a basic knowledge of Italian. My work involved mainly speaking English to the two-year old boy and playing with him. In the summer we spent every day in the swimming pool. I was free for four hours in the afternoon and every evening after 8pm. But once I picked up the language,

I had the best summer of my life. I could go out, meet lots of people and have beach parties at night. Basically it was one big holiday.

Apart from the language barrier, another alienating factor which au pairs have come up against is the extreme security consciousness of some families. Many of the families which employ home helps in Italy tend to be more wealthy than in northern Europe. The British agency *Au Pairs Italy* claims that many of the families registered with them are in the 'upper income brackets and include members of the nobility and some of Italy's most distinguished families'. Although some are looking for qualified nannies and governesses, many simply want a well-behaved English-speaking au pair. Working in an extremely privileged environment has several repercussions, good and bad. It often means that the mother does not go out to work. Also anxiety about burglars, terrorists and kidnappers can verge on paranoia. Some families even hire bodyguards once their children start school. They want you to amuse the children at home rather than take them out onto the dangerous streets. At the very least you may find yourself spending a good part of your day locking and unlocking windows and doors.

Susie Walton deeply resented that her wealthy Neapolitan employers would not entrust her with the keys to the several layers of doors and gates at their seaside villa. Whenever she went out she had to rely on someone being at home to let her back in. Such families are also very reluctant to allow their au pairs to bring friends into their homes. Susie was told that she was not allowed to meet more than two friends on the beach at any one time.

The advantages of living amidst great wealth are more obvious than the drawbacks. Most families have villas by the sea or in the mountains where they can escape from the heat and tourist crowds of Rome, Florence, Venice, etc. In fact even if you are working in a more modest household, chances are you will accompany the family to their holiday retreat. There are quite a few summer-only jobs available in Italy. Families with two houses often repair to their country retreat on weekends which can cut into your social life as Joanne Moscrop soon found:

The family had a house on Lake Garda (for the week) and a house on Lake Como (for the weekends). This meant bringing clothes and toys backwards and forwards, and I found the children extremely naughty while we prepared them. Also this packing up cut into what was supposed to be my free time. Most of the friends I made were in Lake Como, but we spent more time at Lake Garda which was deserted out-of-season.

Often families have other domestic staff to do all the cleaning, leaving you free to spend time looking after and teaching the children. Louise Rollett, who spent a summer working for a fabulously wealthy Florentine family, appreciated the opportunity to live in a style which would be otherwise impossible and to spend time on the Tuscan coast and other glamorous resorts. But she did not enjoy the social no man's land between servants and employers. She found her employers formal and forbidding. Although she valued the overall experience, in the end she found the life very lonely.

Fixing up a Job

The majority of European au pair agencies deal with Italy, so you should have no trouble arranging a placement. In Britain *Au Pairs-Italy* has been specialising in Italy since 1975 and has a large number of established clients throughout the country. The families in Italy deal directly with Mrs. Knoops of

Au Pairs Italy rather than going through a mediating agent in Italy. The agency frequently revises and publishes a list of actual vacancies which helps you to choose a suitable location and family, e.g. 'Mother's help for boy 11 and girl 8 until end August, urgent! — *Palermo*' or 'Au Pair for girl 3, baby due end March — *Rome*'. There is an optional services charge of £30 which covers the cost of translations where necessary, information about insurance, addresses of other au pairs in your region and post-placement advice.

Angie Copley fixed up her job in Sardinia through Au Pairs-Italy:

After finding the address of Au Pairs Italy in your book, I wrote to them and before I knew it they had found me a family. When I arrived, the family met me and took me to their house. Some house. It wasn't just a house but a castle where the Italian royal family used to spend their holidays. What was even better was that the family had turned it into a hotel, the best possible place for meeting people.

Another agency in the UK which specialises in Italy is the *English-Italian Agency* which does not charge for making placements in Italy via its partner in Turin, *The English Agency*. They offer summer placements for a minimum of one month as well as year-long placements. Another Italian specialist is *English Solutions* in Brighton which is run by an Italian man Marco Piras.

If you want to work directly with an agency in Italy, choose one which is based in the city or region where you hope to work, for example the *Sunshine Agency* for Sicily, *A.R.C.E.* for Genoa, and so on. There can sometimes be substantial delays between submitting your application and receiving details of a family, but on the other hand you may be given as little as a fortnight to get yourself organised for departure once the family's details are sent.

Make sure first that you won't be liable to pay a hefty registration fee. Two Bologna agencies are *Au Pair International* and *Easy Travel — Giovani in Europa*.

The San Silvestro Church in Rome used to host an au pair club, but that has ceased. One of the priests recommends two au pair agencies: Mix Culture Au Pair Agency (Via Baccina 16; 06-67 83 887) and Angels Babysitting Services (06-70 20 244).

A few Italian agencies only arrange for Italian girls to go abroad, for example *Soggiorni all'Estero per la Gioventu* which arranges paying guest but not au pair stays for foreigners coming to Italy.

If you are not going to use an agency, the *Lady* magazine (as usual) carries plenty of adverts from Italian families. If you are already in Italy you can check the classified adverts in English language journals such as *Wanted in Rome* mainly aimed at the expatriate community. Language school notice boards are always worth checking; at the Centro di Lingua & Cultura Italiana per Stranieri where Dustie Hickie took cheap Italian lessons in Milan, there was a good notice board with adverts for au pairs, dog-walkers, etc.

The links between Italy and the US are very strong and often an Italian family will notify friends in the US to find them an au pair. Janet Renard saw a notice on the bulletin board of her university in Illinois and arranged to be interviewed by a friend of the employer. Even after confessing that she had little experience with children, could not speak Italian and had no idea where Sicily was, the family invited her to come.

Leisure Time

The majority of au pairs enrol either in an Italian language class or, especially in Florence, in a course on art and civilisation. As usual most of these close down for the summer. There is usually no problem fitting classes in during the school year, since in most cities, children are at school from 8am to 4pm. Course fees are expensive, but they normally guarantee a good social life. You may be able to negotiate some free Italian lessons in exchange for helping with English classes.

In fact most things in Italy are expensive. For example Dustie Hickey used to go swimming in Rimini and had to pay about £4 a session (after purchasing the compulsory hat and flip flops). Most au pairs find no difficulty in making friends, though of course every situation differs. For example Frances Thirlway had a wonderful social life in a fairly isolated village near Naples. Although her duties did not finish until 9.30 or 10pm most nights, she simply strolled out into the square where she was sure to bump into some of the local teenagers she knew. With relatively little money, she appreciated that their social life seemed to be conducted over ice creams rather than alcohol. This obviously does not work for everyone since Janet Renard's village in Sicily (Mondello) is a seaside resort which flourishes in the summer but was deserted while she was there.

Italian families can be among the most warm and welcoming of any in the world. For every family which treats you as a servant, dozens of others will treat you as one of the family and will spurn protestations of gratitude for any generosity. Being treated as one of the family may have its drawbacks as Janet Renard found in Sicily:

> *I had my own room but quickly learned that a closed door was considered an affront; for nine months, I gave up privacy. On free afternoons when I wanted to read or write, Marcella would often ask if I could watch the baby for 'just five minutes' which meant half an hour or much more. They said it was their way of making me part of the family.*

If you are treated like a daughter, you may find your social life being a little cramped, since outside the major cities (and especially in Calabria and Sicily) it is not the 'done thing' for respectable young women to go out unescorted in the evenings. In some places the compulsory evening activity is the *passiagata* when everyone dresses up and promenades up and down the main street for several hours.

Susan Powell spent a thoroughly enjoyable year working for a family (again in Sicily), who disapproved strongly of her plans to go off alone to sightsee on the island. They insisted on driving her wherever she wanted to go and organised family excursions for her benefit; she greatly appreciated this, but if she hadn't been getting on with them so well, it would have been a real nuisance.

The problems which young women alone encounter on the streets of Italy are legendary, as recounted by Janet Renard:

> *Going places was also difficult because my friend (another American 'babysitter') and I were so often followed by men whom we didn't want following us. Whether we were shopping, going to the opera in Palermo or riding bikes, we were followed. In the end we curtailed activities outside the neighbourhood and relied on each other's company.... until I met a Sicilian boyfriend who lived three hours away in a small town. My visits there on Sundays (by bus) introduced me to the best aspects of Sicily, the people, the countryside, the sea.*

In big cities it is an advantage to live close to public transport routes so as to cut down on long unaccompanied walks. The house in Rome where Emily Hatchwell stayed for six months was a ten-minute walk from the end of the bus line. Every time she walked this route, at least three cars would stop to ogle and hassle. Emily felt confident and fearless for the first couple of months which she thinks is the best protection (just as in New York City). But after a conversation with a scaremongering Englishwoman, she lost her nerve and had several unpleasant incidents, when men got out of their cars and grabbed her arms on either side; fortunately she managed to break free both times. So perhaps employers are not entirely misguided when they take an overprotective attitude to their au pairs.

Travel

Check the adverts in the national papers, *Time Out* or free London magazines like *TNT* for bargain flights to Rome, Milan, etc. One way last minute flights to Rome or Milan are advertised for £89, though you are more likely to have to pay more. Discounted returns cost about £170, though there may be a maximum validity of three months. This is less than the Eurotrain (under 26) rail fare to Rome. Three travel agencies which specialise in Italian destinations are Italy Sky Shuttle (227 Shepherds Bush Road, London W6 7AS; 0181-748 1333), Anglo Italian in Birmingham (0121-452 1188) and Linea Diretta (0171-376 2055).

Directory References

For agencies based in Italy, see: **3 Esse** (Gallarate), **A.C. Link** (Brescia), **L'Aquilone**(Milan), **ARCE** (Genova), **Au Pair International** (Bologna), **Easy Travel** (Bologna), **Intermediate** (Rome), **Learn & Travel** (Bologna), **Sunshine Agency** (Palermo) and **The English Agency** (Turin).

For au pair agencies based in Britain, see: 1st for Au Pairs, Abbey Au Pairs, Academy Au Pair & Nanny Agency, A.C. Au Pairs, AMITI International, Angels International, Anglo Continental, Anglo Nannies, Anglo Pair, Au Pair Agency (Edgware), Au Pair International (Uckfield), Au Pairs in Italy (specialises in Italy), Au Pairs of Surrey, A.Z.E. Au Pairs, Bloomsbury Bureau, Bunters Agency, Childcare International, Church View Nanny Agency, Delaney, Edgware, English Italian Agency (specialises in Italy), English Solutions (specialises in Italy), Euro Employment Centre, European Au Pair Agency, Euro Pair, European Connections (specialises in Italy), Family Match, Girls About Town, Helping Hand Agency, Helping Hands (Essex), Home From Home, Hyde Park International, Janet White, Johnson's Au Pairs, Jolaine, London Agency, Nanny & Au Pair Connection, North South, PEC, People & Places, Problems Unlimited, Quick Help, Richmond & Twickenham, Simply Domestics, Solihull, Students Abroad, Tarooki, Top Notch Nanny Agency, UK & Overseas, Universal Care, Wealden Nannies

Other agencies abroad which send au pairs to Italy are:
Australia: Au Pair Australia, Australian Nanny & Au Pair Connection
Austria: Auslands Sozialdienst, Okista, Irmhild Spitzer
Belgium: Stufam
Canada: Au Pair in Europe
Croatia: Glogovic
Czech Republic: Au Pair International CZ, Student Agency
France: Accueil International, Alliance Culturelle Internationale, l'ARCHE, Au Pair Service, Euro Pair Services, France Au Pair, Goelangues, Good Morning Europe, Institut d'Echanges Franco-Europeens, Inter-Séjours, Relations Internationales, Soames
Germany: AU-PAIR e.V., IN VIA, Rodata
Greece: Au Pair Activities

Hungary: Avalon '92
Ireland: Careers Information Service (Limerick), Dublin School of English, Irish Nanny Services, Job Options Bureau, Langtrain International, Swan Training Institute
Slovakia: Agentúra Nomati
South Africa: All Aboard, Au Pair Discover C.C.
Spain: Agencia Intercambios Culturales, Centros Europeos Galve, Intercambio 66
Sweden: IRCA
Switzerland: Freundinnen Junger Madchen, Pro Filia, Swiss-O-Pair
USA: Accord Cultural Exchange, Alliances Abroad, InterExchange

Netherlands

The Regulations

Until January 1986 the Dutch legal system did not recognise the au pair arrangement since it was felt that it was inherently exploitative. However due to the lobbying of various youth and student organisations, au pairs have been permitted to come to the Netherlands, provided the Council of Europe guidelines are complied with and the main purpose of the au pair stay is to learn about the Dutch language and culture rather than to work full-time.

Au pair positions are available to young women and men aged between 18 and 25 who can commit themselves to stay at least six months in most cases, though there are a few opportunities for summer stays. The maximum stay is one year. In addition to the statutory time off, the au pair must be given free time to attend a course (not necessarily the Dutch language), and must have health insurance provided by the family.

Citizens of EEA countries plus Switzerland, Australia, Canada, Japan, New Zealand and the USA do not have to apply for any special permits before they arrive in the Netherlands. They simply register with the immigration police *(Vreemdelingenpolitie)* within eight days of arrival in the municipality *(gemeente)* where they will be au pairing. You should be accompanied by your host family who will sign a declaration that they can support you throughout your stay and in some cases will be liable for the cost of your return trip if necessary. Once the forms are in order you should be granted a residence permit *(Verblijfsvergunning)* for a fee of 125 guilders which will be for a maximum of one year. The registration office for foreigners in Amsterdam *(Bevolkingsregister)* is at Bylmerdreef go (Vreemdelingendienst), 1102 CS Amsterdam.

Applicants from other countries not listed above must apply for an authorisation for temporary stay *(Machtiging tot Voorlopig Verblijf* or *mvv)* from the Dutch Embassy in their home country. In order to obtain the *mvv* you must submit a hand-written letter of invitation from the family setting out your rights and obligations, a promise that you will provide yourself with full health insurance and that you have no criminal record. It will take up to three months for the *mvv* to come through. Having an *mvv* will make it easier for you to obtain the residence permit after arrival. The residence permit will restrict you to remaining in the Netherlands only as an au pair, though it is possible to change host families.

It is also possible to get a residence permit without having obtained an *mvv* in your home country. In this case you must apply for the residence permit within three days of arriving in your *gemeente* (municipality) and will have to pay an application fee, which will not be refunded if your application is denied.

The Dutch Immigratie- en Naturalisatiedienst (IND) publish special booklets on the *mvv* and the guarantor's declaration which can be ordered by writing to the IND: Stafafdeling In-en Externe Betrekkingen, Postbus 30125, 2500 GC Den Haag (070-370 3124/fax 070-370 3134). You can also obtain the IND-Info sheet on au pairing from the Consular Section of the Dutch Embassy.

Satisfying the bureaucrats may take up a lot of time and energy and, especially in rural areas, use up lots of petrol. Jill Weseman (an American who worked as an au pair in Groningen) came to regret her decision to follow the letter of the law:

> My advice is avoid going to the police to register for a residence permit. It's more trouble than it's worth, and your chances of getting caught are very slim. The au pair before me never registered, with no repercussions. The amount of paperwork I was required to present to the police was ridiculous. It took six visits plus several phone calls before I was 'official', at which point my passport was filled with meaningless but huge stamps.

Health and Insurance

The residence permit will be granted only after the authorities are satisfied that you have adequate medical insurance. Nationals from outside Europe and some other countries are required to have a tuberculosis test.

It is a wise precaution to have the E-111. As usual it should be presented to the local sickness insurance fund (*Algemeen Nederlands Onderling Ziekenfonds* or ANOZ). In case you do need treatment, you should have several photocopies of the E-111 to give to the doctor and chemist.

Working in The Netherlands: Pros and Cons

Despite the fact that the state provides excellent day care facilities for working mothers, the demand for au pairs seems to be growing, so that an increasing number of agencies make placements in the Netherlands; for example all the major au pair sending organisations in the USA now send au pairs to Holland.

Au pairs in Holland usually enjoy favourable work conditions, although it has to be said that some sending agencies mention a figure of 40 hours of childcare per week rather than the usual 30. The minimum rate of pocket money, 500 guilders per month, has not increased much over the past eight years but it still represents the equivalent of £40 a week. Some families pay 550 guilders a month and many pay extra for babysitting, e.g. 2.50 guilders an hour.

The Netherlands has a strong tradition of social liberalism and egalitarianism, so you are unlikely to be treated as a skivvy. In fact the progressive policies and attitudes of the Dutch are what attract many young people from all over Europe to spend time in the country, especially Amsterdam. Other cities where families request au pairs include Den Haag, Groningen, Rotterdam, Eindhoven and Utrecht.

Even without any knowledge of Dutch, you shouldn't encounter too many problems with communication, since the standard of English is remarkably high, except in rural areas.

Fixing up a Job

In 1995 the main au pair placement organisation for the Netherlands, Exis-KLIX, became a division of *Travel Active Programmes*, which does not at present have an incoming programme for au pairs. The major agency which makes placements with Dutch families is the Groningen agency *Activity International* which acts as the partner for a large number of European and North American agencies. Although it places au pairs in families throughout the country, it is more strongly represented in the north. A possible method for placement in southern Holland (e.g. Maastricht) might be to try one of the Belgian agencies.

Activity International in Groningen is an energetic private agency which is a founding member of the IAPA and runs a number of exchange programmes for Dutch young people. Jill Weseman from the States was very pleased with their service and also with her experiences as an au pair in a village of just 500 people 30km from Groningen:

> *After graduation I accepted an au pairing position in Holland, mainly because there is no prior language requirement here. I really lucked out and ended up with a family who has been great to me. Though the situation sounds difficult at best — four children aged $1\frac{1}{2}$, 3, 5 and 7, one day off a week and a rather remote location in the very north of Holland — I have benefitted a great deal. The social life is surprisingly good for such a rural area.*

Among the bonuses which Jill received from her host family was the chance to spend the summer on their yacht on the south coast of France and then a return airline ticket to Japan to allow her to visit a friend. Jill's job was set up by *AuPair Homestay* in Washington.

Leisure Time

The cultural and café life of the Netherlands is very vigorous and au pairs should have no trouble finding amusement. Public transport is good so that even travelling to a nearby town for entertainment should pose few problems. Jill describes some of the good times:

> *Discos are packed on weekends and Americans are pretty rare here, so my company is a novelty. When I feel like catching the train or borrowing the family van and going to Groningen, a booming university city, I am always rewarded. There are a couple of other American au pairs there, and we always have a great time in the incredible discos and 'gezellig' (cosy) pubs. The energetic students give Groningen the reputation as the liveliest Dutch city next to Amsterdam. The nightlife doesn't die down until 6am (especially on Thursday nights).*

The density of au pairs and nannies is too low for au pairs to rely on each other for their day-to-day social life; however most Dutch young people speak fluent English so you shouldn't feel too socially isolated. Activity International runs the Go Dutch Club which all au pairs in Holland are invited to join for a fee. It organises several group outings a year, for example trips to the islands off the north coast.

Language classes are widely available, mostly for the benefit of aspiring migrants to Holland, people from countries like Somalia, Poland, Vietnam and Turkey, many hoping to take advantage of the generous hand-outs given to the unemployed *(verkloos)*. A list of language and other education courses can be obtained from the Foreign Student Service (FSS), Oranje Nassaulaan 5, 1075 AH Amsterdam. FSS also had information about International Student Clubs which were founded in the sixties in university towns and offer counselling and recreational activities for all students.

Holland is a compact country with such a well developed network of cycle tracks that cycling is a highly recommended way to spend your free time. Anyone considering staying for six months or more should consider buying a bicycle, which shouldn't cost much more than 100 guilders second hand. Alternatively you can hire them cheaply from railway stations.

Travel

The cheapest way to get to the Netherlands is by coach from London Victoria, and there is lots of competition on the London-Amsterdam route. Expect to pay from £25 one way, £39 return. The train is only slightly more. The route taken by the cheap coach companies is usually Dover-Zeebrugge (which is a cheaper crossing then Harwich to the Hook of Holland), a journey which takes 12½ hours.

New no-frills airlines have begun to serve Amsterdam offering fares which rival the land route. For example Easyjet (0990 292929) flies daily between Luton Airport and Amsterdam for a one-way fare of £35, cheaper at short notice.

Directory References

For an au pair agency based in the Netherlands, see: **Activity International** (Groningen).

For agencies in Britain which deal with the Netherlands, see: Academy Au Pair & Nanny Agency, Au Pair Agency (Bournemouth), Au Pair International (Uckfield), Au Pairs of Surrey, Bunters Agency, Childcare International, Edgware, Girls About Town, Nanny & Au Pair Connection, People & Places, Quick Help, Solihull, Students Abroad, Top Notch Nanny Agency, UK & Overseas.

Other agencies abroad which send au pairs to the Netherlands include:
Australia: Au Pair Australia
Austria: Auslands-Sozialdienst
Belgium: Services de la Jeunesse Feminine, Stufam, Windrose
Canada: Au Pair in Europe
Czech Republic: Au Pair International CZ, Student Agency
France: Butterfly et Papillon
Germany: APSI
Hungary: Avalon '92
Ireland: Au Pair Bureau of Ireland, Langtrain International
Israel: Hilma's
Italy: L'Aquilone
South Africa: All Aboard, Au Pair Discover C.C.
Spain: Agencia Intercambios Culturales
Sweden: IRCA
Switzerland: Swiss-O-Pair
USA: Alliances Abroad, AuPair Homestay, InterExchange, WISE

Scandinavia

The Regulations

Sweden and Finland are now full members of the European Union, as Denmark has been for many years. Norway and Iceland have decided to stay outside the Union but are part of the European Economic Area (EEA) and therefore permit the free movement of goods, services and labour from the EU. European citizens are now entitled to enter any Scandinavian country for up to three months to look for work.

Although there are many thousands of Swedes, Danes, Norwegians and Finns working as au pairs throughout Europe, the reverse is not true. The au pair system is not well developed in the countries of Scandinavia, probably due to the excellent provision of childcare and also the limited appeal for foreign young people of learning the Swedish, Danish, Norwegian, Finnish or Icelandic languages. However there are some opportunities and a few organisations that can help you to arrange an au pair placement in Scandinavian countries, which is one of the few ways to afford an extended stay in this very expensive region of the world.

Qualified nannies should register with an agency which has openings in Scandinavia from time to time, for example Hyde Park International, Monroe Nannies or Regency Nannies.

DENMARK

The Regulations

EU nationals who intend to stay longer than three months should apply for a residence permit *(Opholdsbevis)* from the Copenhagen Overpraesidium (Hammerensgade 1, 1267 Copenhagen K; 33 12 23 80). Although the office stays open until 3pm most days, it is better to go as close to opening time at 9am as possible. Take the approved form (which you can request by post ahead of time), two photos, passport and, if possible, a contract of employment or, alternatively, proof of means of support. If your application is straightforward, you should be sent the permit within a week.

Non-EU nationals will find it more difficult, though au pairs are eligible. The office to which non-EU citizens in the capital should apply for residence and work permits is the Danish Immigration Service, *Direktoratet for Udlaendinge* (Aliens Department), Ryesgade 53, 2100 Copenhagen O (35 36 66 00) or from the local police in other towns.

Another essential document you will need if you will be staying in Denmark for more than three months is a *(personnummer* or CPR) which is simply a personal registration number which you are supposed to apply for within five days of finding accommodation. In Copenhagen this can be obtained from the Folkeregistret, Dahlerupsgade 6, 1640 Copenhagen V (33 66 60 95). This will entitle you to use the Danish health service and to enroll in subsidised Danish classes. Au pairs plus earn about 600 kroner a week for working 35 hours a week, and full-time mother's helps earn 600-700 kroner. It is customary for au pairs to be given a week's paid holiday after six months.

Any temporary resident in Copenhagen should take advantage of the youth information centre Use It, Rädhusstraede 13, 1466 Copenhagen K (33 15 65 18). They publish an excellent booklet in almost faultless English called *Short Cuts* (kr40 plus kr20 postage abroad) which has lots of hard and detailed information about red tape procedures. USIT can advise on language courses; they publish a leaflet 'Danish for Foreigners'. Some communes (local councils) offer free Danish lessons to foreigners, and in other cases your family will pay for language classes.

Fixing up a Job

Conditions for au pairs in Denmark are generally congenial. On top of the monthly pocket money of 2,200 kroner, you should be given health insurance and are entitled to join free language courses in Danish.

The major au pair organisation in Denmark is *Exis ApS* which sends Danish young people abroad and also places foreign applicants with families in Denmark and all the countries of Scandinavia. They do not charge a fee to incoming au pairs but charge Danes whom they send abroad 600-750 kroner per placement.

If arranging a placement independently, place a free advertisement in English or Danish in the twice-weekly Copenhagen paper *Den Bla Avis* (meaning The Blue Paper), a member of the Free Ads Paper International Association; it comes out on Monday and Thursday. The free Copenhagen paper *Sondagsavisen* carries a good number of ads for casual work. If you know a Danish speaker, check adverts in the jobs *(erhvervs)* section of the Sunday and Wednesday editions of *Berlingske Tidende* and *Politiken* newspapers. Advertisements in English are accepted by these papers. There is usually a fair sprinkling of adverts for au pairs and home helps.

SWEDEN

EU and EEA nationals may now enter Sweden to look for work as in any other member state of the Union. The best chance non-EU nationals have is to obtain a special work permit for seasonal employment. This allows foreign people to undertake vacation employment for up to three months between the 15th of May and 15th October. The permit, if granted, will specify which field you intend to work in (e.g. au pairing) but you are allowed to change employers within that category.

When applying to your local Swedish Embassy for the permit, you must submit a written offer of work on form AMS PF 1704, at least two months before your proposed arrival. Au pairs are subject to the same regulations as all other foreign employees so non-EU nationals must obtain a work permit before leaving their home country. It would help your application if you could show that your employer had enrolled you in Swedish language classes. Immigration queries should be addressed to Statens Invandrarverk (Swedish Immigration Board), Box 6133, 60006 Norrköping (15 60 72). Americans may be able to obtain relevant information from the Swedish Information Service, 1 Dag Hammarskjold Plaza, 45th Floor, New York, NY 10017-2210.

The Swedish au pair agency *IRCA International/Sprakcenter* mainly arranges au pair placements abroad for Swedes, but also makes a few year-long and summer placements with Swedish families. However, the manager (Anitha Jacquemot) wrote in 1997 saying that they were experiencing more difficulty in placing au pairs in Sweden than previously. Some UK agencies which in the past have been willing to try to place applicants with Swedish families now say that they are unable to do so. One reason for the lack of demand is the extremely good state provision of day care centres in Sweden.

Once you arrive, it is worth checking university notice boards for baby-sitting openings. A large proportion of Swedes speak English so, in general terms, you should have no trouble making your desire to find a live-in position known. The same wealthy class which employed Woden Teachout from Vermont on her cleaning lady's tour of Swedish mansions is often willing to hire live-in childcare. In fact the last family for whom Woden cleaned gave her free room and board in exchange for acting as a companion to their ten year old daughter. The most efficient way to get an au pair job in Sweden is to advertise in the Sunday edition of *Dagens Nyheter*.

NORWAY

The situation is promising for au pairs of all nationalities (provided they speak some English), though the red tape is still considerable for non-Europeans. *Atlantis,* the Norwegian Foundation for Youth Exchange, runs a programme for about 100 incoming au pairs who must be aged 18-30 and willing to stay between six months and two years. The first step is to write to the foundation or one of their partner agencies for an information sheet and application forms. Its literature warns that 'due to government regulations, this programme has been subject to annual changes' so it is essential to contact Atlantis before making any plans. Furthermore the number of participating families has diminished from 400 to 350 in recent years. Atlantis charges foreign au pairs a substantial registration fee of kr1,000, a quarter of which is non-refundable even if you are not placed or if you cancel.

The main au pair sending agencies in North America send au pairs to Norway via Atlantis. When a family has been found for someone from outside Western Europe, the agency in Norway obtains an agreement of which four copies are forwarded to the au pair, together with an invitation letter. These must be presented to the Norwegian Embassy in the applicant's home country, together with an original birth certificate. At least three months should be allowed for these procedures. Upon arrival in Norway you must register with the local police within a week. EEA nationals can apply for a residence permit after arrival.

Jill from Maryland decided to become an au pair in Norway after she was already in Europe and could not make her status official. In any case she headed north to stay with a family in Mosjoen north of Trondheim. She found that she didn't really have enough to do (since Norwegians receive paid maternity leave for up to a year and so the mother was at home), but she did enjoy hitching and exploring the local area, especially Bodo and Kjerringoy.

The Council of Europe regulations are scrupulously observed in Norway since Norway is one of the few countries to have ratified the agreement (principally to protect their au pairs abroad). So au pairs in Norway are normally not asked to work more than six hours a day, are covered by social security which the family arranges and so on. The pocket money in Norway is a minimum of kr2,800 per month, which sounds generous until you realise that it will probably be taxed at 25%-30%, leaving a net wage of kr2,000-2,200.

The majority of families are in and around Oslo, Bergen or the other cities in Norway, although applicants are invited to indicate a preference of north, south, east or west on their initial application. Virtually all employers will be able to communicate in English.

Another programme administered by Atlantis is not specifically for au pairs but is based on a similar principle. The Norwegian Farm Guest Programme allows young people to spend two to three months living with a farming family free of charge in exchange for helping around the farm. The programme is open to people aged between 18 and 30 of any nationality, provided they can speak English. The pocket money is not high relative to the Scandinavian cost of living, i.e. 600 kroner for a maximum of 35 hours a week. The length of stay is 6-12 weeks. Application should be made three to four months before your proposed arrival date. The registration fee is as for the au pair programme.

Neil Tallantire worked for a number of winter seasons in Lillehammer, a ski resort 150km north of Oslo. He observed that there is some demand for seasonal live-in help in resort areas and recommends chatting to as many people as possible on the ferry from Harwich to Oslo (via Hirtshals in Denmark):

> *Talk to people. Norwegians are friendly. You should get some job offers; I was offered work on a pig farm and an au pair type job, teaching English to some kids. Both were in resort areas and would allow plenty of time to ski.*

As in Denmark there is a youth information centre known as USIT at Mollergata 3, N-0179 Oslo (2241 5132) but it is open in the summer only. It can recommend cheap accommodation and restaurants and can advise young people on practical problems.

FINLAND

Now that Finland is a full member of the European Union, there are fewer red tape hassles for European au pairs. The country actively encourages nationals from other countries to come as temporary trainees as well. The International Trainee Exchange programme in Finland is administered by CIMO, the Centre for International Mobility (PO Box 343, 00531 Helsinki, Finland; 09-7747 7033/fax 7747 7064) which also runs the Finnish Family Programme. Participants live with a Finnish family for one to three months in the summer or for longer periods up to 18 months starting at any time of the year, helping in their home and teaching the children English. Anyone who is aged 18-25 and who can speak English, German or French is eligible. The school term for Finnish students begins in mid-August so most summer placements come to an end at that time.

The host families' principal motivation for participating in the programme is to improve their English, though it can't be a deterring factor that they also get five hours work from you a day, in their garden or house, including looking after their children. The arrangement is a sophisticated version of the au pair arrangement and is open to men as well as women. Teaching English usually involves no more than just talking. Most Finns have a good knowledge of English.

In addition to free room and board, you will be paid pocket money of between FIM1,000 and FIM2,000 per month (£130-£260). Bob Seymour enjoyed the Finnish Family Programme immensely:

> *The location of my family in the forests of northern Finland was so idyllic and the atmosphere so congenial that I refused to accept the pocket money, since I reckoned it to be payment enough that I could live there free for two months.*

Readers in other countries should write to CIMO for their list of cooperating organisations in 13 countries who will be able to help prospective au pairs obtain the necessary work and residence permit before entering Finland. American applicants should apply through *InterExchange*.

A few years ago the student exchange organisation Allianssi (Olymdiastadion, Eteläkaarre, 00250 Helsinki; 348 2422) had a small incoming programme but that has been dissolved.

The alternative to an agency is to fix up something privately. Several years ago Natasha Fox exploited the Scandinavian desire to improve their English:

> *I found work as a nanny in Finland simply by placing advertisement cards in a few playgroups. The best area to place them in Helsinki is Westend, Espoo, about 15 minutes bus ride from the city centre. This is the most affluent area of the capital and I found a nanny job paying £110 a week for working 8am-4pm Monday to Friday. Most Finnish parents want their children to learn English so you may get hired on the strength of this.*

Natasha goes on to recommend asking some locals to translate newspaper advertisements for you. The main daily *Helsingin Sanomat* carries details of several domestic vacancies each day, and it is worth ringing up and asking if they would like an English-speaker for the benefit of the children.

If you advertise yourself, try to write it in Finnish, so you won't give the impression of being an arrogant foreigner. (You probably won't have to speak a word of it in the job.) This is the text of the advert Natasha used:

> *Haluaisitko 'vaihtaa vapaale', lasten hoidon lomassa? Iloinen, vastuullinen Englandtilais-tytto antaa sinulle mahdollisuuden! Olen vapaa useimpina päivinä/iltoina.*

This translates as, 'How would you like a break from the kids? Responsible cheerful English girl will give you the chance! I am free most days and evenings.'

ICELAND

Interest in au pairing in Iceland is increasing, especially on the part of Americans who can participate in the programmes run by *WISE* or *AuPair Homestay*. WISE's partner agency running the Au Pair in Iceland programme is Vistaskipti & Nam. The only European agency we know of which offers a realistic hope of placing au pairs in Iceland is *Exis* in Denmark who say that au pairs receive free flights from Europe and pocket money of kr2,000 per month, though this is more likely to apply only to Scandinavian nationals.

The Au Pair in Iceland programme accepts au pairs aged 18-25 for periods of 9-12 months starting in August/September and for 6, 8 or 12 months from January. The minimum pocket money is 23,700 kronur per month (about US$330). Families undertake to reimburse half the travel costs if you stay 6-9 months and the full cost if you stay 9-12 months, to a maximum of 50,000 kronur. The mediating agency arranges all the paperwork and arranges for a residence permit.

Travel

Travel to and around Scandinavia is very expensive. There are no bargain flights, so the cheapest way is to go by ferry and by land. There is a year round ferry service on the Fred Olsen line (which gives good discounts to students) from Harwich to Oslo. If you have a chance to talk to people on the ferry you may find it is possible to arrange a long distance lift. Otherwise the hitching in Scandinavia isn't too bad, though beware of the very short winter days in the north and the vicious mosquitoes in the summer.

Unfortunately rail fares within each country are high. Information and bookings can be made in advance if required through Norwegian State Railways, 21/24 Cockspur Street, London SW1Y 5DA (0171-930 6666).

Directory References

For au pair agencies based in Scandinavia with incoming programmes, see: **Atlantis** (Norway), **EXIS ApS** (Denmark) and **IRCA** (Sweden).

For agencies in Britain which deal with Scandinavia, see: Au Pair International — Stockport (to Finland, Sweden & Norway), Au Pair International–London (to Denmark & Sweden), Au Pairs of Surrey (to Finland), Edgware (to Denmark), Helping Hand Agency (to Sweden), Helping Hands — Essex (to Denmark), Nannies Now (to Finland & Sweden), North South (to Sweden), Quick Help (to Norway), Solihull (to Denmark, Norway & Sweden), Students Abroad (occasionally), UK & Overseas (to Denmark, Norway & Sweden).

Other agencies abroad which send au pairs to Scandinavia are:
Austria: Okista (to Norway & Iceland)
Belgium: Stufam (to Denmark & Norway)
Canada: Au Pair in Europe (to Norway, Finland, Denmark & Sweden)
Czech Republic: Au Pair International CZ (to Denmark, Norway & Sweden)
France: Au Pair Service, Inter-Séjours (to Denmark)
Germany: APSI, AU-PAIR e.V. and Rodata (to Norway)
Greece: Au Pair Activities (to Denmark & Finland), Galentina's (to Norway, Sweden, Denmark & Iceland)
Hungary: Avalon '92 (to Norway)
Ireland: Au Pair Bureau of Ireland & Langtrain International (to Denmark)
Italy: L'Aquilone (to Denmark & Norway)
Slovakia: Agentúra Nomati (to Denmark, Norway & Sweden)
South Africa: All Aboard (to Sweden), Au Pair Discover C.C. (to Norway & Sweden)
USA: AuPair Homestay (to Iceland, Norway and Finland), InterExchange (to Norway & Finland) and WISE (to Norway & Iceland)

Spain & Portugal

The Regulations

European au pairs who intend to stay for more than three months must apply for a residence card *(Tarjeta de Residencia)* within 30 days of arrival. Application should be made to a regional police headquarters *(Comisaría de Policía)* or a Foreigners' Registration Office *(Oficina de Extranjería)* which in Madrid is at Calle Moratin 43. The documents necessary for the *residencia* are a contract of employment, three photos, a passport and (sometimes) a medical certificate. This information is confirmed both in the hand-outs from the Labour Counsellor's Office of the Spanish Embassy (20 Peel St, London W8 7PD) and in 'Settling in Spain' (revised May 1996) from the British Consulate-General in Spain (c/ Marqués de la Ensenada 16-2°, 28004 Madrid). These notes also include addresses of all 15 British Consulates in Spain.

Most of the Spanish agencies limit their placement services to Europeans though some do work with North American and other nationalities. Non-EU nationals who wish to work as au pairs should apply for a student visa before leaving their country of residence. Officially the Spanish Embassy requires both an offer of employment from the family and a letter from the school where the au pair is enrolled to study Spanish but in fact only the former is required, since the authorities recognise that it is usually impracticable for au pairs to enrol in classes before arrival in Spain. The right to remain in Spain will be extended only for periods of three months at a time, so this procedure will have to be repeated every three months. Non-EU au pairs and nannies who come to an informal arrangement with a family in Spain will have to leave the country every three months in order to renew their tourist visa on re-entry.

Portugal has the reputation for being more lenient towards au pairs who, like live-in English tutors and governesses, traditionally worked without worrying about obtaining a work permit. So few au pairs go to Portugal that the *Ministerio do Trabhalho* it seems does not concern itself too much with live-in childcarers from developed countries. Those who wish to apply for a residence permit in Lisbon must go to the *Servico de Estrangeiros e Fronteiras* (Av. António Augusto Aguiar 20, 1000 Lisbon; 1-523324).

Health and Insurance

An E-111 is sufficient to cover urgent medical treatment in Spain. As soon as you arrive in Spain, take your E-111 to an office of the Instituto Nacional de la Seguridad Social or INSS and obtain a list of participating doctors (which are more widely scattered than is convenient). Some of the agencies in Spain recommend that the families registered with them arrange insurance cover for their au pairs but this can by no means be relied upon.

All British passport and E-111 holders are entitled to receive treatment at Portuguese health centres *(Centro de Sáude)* and state hospitals, though varying charges will be made which would be better covered by a comprehensive private insurance policy.

Working in Spain: Pros and Cons

Spain's demand for au pairs and mother's helps is booming. Many UK and European agencies have added Spain to their list of destination countries, and the number of Spanish agencies has increased significantly. The last 15 years have seen unprecedented economic growth in Spain, as business and industry forged ahead in the wake of European unification and the Barcelona Olympics. This has fuelled a huge demand for the English language and many Spanish families want a young English speaker to interact with their children on a daily basis. The emphasis on conversational English means that a certain number of families are happy to consider young men for live-in positions.

Gone are the days when all the live-in positions in Spain were taken by Irish girls because of their Catholicism (though the Associacion Catolica Internacional Servicios Juventud Femenina continues as one of the largest agencies in Spain). An amusing and vivid account of what it was like to be a 'governess' in Spain in the 1920s and 30s is provided in the book *No More than*

Human by Maura Laverty, in which she claims that a whole generation of aristocratic Spanish children grew up with Irish accents.

The chances of being able to arrange an au pair placement in Spain, even at short notice, are very good. In many cases requirements are minimal, e.g. a knowledge of Spanish or experience of childcare may not be necessary. The majority of jobs are in the cities and environs of Madrid and Barcelona, though jobs do crop up in glamorous resorts like Marbella, Majorca and Tenerife from time to time.

Despite the efforts of the many agencies and youth organisations active in Spain, the rules of au pairing are probably less strenuously enforced in Spain than in most other countries and hours tend to be on average longer than in other countries. Some au pairs report that they have ended up working the same hours as a mother's help but for au pair pocket money (which is normally paid on a monthly basis in Spain). The minimum pay at present is 24,000 pesetas a month, though families in the major cities pay more (for example the rate in Barcelona is 26,000-27,000 pesetas) and ones in popular tourist areas may pay less. No perks are built into the arrangement, so au pairs can't count on getting any paid holidays, subsidised fares or a contribution towards their tuition fees except at the discretion of their employers.

As noted above, many families will want you to speak English making it more difficult to learn Spanish. Another possible pitfall for serious linguists is that in some areas, principally around Barcelona, the dominant language is Catalan, which is incomprehensible to most speakers of Spanish. Basque is spoken in the north around Bilbao, however since only 2% of the population of Spain are Basques, you are unlikely to encounter the language much.

Society remains fairly conservative in both Spain and Portugal (as throughout the Mediterranean) and a relatively small proportion of women go out to work. Good daughters stay at home helping their mothers, and so there may be a certain level of intolerance of independent behaviour. One advantage of the traditional closeness of the extended family is that there is often an aunt or grandmother on hand to help with the childcare if the au pair wants some time off.

On the other hand many city families are as liberal as their counterparts elsewhere in Europe and Judith Twycross had no complaints about her situation in Seville which had been arranged through *North South Agency*:

> *The family treated me very well; they treated me as an equal with consideration for my need for privacy and free time. I was free to come and go as I liked during my spare time. Lunch was the main family meal of the day and I was expected to be there for it. I was rarely needed to babysit but, on the times I was needed, I was asked in advance. I also dogsat a couple of weekends when the rest of the family went away.*
>
> *I was very lucky because the family had a maid and the only domestic duties I had were to tidy the girls' rooms and prepare breakfast for them in the mornings and a light tea when they got back from school. I had to give an hour's English class to the younger daughter and spoke to the elder daughter, who was already fluent, only in English. I was able to practise my Spanish with the parents and the maid, so didn't mind speaking English to the children, to whom I continued to give lessons for the rest of my stay in Spain, even after I stopped au pairing and began teaching English.*

An extreme social elite remains in Spain and they are likely to maintain their distance from their home helps. Sally Stanley found this to be the case with her employers who ran a top hotel in Marbella and seemed to be out most evenings attending charity balls:

Although we were living together in a small flat, the mother's world remained completely remote from mine. There was no attempt to make me feel like part of the family, and I couldn't help but bristle whenever her treatment of me as paid help became especially glaring. Fortunately I got on fairly well with the three children (though they were terribly spoiled) who all spoke English, as they had had English nannies since birth — it was that kind of family.

Working in Portugal

European au pairs are much less common in Portugal than nannies and childminders from former Portuguese colonies like Mozambique and Brazil, as well as other developing nations. Virtually no British agencies undertake placements there. Yet the decade of the 1990s has seen very fast growth in the Portuguese economy, and there may yet come a time when well-to-do Portuguese families look to British and other agencies for childcarers, even if the attractions of learning Portuguese are unlikely to increase.

However there are such sizeable expatriate British communities in the two main cities of Lisbon and Oporto as well as on the Algarve (the south coast) that there is some demand for English-speaking nannies and mother's helps in these households.

Fixing up a Job

The huge number of British nanny and au pair agencies which deal with Spain indicates the extent of the demand in Spain for childcare at all levels. One of the biggest agencies in Spain with partner agencies around the world is *Relaciones Culturales Internacionales,* which is a non-profit club allied to the Ministry of Culture and the Ministry of Education and member of the IAPA. RCI has many openings throughout the year. Although Noel Kirkpatrick wasn't really an au pair, he found them very helpful:

RCI helped me tremendously during my time here in Madrid e.g. finding students for me to teach and a family with whom to live this summer.

One of the most energetic agencies is *G.I.C.*, a founding member of the International Au Pair Association and one which is determined to set a standard for other au pair agencies to try to rescue the reputation of au pairing in Spain. Another important agency whose quality of service has been praised is *Centros Europeos* about which Katie Burford wrote in the fortnightly newspaper *Overseas Jobs Express* in 1996:

The choice of au pair agency is important. We were lucky to find Centros Europeos of Madrid which, for 15,000 pesetas, placed us in a good location and followed up to make sure we were acclimatising. I met another girl who had paid ten times what I had, and other au pairs whose agencies had turned a cold shoulder at the first sign of problems.

Madrid does not have the monopoly on au pair agencies. Barcelona is an increasingly attractive destination. In addition to the two Barcelona agencies listed in the Directory *(Interclass* and *International Au Pair Intercambio)* try also Delivery Au Pair and Oh Europa (among whose partner agencies is *Au Pair Connections* in Southampton). Tenerife must be one of the most popular destinations for disaffected northern Europeans; if interested in au pairing here, try the Canary Islands Bureau (Urb. Santiao B.4 — 5° dcha, 38005 Santa Cruz de Tenerife). Another agency to try is Au-Pair Spain run by Rosalia

154 Country Guide

Au Pair in Spain

by

Pintor Sorolla Apt #. 1080
Monte Vedat 46901-Valencia
Tel. +34-6-156-5837 (Also fax)
email:gic@redestb.es

☺ Are you a good German/English speaker aged between 18 and 28 – Western Europe –
willing to spend 1, 2 or 3 months in Spain starting in June, July or August?
☞ You will receive a minimum of 24,000 pesetas a month for 30 hours of weekly child care of babies and infants or private tutoring of Pre school and youngsters and light domestic help
☞ You will have free time to learn Spanish and at least one and a half days free a week.

To qualify you must:
- Have practical baby sitting or Au Pair experience.
- Be a non smoker.
- Pass an interview with one of our partner Au Pair Agencies of the I.A.P.A. (International Au Pair Association) in your country.
- Fulfil the requirements that the Au Pair regulations establish.

For details:
e mail your CV and a letter of introduction to us with your questions and information required

email:gic@redestb.es

I A P A

Other Programmes offered by G.I.C. Au Pair Agency are: Au Pair in America and Europe for western Europeans

GIC is a founder member of the IAPA (International Au Pair Association)
The first legal Au Pair Association in the world

Molina (Serrano Clavero 2, 46340 Requena, Valencia; 96-230 50 82/fax 96-230 25 63).

Au pair arrangements can of course be made without a mediating agency. The many language institutes and schools in every town and city can prove a good source of local families looking for an English-speaking live-in helper. If you want to make informal contacts and meet expatriate families who might be looking for live-in childcare, you could visit a mothers' and toddlers' group like the one held every week at the English-speaking St. George's Church at C/ Nunez de Balboa 43, Madrid.

A possible way of fixing up a job ahead of time would be to advertise in the free ads paper *Segundamano* (equivalent to *LOOT* in London). One summer Nan Bevan from California tried this means of fixing up an au pair position and described the responses to her ad as 'more than fruitful'. If you are on the spot, check local advertisements in the English language press. For example the *Daily Bulletin* of Majorca and the *Costa Blanca News* carry job adverts which occasionally include requests for au pairs. You can place your own advert, though newspapers are not allowed to accept 'Employment Wanted' ads from outside Spain. Unfortunately the useful notice board which the English language Turner Bookshop used to have at its old location in Madrid has not resurfaced in its new one on Calle Principe de Vergara.

Although Portuguese agencies do exist which are involved in au pair placement, they keep a very low profile and are reluctant to publicise details. The International Friendship League (R. Ruy de Sausa Vinagre 2, 2890 Alcochete; 234 1082) did at one time claim to arrange au pair stays in Portugal, but recent confirmation was not forthcoming. Neither is it known whether Turicoop (Rua Pascoal-Melo, 15-1°, 1100 Lisbon; 531804) is still involved in au pair placement. The best chance of obtaining information is to make contact with student travel organisations like the Associacao de Turismo Estudantil e Juventil, PO Box 4586, 4009 Oporto, or the Instituto Portugues da Juventude, Avenida da Liberdade 194, 1250 Lisbon. Try also Intercultura, Avenida Almirante Reis 219-r/c Esq, Apartado 1395, 1011 Lisbon Codex.

It may be possible to arrange a job with a family after arrival in Portugal by making enquiries among expatriates. It is a good idea to scan the advertisements in the weekly *Anglo-Portuguese News* (Apartado 113, 2765 Estoril; 466 1551). You can place your own advert in this widely circulating paper though the rates are fairly expensive. Also check the fortnightly English language *Algarve News* which has a handful of employment classified adverts (PO Box 13, 8400 Lagoa; fax 82-341201).

Leisure Time

State schools offer Spanish language instruction more cheaply than private schools, though of course they will be closed in the summer. Prices vary wildly among schools, so it is worth comparing several, since it is possible to spend over half your monthly pocket money on fees. For a list of courses, request a copy of 'Spanish Courses for Foreigners in Spain' from the Ministerio de Educacion y Ciencia, Ciudad Universitaria, 28040 Madrid. The Spanish Institute in London (102 Eaton Square, London SW1W 9AN) can also send a list of schools and a separate list of summer courses, though these are normally full-time and expensive and therefore of no interest to au pairs.

Judith Twycross did not have to depend solely on her Spanish classes at a local institute twice a week for her social life:

I took Saviana classes in the afternoons for a month before the Seville feria. I went out at night three or four times a week to the cinema or bars where it was easy to meet other people, both Spanish and other foreigners. In the summer I was given a free swimming pass for the local swimming pool. I made the acquaintance of quite a number of other au pairs and found that while a number of us had a lot of freedom, others were working all night and day (often in families with pre-school children) for next to nothing.

In Madrid, Barcelona and tourist-exploited areas, it may be difficult to break the ice with the locals. The impact of tourists (over 40 million of them per year) from the more permissive societies has prompted some Spanish men to turn their backs on their own over-protected women and consider foreign women fair game. This is all very well for the good-time girls who have set their sights on one of those beady-eyed Spanish waiters, but unfortunate for those interested in harmless friendships. As in Italy, you will have to learn how to repel unwelcome advances.

Travel in Spain is relatively cheap. RCI have a travel bureau which can book tickets for you. Hitch-hiking is reputed to be less favourable than elsewhere in the Mediterranean, possibly because of a fear of Basque terrorism in some areas.

Travel

You should have no trouble booking a cheap flight to Spain. Charter and specialist discount operators sell low-season return flights for as little as £61, and it might be worth using this as a one-way fare especially since coach and rail fares to Madrid work out to be considerably more. If you are prepared to leave at short notice, ask any travel agent for last minute bargains.

Directory References

For agencies based in Spain, see: **Agencia Intercambios Culturales** (Majorca), **Centros Europeos Galve** (Madrid), **G.I.C.** (Valencia), **Interclass** (Barcelona), **International Au Pair Intercambio** (Barcelona), **O'Neill School** (Vizcaya), **Relaciones Culturales Internacionales** (Madrid) and **S & C Asociados** (Seville).

For au pair agencies in Britain that deal with Spain, see: 1st for Au Pairs, Academy Au Pair & Nanny Agency, A.C. Au Pairs, AMITI International, Angels International/Spanish Angels, Anglo Continental, Anglo Pair, Au Pair Agency (Edgware) including Majorca, Au Pair Connections (specialises in Spain), Au Pair International (Uckfield), Au Pairs of Surrey, A.Z.E. Au Pairs, Bloomsbury Bureau, Bluebell, Britannia Agency, Bunters Agency, Childcare International, Church View Nanny Agency, Delaney, Edgware, Euro Employment Centre, Euro Pair, Family Match, Girls About Town, Glogovich, Helping Hand Agency, Helping Hands (Essex), Home Concern (specialises in Spain), Home From Home, Hyde Park International, International Catholic Society for Girls, Janet White, Jolaine, London Agency, Mondial, Mum's Army, Nanny & Au Pair Connection, North South, PEC, People & Places, Portland, Problems Unlimited, Quick Help, Richmond & Twickenham, Simply Domestics, Solihull, Students Abroad, Tarooki (including Tenerife), UK & Overseas, Universal Care

Other agencies abroad which send au pairs to Spain include:
Australia: Au Pair Australia
Austria: Auslands-Sozialdienst, Okista and Irmhild Spitzer
Belgium: Services de la Jeunesse Feminine, Stufam
Canada: Au Pair in Europe in Canada
Croatia: Glogovic
Czech Republic: Au Pair International CZ, Student Agency
France: Accueil Familial des Jeunes Etrangers, Accueil International, Alliance
   Culturelle Internationale, l'ARCHE, Au Pair Service, Butterfly et Papillon, Euro Pair Services, France Au Pair, Goelangues, Good Morning Europe, Institut d'Echanges Franco-Europeens, Inter-Séjours, Programme 'Au Pair in Spain', Relations Internationales, SILC, Soames
Germany: APSI, AU-PAIR e.V., IN VIA, Rodata
Greece: Au Pair Activities (also to Portugal), Galentina's (has agent in
   Portugal)
Hungary: Avalon '92
Ireland: Au Pair Bureau of Ireland, Careers Information Service (Limerick),
   Dublin School of English, Job Options Bureau, Langtrain International, Swan Training Institute
Israel: Hilma's (to Portugal)
Italy: A. C. Link, L'Aquilone, ARCE, Learn & Travel, Soggiorni All'Estero per
   la Gioventù
Slovakia Agentúra Nomati
South Africa: All Aboard
Sweden: IRCA
Switzerland: Freundinnen Junger Madchen, Pro Filia
USA: Accord Cultural Exchange, Alliances Abroad, InterExchange

Switzerland

Regulations

The employment of foreigners in Switzerland is organised almost as precisely as their watches. Au pairing is not the casual arrangement it is in some other European countries but is carefully controlled by various rules and regulations. As mentioned in the introductory section, the Swiss invented the au pair arrangement last century and so have had plenty of time to work out the rules. Although Switzerland is not a member of the EU or EEA, it has now joined the European Free Trade Agreement (EFTA) and intends to allow the free exchange of labour some time after 1998. A free booklet *Living and Working in Switzerland* from the Swiss Embassy does not mention au pairs at all.

In Switzerland, there is no separate document for working. A residence permit *(Aufenthaltsbewilligung* or *autorisation de séjour)* covers both the right of abode and employment. This document can be obtained locally by au pairs but only if they have arrived in Switzerland with an *assurance d'autorisation de séjour* either from the Swiss Embassy or sent ahead by the Swiss agency. When a Swiss family decides to hire you, they must apply on your behalf to the local *Controle des Habitants* or cantonal Aliens Police for this document, preferably several months before your proposed arrival. They must pay a substantial fee when applying. Note that there is no quota for au pair permits as there is with other kinds of employment.

In order to qualify for an au pair permit, you must be between 17 and 29 (18 is the minimum in Geneva; 27 is the maximum in Ticino), have a European or North American passport, be willing to stay an entire year and study seriously one of Switzerland's three main languages (German, French and Italian) in which you are meant to have a basic grounding before you arrive in the country. (The agency *Agenzia Inter Au-Pair* in Italian-speaking Switzerland may be able to place au pairs for six months or for just the summer.) You are expected to spend no less than four hours per week at a language school and attendance may be checked. Your one year contract can be broken only in exceptional circumstances and you must give at least one month's notice. At the end of your year, there is the possibility of renewing for a maximum of six months.

The standard au pairing conditions as set out in the articles of the European Accord on Au Pair Placements are observed, with maximum working hours of 30 per week, etc. Other regulations are in place to protect the interests of the au pair, and many are quite generous, including good pocket money and paid holidays (details below). Some families also pay half the course fees plus the cost of travelling to classes.

Sometimes families will want a home helper urgently especially if they work in the tourist industry. It may be possible to get a seasonal permit for a short-term job in this category as Mary Hall did in Wengen. The family of hoteliers which hired her had no problem getting her a four-month seasonal *Permis L*. If you accept a job without a permit, your employers will not be bound to provide all the perks set out (and enforced) by the Swiss agencies.

If you are having any employment problems, you are entitled to consult the local advisory centre on your rights. Any unresolvable difficulties or legal problems should be referred to the cantonal office which arbitrates in such cases, for example the Kantonal Züricherische Arbeitsgemeinschaft für den Hausdienst in Zürich (Klosbachstr. 10; 1-383 53 22) or in Geneva the Office d'Orientation et de Formation Professionelle Services 'Jeunes Travailleurs', rue Prévost-Martin 6, (22-705 03 05).

Health and Insurance

There is no reciprocal agreement on health care between the UK and Switzerland. Therefore au pairs have to be absolutely sure that they are covered by the Swiss system. This will turn out to be quite expensive but essential. Because of the high degree of regulation of the au pair system, agencies and families generally play by the rules.

Deductions for insurance and contributions are calculated on the basis of the au pair's gross salary, which is the sum of the pocket money of SFr600-700, and board and lodging considered to be worth SFr810. Payment must be made to cover health insurance, which amounts to between SFr90 and SFr190. In some cantons the bill is split equally between family and au pair; in other cantons the au pair pays it all. Swiss health insurance does not cover dental treatment which is exceedingly expensive. The family must pay for accident insurance. You may also be liable for a cantonal tax (unless you are lucky enough to have an employer who shoulders these incidental expenses for you or if you have not yet turned 19). In Zürich the deduction for taxes amount to about a fifth of your earnings.

Working in Switzerland: Pros and Cons

Anyone who wants to spend a complete year abroad to learn French, German or Italian should certainly consider au pairing in Switzerland where working conditions are very favourable. The 'pocket money' varies somewhat from canton to canton, but is higher than anywhere else in Europe. For example in the canton of Geneva the minimum is SFr710 per month, whereas in Ticino and Lausanne, it is must less. Bear in mind that the monthly earnings of more than £300 will be severely reduced by compulsory deductions (see section above). The minimum amounts are adjusted every year to remain in line with the price index (which is published in November in Geneva).

There are other perks for Swiss au pairs which are unheard of elsewhere. For example you are entitled to four weeks paid holiday during your year and five weeks if you are less than 20 years old. When on holiday you get not only your weekly net salary but also financial compensation for the meals which you are not eating with the family. This daily food allowance is SFr18 in both Geneva and Zürich. So if you took two of your four weeks off to tour the French Alps, visit Bavaria, travel home to England or whatever takes your fancy, your holiday earnings would go a long way to offsetting the cost of the travel. The cost of living in Switzerland is among the highest in the world so unless you lead a fairly spartan life you probably won't be able to save much from your wages. But becoming an au pair is one of the easiest ways of being able to afford an extended stay in Switzerland.

As mentioned above, families are often required to pay at least half your language school fees which will be (in total) between SFr500 and SFr1,000 for six months of three or four lessons a week.

An au pair stay in Switzerland is not necessarily a bed of roses however. The Swiss national character, with its very hard-working and orderly approach to life, is not to everyone's taste. Many families comprise two working parents, in which case the au pair will be expected to work 35-40 hours per week and sometimes more. There is also a streak of chauvinism in many Swiss which can lead to a certain smugness and even xenophobia. It is certainly a conservative country where women did not get the vote until 1971 and almost all political activity is banned from university campuses. After au pairing for the winter season in Wengen, Mary Hall ended up agreeing with the clichés about the Swiss, that they are very organised and particular, money-mad and hard to befriend.

You may find yourself hemmed in by rules, for example being asked to keep all the receipts for any expenditures you make on behalf of the children or for shopping. The bumph from one of the major agencies in Switzerland states that au pairs 'should not simply take fruit without asking first', or in fact help themselves to anything in the fridge, larder or pantry.

Most reports indicate that farming families tend to be warmer and more welcoming than city families, though equally hard-working. Gillian Forsyth, who applied through the Landdienst-Zentralstelle described below, found her family placement hard work since she had to muck in with both farm and domestic duties:

The farm was extremely isolated and the only chance to leave it was on market day, when I sold the cheese we made. Life was very primitive - no electricity for example. However as we got up at 5am, we went to bed before dark. My duties included milking the goats, feeding the animals and making hay, as well as cleaning and looking after the baby. As far as improving my French was concerned, the job was not ideal as I was often alone with the goats or the baby.

Another disadvantage for budding linguists is that Swiss German is very different from high German and can be unintelligible to students of German who have never been exposed to it before. *Hochdeutsch* is taught in schools in Switzerland and so most Swiss Germans can speak it if required. If you are placed in a family working at one of the many international organisations with headquarters in Geneva, you may find that the language of the household is English.

Fixing up a Job

The major au pair agencies in Switzerland, *Pro Filia* (the Swiss branch of the Catholic organization ACISJF) and *Freundinnen Junger Madchen* (or *Amies de la Jeune Fille* in French) have been in operation for over a hundred years. Both agencies are eminently respectable and make their placements strictly by the book. Pro Filia has several offices throughout Switzerland some of which are mainly concerned with sending Swiss girls abroad. Both charge substantial placement fees.

Several other agencies operate on a more local scale such as *Heli Grandjean's Placement Au Pair* and *Swiss-O-Pair*. The latter specialises in Geneva and places many au pairs with families in France within commuting distance of Geneva (about 40,000 people cross the border on a daily basis). This is a popular option not only because it simplifies the visa problems but because families in France are often less formal than their counterparts in Switzerland. Also the pocket money of 1,800-2,000FF is higher than the French average (though up to £100 less than the Swiss average). At the other end of the country is the Italian-speaking canton of Ticino in which *Agenzia Inter Au-Pair* is located. It seems that the system is not so strictly regulated in Ticino.

Seasonal au pair jobs do exist, especially in ski resorts, where there is a demand for casual babysitters as well. Mark Stephenson noticed 'reams of requests for au pairs and nannies' in the tourist office of a French-speaking ski resort. While cycling from Scandinavia to Spain, Mary Hall (a nurse by training) decided to stop off in the Swiss Alps for the winter and look for work:

> I arrived in Interlaken at totally the wrong time, since it was in between seasons at the beginning of November when all the hotel managers have gone on holiday. I went round all the hotels which were open without success. A friend advised me to get a phone card, the Yellow Pages and ring around. He also said to speak with a smile which seemed to work as I got a couple of offers straightaway. I accepted the first one and ended up in Wengen looking after the spoilt daughter of some hotel owners. They asked me to name a price; I had no idea what the going rate was and named a figure that was obviously too low because they accepted it immediately. They said that they would pay for my work permit and train pass (which never happened) but they did hire me skis for the season. I can't say I enjoyed the job or my relationship with the child and her parents, though they were fair with wages and days off.

You may see notices posted in resorts (check at tourist offices) or in places where expatriates tend to meet, such as the American Library and Church in Geneva (3 rue de Monthoux) which has a notice board where live-in jobs are often posted. Alternatively you can post your own request for a family placement.

The Swiss office for Voluntary Farm Work (Landdienst-Zentralstelle, Mühlegasse 13, Postfach 728, 8025 Zürich; 1-261 44 88) can fix up young people who know some German with a job on a Swiss farm lasting from three to eight weeks starting in early August. Female participants in the programme often find that their duties are closer to those of an au pair than a farm assistant, though there is no guarantee of this when you apply. Participants are paid SFr20 a day.

Leisure Time

There are plenty of language courses in all Swiss cities and towns. One of the most important organisations is Migros which has schools throughout Switzerland. Some families pay part or even all of your course fees, though this is not compulsory in most cantons. (According to FJM, families in Zürich are obliged to register their au pairs in language courses and pay the fees.)

Mary Hall did not find the Swiss very friendly or helpful, though she would be willing to work there again (as long as it wasn't as a nanny!):

> On the plus side, I learnt how to ski. Wengen and the Jungfrau region is absolutely gorgeous. There has never been such a good stress-reliever as sitting in the sunshine with my employer's fat out-of-condition dog for company. Oh I also learnt (kind of) how to play the organ at the local church since they were desperate for any kind of effort, regardless.

Despite the high cost of domestic travel by train and postbus, you should have the chance to visit some of Switzerland's more scenic corners. In some cantons, the cost of local travel can be reduced by acquiring a *carte d'indigène* from the *Fremden-polizei* (aliens police) (for which permit-holders are eligible) which allows you to travel on public transport at a subsidised local rate (and also to buy a cheap seasonal ski pass if you happen to be working over the winter in a ski resort).

Travel

You can find one-way flights from London to Geneva or Zürich advertised for £79, return for £100. The easiest rail destination in Switzerland is Basel, which is on the principal Calais to Milan route. Many Swiss families will pay their au pair's fare home (within Europe) on completion of a one-year contract, though this should not be taken for granted.

Directory References

For agencies based in Switzerland, see **Amies de la Jeune Fille** (Lausanne), **Agenzia Inter-Au Pair** (Ticino), **Freundinnen Junger Madchen** (Zürich), **Heli Grandjean** (Colonge-Bellerive), **Pro Filia** (Zürich) and **Swiss-O-Pair** (Bernex).

For au pair agencies in Britain which deal with Switzerland, see: Abbey Au Pairs, Academy Au Pair & Nanny Agency, Anglo Nannies, Au Pair International (Uckfield), Au Pairs Echange, Childcare International, Edgware, Euro Employment Centre, Helping Hands (Essex), Home From Home, Janet White, Nanny & Au Pair Connection, North South, Solihull, Top Notch Nanny Agency, UK & Overseas and Wealden Nannies.

Other agencies abroad which send au pairs to Switzerland are:
Austria: Auslands-Sozialdienst
Belgium: Services de la Jeunesse Feminine, Stufam
Canada: Au Pair in Europe, Paragon Personnel
Germany: AU-PAIR e.V., IN VIA, Rodata
Greece: Au Pair Activities
Ireland: Au Pair Bureau of Ireland, Careers Information Service (Limerick), Irish Nanny Services, Job Options Bureau, Langtrain International
Italy: L'Aquilone, Learn & Travel
South Africa: All Aboard
USA: AuPair Homestay

Turkey

The Regulations

Although Turkey is an Islamic country, its sights are set on Europe and on some day joining the European Union. These aspirations, together with a remarkable expansion in tourism, mean that the privileged classes are very keen to learn English. This in turn has contributed to an increase in the demand for foreign nannies. Au pair-type jobs in Turkey normally involve more tutoring of English than domestic chores. Parents are desperate to give their children every possible advantage in the fierce competition for university places in Turkey. So English-speaking nannies are all the rage among the wealthy of Istanbul (of whom there are a considerable number) and to a lesser extent Ankara.

Many jobs begin as three-month summer jobs which, if successful, develop into longer contracts. British nannies normally work on a three-month tourist visa which will have to be renewed every three months, usually by leaving the country and obtaining a fresh tourist visa after paying £10 (in cash) at the point of re-entry; the employer should be asked to arrange and pay for these visa trips. Alternatively you can apply for an extension at an immigration office, where you will have to show that you have the means to support yourself. Your host family might be prepared to vouch for you in the capacity of 'friend'.

Working in Turkey: Pros and Cons

The pocket money quoted for Istanbul is higher than it is for Europe, i.e. £50 a week, while au pairs plus are promised £100 (for 45 hours a week) and nannies earn from £150. The high salaries quoted sound very attractive, though the reality can be less so. After spending seven months nannying in Istanbul, Michelle Lindsay claimed that she knew of no happy nannies working there. She and five others felt betrayed by their London agency who misled them as to what to expect and who offered no support when the situation went sour.

Cultural differences may account for some of the problems. It seems that Turkish families do not hold much truck with the concept of giving notice and there are numerous cases in which once a nanny tries to resign she is told to leave immediately and her back wages may not be paid.

Having tired of low paid washing up jobs in London, Sonia Douglas from Australia answered an advert in *TNT* and found herself on a plane to Istanbul the following Wednesday to take up a live-in nanny job paying £250 a week. With the calculator in her head ticking over and coming up with an annual figure of £11,000 in savings (easily enough to fund a further year of world travels), she was very excited about her new job, even though she had never considered Turkey as a place to work. The impression she formed after a short time was that life for a nanny in Turkey does not allow much more freedom than elsewhere in the Middle East:

Firstly I must say that I will never marry for money. I seem to be regarded as an English-speaking toy for the wealthy offspring and have had to get used to a complete lack of freedom and independence. Although surrounded by the finer things in life (and, believe me, I mean fine), I sometimes find myself in the depths of despair, partly due to a diminished self-esteem. Basically you are paid to talk English and play with the children. Nowhere in your contract is it stated that you will be required to make decisions or (heaven forbid) think. I feel as though my employers have bought my life for the duration of the contract. I've had to overcome my initial shock at the degree to which the children are spoilt and babied, but I've learned to bite my tongue. It is exhausting, trying and a phenomenal test of your durability.

Although the culture shock can't have helped, some of Sonia's difficulties might have occurred if she had accepted a live-in job anywhere, since she had become used to a very high degree of independence as a 24-year old world traveller.

And of course there was a brighter side as she admits:

When the children go back to school, the living is easy. Your days are free (though life might be rather monotonous without a new goal or venture to pursue). You can always rely on the other nannies to meet you for coffee or more appropriately cay (tea) or with whom you can wander through the Grand Bazaar. It is a friendly and supportive network.
Since I've been in Istanbul, I've had a soft comfortable bed, an abundance of Turkish food, summer days spent splashing in the pool, various outings and even a sailing holiday in Bodrum without spending a single Turkish lira. The potential

to save is astounding. There's a magic about Istanbul. I've fallen for this city, but I value my freedom also. What a dilemma.

Sonia's high salary is partly due to her qualification as a primary school teacher, but apparently there were nannies earning £200 a week whose only qualification was that they were native English speakers.

One persistent problem is that it is generally not acceptable for young women to go out alone in the evenings. But Turkish families are normally very generous and allow their live-in childcarers to share in family life on equal terms, even in their free time.

Fixing up a Job

A few agencies in Britain have links with Turkish families, but in no other country do agencies claim to be able to place candidates in Turkey. The Istanbul agency *Dogan International Organisation* regularly places English and German au pairs (who must be women aged 18-40) with Istanbul families for a minimum of six months. Although it prefers applicants to be in Istanbul already, it accepts overseas applications one or two months before arrival, provided the necessary documentation is included, i.e. education certificates, character and childcare references and a recent medical certificate.

Summer posts are often available through the *Solihull Au Pair Agency* and other agencies. An end-of-contract bonus can sometimes to earned. Saday Educational Consultancy (Necatibey Cad. 92/3 Karakoy, Istanbul; 212-243-2078/fax 212-249 7037) has introduced a working holiday scheme for up to 500 English-speaking young people. They live with well-to-do Istanbul families as a tutor guest for 4-12 weeks year round. The family pays all their expenses plus weekly pocket money of £20 in exchange for tutoring members of the family for about 30 hours per week. Saday has two offices in the UK as well as in Istanbul: 3c Randolph St, London NW1 0SS (tel/fax 0171-284 2949) and 24 High St, Rolvenden, Kent TN17 4LN (tel/fax 01580 240156).

If in Turkey, it can be worth checking the English language newspaper *Daily News* for adverts placed by agencies or families.

Directory References

For agencies based in Turkey, see: **Anglo Nannies** (London and Istanbul) and **Dogan** (Istanbul).

For agencies in Britain which deal with Turkey, see: Anglo Nannies, Anglo Pair, AMITI International, Au Pair & Student Placement Agency, Helping Hand Agency, Hyde Park International, Nanny & Au Pair Connection, Solihull, Students Abroad and Tarooki.

United Kingdom

As many as 100,000 live-in child-carers work in England, Scotland and Wales at any one time. This chapter is primarily aimed at foreign young people who want to come to Britain as au pairs, nannies or mother's helps. However working with families in Britain is not the sole preserve of foreign women and men. British school leavers and others may want to spend six or twelve months working as a mother's help to gain their first experience of employment and more specifically of childcare, or perhaps just to see a different part of Britain. Some may find it difficult to find other work depending on what part of the country they come from and many choose to move south as mother's helps to spare themselves the trauma of trying to find accommodation in the London region. Those who are unemployed should enquire at their local Jobcentre about the possibility of claiming travel expenses to the home of the family who hires them. There is no regulating body for such jobs and most candidates entrust their search for a suitable family to a reputable agency to whom they can turn in the event of exploitation or other problems.

The Regulations

The Home Office publishes a leaflet on au pairing (dated October 1994) which may be obtained by writing to the Home Office, Lunar House, 40 Wellesley Road, Croydon, Surrey CR9 2BY. The leaflet's contents are not very earth-shattering and most of the information is contained below.

Au pair stays are available to single women and (since 1993) men between the ages of 17 and 27 who come from one of the following European nations: Andorra, Austria, Belgium, Bosnia-Herzogovina, Croatia, Cyprus, Czech Republic, Denmark, Finland, France, Germany, Greece, Hungary, Iceland, Italy, Liechtenstein, Luxembourg, Macedonia, Malta, Monaco, Netherlands, Norway, Portugal, San Marino, Serbia, Slovakia, Slovenia, Spain, Sweden, Switzerland and Turkey. Poles and nationals of the Russian Republics are excluded, despite constant lobbying, because they are regarded as being more likely to overstay their visas and seek illegal work. Note that this list is applicable only to au pairs who are meant to work no more than 25 hours a week. The only nationalities who are permitted to work full-time as au pairs plus or mother's helps are EU nationals.

Citizens of the Commonwealth and the US may be eligible to work with families (see below) but not officially as au pairs since the au pair system presupposes the motivation of learning a language. In fact no check is made on European au pairs though they may have to show that they have been attending a course if they seek to extend their permission to stay in Britain, up to a maximum of two years.

Many girls from other countries would dearly love to come to the UK as au pairs. Many consider the reasoning of the Immigration & Nationality Department's for the exclusion unconvincing:

> By tradition the au pair arrangement of girls living in a family abroad to learn the language of their hosts and the way of life in that country has been a Western European arrangement. While the aspirations of girls from outside Western Europe are understandable, it was considered that those who came from further afield were more vulnerable to exploitation and that a number of girls were coming ostensibly as au pairs but in reality to do more substantial work, often with a view to long-term residence.

Often British families and non-European girls make an independent arrangement but both sides should be well-primed to avoid what happened in the following story. While a couple from London with a young baby were on holiday in Argentina they met Maria. They arranged to take her on as their au pair a few months later. She arrived at Heathrow with just $250 and a 12-month open return ticket, asking (in very poor English) to stay nine months.

Questioning elicited from her a confession that she had arranged to work as an au pair. The employing mother (who speaks Spanish) was contacted by immigration and immediately drove to Heathrow where she was accused of trying to import slave labour. Maria was given permission to stay in England as a tourist for no more than 7 days and then had to return to Argentina. The whole episode cost the ill-informed employers £1,000.

Finally in 1993, the 1971 Immigration Act which defined au pairs as 'female' was amended so that male au pairs are now entitled to seek placements in the UK. In the case of other kinds of domestic employment in private households, preferences of gender can be expressed in advertisements in cases where a job involves a certain amount of physical or social contact with someone in the family or having knowledge of intimate details of someone's life.

In most cases, young people arriving from EU countries will automatically be given permission at entry to stay for six months in any capacity. If they intend to stay longer they should apply for a residence permit by submitting their passport and form EC-1 (available from any Jobcentre or police station) to the Home Office before the six months expires. But EU nationals are entitled to reside in any Community country, so refusal is rare.

Citizens from countries on the approved list which are not in the EU must show the letter of invitation from the family at entry and be prepared for a grilling by immigration officials. In cases where the official is not satisfied, perhaps because the letter is too sketchy, the family or agency may be rung up and asked to corroborate the au pair's story. If the reply is satisfactory, permission is normally given to enter for the duration of the contract. The stamp in your passport may indicate that you must register as an alien within seven days at the local police station. A fee of £34 must be paid by the au pair though occasionally the family will be willing to underwrite this irritating expense. The Special Aliens Registration Office in London is at 10 Lamb's Conduit Street in Bloomsbury. The maximum period which non-EU nationals are permitted to be au pairs is two years, whether consecutive or aggregated.

If a non-EU au pair wishes to extend her stay, she must apply, preferably on a special form, by post or in person to Lunar House or in person to one of the Public Enquiries offices in Harwich, Norwich, Southampton, Liverpool or Glasgow. The latter course generally results in less delay and shorter queues but check the opening hours ahead of time.

Any au pair who is confused about the regulations or her rights in any capacity might find it helpful to visit a Citizens Advice Bureau, manned by volunteers who will patiently sift through the regulations and try to interpret them.

Citizens of Commonwealth countries, principally Australia, New Zealand and Canada are entitled to apply for a working holiday visa, which will allow them to work in any casual capacity for a maximum of two years. The age limits of 17-27 are the same as for European au pairs. Canadian students may participate in a Student Work Abroad Programme (SWAP) administered by the Canadian Universities Travel Service known as Travel CUTS. After paying the registration fee, eligible students are allowed to come to Britain to look for any kind of work including domestic work. Commonwealth citizens do not have to register as aliens.

There is a similar Work in Britain programme for American college students over 18. The Council on International Educational Exchange, 205 East 42nd Street, New York, NY 10017, allocates 'blue cards' to up to 3000 applicants (for a fee of $225) which entitles them to enter Britain at any time of the year to work for up to six months starting at any time of the year.

Anyone who is not from any of the countries dealt with above is not permitted to work as an au pair, mother's help or nanny in Britain. For all kinds of employment, a work permit must be obtained from the Department of Employment for a specific post before arrival in the country. The Home Office unflinchingly states that 'permits are no longer issued for domestic employment'.

Health and Insurance

The National Health Service offers emergency treatment to anyone and will also provide health care to EU nationals and some others residing in Britain. Au pairs should register with a local doctor when they arrive, perferably the same one whose surgery the family attends. The standard fee for prescriptions at present is £5.10 with the exception of contraception which is free. Dental care by NH-registered dentists is only partially subsidised; also very few dentists will accept new NHS patients onto their books since they are under no obligation to do so and earn more money from their private patients.

Au pairs from countries outside the EU may find that there are reciprocal agreements between their country and Britain. However there are exceptions, for example Switzerland and Turkey, and so nationals of these countries should be sure to insure themselves privately.

Au pairs are not liable to pay National Insurance contributions, though they may make voluntary contributions if they wish to retain their rights to future benefits in their home countries. Further advice may be obtained from the local Department of Social Security (DSS).

Contributions will be due for other positions however. Professional nannies must pay tax and contributions in the usual way and should present their P-45 form to a new employer. Anyone earning over £62 a week should pay National Insurance Contributions at a rate of 2% on the first £62, and 9% on earnings above this. Anyone who earns more than £4,045 per year (about £77 a week) must also pay tax. The employer must match these payments which can make it expensive for a law-abiding person to hire a mother's help; as a result many employers (indeed the majority) neglect this obligation, which may mean that their employees lose their entitlement to unemployment benefit, sick pay, maternity benefit and perhaps even their state pension. Occasionally nannies who do short stints for different families can claim to be self-employed which means that the employer does not have to pay contributions. Qualified NNEB nannies may want to consider a specialist insurance policy for nannies offered by Robert Barrow Ltd. (24-26 Minories, London EC3N 1BY) which will protect them from lawsuits for negligence among other things.

All live-in child-carers are liable to pay the council tax (which replaces the poll tax). Full-time students pay only 20% of the total; full-time is defined as 21 hours a week (including homework) for a year's course. It is also possible to claim a reduction on the basis of low income. If you are staying less than six months, there is every chance that your employer will not register you.

Working in Britain: Pros and Cons

The demand for English tuition is enormous among young people from continental Europe and living in Britain is one of the easiest and best ways to achieve that end. Many come for intensive summer courses but often find that they spend most of their time socialising and therefore their English improves little. Coming as an au pair gets round the problem and most find that their English improves dramatically.

The demand for live-in childcare continues to increase and any woman aged 17-27 from one of the approved countries should have no trouble fixing up a placement. Summer stays can usually be arranged if the interested au pair applies in plenty of time, and there are even some openings for just the Christmas and Easter holidays as well as the summer vacation. Quite often these short stays are available on a demi pair basis i.e. 10-12 hours of work a week for a reduced amount of pocket money. *Belaf Study Holidays* in Wiltshire specialises in this arrangement. Summer stays are easier to arrange for those who are available by mid-June and able to stay for at least ten weeks.

The weekly pocket money has risen slowly over the past few years to an average between £35 and £40, which brings it into line with most of the rest of Europe. Usually those with a driving licence or who have longer working hours because both parents work earn £40. Few families offer any bonuses such as helping with school fees or paying for travel (though one or two agencies in the provinces request that their client families pay the au pair's travel from London).

Full-time live-in helpers earn more than this. Mother's help wages start at around £80 and qualified nannies seldom earn less than £120 a week.

One disappointment for many au pairs is that they must live a considerable distance from central London. One agency goes so far as to say that almost no English-speaking families live in the city centre these days. There are of course plenty of middle class suburbs within easy reach of London with a high au pair population, but there is also a great demand in the Home Counties of Surrey, Essex, Hertfordshire, Buckinghamshire and Berkshire where access to London is not necessarily difficult but can be expensive.

If you are less interested in the London region than in one of the more scenic areas of Britain, sift through the agencies in the Directory section and find one based in the area which interests you, for example *Pec Au Pairs* in Shropshire, *Abbey Au Pairs* in Poole, *Homelife* in Cardiff. Unfortunately there are very few in Scotland; however a few in the Directory specify Scotland.

British families differ as much from one another as French, German or Israeli ones, but a characteristic reserve and a jealous attitude to privacy are noticed by many au pairs, especially at first. Barbara Henson, an ebullient American, soon learned that her employers in South London did not expect her to share their evenings, and so she either had to take her dinner up to her room or go out. This is not typical, but English people do on the whole find it harder to share their homes with strangers than other nationalities do.

Children's feelings and preferences are easier to interpret than their parents'. Another problem Barbara encountered (and one which is particularly noticed by North Americans) is how to gauge the tone and intention behind the polite facade. For example, 'help yourself to the chocolates/drinks cupboard/fridge at any time' may mean, 'have one if you must'.

British children do not always conform to the stereotype of the well-behaved English child of story books. On the other hand, British children do tend to be less spoiled than, say, Italian or American children and most are relatively obedient. After a couple of years of working for American families, Carla Mitchell took a temporary job with an English family and recalls her amazement when the children dutifully trooped off to bed after a single request.

And if British parents expect a lot from their children, they will not be very tolerant of slack discipline in their live-in helpers. Deserved or not, they are reputed to be demanding employers; for example the large French agency *Contacts* warns applicants that the English are *tres exigeantes*. Whether or not any of these generalisations is useful is another question, and one which may well have been answered by the English poet William Blake who wrote that to generalise is foolish, whereas to ᵣ ᵣticularise is the distinguishing feature of mankind.

Fixing up a Job

Au pair and nanny agencies proliferate in Britain and by law none can charge a placement fee for placing girls in Britain, only for placing girls with families abroad. There is no single listing of all registered agencies. A selection belong to the Federation of Recruitment and Employment Services or the International Fellowship of Au Pair Agencies (see Introduction). Most Yellow Pages will reveal a few domestic agencies under the new heading 'Nanny and Childcare Agencies'. Many are run as small businesses by one or two people, sometimes working from home, and these often provide a more personal service than the larger au pair 'factories', though naturally they will have a smaller choice of families.

Certain nationalities should endeavour to apply directly to an agency in Britain rather than through an agency in their own country. France is one such country, since many French agencies charge large registration and placement fees, sometimes over 1,000FF which does not guarantee an attentive service. There are a number of agencies in London which specialise in placing nannies from Australia and New Zealand.

There are many other ways of finding out about vacancies, once you are in Britain. The *Lady* magazine published each week carries pages of advertisements for both agencies and individual vacancies throughout the country. The *Horse & Hound* sometimes includes adverts for domestic helpers normally in rural areas which might have a special appeal. Newspapers catering to wandering colonials often prove fruitful such as *TNT* and *New Zealand News*. Some of the jobs will be in London but many will be in country areas. An example taken at random from *New Zealand News* gives a flavour of the opportunities available:

Do you like children, horses and country life? We live in a beautiful country house, 20 minutes from Oxford, Reading and Henley, and need someone to come and help out. Relaxed fun and loving family.

In London you can make use of notice boards such as the one at New Zealand House in the Haymarket and the one by Earls Court tube station which is where Ms. T. P. Lye from Malaysia found three possible live-in jobs after just one look, and accepted a job taking one child to and from school in exchange for free board and lodging. (These days it seems to have more accommodation than jobs).

Student Union notice boards are often a worthwhile source of positions. Simon Willis, an Australian on a working holiday visa, had the good sense to check one of the notice boards at London University and persuaded the advertiser (with difficulty) to take him on to look after two-year old Jessica. University news sheets are often used by academically-minded families looking for home helps. Anyone who keeps his or her eyes open is bound to come across openings of potential interest.

Leisure Time

In the London area most agencies can recommend social clubs, some specifically for au pairs. The Catholic organisations run especially energetic programmes. For example the *International Catholic Society for Girls* whose St. Patrick's Centre is just off Oxford Street, puts on films, discos, sporting events, discussions, folk evenings and excursions, and offers au pairs a special membership rate of £2 per month. St. Patrick's has 1,000 members representing 87 nationalities among whom the average age is 23. German-speaking au pairs might prefer the *German Catholic Social Centre* in London which sends out a monthly programme of events (in German) which includes activities as diverse as special masses and pub crawls, as well as excursions outside London.

A more secular organisation in London is International Students House at 229 Great Portland Street which has a bistro with live music, bar, TV lounge and active sports programme. You might also make enquiries at the University of London Union on Malet Street which sometimes extends membership to non-students for a nominal fee. It has a pool, gym, bars, banks, discos, etc. and is a regular venue for rock concerts and dances. A student membership in the London Central YMCA might also be affordable for a term. Smaller agencies often hold occasional au pair get-togethers, perhaps at Christmas or the end of the school year.

Of course it is not necessary to join a club to have a social life. English people can be surprisingly friendly in pub situations so it is a good idea to visit a few pubs in your local area until you find one with a congenial atmosphere or watch for posters advertising pubs with live music.

A wide range of language courses is available in almost every city in Britain. Predictably state-run courses are significantly cheaper than private ones, so most au pairs prefer to investigate what is on offer at the local adult education centre, technical college or college of further education. It is necessary to enrol at the beginning of each term which run September to December, January to March and April to June/July. Unfortunately local authority courses in London tend to be oversubscribed, so make enquiries as soon as you know your requirements.

There are of course plenty of private schools but their fees are usually beyond the means of au pairs. More intensive courses involve 15 hours of instruction per week and cost from £110 per month. In all cases the fees will be due in advance. Some families may be willing to lend you the money and deduct it from your pocket money.

The standard qualification is the Cambridge First Certificate, Advanced and Proficiency. Exams are held twice a year in December and June, though you must enter for the exam in the preceding October or March. The sitting fee will be about £70.

Directory References

The vast majority of au pair agencies in the UK and Europe place foreign applicants in British families as well as arranging for British au pairs to go abroad. A few specialise only in incoming au pairs. Nanny agencies by contrast usually deal exclusively with positions in Britain.

United States of America

The Regulations

For many years thousands of European nannies and mother's helps had been going to the US to work, many of them working on tourist visas and therefore breaking the immigration law of the United States. This situation had long been recognised as unacceptable and finally in 1986 the US Information Agency (USIA) initiated an experimental legal au pair programme, which allowed young women and men with childcare experience to work for an American family for one year. (The numerous conditions of participation will be dealt with in detail below.) The programme has survived and expanded despite some controversy, most recently after the charge of murder was brought against one of the participants. Many childcare professionals in the US see the supply of European au pairs as cheap labour.

The Visa Branch of the United States Embassy (5 Upper Grosvenor St, London W1A 2JB) sends a standard letter to enquiring au pairs which states that working as an au pair, even if only in exchange for room and board, is prohibited under the terms of the temporary visitor visa (B-1/B-2). This means that the only legal visa available to prospective nannies, mother's helps and au pairs is the J-1 visa. By participating in approved Exchange Visitor Programs, European au pairs can obtain a J-1 visa valid for one year; this is the same visa as is available through Camp America or BUNAC. These programmes are allowed to exist because of their purported educational value in the interests of international cultural exchange, and the au pair programme is no different. Its stated goal is to 'encourage intercultural understanding by living with an American family'. The conditions of the J-1 visa include not undertaking any paid work outside your job with a family and that you must return home at the end of your year's contract. As a guarantee that you will fulfil your obligations, USIA requires that all au pairs pay a deposit (normally $500) to their sponsoring organisation which is returned on the successful completion of the contract. For those who are unable or unwilling to stay an entire year, the Family Companion summer programme administered by *Camp America* and described in this chapter might be preferable.

All the approved programmes are authorised to issue Form IAP-66 which is the 'Certificate of Eligibility for Exchange Visitor (J-1) status' to applicants who satisfy the requirements of the programme. Applicants must then submit this form and their passports to the Visa Branch of the US Embassy. The procedure for obtaining the J-1 visa can be protracted and complicated, but is usually successful in the end, since you will have the guidance and support of a sponsoring organisation throughout. The American Institute for Foreign Study (whose programme is included in the Directory under *Au Pair in America*) is the largest one, sending more than 4,000 au pairs and mother's helps to the States every year.

The only other visas which might be relevant in a few cases are the Q-visa 'International Cultural Exchange' and the H-2 'Temporary Worker' visa. For the H-2, the prospective employer in the US must file an application on Form I-129B ('Petition to Classify Non-Immigrant as Temporary Worker or Trainee') with their local Immigration and Naturalization Service (INS) office and present a strong case that a genuine effort has been made to fill the vacancy with an American citizen. While the application is being processed (usually between four and six months) there is no way of checking on the progress of the application. The Q visa is intended for foreign workers who will be providing practical training or sharing the history, culture and traditions of their country. Unfortunately this visa is not available to nannies, even one who wants to share her culture.

Inevitably there will be some people who cannot qualify for a visa but nevertheless want to work as an au pair or nanny in the US. In view of the publicity surrounding high-profile Washington politicians who have been caught employing illegal house staff as nannies and cleaners (mainly from Latin America), it would be wise to tread carefully. It is illegal for an employer to hire an alien. The nanny working illegally would therefore be putting her host family at risk. It would take only a nosey and hostile neighbour alerting the local INS before the authorities might start to investigate. Workers caught working illegally risk being deported and barred from travelling to the States for a minimum of five years.

Apart from the ongoing danger of being caught while you're working, the grilling you may get upon entry to the country is enough to put off many people. The suspicion has been that any young woman arriving alone from Britain or Ireland was coming to work with a family. Luggage may be carefully searched for incriminating evidence such as a letter of invitation from the family or summer clothing when you have claimed you are coming for just a short holiday in March. Unless girls have been tutored by someone familiar with immigration procedures, they can end up being turned back at the airport. Those who have been primed invent plausible stories often backed up by corroborating evidence such as a return ticket (later to be turned in for refund) or a letter from a college or employer on headed paper stating that the bearer must return to England by a certain date. Your case will be strengthened if you are dressed smartly, have plenty of money and a return ticket (perhaps one which can be extended or refunded after arrival), and perhaps a list of people you intend to visit on your tour. (Do not invent these because if the immigration officer is suspicious, he or she won't hesitate to phone them.) Some girls go to extraordinary lengths, such as wrapping up a wedding gift to support their story that they have come to the States to attend the wedding of cousin Betty Lou.

Since the authorities are bound to be suspicious if you ask for a very long stay, be content with whatever they give you. It is possible to apply for an extension of your tourist visa from the local INS later. At entry Susie Walton was granted permission to stay three months. She then got a six-month extension of her tourist visa from the INS in Minneapolis — admittedly her employer did know a senator — and then applied for another one. After keeping her passport for two months (which serves the purpose of an extension in itself) her request was denied and she was given 15 days to leave the US, which she did. Overstayers have been known to 'lose' their immigration card showing the date of entry. If you are staying on with an expired tourist visa, it can be difficult to cross borders into Canada or Mexico and then return again.

The Visa Waiver Program introduced means that ordinary holidaymakers can enter the US without having to obtain a tourist visa beforehand. The visa concession does not apply to anyone intending to work or stay for a lengthy time since only those with non-refundable return air tickets on participating carriers are exempt from the visa requirement.

CHILD CARE AMERICA

The legal way to live in the U.S.A. and care for children. A secure family environment. Learn about America and experience different cultures.

- One year commitment
- Return flight paid
- Two week vacation
- Med. Ins. paid
- Visa provided
- Choice of family
- Part-time college course
- Local Counsellor support
- Drivers/Non-smokers
- Age 18–26
- Start anytime
- Increased salary for qualified nannies

Contact
Childcare International Ltd.
Trafalgar House, Grenville Place, London NW7 3SA
Tel: 0181-906 3116 • Fax: 0181-906 3461
E-mail: office@childint.demon.co.uk
Web: http://www.childint.demon.co.uk
Emp. Agy

Health and Insurance

Everyone has heard horror stories of visitors to North America becoming destitute after having to pay enormous medical bills because they had insufficient insurance. All but the poorest Americans belong to health insurance schemes, and it is imperative that you be covered. Although the approved au pair programmes include a basic medical and accident insurance policy, health care in the United States is so exceedingly expensive, that it would be unwise to depend on it; top-up policies are available from programme organisers.

Au Pair in America offers medical cover of $100,000 ($200 deductible) and personal liability of $100,000 for 12 months, which is included in the cost of the programme. Its upgrade policy costs $240 and provides $500,000 medical cover and personal liability as well as $1,000 baggage and personal effects insurance for 13 months. For Camp America's Family Companion programme the cost is £130 for up to five months medical coverage (to the value of $250,000). Baggage cover is optional for an addition £41 (with $2,000 coverage). If you intend to indulge in high-risk activities such as skiing you will need an even more expensive policy.

Working in the US: Pros and Cons

As anywhere, you may find that you and your employers are not entirely compatible. But most people are won over by the generosity of American families and by the way that they are treated as equals. The democratic habits of thought for which the US is justly famous carry over into the family situation where a spirit of egalitarianism normally prevails. British women are especially popular as a status symbol, a curiosity and as representatives of a culture which Americans subconsciously admire (without necessarily understanding it very deeply). The affection which American families develop for their European au pairs and nannies seems to be more long-lasting than in any other country. It is not unusual for families to offer to sponsor their live-in helper for a 'green card' which entitles foreigners to settle in the US as 'resident aliens'. Karin Huber, a young Austrian woman, spotted an advertisement in the Saturday edition of *Süddeutscher Zeitung* and after several months of corresponding accepted a job with a family living on Long Island:

> The minute we met at the airport, I knew I'd get on with them. After ten very enjoyable months, they offered to sponsor me, which means the family pays an immigration lawyer to try to get a green card on behalf of an employee. This can take two or three years, during which time you can't leave the US. I didn't want to go that long without seeing my family so I went home to Austria. But I still keep in touch with that family; in fact they phone me once a week.

Susannah Walton's experiences echo Karin's and in her case, her Minnesota employer tried to persuade her to stay by offering to pay for her to take courses at the local university.

Many live-in helpers get the chance to travel around the US either on family vacations or sometimes just as a reward for services rendered, as in the case of Yvonne Standard who, after caring for the children single-handedly for a month, was sent to Florida for a week's vacation. There she was supposed to be chaperoned by the children's 75-year-old grandfather, though it was generally thought by the gossips in the hotel that he was Yvonne's sugar-daddy.

Set against all this generosity and reasonableness, there are the usual stories of extreme neuroses among employers. After having been in California for a while, Paul Young decided to try to market himself as a domestic employee, willing to drive and cook in a household. After advertising in the rich county of San Anselmo, he received a disappointing response, mostly from disabled people offering $100 a week. He chose the most lucrative position paying $320 a week cash-in-hand, but was far from thrilled with his choice. His employer was the worst kind of snobbish spoiled American; even the dog was horrible and, in Paul's view, needed (and pro¹ ably got!) a psychiatrist. He concluded that a sane wealthy American is a contradiction in terms and recommends checking out the situation carefully before committing yourself.

Ann McCann found herself working in a horrific situation:

> *I was told by an agency in London that the family had five children though by the time I got there a sixth had arrived! Both parents drank. The wife would call her husband at work and if he'd been drinking, she would start drinking so that when he came home they'd be equally smashed. The parents ate at the country club almost every night while the children had hot dogs and hamburgers, never any vegetables or fruit in the house. I lasted six months and then gave my notice.*

This unhappy story is far from typical but the United States does have one of the highest divorce rates and so your chances of working for people whose marriage is breaking up (or has done) are higher than elsewhere in the world. You might also find yourself working for what is sometimes known as a 'merged' family, i.e. couples on a second marriage with children from the first.

Another cliché about American life is its extreme mobility and you should not be unduly surprised to find that your employers aren't much more familiar with the town they are living in than you are, since they too may have arrived very recently. Another cultural difference you may encounter is the high profile which religion has in public and private life, so you should be prepared to exercise more tolerance than usual.

Most nannies and au pairs who have worked for American families agree that it is possible to identify certain typical traits in American children. They tend to be noisy and rambunctious with a proclivity to interrupt adult conversation more often than would be tolerated in Europe. They are energetic, self confident and fearless. Their wishes tend to be indulged to an excessive degree which makes the task of imposing a workable routine difficult in some cases. Carla Mitchell experienced an extreme version of this:

> *Soon after I arrived the mother told me that I was not to use the word 'no' to the children (who were aged 3 and 6) because she didn't want them learning to say no. This made disciplining them virtually impossible. They would scream whenever thwarted and stop screaming only when the adults capitulated, which the parents did almost instantly. I took a tougher line at first but by the end they wore me down and I too started handing over chocolate biscuits on demand. When I tried to discuss the discipline problem with the parents they seemed surprised and offended that I should criticise their beautiful children.*

When Carla returned to England, she took up a temporary nannying job. When her new charges' bedtime was approaching, she found herself becoming tense and anxious, anticipating the inevitable battle of wills and nerves. This was a case of tilting at windmills since the English children sweetly said 'goodnight' and took themselves off.

Carol Rowan followed her American employers from a German army base back to their home in Colorado Springs to continue looking after 2½ year old Kelsey whose behaviour was often impossible due to a lack of parental discipline. Her doting parents didn't even interfere and say **No** when she was teetering on a window ledge. One of her many acts of vandalism was to write on walls and so it was agreed with the parents that she not be allowed any pens. An hour later Carol found her writing on the wall. She confronted the father whose feeble reply was, *But it's a green pen*. What use is an NNEB training in such circumstances?

The fixed level of pocket money paid on official au pair programmes to America has now been brought into line with the US minimum wage requirements. At the time of writing the weekly payment was $128.25 which was expected to rise to $139.05 subject to US Government Approval. Au pair programme participants are supposed to work 45 hours a week.

The perks of the programmes vary slightly but always include a free transatlantic flight plus one-way or return from New York to your family, up to $500 to cover fees for a course of your choice, and one or two weeks paid vacation. Sometimes, with your consent, a family vacation will count, though there are definite disadvantages to this (see *Leisure Time* below).

Fixing up a Job

There are five main au pair recruitment organisations active in Britain, all of which have entries in the Directory (listed under *Directory References* at the end of this chapter). Agencies in the Directory which include the US as one of their destination countries are simply appointed interviewers for one of these programmes.

The basic requirements for these programmes are that you be between 18 and 26, speak English to an acceptable standard, have practical childcare experience (a babysitting reference is usually sufficient), be a non-smoker and a car driver. The majority of candidates are women though young men with relevant experience (e.g. teaching sports at a children's camp) may be placed. The job entails working 45 hours a week (including babysitting) with at least one and a half days off per week plus one complete weekend off a month. Au pairs who will be working for a family with a child less than two years of age must show that they have had at least six months of prior infant childcare experience.

If you are interested in going to the US for a year as an au pair it is worth requesting literature from all of the agencies, since details do differ. For example EIL offers to pay for a transatlantic phone call twice a month, an insurance policy with no deductible and a $100 cash bonus to those who are qualified to look after children under two. Au Pair in America encourages a thirteenth month of pure travel (at your expense) arranging return flights accordingly and including the extra month in the top-up insurance policy. Another difference between programmes pertains to the strings attached to the refunding of the goodwill deposit or training fee of $500 or £350.

All the programmes include free return flights. Most participants travel with groups of other au pairs on their programme, though some do travel alone. The most popular departure times are between January and March or between June and September, with the starting date of the majority of jobs coinciding with the beginning of the school year in September. A new requirement of the programme is that on arrival in New York all au pairs attend a four-day training and orientation course in which they receive at least eight hours of child safety instruction and 24 hours of child development instruction.

Interviews are a necessary stage in the application process. In addition to the interviews there will be a lot of form-filling, reference-gathering and letter-writing involved before you will be chosen. You will probably have to prepare a standard autobiographical essay or an account of how you would amuse two children on a rainy winter day. (If you're short of ideas, see Appendix V.) The time taken between applying and arriving is usually eight to ten weeks.

Michelle Francis advises prospective au pairs not be take the information in the brochures too literally:

> During my interview I discovered that it is not necessary to have any 'real' childcare experience; babysitting was quite sufficient as long as you could back it up with a good reference. I personally hadn't done any childcare for two years. The brochure also states quite clearly that au pairs are not allowed to choose their destination. However, once I'd arrived, I discovered that many au pairs (particularly those from the Continent) had requested a destination and/or ages/ numbers of children preferred. Many got what they asked for. Some friends even asked to be placed together and were within a few miles of each other.

EIL Ltd. say that they will try to place friends who apply together in the same vicinity.

After your application has been accepted, it will be circulated among American families. The normal procedure is for any family who is interested in your application to ring you for a chat to see if you are vaguely compatible. If you are interested in them there may be a subsequent phone call when more specific details can be discussed.

Once you are *in situ*, follow-up is provided in both cases by community counsellors who meet about once a month with the au pairs in their region. These meetings are both social and of practical benefit since any problems can be aired here. The counsellors are also responsible for advising on local education facilities of which au pairs are expected to take advantage. In fact families pay up to $500 towards the cost of classes in whatever subject the au pair chooses to pursue for at least three hours a week from Tae KwonDo to American literature.

With hindsight, Michelle makes the following recommendations to au pairs who are still at the stage of choosing a family on the basis of phone calls:

> I would advise anybody considering embarking on such a trip to establish exactly what will be expected of them, how many nights babysitting at the weekends, do they believe in curfews and what restrictions would be put on the au pair regarding use of the cars and socialising. My situation was not as bad as other au pairs I met: one had a curfew of 10.30pm, another had to do all the housework, cooking and cleaning for a family of six, while another had to hoover the carpet in stripes and fold all the towels and underwear in a particular way. As it is really difficult to get to know somebody by just a telephone call, it's much better to ask as many day-to-day questions as possible.

The penalties for breaking the terms of the contract are harsh. The hefty deposit is really a bond to guarantee that you don't flit and use your J-1 visa to take up other work. Not only will your bond be forfeit and your return ticket and insurance cancelled but the US Immigration and Naturalization Service will be alerted, so the legal consequences can be serious.

Compared to all this the requirements of the ten-week Family Companion Programme operated by *Camp America* are relatively lax. Like Au Pair in America, this comes under the umbrella of AIFS. A genuine interest and positive attitude to children will suffice for this programme and also a driving licence is not absolutely essential. The pocket money is lower than on the one year programme, i.e. $400 for the entire ten weeks, plus a free flight. There are about 400 places altogether.

This exhausts the official avenues for fixing up a family job in the States. Otherwise it is a question of answering or placing adverts as Ana Maria

Güemes, a recent graduate in tourism administration in Mexico City, did in Houston:

> *I soon learned how difficult it would be to find an employer without having a green card or social security number, so I ended up going through the newspapers looking for something suitable like babysitting. The job I got for the vacation month of August was a live-in job looking after two children. I had the weekends off and was paid $100. At the end of the month I was asked to stay for the year but I preferred to go north.*

Some informal arrangements are advertised on the notice boards of popular travellers' hostels. There is a very active and helpful network of nannies outside the official programmes, and you may well benefit from their advice as Kim Wetherel did:

> *When the rich Dallas family I was working for announced that I would also have to look after their visitors' baby, I said I'd be leaving in a week. Fortunately I had made plenty of other nanny friends and their families were willing to put me up while I looked for another job. For two weeks I sunned myself, and through word of mouth went for interviews. Eventually I got a job with the nicest people I've ever met who ended up feeling like a sister and a brother-in-law.*

Leisure Time

The United States holds much fascination for many Europeans and it can be a great pleasure satisfying your curiosity and experiencing the real thing rather than the television version to identify truths and falsehoods about the Great American Myth. Of all the clichés about Americans, perhaps the one with the most foundation in truth is that they are open and friendly. It is very easy to meet Americans. They are not suspicious when foreigners address them, and they love to talk to strangers on buses and in restaurants. They are not critical or subtle and will accept overtures of friendship at face value. Especially if their own ancestry is British they will be delighted to befriend you, perhaps because they regret the lack of history in their own culture. If you want to get on well with the locals try to be full of praise for the United States. Although many Americans have a hearty sense of humour, they seldom direct it at themselves or their country.

There may be a few impediments to developing a social life quickly, especially if you happen to start a job in the Midwest in the depths of winter. One is that you will probably be dependent on a vehicle. Most American families live in suburbs which can be many miles from the centres of nightlife. It is virtually impossible to get a live-in job in the US without being able to drive, and it is not unusual for the au pair or nanny to have unlimited access to a car.

But even with the use of a car, life in some American settings can be very dull. Barbara Schmuk travelled from Austria to take a job with a family in Vermont on the understanding that they would be moving to New York after a month. But this move never materialised so Barbara was left with hardly any company beyond that of her $2\frac{1}{2}$ year old charge and the mother (even the father commuted into New York on a weekly basis). She didn't know what to do in her spare time, except ski, which was something she could do in Austria anyway. She stuck at the job three months before moving to New York where she found another job in Manhattan and so never again had to worry about how to fill her leisure time.

Au pairs who are used to the conviviality of British pubs might find the

American counterpart a little disappointing. Social drinking in the States does not revolve around neighbourhood pubs; in fact there *are* no neighbourhood pubs since suburbia is almost devoid of bars. People tend to go to bars not for a quiet chat with friends, but for an expensive night out on the town, which can soon cut into the savings of a $139-a-week au pair. Nevertheless British au pairs and nannies are a familiar sight at certain singles bars in Boston, New York, Los Angeles and so on. You should bear in mind that the minimum drinking age in half the states of the Union is 21, though some British visitors have managed to acquire ID cards which exaggerate their age for this purpose.

Au pairs on the authorised programmes will be given a directory of all the participants, some of whom they will already have become acquainted with at the orientation. The Community Counsellor might also be able to suggest local clubs and sports centres where you can meet other people. The local YM/YWCA is always a good bet. Michelle Francis soon developed a busy social life in Seattle (too busy as it turned out): 'The au pairs who were already there (approximately 50) really did work to help me fit in, always telephoning me, introducing me to other people, clubs, bars, etc.'.

With two weeks of paid holiday and regular weekends off, you should be able to see at least some of the sights. As mentioned above, vacations with the family can be a real perk; however they are not necessarily a holiday for you if your duties continue. It had been one of Carla Mitchell's lifelong dreams to see Disneyland and she became excited when the family she was working for announced that as part of their visit to California (where they stayed in a hotel on Rodeo Drive in Los Angeles) they were going to visit Disneyland. But the day was spoiled for Carla by the presence of her two badly behaved charges who whined continuously. If there is something you are especially eager to see, it is probably wise to organise an independent visit.

Travel

As mentioned above, anyone participating in the approved au pair programme will have their return flights organised and paid for. The programme permits a 13th month of pure travel (at the au pair's expense) though the agencies will be able to suggest ways to travel economically. EIL even sells a seven-day Greyhound bus pass for $99 which is cheaper than the £110 pass being sold by the British office of Greyhound at the time of writing (01342 317317).

The company Cultural Hi-Ways (PO Box 4191, Wallingford, CT 06492-7560; 1-800-819-7683) specialises in arranging holiday tours for au pairs and nannies, including three-day trips to Niagara Falls ($189 from Michigan) to a coast-to-coast trip (about $1,600 for three weeks). Their web-site can be found at http://www.cultural-hi-ways.com. Suntrek Tours offer discounts to au pairs on some of their trips.

If you are not participating in an au pair programme and want to travel to the USA, it will be a question of checking adverts in the daily press and consulting a reliable discount travel agent. Having a return ticket will make things much easier for you at immigration. Make sure that your ticket is an open return or one which can be altered or cashed in without an exorbitant penalty if you do not intend to make use of the return half. Lots of lesser known scheduled airlines such as Air India and Kuwait Air sell off seats quite cheaply.

NORTH AMERICA
... on the wild side!

USA • CANADA • ALASKA • MEXICO
Adventure and Fun!
Camping & Hotel Treks / 1–13 Weeks
Small International Groups
(13 People Maximum)
GUARANTEED DEPARTURES
$ $ $ Au Pair discounts $ $ $

DISCOVER AMERICA
For your free catalog contact SUNTREK:

USA/Canada	Germany	Britain	Switzerland
Sun Plaza	Sedanstr. 21	Greyhound Int'l.	Birmensdorferstr. 187
77 West Third Street	D-800 Munich 80	Sussex House	CH-8003 Zurich
Santa Rosa, CA 95401	Phone: 089 480 28 31	London Road	Phone: 01 462 61 61
Phone: (707) 523-1800	Fax: 089 480 24 11	East Grinstead RH19 1LD	Fax: 01 462 65 45
Fax: (707) 523-1911		Phone: 01342 317317	
Reservations Toll-Free		Fax: 01342 328519	
1 (800) 292-9696			

"SPECIALIZING IN ADVENTURE TRAVEL SINCE 1974"

Directory References

The main au pair placement organisations in the USA are: **AuPairCare** (San Francisco and Hove), **AuPair Homestay** (Washington) whose UK partner is **EIL** (Malvern), **Au Pair in America** (London), part of AIFS in Connecticut; **Au Pair Programme USA/EXCEL** (Salt Lake City) whose UK partner is **Childcare International Ltd**, **EF** (Boston and London) and **InterExchange** (New York) whose UK partner is **Tinies U.K. Ltd** (Reading). A summer programme is run by **Camp America.**

For au pair agencies in Britain which interview for US au pair programmes, see for example: Anglo Nannies, Au Pair International (London), A.Z.E., Bluebell, Childcare International, Edgware, Elizabeth Elder Recruitment, Homelife, Hyde Park International, Janet White, Nannies Now, PEC, Portland, Solihull, Students Abroad and UK & Overseas

Other agencies abroad which send au pairs to the USA are:
Australia: Australian Nanny & Au Pair Connection, Dial-an-Angel, International Nannies Services
Austria: Okista, Irmhild Spitzer
Belgium: Windrose
Canada: Au Pair in Europe
Czech Republic: Au Pair International CZ, Student Agency
France: Accueil Familial des Jeunes Etrangers, Accueil International, Butterfly et Papillon, Euro Pair Services, France Au Pair, Goelangues, Good Morning Europe, Relations Internationales, SILC, Soames

Germany: AU-PAIR e.V., Au Pair in Germany/GIJK, EuroPractica
Greece: Au Pair Activities, Galentina's
Hungary: Avalon '92
Ireland: Au Pair Bureau of Ireland, Careers Information Service (Limerick), Job Options Bureau, Langtrain International
Italy: A.C. Link, L'Aquilone, 3 Esse, Au Pair International, Learn & Travel
Netherlands: Activity International, Travel Active
Poland: ADA
Slovakia: Agentúra Nomati
South Africa: All Aboard, Au Pair Adventure C.C., Au Pair Discover C.C.
Spain: G.I.C., Intercambio 66, Interclass
Sweden: IRCA
Switzerland: Agenzia Inter-Au Pair

The Rest of the World

Occasionally vacancies crop up in other corners of the world outside the countries treated individually. Qualified or experienced nannies have a better chance of getting unusual posts such as working for a Saudi sheikh, for a British diplomatic family abroad or in fact anywhere where there are wealthy people. Another possibility is to arrange a live-in position in which the primary duties are to improve the children's knowledge of English. This is commonplace in Turkey, Egypt and elsewhere. AuPair Homestay in Washington includes Argentina on its list of destination countries for au pairs as well as the usual European ones. Several overseas agencies cooperate with *All Aboard* in South Africa, not only to place South African au pairs in, say, the Netherlands and Israel, but to place nannies in South Africa.

Anyone with a childcare or teaching background might consider working in some distant part of the world from Central America to Central Europe in a voluntary capacity. For example an orphanage in a remote part of Guatemala takes on volunteers to look after orphaned toddlers; details are available from the office in the capital (Angelina de Galdamez, Casa Guatemala, 14th Calle 10-63, Zona 1, Guatemala City). Another example would be to spend time working for a voluntary organisation in Croatia; for example Project Pakrac, Hrvatskih Velikana 11, 34 550 Pakrac, Croatia (tel/fax 03483 435) could use nannies and nursery teachers to work on its children's schemes.

Middle East

Specific vacancies are often advertised in the specialist press, i.e. The *Lady* and *Nursery World*. Of course the wealthiest families want professional Norland nannies but there are plenty of lesser nobility — the House of Saud alone comprises over 800 members — and other wealthy families eager to hire an English-speaking woman for reasons of prestige. Those who are attracted by the high wages paid in the Middle East should be warned that many nannies become unhappy due to the boredom and hardship of living in a strict Islamic society.

Trained and experienced nannies willing to live a relatively cloistered life should contact nanny agencies and check adverts in the *Lady* magazine. Nanny agencies which make placements in the Middle East include Anglo Nannies, Hyde Park International and Monroe Nannies. Nurses are regularly recruited for Saudi Arabia by agencies in London, though working conditions are said to be much less satisfactory than they were a few years ago, with stories of wages being paid several months late. There is very little job security, even when you have a signed contract.

Recruitment consultants which find professional staff for all kinds of work in the Middle East are sometimes asked to find nannies. Watch the advertisements in *Overseas Jobs Express,* the fortnightly newspaper published in southern England.

Eastern Europe

Under Communism the state provided such good childcare facilities for working parents that there is no tradition in the new democracies of Eastern Europe of live-in childcare (despite the huge demand for learning English). In general, the middle classes of Hungary, Czech Republic and Poland live in much more cramped accommodation than in western Europe and even if they could afford to take on an au pair, they could ill afford the space that she would require.

This is changing as individuals who have prospered in a market economy acquire more disposable income and bigger houses. Agencies in the UK which claim to have posts in Eastern and Central Europe are likely to be professional nanny agencies supplying nannies to expatriates earning international salaries in Moscow, Bratislava or any of the cities which have proved to be magnets for foreign businessmen.

There are scores of au pair agencies throughout Eastern Europe, but these are primarily concerned with the placement of their nationals in the rest of Europe and North America not placing foreign au pairs in local families. One important exception is the Budapest agency *Avalon '92* though they work with many expatriate families rather than Hungarian ones.

AVALON '92
agency

**Au Pairs – Nannies –
Mother's Help – Housekeepers**

Positions in Hungary and all over Europe (Minimum stays 6–12 months)

1075 Budapest, Karoly krt. 21, Hungary
Tel: +36-1-342-1534 • +36-1-342-9316 • +36-1-267-8754
Tel/fax: +36-1-351-3010

An organisation in Latvia recruits English-speaking volunteers for various summer projects including the placement of about 50 au pairs in and around the capital Riga. The International Exchange Center (2 Republic Square, 1010 Riga, Latvia; 702 7476/fax 783 0257; e-mail: iec@iec.vernet.lv) says that au pairs will work for four to six hours a day in exchange for board and lodging and minimal pocket money (by Western standards). The minimum stay is one month though longer stays are possible. Applications should be sent early in the spring; there is a registration fee of $50. Participants are considered part of a cultural exchange and so visas are easily obtained at the border.

Until recently, the only agency in Central or Eastern Europe which claimed to make local placements was *Avalon, 92* in Budapest: however, the *Student Agency* (see advertisement above) is at the time of going to press planning to start placing girls with Czech and Slovak families. UK agencies which send candidates to Hungary are: Au Pair and Student Placement Agency, A.Z.E. Au Pairs, Edgware and UK & Overseas. Outside the UK, the Centre de Langue et Culture Russe/EIEC sends people to Russia in various capacities, including as nannies/au pairs).

Worldwide

Agencies which claim to operate outside Europe as well as throughout it tend to be professional nanny agencies which fill high-level vacancies, often for British families posted abroad. Among agencies which claim to have clients all over the world are: Anglo Nannies, Bees Knees, Cinderella, Homelife, Hutchinson's, Hyde Park International, Kensington Nannies (except USA), Knightsbridge Nannies, Lloyd's, Monroe Nannies, North London Nannies, Occasional & Permanent, Park Lane Nannies, Regency Nannies, Sinclairs, Tinies, Top Notch Nanny Agency and Yorkshire Nannies.

PART III

Directory of Agencies

Alphabetical Listing of 235 Agencies specialising in jobs for au pairs, nannies and mother's helps in the U.K., Europe and overseas.

The information given in this section has been provided by the agencies concerned. It should be checked personally when applying for a job.

1ST FOR AU PAIRS
2 Ashburnham Close, Worthing, West Sussex BN13 3QA. Tel/fax: 01903 530330. Fax: 01903 531256.
In business since 1992. Member of IFAA.
Placements: 350 au pairs, au pairs plus, nannies and mother's helps.
Jobs in: France, Italy, Spain and UK.
Male applicants can be placed.
Minimum stay: 6 weeks in summer, otherwise 3 months.
Wages/pocket money: £35-40 per week for au pairs; £55 au pairs plus/family help.
Qualifications: must like children and have some knowledge of target language.
Application procedure: medical certificates, photos, 2 written references and 'dear family' letter required. Average processing time between 24 hours and 2 weeks.
Other services: advice on language schools. Contact with other au pairs encouraged. Back-up provided.
Fees: nil (incoming), £40 outgoing.
Contact: Alex Cameron, Proprietor.

3 ESSE AGENCY
Via Francesco Baracca 18, 21013 Gallarate (VA), Italy. Tel/fax: 331-771065.
In business since 1992.
Placements: 150/200 au pairs.

Jobs in: Italy (for Europeans) especially the north; also other European countries, USA, Canada, Australia and New Zealand for Italians. Male applicants can be placed in some countries, viz. England, France, Germany and New Zealand.
Minimum stay: 6 months, sometimes less in Italy; 3 months in Australia and New Zealand (combined English language course and staying with host family); 6 months in Europe; 1 year in North America. Summer stays of 2-3 months are available in Europe and USA (on Camp America — see entry).
Wages/pocket money: about 100,000 lire per week in Italy; varies elsewhere. No pocket money paid in New Zealand and Australia; compulsory language course in New Zealand costs participants about NZ$2,000 for 3 months and NZ$3,500 for 6 months.
Qualifications: must have basic knowledge of the language, childcare experience (for some countries) and be at least 18 years old. Maximum age varies with country (26, 27 or 30 in the case of Italy).
Application procedure: within EU, need 2 references but no interview; average processing time is 15-60 days. For USA, need 3 references and interview; placement takes about 2 months. For Canada, need 5-6 references and interview; placements takes 4 months.
Other services: full support service by partner agencies. In Italy, advice can be given on finding low cost language courses.
Fees: nil for those who apply directly for placement in Italian families. 50,000 lire enrolment fee plus 250,000 lire placement fee for Italian au pairs going to Europe. 100,000 lire enrolment fee plus 300,000 lire placement fee for Canada. US fee is nil. 100,000 enrolment fee for New Zealand and Australia plus cost of course (as above).
Contact: Daniela Socci, Owner.

AARON EMPLOYMENT AGENCY — now incorporated into Global Au Pairs

ABBEY AU PAIRS
8 Boulnois Avenue, Parkstone, Poole, Dorset BH14 9NX. Tel/fax: 01202 732922.
In business since 1988.
Placements: 100 au pairs.
Jobs in: UK, France, Italy, Austria, Switzerland, Germany.
Nationalities placed: Europeans in accordance with Home Office regulations.
Minimum stay: 6 months although summer stays are available.
Wages/pocket money: £35 per week.
Qualifications: ages 18-27 years. Basic knowledge of destination language essential. Genuine liking of children a distinct advantage.
Application procedure: after all necessary documents and references are received, applicants can usually be placed within weeks. Interviews preferable; otherwise telephone contact is encouraged.
Other services: 'pastoral visits' are made after arrival in England, and advice is given on language schools, activities and whereabouts of other au pairs.
Fees: £40 if placed abroad; otherwise nil.
Contact: Ursula Foyle, Proprietor.

ACADEMY AU PAIR & NANNY AGENCY
42 Cedarhurst Drive, Eltham, London SE9 5LP. Tel: 0181-294 1191. Fax: 0181-850 8932.

In business since 1990. Member of FRES.
Placements: au pairs, au pairs plus, nannies, mother's helps and housekeepers.
Jobs in: France, Germany, Spain, Italy, Netherlands, Belgium, Austria, Switzerland, Canada, Australia and occasionally other countries.
Nationalities placed: all that are legal.
Minimum stay: 6 months. Summer stays are available in Europe.
Wages/pocket money: £35-40 per week for au pairs; £100+ for mother's helps; £180+ for nannies.
Qualifications: au pairs must speak language of chosen country. Non-smokers preferable. Nannies must be qualified. Mother's helps must have some sole charge experience.
Application procedure: medical certificates, photos, 2 references and life story. If within the UK, interviews are essential; telephone and letter contact otherwise. Applications processed within one week.
Other services: welcome pack sent on arrival. Advice on language classes and insurance available.
Fees: £40 upon acceptance.
Contact: Susan Sheehan.

A. C. AU PAIRS
2 Ashburnham Close, Worthing, West Sussex BN13 3QA. Tel/fax: 01903 530330. Fax: 01903 531256.
Business established in 1997. Member of IFAA.
Placements: au pairs, mother's helps and demi pairs.
Jobs in: EU countries, especially Spain, also France and Italy.
Nationalities placed: all that are legal.
Minimum stay: 6 months. Summer stays may be available.
Wages/pocket money: minimum £35 per week in local currency.
Qualifications: experience with children desirable.
Application procedure: written references checked by telephone. After being interviewed, successful applicants are given list of families from which to choose.
Fees: £40 plus cost of requested phone calls.
Contact: Alex Cameron, Owner.

ACCORD CULTURAL EXCHANGE
750 La Playa, San Francisco, California 94121, USA. Tel: (415) 386-6203. Fax: (415) 386 0240.
In business since 1985.
Placements: au pairs, demi-pairs, language students, home-stays, live-in English tutors, unpaid interns.
Jobs in: France, Germany, Italy, Austria and Spain.
Nationalities placed: Americans.
Male positions are available.
Minimum stay: one semester, one year (mid-September to the end of May) or summer only (June to August).
Wages/pocket money: $220-$350 per month.
Application procedure: after acceptance, phone calls with potential host families are arranged. If applicant chooses to proceed, they pay fees.
Other services: help given registering with language courses. Agency will move au pairs to hotel in the event of problems until a different family can be found. Agency will accept reverse charge calls in a crisis.

Fees: $1,800 for one-semester or one-year placement. Summer programme $750.
Contact: Michael Howard, Director.

ACCUEIL FAMILIAL DES JEUNES ETRANGERS (AFJE)
23 rue du Cherche-Midi, 75006 Paris, France. Tel: 1-42 22 50 34. Fax: 1-45 44 60 48.
Nearest métro: Sèvres-Babylone.
In business since 1948.
Placements: about 1,600 au pairs and paying guests.
Jobs in: France (Paris mostly and also university towns). Also Britain, Ireland, Germany, Italy, Spain and USA for French girls.
Nationalities placed: no restriction.
A few male placements are made.
Minimum stay: 6 months, though 9 months preferred (September-June). Summer stays of 1, 2 or 3 months arranged outside Paris between mid-June and mid-September.
Wages/pocket money: 1,650FF per month plus Paris transport pass.
Qualifications: ages 18-30 years (18-25 preferred). Some experience of childcare needed. Driving licence welcome.
Application procedure: files circulated among families who contact girls direct. Interviews arranged if candidates already in France. (In this case placements usually made within 16 days). Non-EU applicants must apply for a Long Stay Au Pair Visa in their home country and allow several months for processing. Must submit school diploma translated into French by official translator. Non-EU applicants must also submit recent medical certificate in translation. Applications for summer stays should be sent before the end of March.
Other services: help with visas, contracts and social security given. Also advice on language courses (e.g. Alliance Francaise, Institut Catholique, Sorbonne, Ecole de l'Etoile, etc). Agency organises cultural activities in Paris once a month.
Fees: 650FF for EU candidates; 800FF otherwise (includes 250FF non-refundable deposit).
Contact: Nicole Riollot, Director.

ACCUEIL FRANCO-NORDIQUE
28 rue Vignon, 75009 Paris, France. Tel: 1-42 66 53 02/47 42 45 04. Fax: 1-42 66 53 32.
In business since 1966.
Placements: 300 au pairs.
Jobs in: France only, especially Paris region.
Nationalities placed: all, especially Scandinavians but would like to place more au pairs from UK.
A few male positions are available.
Minimum stay: 6 months. Summer stays are available, but limited.
Wages/pocket money: 1,700FF per month plus *carte orange* for free Paris transport.
Qualifications: childcare experience and some knowledge of French generally required. Age limits 18-30.
Application procedure: application forms and information in English. Application dossier includes photos and secondary school diplomas (with certified translations into French). Agency arranges correspondence, phone conversation and, if possible, a meeting between applicant and host family.

Other services: assistance given with visa and/or work permit. Agency has its own language school offering courses year round at all levels including for the state diploma (D.E.L.F.). Cultural programme with excursions is offered to all au pairs and students. Work and study programme also arranged for university students who can exchange 12 hours of work for free accommodation.
Fees: 400FF.
Contact: Jacqueline Gauthier Sainte Marie, Director.

ACCUEIL INTERNATIONAL
2 rue Ducastel, 78100 St. Germain en Laye, France. Tel: 1-39 73 04 98. Fax: 1-39 73 15 25.
In business since 1983.
Placements: 450 au pairs principally, plus au pairs plus.
Jobs in: France. Plus French women can be placed in Spain, UK, Ireland, Germany, Austria, Italy and USA.
Nationalities placed: Western Europeans, South Africans, Americans.
Male applicants can be placed.
Minimum stay: 6 months. Summer stays: 1-3 months.
Wages/pocket money: 1,700FF per month for au pairs (30 h.p.w. plus 2 or 3 evenings of babysitting); 2,300FF for au pairs plus (35 h.p.w. plus babysitting). All receive Paris transport card.
Qualifications: childcare experience essential for nannies. Ages 18-30 years. Driving licence useful. Should be able to speak some French.
Application procedure: placements are usually made 2-4 weeks after application, 2 character references and health certificate have been submitted. Office staff speak English and German as well as French.
Other services: agency has its own language school (Yvelines Langues) at the same address which offers courses at all levels lasting from 2 weeks to 1 year; three 1½ hour classes a week. Agency can also recommend other schools in Paris.
Fees: for those who apply direct 850FF for 6 month stays, 650FF for summer stays.
Contact: Edith Drilhon, Director.

A.C. LINK
Via F. Ugoni 7/B, 25100 Brescia, Italy. Tel/fax: 30-375 4471.
In business since 1990. Member of IAPA.
Placements: au pairs and mother's helps.
Jobs in: Italy; also USA, England, France, Spain, Germany and Austria.
Nationalities placed: Europeans placed in Italy; Italians sent abroad.
Minimum stay: 6 months; 3 months in summer.
Wages/pocket money: 100,000 lire per week.
Qualifications: minimum age 18. Must be well-educated, mature and have proven childcare experience. Knowledge of Italian not always necessary. Italians going abroad should have some knowledge of relevant language.
Application procedure: interviews always required (in person or by phone). References are occasionally checked. Placements are usually processed quickly.
Other services: assistance given with booking flights and advice on language classes.
Fees: 278,000 lire.

ACTIVITY INTERNATIONAL
PO Box 7097, 9701 Groningen, Netherlands. Tel: 50-31 30 666. Fax: 50-31 31 633. E-mail: aupair@noord.bart.nl. Address for personal callers: Steentilstraat 25, Groningen.
In business since 1986. Founding member of IAPA.
Placements: 600 nannies and au pairs.
Jobs in: Netherlands; plus Europe, USA and Australia for Dutch girls.
Male positions are occasionally available.
Minimum stay: 6 months. Summer stays are occasionally available.
Wages/pocket money: 500 guilders per month.
Qualifications: childcare experience normally required.
Application procedure: placement normally takes 4-6 weeks.
Other services: agency also operates as international employment agency for Dutch young people who want to go abroad.
Fees: 125 guilders.
Contact: Mrs. Jose Hendriksen, Director.

ADA s.c.
ul. Wspolna 4a, Room 24, 35-205 Rzeszow, Poland. Tel: 17-520329. Fax: 17-520925. E-mail: adaintertele.pl
In business since 1994.
Placements: about 50 au pairs.
Jobs in: USA.
Male au pairs cannot be placed.
Minimum stay: 12 months.
Wages/pocket money: minimum US$115 per week.
Qualifications: ages 18-26. Must be able to speak English, have experience of childcare, driving licence, secondary school education, clean criminal record and non-smokers.
Application procedure: detailed application package will be sent on request.
Other services: cooperating agent in US (Au Pair Programme USA/Childcrest) provides insurance, ticket, English classes, J-1 visa and other supporting services.
Fees: US$75 and training deposit.
Contact: Wieslaw Sudol, Manager.

AFJE - see Acceuil Familial des Jeunes Etrangers

AGENCIA INTERCAMBIOS CULTURALES Y AU PAIR
San Joaquin No. 17, 07003 Palma de Mallorca, Baleares, Spain. Tel/fax: 71-75 51 24.
In business since 1987.
Placements: 500 au pairs.
Jobs in: Spain (mostly Majorca); plus France, England, Italy, Austria, Germany, Ireland, Netherlands, etc.
Nationalities placed: Europeans.
Male positions are available.
Minimum stay: school year preferred. Summer stays are available.
Wages/pocket money: minimum 28,000 pesetas per month.
Qualifications: childcare experience needed.
Other services: can advise on local Spanish courses.
Fees: on application.
Contact: Catalina Garces, Director.

AGENTURA NOMATI
Smetanov Háj 290/22, 929 01 Dunajská Streda, Slovak Republic. Tel/fax: 709-527786.
In business since 1995.
Placements: 150 au pairs, demi pairs, au pairs plus, nannies and mother's helps.
Jobs in: Belgium, Canada, Denmark, England, France, Germany, Ireland, Israel, Italy, Norway, Spain, Sweden and USA.
Nationalities placed: Slovaks, Czechs, EU nationals, Canadians and Americans.
Male applicants can seldom be placed.
Minimum stay: 6 months (longer preferred). Summer stays are minimum 2-3 months. 1 year for Canada and USA.
Qualifications: ages 18-26. Must have very good childcare experience and language skills.
Application procedure: interviews always required without exception. Must have 4-6 references (childcare and character). Applicants must be free of health problems and present a clear police check. Applications processed in days or weeks.
Other services: support services include arranging insurance, travel tickets, providing information about destination culture and loan of videotape for au pairs, free consultations, arranging meetings with returned au pairs, free English translations, etc.
Fees: varies according to country.
Contact: Norbert Tinka, Proprietor.

AGENZIA INTER-AU PAIR
Via Pezza Venerdi 5, CH-6616 Losone, Ticino, Switzerland. Tel: 91-791 66 75. Fax: 91-791 08 42.
In business since 1981.
Placements: 40 au pairs.
Jobs in: Italian-speaking Switzerland; plus Germany, UK, France and USA.
Nationalities placed: Western Europeans.
Male positions are seldom available.
Minimum stay: 1 year. Summer stays: 2-3 months.
Wages/pocket money: SFr400 per month.
Qualifications: childcare experience very helpful. Ages 18-27 years.
Other services: work permits and language courses arranged before arrival. Meetings arranged with other au pairs.
Fees: nil.
Contact: F. Betté.

ALBANS AU PAIR AGENCY
41 Station Road, Arlesey, Bedfordshire SG15 6RG. Tel: 01462 731099. Fax: 01462 733401.
In business since 1987.
Placements: 200 au pairs.
Males may be placed.
Jobs in: England only.
Nationalities placed: mostly French but also other Europeans.
Minimum stay: 2-3 months; summer stays are available in limited numbers.
Wages/pocket money: £40 per week.
Qualifications: basic knowledge of English essential. Ages: 18-27.

Application procedure: complete applications are usually processed within 3 weeks. Interview desirable if the girl is in the UK. Agent in France is Mme. Maillard, Albans Au Pair Agency, St. Martial, 82000 Montauban (5-63 66 91 95).
Other services: French-speaking agent can advise on colleges and organises occasional au pair evenings in major towns.
Fees: nil if applicant is in UK; French registration fee is 200FF and the placement fee is 800FF.
Contact: Mrs. Colette Elliott, Proprietor.

THE ALBANY AGENCY
21 Albany Close, Bushey, Herts. WD2 3SG. Tel/fax: 0181-950 4025.
In business since 1987.
Placements: au pairs and demi pairs.
Jobs in: France, Italy, Spain and UK.
Minimum summer stays: 2-3 months.
Wages/pocket money: minimum £35 per week.
Qualifications: childcare experience needed.
Fees: £40 on acceptance.
Contact: Mrs. Melissa Taylor, Proprietor.

ALL ABOARD WORKING HOLIDAYS
PO Box 12188, Benoryn 1504 (33 Hartshorne St, Rynfield, Benoni 1501), South Africa. Tel: 011-425 3312/082-672 0677. Fax: 011-425 1941.
In business since 1992.
Placements: au pairs and, in a few cases, mother's helps and nannies.
Jobs in: foreigners placed in South Africa; South African au pairs in Netherlands, Belgium, Germany, France, Italy, Spain, Sweden, Switzerland, Austria, Prague and USA; mother's helps in England, and nannies and summer au pairs in Greece.
Nationalities placed: British, European and Australian in South Africa. South Africans sent abroad.
Male au pair positions are available in some countries.
Minimum stay: normal minimum of 12 months. 3-month summer placements in Italy, Greece and France.
Qualifications: ages 18-28. Must enjoy children.
Application procedure: send s.a.e for application forms.
Other services: agency recommends au pair orientation courses in Durban (run by Mrs. Karen Southwell; tel 031-843347, 2-5pm) and childcare courses in Johannesburg (run by Mrs. Bev Wilson; tel 011-482 3378, mornings only). Au pairs are given list of addresses of other au pairs in their area. Insurance available to South Africans for R390. Advice given on visas (which can cost up to R200).
Fees: registration fee for outgoing au pairs R500 plus placement fee R180.
Contact: Mrs. Christine Baverstock.

ALLIANCE CULTURELLE INTERNATIONALE (A.C.I.)
4 Av, Félix Faure, 06000 Nice, France. Tel: 4-93 13 44 13. Fax: 4-93 92 58 85.
In business since 1963. Authorised by Préfecture Des Alpes Maritimes.
Placements: 300-400 au pairs.
Jobs in: France, UK, Germany, Italy and Spain.

Nationalities placed: Europeans with knowledge of English.
Male applicants cannot be placed.
Minimum stay: 6-12 months. Summer stays 2 months minimum.
Wages/pocket money: 1,650FF per month.
Application procedure: application should be made 2-4 weeks in advance. 2 references, medical certificates, letter of motivation and 4 photos needed.
Other services: back up via partner agencies abroad, e.g. Bloomsbury Bureau in London (see entry).
Fees: 700FF.
Contact: Mme. Antoinette de Yarcy, Principal.

ALLIANCES ABROAD
2830 Alameda, San Francisco, CA 94103, USA. Tel: 415-487-0691. Fax: 415-621-1609. E-mail: AllianceA@aol.com. Web-site: http://www.studyabroad.com/alliances
In business since 1992.
Placements: au pairs, homestays and some mother's helps.
Jobs in: France (especially Paris, Lyon, Nice or Burgundy), Spain (Madrid), Germany (Munich, Bonn or Hamburg), Italy (Genoa or Milan), Germany, Netherlands and England (London, Bournemouth or Manchester). Possibility of Australia.
Nationalities placed: Americans.
A few placements of males are available.
Minimum length of stay: 3-12 months. Some summer stays of 2 months are available.
Wages/pocket money: US$200-300 per month.
Qualifications: ages 18-26. Some childcare background welcome. Must be registered student in some cases. No language requirements.
Application procedure: phone interviews. 6-8 week processing time. 3 references required.
Other services: basic medical insurance (including repatriation) provided. Enrolment in language classes can be arranged (e.g. $150 for 3 months in Madrid).
Fees: $75 application fee plus $625 placement fee.
Contact: Victoria Lynden, President.

AMIES DE LA JEUNE FILLE
Rue du Simplon 2, 1006 Lausanne, Switzerland. Tel: 21-616 29 88.
In operation since 1888.
Placements: au pairs and mother's helps.
Jobs in: Switzerland (French-speaking Lausanne area mainly). Swiss girls sent to Europe and Canada.
Nationalities placed: Europeans, Canadians and Americans in Switzerland.
Minimum stay: one year.
Wages: from SFr700 per month (for 30 hours of work per week).
Qualifications: childcare experience if possible. Must be aged 18-25 years, have some knowledge of French and be prepared to fund four hours of tuition in French per week. Driving licence sometimes required.
Application procedure: must submit full dossier including references and recent medical certificate at least two months in advance to allow time for work permit to be granted. Postal and telephone contact encouraged; all au pairs receive written agreement setting out duties before leaving home.

AMITI INTERNATIONAL
75 Lascelles Road, Slough, Berks. SL3 7PW. Tel/fax: 01753 817311.
In business since 1995.
Placements: 150-200 au pairs and au pairs plus.
Jobs in: UK (mostly in Home Counties near London), France, Spain, Italy, Turkey.
Nationalities placed: EU nationals plus other Europeans in accordance with Home Office regulations.
Male positions are rarely available.
Minimum stay: 6-24 month stays preferred; or 2 months in the summer (between May and September).
Wages/pocket money: £35-40 per week for au pairs; £45+ for au pairs plus.
Qualifications: ages 18-27. Childcare experience preferred. Driving licence helpful. Non-smokers preferred. Should have some knowledge of language of chosen country.
Application procedure: write for registration pack. Photos, medical certificate and 'dear family' letter required. A fax number is very helpful.
Fees: £40 if going abroad; nil in UK.
Contact: Wendy Wilson, Manageress.

ANGELS INTERNATIONAL AU PAIR AGENCY

A Division of Spanish Angels Au Pair Agency
31 Bushfield Crescent, Edgware, Middx, HA8 8XQ
Tel: 44 181 958 7002 or 7003   Fax: 44 181 958 7000   I.F.A.A. Member
E.Mail: admin@angelsint.demon.co.uk

The Agency That Cares

Demi Pairs, Au Pairs, Au Pair Plus and Mother's Helps. Temporary, short term or long term. All nationalities. Placements around the UK but mostly **London** and surrounding areas. References checked for both families and girls.
Excellent back-up service. **24-hour emergency contact**. Personal service for both families and girls. Parties arranged for the girls to meet new friends.

ANGELS INTERNATIONAL AU PAIR AGENCY
31 Bushfield Crescent, Edgware, Middlesex HA8 8XQ. Tel: 0181-958 7002/3. Fax: 0181-958 7000. E-mail: admin@angelsint.demon.co.uk.
Division of Spanish Angels Au Pair Agency. Member of IFAA.
Placements: demi pairs, au pairs, au pairs plus and mother's helps.
Jobs in: England (mainly London and surrounding areas), Spain, Greece and Italy.
Nationalities placed: all nationalities but mostly Croatian, Slovakian, Czech, Spanish, French and Italian.
Males can be placed if they have childcare or care-work experience.
Minimum stay: 2½ months for summer placements, 6 months all other times but preferably 1 year.
Wages/pocket money: normal rates for all categories.

Qualifications: ages: 17/18-27. Childcare experience not always necessary. Basic English. Happy, flexible and helpful attitude.
Application procedure: application form, 4 passport photographs, 2 references (one childcare, one character from a teacher, previous employer, etc.), a 'dear family' letter and if possible a CV.
Other services: 24 hour emergency help available. Information pack on arrival and phone numbers of other au pairs. Agency checks to see that all is well during first few days of placement. Parties for au pairs arranged regularly.
Fees: nil for those coming to UK.
Contact: Karen Martin, Proprietor.

ANGLIA AU PAIR AND DOMESTIC AGENCY
70 Southsea Avenue, Leigh-on-Sea, Essex SS9 2BJ. Tel/fax: 01702 471648.
In business since 1981.
Placements: 300 au pairs, nannies, mother's helps and demi pairs.
Jobs in: UK (London and throughout), Europe and worldwide.
Nationalities placed: those approved by Home Office, plus Australians, New Zealanders, Canadians and Americans.
Males who can cook and drive occasionally placed in childless families.
Minimum stay: 3 months, preferably 6. Summer stays: minimum 2 months.
Qualifications: age limits 18-27 years (no upper limit for nannies and mother's helps). Childcare experience needed (except for au pairs).
Application procedure: applications usually processed within 2 weeks, except for summer jobs which must be applied for early. Medical certificate and 2 references needed. Interviews arranged wherever possible; otherwise written and telephone contact.
Fees: £40 (non-refundable) when British girl accepts au pair job abroad; otherwise free.
Contact: Mrs. Jill Corbett, Principal.

ANGLO CONTINENTAL AU PAIRS PLACEMENT AGENCY
POSITIONS AVAILABLE

Au Pairs, Mothers Help:– Long term 6–24 months.
South African, New Zealanders, Australian, Netherlands, Swedish, German, Austrian, Spain, Italian, Croatian, Slovakian, Czech, Hungarian, French.
Require 3 references, Dear family letter, 4 photographs, Medical Certificate, SAE or 4 IRCS.
Short term summer holiday placements for UK placements.
AU PAIR – £35–£40, 5 hours a day, 5 days a week, two nights a week babysitting, light housework, board and lodgings.
AU PAIR PLUS – £45–£55, 7–8 hours a day plus afternoons. 2 days a week light housework

Applications to: SHARON WOLFE PROPRIETOR
21 Amesbury Crescent, Hove, East Sussex BN3 5RD, England   Tel: 01273 705959   Fax: 01273 705959

ANGLO CONTINENTAL AU PAIRS
21 Amesbury Crescent, Hove, East Sussex BN3 5RD. Tel/fax: 01273 705959.
Placements: au pairs, au pairs plus and mother's helps.
Jobs in: Italy, Spain and UK.

Nationalities placed: British au pairs sent to Europe; South African, New Zealand, Australian, Scandinavian, Eastern and Western European au pairs placed in UK.
Minimum stay: 6-24 months. Short-term summer stays can be arranged for UK placements.
Wages/pocket money: £35-£40 per week for au pairs; £45-£55 for au pairs plus; £80-£120 for mother's helps.
Application procedure: 2 references, 'dear family' letter, 4 photos, medical certificate, s.a.e. and 4 IRCS needed.
Other services: coach travel and medical insurance can be arranged. Agency also recruits staff for fruit picking and hotel work in Britain.
Contact: Sharon Wolfe, Proprietor.

ANGLO NANNIES LONDON

Offices in London and Istanbul
Nannies, M/nurses, M/Helps, Governesses, H/Keepers, Au-Pairs
Interviewers for Au-Pair in America

London office	Phone: **0181-944 6677**	Istanbul office	Phone: **0212-2651878**
	Fax: **0181-944 5838**		**0212-2651879**
			Fax: **0212-2654340**

London office: *20 Beverley Avenue, London SW20 0RL*
(Employment Agency)

ANGLO NANNIES LONDON
20 Beverley Avenue, London SW20 0RL. Tel: 0181-944 6677. Fax: 0181-944 5838. Istanbul office: Bebek Yolu Sokak, Ebru Apt 25/2, Etiler-Istanbul; 0090-212-265 1878 or 0090-212-265 1879. Fax: 0090-212-265 4340.
In business since 1989.
Placements: nannies, maternity nurses, governesses, au pairs and mother's helps.
Jobs in: Turkey mainly, also USA, France, Italy, Switzerland, Middle East and worldwide.
Minimum stay: mostly permanent positions (minimum 1 year). Summer jobs also available (June to September).
Wages/pocket money: £35-£45 per week for au pairs; £50+ for au pairs; £100-£150 for mother's helps; £150-£350 for nannies; £250-£400 for governesses; £350+ for maternity nurses.
Qualifications: childcare experience needed in most cases. Families prefer car drivers over the age of 20.
Application procedure: all applicants are interviewed personally.
Other services: nanny circle in Istanbul.
Fees: nil.
Contact: Mrs. Omur Yeginsu, Director.

ANGLO PAIR AGENCY
40 Wavertree Road, Streatham Hill, London SW2 3SP. Tel: 0181-674 3605. Fax: 0181-674 1264.
In business since 1985.
Placements: 100 au pairs only.
Jobs in: UK, Turkey, France, Germany, Italy and Spain.
Nationalities placed: Europeans.
Male applicants very rarely placed.
Minimum stay: 6 months (3 months for Turkey). Summer stays are sometimes available for minimum 6 weeks.
Wages/pocket money: £35-£50 per week in the UK; average abroad of £35 per week.
Qualifications: ages 17-27 years. Childcare experience generally needed.
Application procedure: interviews generally required, plus 2 character references and a medical certificate. Agency arranges correspondence, phone conversation and when possible meeting between applicants and host family.
Fees: £40 for applicants going abroad; otherwise nil.
Contact: Mrs. G. Kirtley, Proprietress.

APB
33 Hilda Gardens, Denmead, Hampshire PO7 6PQ. Tel: 01705 269124. Fax: 01705 230259.
In business since 1992. Member of FRES and IFAA.
Placements: from 50 au pairs.
Jobs in: UK.
Nationalities placed: Europeans.
Male positions are available.
Minimum stay: 6 months. Summer stays are available.
Wages/pocket money: £35 per week.
Qualifications: childcare experience not always essential.
Application procedure: phone contact with families arranged, depending on fluency of the au pair.
Contact: Miss Susan Bunce, Proprietor.

APEC (Association pour la Promotion des Echanges Culturels)
39 rue Gounod, 92210 St. Cloud, France. Tel: 1-46 02 90 83. Fax: 1-49 11 18 82. E-mail: apec@imaginet.fr
In business since 1976.
Placements: 700 au pairs, demi pairs and mother's helps.
Jobs in: France only, mostly Paris area. Summer au pairs in country and seaside.
Nationalities placed: all EU countries plus Scandinavians and Americans.
A few male placements made in summer and winter.
Minimum stay: usually 6-12 months (September 1st to June 30th preferred). Summer stays: from one month. Possibility of 2-week stays over Christmas and Easter.
Wages/pocket money: 1,700FF per month plus *carte orange* for free transport within Paris.
Qualifications: age limits 18-30 years. Health certificate and a minimum of 3 years study of French required. Driving licence appreciated.
Other services: agency can organise a 'work and study' programme whereby participants live free with a French family in exchange for 12 hours of work a week and attend French civilisation classes at the Sorbonne.

Fees: 600FF/£65.
Contact: Mme. Elisabeth-Charlotte Ackermann, Director.

APSI/AU PAIR SERVICE INTERNATIONAL
Nelkenweg 6, 74391 Erligheim, Germany. Tel: 7143-87 00 78. Fax: 7143-87 00 79. E-mail: kosicki@t-online.de
In business since 1995/6. Applying for membership in IAPA.
Placements: au pairs.
Jobs in: Germany for incoming au pairs. German au pairs are sent to Ireland, UK, France, Greece, Spain, Italy, Belgium, Scandinavia and others.
Nationalities placed: no restrictions provided they can enter the country legally.
Male placements in Germany are possible for candidates with strong background in childcare and housework, though rare.
Minimum stay: 6 months minimum, 9/10/12 months preferred. No summer placements in Germany.
Wages/pocket money: DM450 per month plus monthly ticket for public transport.
Qualifications: ages 18-27 for EU/EFTA applicants; otherwise upper limit is 24. Basic knowledge of German (or host country language) needed though exceptions sometimes made for native English speakers. Childcare experience and light housework skills needed. Driving licence useful but not obligatory.
Application procedure: dossier includes references, medical certificate, 'dear family' letter and photos and should be sent 3 months before desired starting date. Telephone interview may be arranged.
Other services: assistance with visa procedure, advice on language courses and insurance. Emergency phone line. Rematch of families and applicants made if necessary except in cases of grave misconduct.
Fees: nil for incoming au pairs. German au pairs sent abroad are charged DM92 for summer stays and DM150 for all other placements during the year.
Contact: Charlotte Kosicki, Director.

L'AQUILONE AU PAIR BUREAU
Via Giovanni Pascoli 15, 20129 Milan, Italy. Tel: 2-29 52 96 39. Fax: 2-29 52 21 75. E-mail: aquilone@azienda.net. Web-site: www.s.snf.it/aquilone
In business since 1987.
Placements: 200 au pairs, au pairs plus, mother's helps and nannies.
Jobs in: Italy; also UK, Ireland, Germany, Austria, Spain, Greece, France, Belgium, Switzerland, Netherlands, Denmark, Norway and (from 1988) USA, Australia and New Zealand).
Nationalities placed: mainly EU.
Male applicants can be placed.
Minimum stay: 8-9 months during the school year; 2–3 months in summer.
Wages/pocket money: 100,000 lire for 30-hour week, 130,000 lire for 36 hours, and 210,000 lire for 48 hours. 2 weeks pocket money kept back as bond. Nannies' salaries are negotiable.
Qualifications: ages 18-28. Must have childcare references. Should have a basic knowledge of relevant language.
Application procedure: applications should be made via agent in au pair's home country, e.g. Avenue Au Pairs, The Gables, 44 The Avenue, Hatch End, Middlesex HA5 4EY (0181-421 5452); Emergency Mums, 23 Hope Terrace, Edinburgh EH9 2AP (0131-447 7744); Inter Au Pair, Astubben 68, 0381 Oslo,

Norway (22-521560) and ACISJF, Ayala 21, 28001 Madrid, Spain (1-431 9442).
Other services: partner language teaching agency in Milan is Linguadue, Corso Buenos Aires 43, 20124 Milan (2-29 51 99 72/fax: 2-29 51 99 73). Can recommend an Italian insurance policy (for non-EU au pairs). Changes of family can be arranged. Monthly parties and excursions arranged for foreign au pairs.
Fees: 80,000 lire if applying from abroad; 50,000 lire if already in Milan.
Contact: Barbara Merra, Proprietor.

ARCE (ATTIVITA' RELAZIONI CULTURALI CON L'ESTERO)
Via XX Settembre 2/44, 16121 Genova, Italy. Tel: 10-583020. Fax: 10-583092.
In business since 1948.
Placements: 120 au pairs and mother's helps in Italy; 150 sent abroad.
Jobs in: Italy; plus Italian au pairs and demi pairs sent to UK, France, Spain, Germany, Ireland, Austria and Australia.
Nationalities placed: EU nationals plus Americans, Canadians and Australians. Non-EU nationals may stay for maximum of 3 months.
Minimum stay: September to June preferred. Summer stays: June to September.
Wages/pocket money: 100,000 lire per week for au pairs, 170,000 lire for mother's helps.
Qualifications: ages 18-30.
Application procedure: must submit medical certificate, 2 references from teacher, priest, previous employer, etc.
Other services: social activities arranged. Advice given on Italian language courses, e.g. at nearby language school Il Mondo, Via Settembre 8/9 amm.to B, 16121 Genova (10-582718).
Fees: nil.
Contact: Chiara Orlando, Director.

L'ARCHE
53 rue de Gergovie, 75014 Paris, France. Tel/fax: 1-45 45 46 39.
Nearest métro: Pernty.
In business since 1958.
Placements: about 1,300 au pairs and demi pairs.
Jobs in: France, England, Italy, Spain, Germany.
Nationalities placed: all. (French girls only placed outside France).
Minimum stay: 6-12 months. Summer stays: 2-3 months.
Wages/pocket money: 1,800FF a month.
Qualifications: ages 18-30. Must have some knowledge of French. Childcare experience helpful.
Application procedure: application dossier (including medical certificate, references, etc.) must be submitted by end of March for summer placements and end of June for position during the following school year. Also possible to arrange meeting with prospective families upon arrival before fixing up a placement.
Other services: advice given on Parisian language schools, e.g. Sorbonne, Institut Catholique and France Langue.
Fees: 500FF (non-refundable if au pair quits).
Contact: Mme. Noel, Director.

ASL (AQUITAINE SERVICE LINGUISTIQUE)
Galerie 'Louis Gabriel,' 199 Avenue Louis Narthou, 33200 Bordeaux, France. Tel: 5-56 08 33 23. Fax: 5-56 08 32 74.
In business since 1978.
Placements: 100 au pairs, demi pairs and mother's helps.
Jobs in: England, Ireland, Spain, Germany and USA.
Nationalities placed: EU nationals.
Minimum stay: 3 months during the summer; one year for the USA.
Qualifications: childcare experience not always needed. Minimum age 18 years.
Other services: language course arrangements can be made. Cancellation and health insurance arranged.
Fees: 820FF.
Contact: M. Gaultier, President.

ASSOCIATION NATIONALE FRANCO-QUEBECOISE
4 Quai du Port, 94130 Nogent sur Marne, France. Tel: 1-43 24 34 66.
In business since 1979.
Placements: 25-30 au pairs in France; 20-25 live-in caregivers in Canada.
Jobs in: France and Quebec, Canada.
Nationalities placed: no restrictions.
Minimum stay: 9-12 months.
Wages/pocket money: 1,630FF per month in France; C$1,000 gross per month in Canada.
Qualifications: childcare experience essential; at least 6 months childcare formation and training required for Canada.
Fees: 700FF for EU nationals, 900FF for non-EU nationals.
Contact: Christiane Bouvard.

ATLANTIS
Norwegian Foundation for Youth Exchange, Rolf Hofmosgt. 18, 0655 Oslo, Norway. Tel: 22-62 60 20. Fax: 22-62 60 61.
In operation since 1987.
Placements: approximately 100 au pairs.
Jobs in: Norway.
Nationalities placed: no restrictions.
An attempt will be made to place male applicants, but it is very difficult.
Minimum stay: 6 months (8-12 month stays preferred).
Wages/pocket money: minimum NOK 2,800 per month.
Qualifications: ages 18-30 years. Must be able to speak English well and have some childcare experience.
Application procedure: usual dossier including 2 references, medical report and letter of introduction.
Other services: agency helps with various stages of work permit application for non-EFTA au pairs.
Fees: NOK 1,000; NOK 750 will be refunded if placements cannot be made or candidate cancels before being placed.
Contact: Ingvill Severinsen or Bente Kleiven (Inbound Department).

AU PAIR ACTIVITIES
PO Box 76080, 17110 Nea Smyrni (19-21 Sardeon Str. 17121 N. Smyrni), Athens, Greece. Tel: 1-93 22 506. Tel/fax: 1-93 26 016.

In business since 1993. Many contacts with IAPA, though not yet a member.
Placements: 30 au pairs, demi pairs and mother's helps in Greece; 50 Greek au pairs sent abroad.
Jobs in: Greece; also USA, UK, France, Spain, Italy, Belgium, Germany, Denmark, Portugal, Austria, Switzerland, Finland and Luxembourg.
Nationalities placed: EU.
Male applicants can rarely be placed.
Minimum stay: 1 month minimum in summer though normal summer stay is from 15th June to beginning of September. Most families prefer someone to stay 9-12 months, though 6 month placements are available.
Wages/pocket money: 13,000 drachmas per week for au pairs (working 30 hours). 24,000 drachmas for mother's helps (working 50 hours).
Qualifications: au pairs must have language skills (usually English for Greece) and willing and happy personalities.
Application procedure: references are always necessary. 'Dear family' letter is very important as are photos and medical certificate. Applications processed in 1-3 months (to allow time to visit and interview the host family).
Other services: insurance is normally provided by host family. Agency sends newsletters to au pairs in Greece and organises meetings and excursions. Agency prides itself on its after-care service and in staying in close contact with au pairs. Good back-up in the event of problems. Au pairs can be met at airport.
Fees: nil.
Contact: Popy Raekou, Owner.

AU PAIR ADVENTURE C.C.
PO Box 46, Muizenburg 7951, South Africa. Tel: 21-729371. Fax: 21-729379. Also: Shop B1, Toaki Vilage, Vans Road, Tokai 7945, South Africa.
In business since 1990.
Placements: nannies, mother's helps and au pairs.
Jobs in: Southern Africans sent to Europe, USA and UK; some jobs in South Africa.
Minimum stay: 6 months. Summer placements sometimes made.
Wages/pocket money: 1,200-3,000 Rand per month (depending on country).
Qualifications: must have contactable childcare referees and speak some English. Ages 18-27 years.
Application procedure: processing between registration and sending a file takes about a week, then a further 1-2 weeks while agent in destination country tries to match application with family, then 2-6 weeks while candidate obtains visa and arranges travel.
Other services: airline ticketing service and insurance can be arranged. Trouble-shooting done by overseas agents.
Fees: R150 registration plus R500 for outgoing placements; nil for placement in South Africa.
Contact: Jacqui Farr (Manager) and Darryl Soule (Managing Director).

AU PAIR AGENCY BOURNEMOUTH
45 Strouden Road, Bournemouth, Dorset BH9 1QL. Tel/fax: 01202 532600.
In business since 1977.
Placements: 300+ au pairs.

Jobs in: France mainly, plus UK and other European countries including the Netherlands.
Nationalities placed: Europeans and other nationalities in accordance with Home Office regulations.
Minimum stay: 6 months. Summer placements also available.
Wages/pocket money: £40 per week.
Qualifications: minimum age 18 years. Childcare experience a great advantage.
Application procedure: 2 references, medical certificate, curriculum vitae and detailed questionnaire needed plus interviews in some cases.
Other services: arrange social activities.
Fees: nil.
Contact: Ms. Andrea Rose, Partner.

THE AU PAIR AGENCY
231 Hale Lane, Edgware, Middlesex HA8 9QF. Tel: 0181-958 1750 or 07 00 00 AUPAIR. Fax: 0181-958 5261. E-mail: elaine@aupairs-r-us.com; also: elaine@aupairagency.com
Established 1986.
Placements: au pairs, demi-pairs, au pair plus and mother's help positions throughout Britain. Au pairs and mother's helps placed in Europe.
Families available in: UK, France, Spain, Majorca, Italy, Belgium and Germany.
Minimum stay preferred: 9-12 months. Summer stays: 10-12 weeks.
Pocket money/wages: £35 per week for au pairs, mother's helps from £100 net, according to age and experience. Equivalent paid in local currency in Europe.
Qualifications: reasonable conversational ability in language of chosen country. Childcare experience preferred for au pairs, essential for mother's helps.
Application procedure: contact for an application form at least 12 weeks before intended date of commencement. CV, references, photographs and medical certificate will be required.
Other services: general advice on schools, au pair clubs and medical facilities available.
Fees: nil to incoming au pairs; £40 if outgoing from Britain (may be increased if government permits).
Contact: Elaine Newman, Proprietor.

VERY RAPID AU PAIR SUPPLY SERVICE

Au Pair & Student Placement Agency
National & International Au Pairs & host families

PART-TIME & FULL-TIME STUDENT EDUCATION & ACCOMMODATION

Host families in UK, EC & many countries of the world

Au Pairs, Nannies & mother's helps from all countries of the world

Flexible part-time or full-time help in the home & with children

Student placements for families requiring minimal assistance

UK pay is £35.00 to £70.00/wk depending on hours

FREE TRAVEL, FREE AIRPOT COLLECTION & FREE COLLEGE EDUCATION AVAILABLE

FREEPHONE NUMBER IN UK, FREE HOTEL ACCOMMODATION IN EMERGENCIES

NO REGISTRATION FEE

> Winner, Residential Services Award 1997
> The company has also appeared on the BBC, supplies
> general guidance to many national and international
> organisations and has supplied editorial for many
> regional and national newspaper groups.

Please contact Dr Elizabeth Bright, M.B., Ch.B., AFOM.
ASPA
NATION HOUSE
NEWPORT ROAD
STAFFORD
ST18 9JH
ENGLAND

I F A A
International Fellowship
of Au Pair Agencies

Tel: +44 (0)1785 780424
Tel: +44 (0)1785 780419
Fax: +44 (0)1785 780157
email: aspa@uk-hq.demon.co.uk

w.w.w.uk-hq.demon.co.uk

NO ADVANCE REGISTRATION CHARGE

Side banners: PLACEMENTS AVAILABLE DURING ALL MONTHS OF THE YEAR — NO MINIMUM OR MAXIMUM DURATION FOR ALL PLACEMENTS

AU PAIR AND STUDENT PLACEMENT AGENCY
Nation House, Newport Road, Stafford ST18 9JH. Tel: +44 (0)1785 780424. Fax: +44 (0)1785 780157. E-mail: aspa@uk-hq.demon.co.uk www.uk-hq.demon.co.uk
In business since 1985. Member of IFAA. Winner, Residential Services Award.
Placements: 400 au pairs, demi pairs, nannies and students.
Jobs in: worldwide including UK and all EU countries, USA, Eastern Europe and Turkey.
Nationalities placed: all approved countries including UK, EU, Poland, Eastern Europe and Turkey. Male applicants can usually be placed.
Minimum stay: No minimum stay. Summer placements available.
Wages/pocket money: Typical UK wage £35-£70 depending on hours and country of placement.
Application procedure: Very detailed application form and references required. Interviews arranged if possible in offices in applicants country. Placements usually made within 2 weeks of receiving application form.
Other services: Insurance and travel arranged. If problems, new family is always offered. Free language school. Free accommodation in emergencies. Free collection from airport/coach station. Freephone number in UK. Free medical advice. Free immigration advice.
Fees: Nil. The host family pays the fees
Students: Please contact above address for full prospectus and fees for all countries.
Contact: Joanna, Helen, Bernie or Paul.

AU PAIR AUSTRALIA
6 Wilford Street, Corrimal, NSW 2518, Australia. Tel: 42-846412. Fax: 42-854896.
In business since 1987.
Placements: au pairs and mother's helps .
Jobs in: Australia, UK and France, Netherlands, Germany, Italy and Spain. Male au pairs can occasionally be placed.
Minimum stay: 6 months. Summer stays sometimes arranged.
Wages/pocket money: A$120-A$250/300 per week (depending on hours, duties and responsibilities).
Qualifications: minimum age 18. Au pairs must have good babysitting experience; nannies must have more childcare experience. Some knowledge of the language is needed. Applicants must be willing to become part of a family. Should be flexible and have initiative.
Application procedure: Australian applicants are given personal or telephone interview before being accepted for overseas placement. 1-3 month process.
Other services: au pairs are introduced to others in their region. Advice given on travel (for Australian candidates) and language classes.
Fees: A$100-A$200 for Australian applicants looking for overseas placement.
Contact: Mrs. Genelle Thomson, Director.

AU PAIR BUREAU — see UK & Overseas Au Pair Bureau

AU PAIR BUREAU OF IRELAND
89 Dublin Road, Sutton, Dublin 13, Ireland. Tel: 1-832 4773. Fax: 1-839 3783.

In business since 1983.
Placements: 80 au pairs and au pairs plus.
Jobs in: Ireland (all parts), France, Spain, Germany, Italy, Denmark, Switzerland, Austria, Netherlands, Belgium and USA.
Nationalities placed: mostly Europeans.
Male positions are rarely available.
Minimum stay: 6 months; 9-12 months preferred. Summer stays occasionally available.
Wages/pocket money: £40 per week for au pairs; £50 for au pairs plus.
Qualifications: minimum one childcare reference, two preferred, stating ages of children. Ages: 18-27 years.
Application procedure: current medical certificate required. Placement takes between 2 weeks and 3 months.
Other services: group meetings sometimes arranged.
Fees: £50 if applying from abroad.
Contact: Mary Kelly, Proprietor.

AU PAIR CARE
Challenge Holidays and Travel, 99/101 Lorna Road, Hove, East Sussex BN3 3EL. Tel: 01273 220261. Fax: 01273 220376.
Sponsoring foundation in San Francisco (see next entry).
Placements: au pairs.
Jobs in: US only.
Nationalities placed: Western European.
Male positions are available.
Minimum stay: 1 year.
Wages/pocket money: $118 a week.
Qualifications: must be aged 18-26, speak fluent English, have completed secondary school, have childcare experience and have a driving licence.
Application procedure: interview compulsory. Applicants will be told within 10 days if their interview has been successful so that they can organise a medical check-up.
Other services: insurance, orientation and local counsellor available.
Fees: good will deposit of £330 will be refunded at end of 12 months in the USA plus £50 refund in UK.

AU PAIR CARE (USA)
One Post Street, Suite 700, San Francisco, CA 94104, USA. Tel: 415-434-8788.
In business since 1991. Member of USIA (United States Information Agency).
Placements: au pairs.
Jobs in: USA.
Nationalities placed: all that have access to international recruiter.
Male applicants can be placed (about 5% of total).
Minimum stay: 12 months.
Wages/pocket money: $128.25 per week.
Qualifications: secondary school graduate. Childcare experience. Ages 20-26. Good English skills. Experienced driver.
Application procedure: processing takes 4-12 weeks after interview and acceptance. Medical examination, photos and 3 references required. Applicants must apply through cooperating agent, e.g. Au Pair Care (see above) or Portland Placements (see entry).

Other services: health insurance, support of local field staff and $500 contribution for education.
Fees: $500 training fee (varies according to country and recruiter). $300 cancellation penalty after family match is made.
Contact: P. Cowan, Program Manager.

THE AU PAIR COMPANY
2 Welch Place, Pinner, Middlesex HA5 3TA. Tel/fax: 0181-429 0311.
In business since 1987.
Placements: about 150-200 au pairs, au pairs plus, demi pairs and mother's helps.
Jobs in: UK only.
Nationalities placed: most Europeans especially French, Spanish, Italian, Scandinavian, Hungarian and Czech, plus South Africans with European passports.
Minimum stay: 6 months. Summer stays: 2-3 months.
Wages/pocket money: £35-38 per week for au pairs; £45-48 for au pairs plus; £22+ for demi pairs; £65-70 for mother's helps.
Qualifications: age limits 17-27. Reasonable knowledge of English (at least 4-5 years study) and a fondness for children required.
Application procedure: 2 references, 4 photos, medical certificate. Agency encourages contact between family and applicant.
Other services: agency advises on language schools and gives addresses and telephone numbers of au pairs in the same area.
Fees: nil.
Contact: Annabel Wagner/Pamela Sinclair.

THE AU PAIR CONNECTION
PO Box 686, Balgowlah, NSW 2093, Australia. Tel: 2-9971 0102. Fax: 2-9971 5579. Offices in Sydney and the Gold Coast of Queensland as well.
In business since 1984. Member of Department of Fair Trading & Consumer Affairs.
Placements: 100-160 au pairs.
Jobs in: Australia only (mainly Sydney, Blue Mountains, Gold Coast and Brisbane).
Nationalities placed: any that are eligible for working holiday visa or other approved work visa.
Very few males can be placed.
Minimum stay: 3 months. Summer stays are available. Highest number of vacancies occur between April and August.
Wages/pocket money: average A$5 per hour ($120-$250 per week).
Qualifications: must love children (experience not necessary). Minimum age 18. Must speak elementary English. Driving licence an advantage.
Application procedure: interview required (lasting 45-60 minutes). References needed.
Fees: nil.
Contact: Joanne Selby, Manager.

AU PAIR CONNECTIONS
39 Tamarisk Road, Hedge End, Southampton, Hampshire SO30 4TN. Tel/fax: 01489 780438.

In business since 1987.
Placements: au pairs, demi pairs and mother's helps.
Jobs in: Europe (mainly southern France and Madrid and Barcelona, Spain); also UK for incoming au pairs.
Male applicants can sometimes be placed.
Minimum stay: 3 months in summer.
Wages/pocket money: £35-40 per week for au pairs.
Qualifications: minimum age 18. Childcare experience and some knowledge of target language needed.
Application procedure: interviews where possible or phone conversation between candidate and family. References needed. Long stay au pairs are placed within 2 weeks (on average) and summer au pairs placed within 2 months.
Other services: advice on language classes given. Help-line available. Agency owner speaks French and Spanish.
Fees: £40 to outgoing au pairs.
Contact: Denise Blighe, Director.

AU PAIR DISCOVER C.C.
601 Pearl House, 25 Heerengracht, Cape Town 8001 (PO Box 7134, Roggebaai 8012), South Africa. Tel: 21-419 5740. Fax: 21-252 703.
In business since 1990. Branches in Johannesburg, Pretoria, Durban, Port Elizabeth and Bloemfontein.
Placements: 1,200 au pairs and mother's helps.
Jobs in: USA, Netherlands, Germany, Belgium, France, Norway, Sweden and Italy. Mother's helps placed in England.
Nationalities placed: all Southern African countries.
Minimum stay: 6 months.
Wages/pocket money: 1,000-1,600 Rand per month in Europe, £110 for mother's helps in UK and US$128.25 for au pairs in USA.
Qualifications: babysitting experience is sufficient. Ages: 18-29.
Application procedure: after all documents are submitted, agency can usually find a family within 1-3 months.
Other services: free monthly Club magazine sent to all registered au pairs in Southern Africa or overseas. Monthly information sessions and workshops held nationwide.
Fees: R225 registration fee (includes subscription to Club Magazine); R650 placement fee (Europe only).
Contact: Bianca Huys-Elemans, Director.

AU-PAIR e.V.
Staufenstrasse 17, 86899 Landsberg am Lech, Germany. Tel: 8191-941 378. Fax: 8191-941 379. E-mail: 08191941378@t-online.de
In business since 1987.
Placements: au pairs and mother's helps.
Jobs in: Germany plus UK, France, Ireland, Spain, Italy, Switzerland, Norway, USA and Canada.
Male applicants cannot be placed.
Minimum stay: 6 months. No summer stays.
Wages/pocket money: DM100 per week (£30 per week in the UK, 1,500FF per month in France).
Qualifications: ages 18-25. Experience in childcare and basic knowledge of the host language needed.

Application procedure: average processing time within the EU is 3-4 months. Have 50 partner agents abroad.
Other services: help given with arranging insurance, travel and language classes. Trouble-shooting advice available.
Fees: DM190 for Europe, DM330 for North America.
Contact: Susanne Caudera-Preil, Director/Manager.

AU PAIR HOMESTAY (USA & ABROAD)
World Learning Inc., 1015 15th St NW, Suite 750, Washington, DC 20005, USA. Tel: (202) 408-5380. Fax: (202) 408-5397. E-mail: imelda.farrell@worldlearning.org
In operation since 1932.
Placements: au pairs.
Jobs in: Argentina, France, Germany, Iceland, Netherlands, Norway, Finland, Switzerland and UK.
Nationalities placed: Americans and Canadians.
Male applicants are accepted.
Minimum stay: 3-12 months.
Wages/pocket money: about $300 per month paid in local currency.
Qualifications: ages 18-26 (maximum extended to 29 in some countries). Must have completed high school, and be an experienced babysitter or childcare provider, willing to help the children with their homework and communicate in English. Basic oral proficiency in target language needed for France, Germany and Switzerland.
Other services: Go 25 Card given to participants. Programme support given prior to departure and throughout au pair's stay abroad. Full health and accident insurance coverage provided.
Fees: $775.
Contact: Imelda Farrell, Program Specialist.

AU PAIR IN AMERICA
Dept. APN, 37 Queen's Gate, London SW7 5HR. Tel: 0171-581 7311 or freephone 0800 413116. Fax: 0171-581 7355. E-mail: info@aupairamerica.co.uk (with address to request a brochure).
Parent organisation (American Institute for Foreign Study) founded in 1967; au pair programme authorised 1986.
Placements: 4,000+ au pairs.
Jobs in: USA only.
Nationalities placed: all nationalities in whose country an established interviewer network exists.
Minimum stay: 1 year placements available all year round. (For summer placements, see entry for Camp America.)
Wages/pocket money: $128.25 per week (expected to increase to $139.05 from 1st October 1997, subject to US Government approval). Guaranteed 2 weeks paid vacation.
Qualifications: ages 18-26 years. Practical childcare experience and a full clean driving licence are essential. A good command of English is required and non-smokers are preferred.
Application procedure: must submit application forms, 12 passport photos, references including at least one childcare reference, a personal essay, medical report, etc. Interview compulsory with local representative. Au Pair in America also organises Open Days in cities around the UK, which both returned and

future au pairs attend. On-the-spot interviews may be available for those with completed application forms.
Other services: free return flights to New York from 18 cities around the world. A 4-day orientation near New York City. Legal J-1 visa and medical insurance are arranged by agency. All au pairs are placed in cluster groups with a local counsellor who arranges social and cultural activities. Participants are required to attend a local college for 3 hours a week during term time; host families contribute up to $500 for tuition fees.
Fees: $50 non-refundable placement fee. $400 Good Faith Deposit and $100 contribution towards medical and personal liability insurance to be paid once confirmation of placement is received. On successful completion of the 12-month programme, au pairs receive a $400 Completion Payment before they leave the US. Optional membership of Club Au Pair costs $65.
Contact: Marcie Schneider, Vice President and Programme Director.

AU PAIR IN EUROPE
PO Box 68056 Blakely Postal Outlet, Hamilton, Ontario, Canada L8M 3M7. Tel: (905) 545-6305. Fax: (905) 544-4121. E-mail: aupair@princeent-.com. Website: http://www.princeent.com
In business since 1976.
Placements: au pairs.
Jobs in: France, Switzerland, Netherlands, Germany, Spain, Austria, Belgium, Italy, Greece, Finland, Norway, Denmark, Sweden, UK, Ireland, USA, Bermuda and Australia.
Nationalities placed: any that are qualified.
Male au pair positions are available in some countries.
Minimum stay: 3-12 months. Summer stays can be arranged.
Wages/pocket money: equivalent of C$75-120 per week.
Qualifications: age limits for au pairs 18-30. Must have experience of childcare and be in good health. Driving licence and knowledge of language preferred. Child or Youth Worker diploma needed for Bermuda.
Application procedure: suggested application deadline is at least 4 months prior to departure. 2 character and 2 work-related references needed by au pairs plus copy of school results.
Other services: 30 cooperating agents in 18 countries plus recruiting offices in Mexico, Guatemala, Brazil and Lithuania. Au pairs are introduced to others in their region. Advice given on medical insurance and travel (via KN Travel, Burlington Heights Plaza, 1505 Guelph Line, Burlington, Ontario, Canada L7P 3B6; toll-free in Canada: 1-800-741-7954).
Fees: C$295 within Canada; US$295 for applicants outside Canada.
Contact: Corinne and John Prince, Directors.

AU PAIR IN GERMANY
Oststr. 8-14, 53173 Bonn (Postfach 20 05 62, 53135 Bonn), Germany. Tel: 228-95 73 00. Fax: 228-95 73 010. E-mail: gijk@gijk.de
Part of GIJK (Gesellschasft für International Jugendkontakte), an exchange organisation for German and other European young people.
In operation since 1983.
Placements: 600 incoming, 1,600 outgoing.
Jobs in: Germany; also Germans sent to US.
Nationalities placed: no restrictions, providing they can enter the country.
Male positions are available (about 30-40 per year in Germany).

Minimum stay: 6 months, preferably 10-12 months. Limited number of summer placements available.
Wages/pocket money: DM400 per month plus transport pass and DM14 per month for cultural events in most cases.
Qualifications: ages 18-27 (maximum is 24 if visa is required). Basic knowledge of German is preferable, though sometimes English or French will suffice. Some childcare experience needed.
Application procedure: informative leaflet available in English, together with list of partner agencies in 19 countries. Must have at least 1 childcare reference. Processing takes less than 6 weeks. Applications for summer positions must be in by 30th April.
Other services: can give general advice on language courses but cannot recommend any in particular. Offer comprehensive insurance package to host family in addition to the compulsory health and accident insurance.
Fees: DM50 for incoming au pairs applying direct. DM97 for German au pairs who are given 3 month placements, DM154 for 6 months, DM250 for 10 months and DM268 for 12 months.
Contact: Birgit Hempelt, Team Leader.

The
Au Pair International
Agency

Each month we place up to 100 Au Pairs, Nannies and Mother's Help throughout the UK and Europe.

7 Thornley Crescent, Bredbury, Stockport, Cheshire SK6 1AX
Tel/Fax: 0161-406-7036/0161-612-2676   e-mail: xad24@dial.pipex.com

---

AU PAIR INTERNATIONAL
7 Thornley Crescent, Bredbury, Stockport, Cheshire SK6 1AX. Tel/fax: 0161-406 7036/0161-612 2676. E-mail: xad24@dial.pipex.com. Scottish office: 179 Sandyhills Road, Mount Vernon, Glasgow G32 9NB. Tel/fax: 0141-763 1163.
Placements: au pairs, au pairs plus, demi pairs, mother's helps and nannies (about 200 of each).
Jobs in: UK and Europe.
Nationalities placed: EU, Andorra, Bosnia-Herzogovina, Croatia, Czech Republic, Liechtenstein, Macedonia, Malta, Monaco, San Marino, Slovenia, Switzerland and Turkey.
Minimum stay: 2 months. Summer stays are available.
Wages/pocket money: £35 per week for au pairs, £50 for au pairs plus, £15 for demi pairs, £70 for mother's helps and £100-£200 for nannies.
Qualifications: ages 17-27 for au pairs; minimum 18 for nannies. Must have basic knowledge of English. Minimum of babysitting experience for au pairs; NNEB or similar qualification for nannies preferred.

Application procedure: suggested application deadline is at least 4 weeks prior to departure. Enquirers should send SAE and IRC.
Fees: nil.
Other services: agency has English Language Centres in South Manchester and Glasgow offering language and activity courses.
Contact: Helen Morrison or David Wilkinson in Cheshire office; Mrs. Elaine Mulgrew in Scotland.

AU PAIR INTERNATIONAL
144 Cromwell Road, London SW7 4EF. Tel: 0171-370 3798. Fax: 0171-370 4718.
In business since 1993. Founder member of IAPA.
Placements: 850-1,000 au pairs and mother's helps.
Jobs in: Europe (especially Germany), Scandinavia and USA; also UK.
Nationalities placed: any that are allowed by immigration regulations. Male applicants can be placed.
Minimum stay: 3-12 months. Summer placements made with difficulty.
Wages/pocket money: £40 per week au pairs; £50-£55 for au pairs plus; £85-£130 for mother's helps.
Qualifications: ages 17-27. Good childcare experience and some English needed.
Other services: branch agencies in Stockholm Sweden and in Germany providing flights, insurance, orientation and counselling. Au Pair Club for au pairs in London plus quarterly magazine.
Fees: £40 plus VAT for placements abroad.
Contact: Sandrine Picquart, Proprietor.

AU PAIR INTERNATIONAL
115 High St, Uckfield, East Sussex TN22 1RN. Tel: 01825 761420. Fax: 01825 769050.
In business since 1981.
Placements: 450 au pairs, au pairs plus, mother's helps and nannies.
Jobs in: France, Germany, Netherlands, Italy, Spain, Switzerland and Greece.
Nationalities placed: EEA nationals. Male applicants are accepted.
Minimum stay: 6-12 months. Limited number of summer vacancies.
Wages/pocket money: £35-£40 per week for au pairs; up to £60 per week for au pairs plus; up to £120 for mother's helps.
Qualifications: minimum age 18.
Application procedure: 2-3 childcare references and 2 character references needed. Personal interviews held wherever possible, otherwise by phone.
Other services: social contact encouraged with other au pairs in area. Offer basic counselling and help to establish friendly working relationship between au pairs and families.
Fees: £40 (for English girls going overseas).
Contact: Christine Pourcin, Proprietor.

AU PAIR INTERNATIONAL
Via S. Stefano 32, 40125 Bologna, Italy. Tel: 51-267575. Fax: 51-236594.
In business since 1986.
Placements: 150 au pairs and au pairs plus in Italy; 130 Italian girls sent abroad.
Jobs in: Italy; plus all EU countries and USA for Italian young people.

Male positions are available for a minimum stay of 6 months.
Minimum stay: 3-6 months. Many summer stays of 2-3 months are arranged.
Wages/pocket money: from 90,000 lire per week for au pairs, up to 150,000 lire for au pairs plus.
Qualifications: experience required for positions caring for children under 2.
Application procedure: application form and information in English. HIV-test often required by employers.
Other services: agency recommends private and state university courses.
Fees: nil in Italy.
Contact: Angela Ritti and Annalisa Boltri, Managers.

AU PAIR INTERNATIONAL
2 Desler Street, Bnei Brak 51507, Israel. Tel: 3-619 0423. Fax: 3-578 5463.
Office open Sundays and Tuesdays 9am-2pm; otherwise use answering machine.
In business since 1976.
Placements: nanny/mother's helps, nannies, mother's helps and housekeepers.
Jobs in: Israel mainly.
Nationalities placed: all (only exception is Filipino nationals). Couples can sometimes be placed but not individual males.
Minimum stay: 6-12 months.
Wages/pocket money: US$650-700 per month for nanny/mother's helps, US$800 + for qualified nannies and experienced housekeepers, and US$600 for mother's helps; all paid in Israeli shekels. Employees get 1½ days off per week, plus 2 weeks paid holiday after one year.
Qualifications: minimum age 18 years. Childcare experience not always necessary.
Application procedure: applications usually processed immediately. References, 4 photos, medical certificate and introductory letter needed. All candidates must have health insurance. Interviews preferred, either by agency director who travels to UK to interview, or by agents. Otherwise letter and telephone contact. After 2 months (which is a trial period), broken contracts will result in forfeiture of wages (amount depends on length of contracted time left).
Other services: agency puts nannies in touch with one another. Can provide ulpan addresses for those who wish to study Hebrew.
Fees: nil within Israel.
Contact: Mrs. Veronica Grosbard, Director and Miriam Grinspan.

AU PAIR INTERNATIONAL CZ
Kuzmínova 336, CZ-278 01 Krapuly n/Vlt 1, Czech Republic. Tel: 205-74 13 17/74 13 18. Fax: 205-74 10 31. E-mail: au.pair@vtx.cz.
In business since 1992. Having bilateral talks with IAPA.
Placements: 300 + au pairs, au pairs plus, demi pairs, mother's helps, nannies and housekeepers.
Jobs in: Belgium, Canada, Denmark, England, France, Germany, Ireland, Israel, Italy, Netherlands, Norway, Spain, Sweden and USA. Possibility of au pairing in the Czech Republic in the future.
Nationalities placed: Czech, Slovak and EU nationals; also Americans and Canadians.

Males can rarely be placed as au pairs but are encouraged to join Camp America, summer workcamps, etc.
Minimum stay: 6 months; longer stays of 9-12 months preferred. 12 months for Canada and the USA. Summer stays are sometimes available.
Application procedure: varies from country to country.
Other services: agency sells coach tickets to England, Belgium, Sweden, Norway, Germany and Turkey. Organises au pair training sessions once a month.
Fees: variable.
Contact: Martin Tlusty, Proprietor.

AU PAIR PROGRAMME USA/EXCEL
6955 Union Park Center, Suite 360, Salt Lake City, UT 84047, USA. Tel: 801-255-7722. Fax: 801-255-7782.
In business since 1984.
Placements: 1,000 au pairs.
Jobs in: USA only.
Nationalities placed: all Western and Eastern European countries, South Africa, Australia and Canada.
Minimum stay: 1 year.
Wages/pocket money: US$139 per week.
Qualifications: aged 18-26 years. Must have childcare experience, knowledge of English and driving licence.
Application procedure: UK applicants should apply through Childcare International Ltd. Other nationalities should write to the US address above for nearest representative.
Other services: arrange visa, health insurance, travel arrangements and provide year long support from a local counsellor.
Fees: nil in UK; other countries vary.
Contact: Shauna Gallegos, European Director.

AU PAIRS ECHANGE
17 Grovewood, Sandycombe Road, Kew, London TW9 3NF. Tel/fax: 0181-332 9634.
In business since 1994.
Placements: au pairs, au pairs plus and demi pairs.
Jobs in: Francophone countries: all regions of France including French overseas territories e.g. La Réunion, plus French-speaking Belgium and Switzerland.
Male applicants can occasionally be placed.
Minimum stay: 2 months in summer.
Wages/pocket money: £35 per week for au pairs; £50 for au pairs plus; nil for demi pairs.
Qualifications: minimum age 18. Childcare experience preferable, at least babysitting.
Application procedure: usual dossier required to be forwarded to one of about 12 agents abroad. French translation service offered by agency.
Other services: agency is run by French nationals who offer advice and information about au pairing in France and beyond. Withdrawal insurance scheme which is refunded if placement is accepted.
Fees: £40 if placement is offered.
Contact: Mlle. Annick Techer, Proprietor.

AU PAIR SERVICE
Les Bruyères du Mont Crépin, 61800 Frêne, France. Tel: 2-33 64 38 78. Fax: 2-33 65 15 93.
In business since 1989.
Placements: 70 au pairs and mother's helps.
Jobs in: France; plus UK, Ireland, Italy, Spain (including Balearics), Norway, Germany, Greece and Austria.
Male positions are rarely available.
Minimum stay: 3/6/9/12 months. Summer stays 2-3 months.
Wages/pocket money: 300-350FF.
Qualifications: ages 18-28.
Other services: agency recommends university language courses.
Fees: 650FF.
Contact: Elizabeth Halbout, President.

AU PAIR SERVICE INTERNATIONAL
Im Brunnengarten 14, 78256 Steisslingen (near Constance), Germany. Tel: 77381 1553. Fax: 77381 665.
In business since 1996.
Placements: nannies, mother's helps, au pair and demi pairs.
Jobs in: Germany and UK.
Male applicants can sometimes be placed.
Minimum stay: 3-12 months.
Wages/pocket money: DM400 per month.
Qualifications: ages 18-25. Childcare references needed. Should have some knowledge of relevant language.
Application procedure: time taken to process applications is between 2-3 weeks and 2-3 months.
Other services: can advise on language classes. Au pair insurance can be arranged by agency.
Fees: DM100; cancellation penalty is DM50.
Contact: Beate Weber, Au Pair Manager.

AU PAIRS ITALY
46 The Rise, Sevenoaks, Kent TN13 1RJ. Tel: 01732 451522.
In business since 1975.
Placements: au pairs, mother's helps, nannies, junior nannies and governesses.
Jobs in: Italy only.
Nationalities placed: anyone with excellent English who does not need a work permit.
Male placements occasionally available.
Minimum stay: 6-12 months usually. Summer stays: 1-4 months, but most are for 2-3 months from middle or end of June/early July.
Wages/pocket money: from 500,000 lire per month for au pairs, up to 2,000,000 lire for nannies.
Qualifications: minimum age 18 years. Babysitting experience minimum requirement; the more experience the better. Knowledge of Italian not necessary; good command of written and spoken English essential. Also must be fond of children, patient, reliable, willing, adaptable and cheerful.
Application procedure: after receiving s.a.e., agency sends information sheets, application form and a list of vacancies throughout Italy, including location,

length of assignment and ages of children. Interviews not necessary. Normally no direct contact between au pair and family until job is fixed up.
Fees: nil. Voluntary service charge of £30 provides various services.
Contact: Mrs. D. L. Knoops, Principal.

AU PAIRS OF SURREY
7 Highway, Edgcumbe Park, Crowthorne, Berks. RG45 6HE. Tel/fax: 01344 778246.
In business since 1954. Now incorporating Avalon Au Pairs, European Au Pairs and Linden Bureau.
Placements: 100+ au pairs.
Jobs in: UK and most European countries (mainly France, Netherlands, Germany, Spain, Italy and Finland).
Nationalities placed: all approved nationalities for UK; British au pairs sent to Europe.
Minimum stay: a few short-term summer placements available; applications due May 31st. Otherwise minimum stay is 6-12 months.
Wages/pocket money: minimum £35 per week.
Qualifications: age limits 18-27 years. Experience required varies among countries.
Application procedure: write for form and leaflet. Photos, statement of medical fitness, references (including 1 from employer or school) and 'Dear Family' letter needed. Should receive details of family within fortnight of proposed starting date. (Summer placements tend to be less predictable.)
Fees: £40 for English au pairs going overseas; nil for au pairs coming to UK.
Contact: Mrs. Wendy Gibbings or Mr. Gordon Gibbings, Proprietors.

AUSLANDS-SOZIALDIENST
Au-Pair Vermittlung, Johannesgasse 16, A-1010 Vienna, Austria. Tel: 1-512 79 41/512 97 95. Fax: 1-513 94 60.
Office hours: Mondays 4-6pm, Tuesday-Thursday 9-12am. Affiliated to the Catholic welfare organisation Caritas.
Placements: mostly au pairs.
Jobs in: Austria, especially in and around Vienna. Austrian girls are sent to England, Ireland, Belgium, Netherlands, France, Greece, Italy, Spain, Switzerland (French or Italian-speaking parts) and Canada.
Nationalities placed: Europeans, North Americans, Antipodeans. Males can be placed if they have childcare and domestic experience.
Minimum stay: 6 months, but only from January onwards; from September minimum stay is 10 months. Summer stays: minimum 8 weeks (these are in high demand).
Wages/pocket money: AS700 per week.
Qualifications: ages 18-25 years. Basic German, medical certificate and childcare experience required.
Application procedure: after all documents have been submitted (including school testimonial), agency can usually find a family within 3-6 weeks. Families often request summer au pairs at last minute.
Other services: help with obtaining work permit. Active social programme for au pairs in Vienna with regular get-togethers and excursions such as ski weekends in the Alps. Agency can also recommend language schools such as IKI or Volkshochschulen.
Fees: AS600.
Contact: Elizabeth Schmid or Eveline Salmhofer.

AUSTRALIAN NANNY & AU PAIR CONNECTION
404 Glenferrie Road, Kooyong, 3144 Victoria, Australia. Tel/fax: 3-9824 8857.
In business since 1989.
Placements: 100-150 nannies, au pairs, mother's helps and housekeepers.
Jobs in: Australia; also France (Paris area and the South), UK (Oxford and London), Italy, Austria, USA and Canada.
Nationalities placed: many, especially British, Irish, Canadian, Dutch and Japanese on working holiday visas.
Minimum stay: 6 months. Summer stays are available but only after personal interview.
Wages/pocket money: A$100-$120 per 30-hour week; A$200-$300 for 40+ hours.
Qualifications: babysitting experience is minimum requirement. Minimum age 18 years. Medical certificate and knowledge of English needed. Driving licence preferred.
Application procedure: minimum 3 references, preferably childcare ones.
Other services: recommends College of Adult Education for learners of English.
Fees: registration fee of A$20 for overseas applicants; A$120 for outgoing.
Contact: Rosemary McCormack, Managing Director.

AVALON AU PAIR AGENCY — see Au Pairs of Surrey.

AVALON '92
Károly krt. 21, Budapest 1075, Hungary. Postal address: PO Box 701-1065, 1399 Budapest. Tel: 36-1-342 15 34/1-342 93 16/1-267 87 54. Tel/fax: 36-1-351 30 10.
In business since 1992. Member of IAPA.
Placements: up to 30 nannies to work in Hungary (mostly live-in but also some part-time or full-time live-out positions). Also 350-400 au pairs placed throughout Europe.
Jobs in: Hungary; Hungarians placed in Great Britain and Germany; also Belgium, Netherlands, Spain, Italy, France and very occasionally to Norway, Austria and Luxembourg.
Wages/pocket money: £100-£130 per month in Hungary, to work 6-8 hours per day, 5 days per week.
Qualifications: ages 21-30 for incoming, 18-29 for outgoing au pairs. Nannies must have childcare experience and be prepared to do housekeeping duties. Must have basic knowledge of one foreign language.
Application procedure: applications to work in Hungary must be sent 60 days in advance. For Hungarian applicants, make telephone contact before visiting Budapest office. References and application forms carefully checked.
Fees: average fee is £50.
Contact: Marianna Joni, Au Pair Consultant or Judith Hajdu.

A.Z.E. AU PAIRS
73 Victoria Street, Slough, Berks. SL1 1TJ. Tel/fax: 01753 576900.
In business since 1993. Member of IFAA.
A.Z.E. is a group of 36 agents in a range of countries formed into a cooperative who trade exclusively among themselves. At time of writing, A.Z.E. had offices

in England, Spain, France, Belgium, Italy, Austria, Germany, Hungary, Czech Republic, Slovakia, Croatia, Macedonia, Turkey and Poland.
Placements: 5,000 au pairs, nannies and mother's helps placed by 36 agents in group.
Jobs in: UK, especially London and the Thames Valley area; also Belgium, France, Germany, Italy, Spain, Hungary and USA.
Male positions are available (about 10% of total placed).
Nationalities placed: all that are legal.
Minimum stay: 2 months in summer.
Wages/pocket money: £40-£70 per week in England, £80+ for mother's helps.
Qualifications: skills matched to jobs.
Application procedure: on average the process takes 6 weeks. Applicants are interviewed by local branch of agency who take up two references and medical certificate. Long-term families are visited by agency. Applicants in other countries should contact above address to find nearest agent.
Other services: newsletters and contact with other au pairs arranged. Advice on college courses given. In some cases travel and insurance advice given.
Fees: varies among agencies in group.
Contact: Tim Child, Director.

A.Z.E. au pairs

The agency with the personal touch.
Top quality au pairs and families for long term and holiday placements throughout Europe.

Offices across Europe

Telephone or Fax: +44 (0) 1753 576900 for details
73 Victoria Street, Slough SL1 1TJ, England

BACKUP RECRUITMENT
Barnwell House, Barnwell Drive, Cambridge CB5 8UU. Tel: 01223 576495. Fax: 01223 516760.
In business since 1987 (new management since 1994).
Placements: 200 nannies, au pairs, mother's helps and housekeepers.
Jobs in: UK only (mainly East Anglia).
Nationalities placed: any that are eligible, especially Spanish, Slovenian, Czech and Slovak.
Male au pair positions are available.
Minimum stay: 6-12 months. Summer stays of 2-3 months are available.
Wages/pocket money: £35 per week for au pairs; from £100 for others.
Application procedure: all UK staff are interviewed. Au pairs write a biography and talk to the family over the phone or (if they are already in UK) are interviewed by family.
Other services: offer language class information. Will assist in relocating au pairs in emergency.

216 Directory of Agencies

Fees: nil.
Contact: Mrs. Mary Chapple, Proprietor.

BEES KNEES AGENCY
53 Church Avenue, East Sheen, London SW14 8NL. Tel: 0181-876 7039. Fax: 0181-876 9185.
In business since 1980. Member of FRES.
Placements: au pairs, nannies, mother's helps, and all domestic staff such as housekeepers, daily helps and married couples.
Jobs in: UK and overseas.
Nationalities placed: Western and Eastern Europeans or others with necessary work permits.
Male positions available for *Garçons familiales*.
Minimum stay: 6 months minimum, 1 year preferred. Summer placements sometimes available.
Wages/pocket money: £35 per week for au pairs.
Qualifications: basic knowledge of English required, or of language in question. Childcare experience needed for nannies and mother's helps.
Application procedure: references, photos and medical certificate required. Interview with family if possible.
Fees: nil to foreign applicants for UK jobs; otherwise £35 plus VAT.
Contact: Simone Crane, Proprietor/Director.

BELAF
Banner Lodge, Cherhill, Calne, Wiltshire SN11 8XR. Tel: 01249 812551. Fax: 01249 821533. E-mail: belafaltd.net
In business since 1975.
Placements: 300 au pairs (long term and summer) and *aide-maman* (work-for-keep scheme for 17 year olds for 3-6 weeks in summer holidays).
Jobs in: UK (southern England, mainly London, Henley-on-Thames, Bournemouth and Berkshire) and France.
Male au pairs cannot easily be placed.
Minimum stay: 4 weeks in summer. Year-long au pair placements can also be made.
Wages/pocket money: £40 per week.
Qualifications: minimum age 18 (17 for *aide-maman* scheme). Must have studied English for 6+ years, be non-smoker and have satisfactory references.
Application procedure: all families are inspected by local reps. Au pair applicants must send references. Placements made almost immediately after receiving application.
Other services: all families are close to local colleges which arrange language classes. Local reps in all areas liaise with girls and families, and deal with problems.
Fees: £50.
Contact: Carole Browne, Director.

BLIGH APPOINTMENTS
131-137 Earls Court Road, London SW5 9RH. Tel: 0171-244 7277. Fax: 0171-835 1251. Also: Level 9, Dymocks Building, 428 George St, Sydney, NSW 2000, Australia; tel: 2-9235 3699.
In business since 1974. Member of FRES.

Placements: nannies, mother's helps, housekeepers and cooks (no au pairs).
Jobs in: UK, occasionally Europe and America.
Nationalities placed: Australians, New Zealanders and South Africans mainly, but no restrictions provided applicant has work visa (not student visa), experience and references.
Minimum stay: variable.
Wages/pocket money: £130-£180 per week live-in, £200-£250 live-out, depending on age and experience.
Qualifications: minimum age 20. Must have childcare experience and provide references.
Application procedure: compulsory interview with consultant.
Fees: nil.
Contact: Louise Bentley.

BLOOMSBURY BUREAU
PO Box 12749, 37 Store St, London WC1E 7BH. Tel: 0171-813 4061. Fax: 0171-813 4038.
In business since 1971.
Placements: au pairs and mother's helps.
Jobs in: all European countries, especially Austria, France, Germany, Greece, Italy and Spain. Foreign au pairs placed in UK.
Nationalities placed: all, including Australians and New Zealanders.
Minimum stay: 12 months preferred, but shorter stays possible at short notice. Summer stays of 2-3 months are available.
Wages/pocket money: £40-£50 per week for au pairs; £100-£120 for mother's helps.
Qualifications: ages 18-28. Should have some childcare experience.
Application procedure: interviews required if candidate lives in London area. Placement takes 1-4 weeks via one of 20 partner agencies abroad.
Other services: advice given on insurance, travel and language classes. Round-the-clock helpline service. Group activities arranged for au pairs in UK.
Fees: £40 for placements abroad.
Contact: Marianne Dix, Principal.

BLUEBELL AU PAIR AGENCY
Jericho, Colpy, Insch, Aberdeenshire AB52 6XB, Scotland. Tel/fax: 01464 841358.

Placements: au pairs, au pairs plus and demi pairs.
Jobs in: Scotland, England, France, Spain, Germany and USA.
Nationalities placed: all that are allowed.
Minimum stay: 6 weeks.
Wages/pocket money: minimum of £35 per week in UK; variable elsewhere.
Qualifications: ages 17-27. Must like children and be prepared to do light housework. Must have reasonable level of target language.
Application procedure: families and au pairs complete an application form and supply references and photos.
Other services: advice given on cheap travel, language courses, health registration and insurance.
Fees: nil for incoming au pairs; £40 for UK au pairs going abroad.
Contact: Andrew Saunders, Manager/Director.

THE BRITANNIA AGENCY
25 Rose Street, Long Acre, Covent Garden, London WC2E 9EA. Tel: 0171-379 5254. Fax: 0171-497 8978. Freephone: 0800 214974.
London interviewing office and student centre. International postal division: PO Box 84, Richmond, Surrey TW9 2LT; e-mail: 5166@CABLEINET.CO.UK
Placements: 500 au pairs.
Jobs in: Spain (Madrid, Barcelona, Bilbao, etc.); also UK.
Nationalities placed: Europeans in accordance with European Convention on Au Pairs.
Male au pair positions are available in some countries.
Minimum stay: 6-12 months. Summer stays of 2-3 months are available.
Wages/pocket money: from £45 per week; car driving au pairs earn up to £15 extra.
Qualifications: ages 18-30. Some childcare experience needed. Should have basic knowledge of relevant language.
Other services: provides 24-hour assistance in case of difficulty. 10%-30% reductions on language courses, travel costs and cultural programme. Au pairs in London gain free membership in the Kensington Committee of Friendship for International Students which runs a full programme of excursions and social events. Membership costs £150 outside UK, £20 inside UK.

BUNTERS AU PAIR & NANNY AGENCY
8 Fern Lea Drive, Macclesfield, Cheshire SK11 8PQ. Tel: 01625 614534. Fax: 01625 617030. Mobile 0378 629658.
In business since 1962. Member of IFAA.
Placements: 150-200 au pairs and au pairs plus. Some mother's helps and nannies placed in UK.
Jobs in: France, Spain, Italy, Germany, Austria, Netherlands, Belgium and the UK.
15-20 positions for male applicants annually.
Nationalities placed: EU nationals and all others that are legal.
Minimum stay: minimum 8-10 weeks over summer; otherwise as long as possible.
Wages/pocket money: £35-£40 per week.
Qualifications: ages 17-27. Childcare/babysitting experience and some knowledge of the language of the country needed.
Application procedure: work with cooperating agencies of long standing. Summer applicants should apply early in the year.

Fees: £40 due on acceptance of a family abroad. Nil for incoming au pairs.
Contact: Caroline Jones, Proprietor.

Au Pair Agency

Tel: 01625 614534
Fax: 01625 617030
Mobile: 0378 629658

member of
International Fellowship of Au pair agencies

Au Pairs placed throughout the UK and Europe.
We offer you a friendly service.

8, Fern Lea Drive, Macclesfield, Cheshire SK11 8PQ, England

BUTTERFLY ET PAPILLON
5 avenue de Genève, 74000 Annecy, France. Tel: 4-50 67 01 33/4-50 46 08 33. Fax: 4-50 67 03 51. E-mail: aupair.France@wanadoo.fr
In business since 1992. Member of IAPA.
Placements: nannies and au pairs.
Jobs in: France; also Germany, Netherlands, Spain, Italy, UK, Ireland, Australia and USA.
Nationalities placed: all.
Males can be placed but rarely.
Minimum stay: 3 months (2 months in summer).
Wages/pocket money: 400FF per week.
Qualifications: ages 18-25 (maximum 30 for nannies). Childcare experience and references needed. Must have equivalent of A levels and some knowledge of French (for France).
Application procedure: complete file of documents and phone interviews.
Other services: language school, homestays and student exchange programme. Advice on insurance and travel arrangements given. On-going back-up service provided.
Fees: nil for those coming via partner agency; otherwise 350FF plus 150FF annual subscription.
Contact: Veronica Sanchez (Au Pair Coordinator) and Pascale Delzeith (Director).

CALGARY NANNIES UNLIMITED
Suite 350, 604 First St SW, Calgary, Alberta T2P 1M7, Canada. Tel: (403) 266-2890. Fax: (403) 265-3287.
In business since 1973.
Placements: 185 nannies and caregivers.
Jobs in: Canada.
Nationalities placed: no restrictions.
Minimum stay: 1 year.
Wages/pocket money: C$612 per month in Canada.
Qualifications: legal requirement that foreign nannies must have had 6 months

childcare training or 1 year's full-time experience. Must speak English or French.
Application procedure: processing takes 2-3 months.
Other services: arranges social functions and puts nannies in touch with each other.
Fees: nil.
Contact: L. Davey, Manager.

CAMP AMERICA - Family Companion Summer Programme
37A Queens Gate, London SW7 5HR. Tel: 0171-581 7373. Fax: 0171-581 7377.
In business since 1968.
Placements: about 400 family companions. (Also arranges other jobs in summer camps).
Jobs in: USA only.
Nationalities placed: Europeans.
Limited number of positions for males.
Length of stay: 10 weeks June to August/September. (For longer stays, see entry for Au Pair in America).
Wages/pocket money: US$450 for 10-week contract plus free London-New York return flight.
Qualifications: ages 18-24 years. Must be students. A liking for children and knowledge of English are required. Driving licence strongly preferred.
Application procedure: interview essential with an appointed Camp America interviewer. Phone/letter communication with family encouraged.
Other services: J-1 visa sponsorship. Office in the US (102 Greenwich Avenue, Greenwich, Connecticut 06830) offers back-up. Obligatory insurance costs £105.
Fees: £50 good faith deposit refunded in pocket money.

CANONS EMPLOYMENT AGENCY — now incorporated into Domestic Recruitments International.

CAREERS INFORMATION SERVICE
Monaleen Road, Castletroy, Co. Limerick, Ireland. Tel/Fax: 61-338644.
In business since 1993.
Placements: 40-50 au pairs, occasionally mother's helps.
Jobs in: USA, France, Austria and Germany; also Italy, Spain, Switzerland and UK.
Nationalities placed: any that are legal.
Minimum stay: 6 months. Some summer stays available in France, Spain and a few in Austria.
Wages/pocket money: 1,700FF per week in France (plus *carte orange*); AS800 in Austria.
Qualifications: ages 18-25. Must have good quality experience (but official training not needed). For France, must have studied French for at least 3 years.
Application procedure: all applicants within 50 mile radius are interviewed. Time taken to receive job offers varies: 1 week for Austria, 3 weeks for France and 4-6 weeks for America.
Other services: can advise on travel, insurance and language classes. Partner is EIL in Cork (and Washington).

Fees: £50 for Europe, £75 for USA.
Contact: G. Cantillon, Director.

CENTRAL LONDON BUREAU (CLB)
Suites 21-23, Kent House, 87 Regent St, London W1R 7HF (1 min from Piccadilly Circus). Tel: 0171-494 2929 (5 lines). Fax: 0171-494 2922 (day or night).
One of the trading names of UK & Overseas Nanny/Au Pair Agency Ltd. (see entry).

CENTRE DE LANGUE ET CULTURE RUSSE DE L'EIEC
2 rue de l'Eperon, 75006 Paris, France. Tel: 1-40 51 87 55. Fax: 1-40 46 90 70.
In business since 1969.
Placements: 25-30 au pairs and demi pairs; also monitors and companions.
Jobs in: Russia only.
Nationalities placed: many, especially French, Canadian and English.
Male positions are available.
Minimum stay: 1 month.
Wages/pocket money: US$100-$2,000 per month.
Qualifications: knowledge of French or English needed, some Russian preferred.
Application procedure: interviews compulsory, but references not needed. Placement normally takes 2 months.
Other services: back-up provided by partner agents in Moscow and St. Petersburg. Advice given on university language courses given.
Fees: 150FF membership fee; 2,000FF placement fee.

CENTROS EUROPEOS GALVE S.A.
Calle Principe, 12-6°A, Madrid 28012, Spain. Tel: 1-532 72 30. Fax: 1-521 60 76.
In business since 1968.
Placements: 300 au pairs and a few demi pairs.
Jobs in: Spain; plus France, Germany, Ireland, Italy and UK.
Nationalities placed: usually Western European.
Minimum stay: school year preferred, 6 months minimum. Summer placements: minimum 2 months.
Wages/pocket money: 7,500 pesetas per week.
Qualifications: age limits 18-27 years. In Spain families prefer girls with good spoken English, French or German (to teach the children after school). A basic knowledge of Spanish very useful.
Application procedure: school or work references required as well as a medical certificate. Personal interviews with Spanish girls only. Time needed to process application between 3 weeks and $2\frac{1}{2}$ months.
Other services: agency organises other programmes, for instance homestays with Spanish families in Madrid, Valencia, Alicante, Segovia and Barcelona, and language exchanges between English, Spanish and French students. Affordable Spanish language courses at all levels offered in Madrid for 3-10 hours per week.
Fees: nil for foreign girls coming to Spain; otherwise 15,000 pesetas.
Contact: Lucia Roperh.

THE CHARLOTTE LOUISE AU PAIR AGENCY — incorporated into Domestic Recruitments International.

AMERICA * CANADA * EUROPE

NANNY – MOTHER'S HELP – AU PAIR

An opportunity to live abroad in a secure family environment, caring for children and helping in the home. Continuous agency support whilst overseas.

For further information please contact:

CHILDCARE INTERNATIONAL LTD
Trafalgar House, Grenville Place,
London NW7 3SA
Tel: 0181 906 3116
Fax: 0181 906 3461
Email: office@childint.demon.co.uk
Web: http://www.childint.demon.co.uk

Member of the
International
Au Pair Association

CHILDCARE INTERNATIONAL LTD.
Trafalgar House, Grenville Place, London NW7 3SA. Tel: 0181-959 3611/906 3116. Fax: 0181-906 3461. E-mail: office@childint.demon.co.uk. Web-site: http://www.childint.demon.co.uk
In business since 1986. Member of IAPA.
Placements: nannies, mother's helps and au pairs.
Jobs in: Europe (Austria, Belgium, France, Germany, Israel, Italy, Netherlands, Spain and Switzerland), USA and Canada.
Minimum stay: 1 year for Canada and the US; 6-12 months in Europe. Short-term summer positions and winter ski au pair placements (December-April) available.
Wages/pocket money: from £40 per week for au pairs to £250+ per week for nannies according to position and qualification.
Qualifications: minimum age 18. Childcare/teaching/nursing qualifications needed for Canada. Knowledge of language an advantage for Europe. Non-smokers and drivers preferred.
Application procedure: write or telephone agency for details.
Other services: full support of local European agents and counsellor support in USA.

Fees: £40 for girls going abroad (except USA and Canada).
Contact: Mrs. Sandra Landau, Director.

CHURCH VIEW NANNY AGENCY
27 Layton Crescent, Brampton, Huntingdon, Cambridgeshire PE18 8TS. Tel: 01480 386076.
In business since 1986.
Placements: 250 au pairs, mother's helps, nannies, etc.
Jobs in: UK, USA, France, Italy and Spain.
Nationalities placed: Europeans, in accordance with Home Office regulations plus Australians and New Zealanders.
Male positions are available.
Minimum stay: 6 months-1 year. Summer stays minimum 6 weeks.
Wages/pocket money: £40 per week in UK, US$129 in US.
Qualifications: minimum age of 17 years for Italy and Spain (with parental consent).
Application procedure: minimum 2 references (including one related to childcare) and medical certificate required. Placement takes 1-5 days in UK and Europe.
Other services: advice on language courses and insurance given. Introduction to other au pairs.
Fees: £25.
Contact: Patricia Turnbull, Partner.

Jobs in Great Britain and abroad for Nannies,
Mother's Helps and Au Pairs.
Short and long term jobs in London, Countryside and overseas.
Friendly families who want willing, child loving, cheerful help.

For more information and advice:
Tel: (00) +44 0181-676 0917/8
(00) +44 0181-659 1689
Fax: (00) +44 0181-778 6906
323 Kirkdale, Sydenham,
London SE26 4QB

CINDERELLA NATIONAL & INTERNATIONAL NANNY AGENCY
323 Kirkdale, Sydenham, London SE26 4QB. Tel: 0181-659 1689. Fax: 0181-778 6906. E-mail: CINDERELLA—NANNIES@comp.com
In business since 1983. Member of IAPA; applying for FRES membership.
Placements: au pairs, au pairs plus, nannies and mother's helps.
Jobs in: UK, throughout Europe and worldwide (including US via Childcare in America).
Male applicants occasionally placed.
Minimum stay: 3 month summer placements; otherwise 6-12 months.
Wages/pocket money: £45-£90 per week for au pairs abroad; £45 for au pairs in England; £100-£150 for mother's helps; £120-£350 for nannies.
Qualifications: must have record of childcare jobs and references.

Application procedure: interviews compulsory (excluding au pairs).
Other services: telephone advice given if problems arise after placement. Free advice service on travel, insurance, etc.
Fees: nil for nanny placements in UK and Europe. £40 admin charge for au pair placements in Europe.
Contact: Liz Rowland, Director.

CONNACHER CHILDCARE
92 Highfield Avenue, Fareham, Hants. PO14 1HX. Tel/fax: 01329 233825.
In business since 1993. Member of IFAA.
Placements: nannies, au pairs and mother's helps.
Jobs in: UK only.
Nationalities placed: specialise in placing Spaniards.
Male applicants can sometimes be placed.
Minimum stay: 2 months. Summer stays are arranged.
Wages/pocket money: £35-40 per week.
Qualifications: must have childcare qualifications and experience.
Application procedure: overseas applicants interviewed by local agent. Process takes 3 weeks on average.
Other services: support from both agencies on all services.
Contact: Kim Montague, Proprietor.

CONTACTS
55 rue Nationale, 37000 Tours, France. Tel: 2-47 20 20 57. Fax: 2-47 20 68 92.
In business since 1968.
Placements: 600-800 au pairs and demi pairs.
Jobs in: France; also French girls sent to Europe and USA.
Nationalities placed: EU preferred.
Minimum stay: 6-12 months. Summer stays of 3 months.
Qualifications: ages 18-25 years; good knowledge of the language needed, and childcare experience preferred.
Other services: agency advises on schools and social activities.
Fees: 1,200FF for summer stays; 500FF for longer stays.
Contact: Lucien Mazik, Director.

COTSWOLD NANNIES
Wood Farm, Nailsworth, Stroud, Glos. GL6 0EU. Tel: 01453 835433. Fax: 01453 835403.
In business since 1983.
Placements: nannies, mother's helps and maternity nurses.
Jobs in: UK (mostly country areas).
Nationalities placed: no restrictions, provided work permit can be arranged.
Minimum stay: 3 weeks. Summer placements available.
Wages/pocket money: £90-£200 per week, depending on age, training and experience.
Qualifications: minimum age 19 years. Childcare experience and driving licence very useful.
Application procedure: minimum 3 references. Interviews when practical.
Other services: advice provided before and after placement.
Fees: nil.
Contact: Paula Pallestri.

DELANEY INTERNATIONAL
Middleton Lodge, Munstead Heath Road, Godalming, Surrey GU8 4AR. Tel: 01483 424343. Fax: 01483 420003.
In business since 1991. Member of FRES.
Placements: nannies, mother's helps, au pairs and demi pairs.
Jobs in: France, Germany, Italy, Spain and Australia.
Nationalities placed: any that are legal.
Minimum stay: 1-3 months in summer.
Wages/pocket money: £35-£40 per week for au pairs; £120-£150 for live-in nannies.
Qualifications: should have some knowledge of relevant language.
Application procedure: most girls are interviewed. Medical certificate required.
Fees: £20 (for English girls going overseas).
Contact: Marcia Delaney, Proprietor.

DIAL-AN-ANGEL PTY LTD
Head Office, Suites 20 & 21, Edgecliff Mews, 201 New South Head Road, Edgecliff, NSW 2027, Australia. Tel: 61-2-9362 4225. Fax: 61-2-9362 4001/9328 2654. E-mail: daangel@s054.aone.net.au. Also 11 offices throughout Australia (see Australia chapter for list of contact phone numbers).
In business since 1967. Member of NAPC and ACM (NSW).
Placements: au pairs, au pairs plus, nannies and mother's helps.
Jobs in: Australia, UK, USA and Canada.
Nationalities placed: Australian nannies sent abroad. Nannies with good English skills can be placed in Australia.
Males with rehabilitation experience are in demand.
Minimum stay: short and long term placements. Summer positions available (early December to late February).
Wages/pocket money: A$250-$500 per week.
Qualifications: minimum age 21. NNEB or equivalent certification needed plus childcare experience. Linguistic skills an advantage.
Application procedure: 2 work asnd 2 character references needed. Interviews essential. Placement can be almost immediate if references can be checed by phone or fax.
Other services: comprehensive insurance for staff Angels. Extensive agency back-up.
Fees: nil.
Contact: Dena Blackman, Managing Director.

DIAL-AN-ANGEL
4&5/21 Station Road, Indooroopilly, Brisbane, Queensland 4068, Australia. Tel: 61-7-3878 1077. Fax: 61-7-3878 2730.
In business since 1966.
Placements: au pairs, etc.
Jobs in: Australia.
Nationalities placed: those with working holiday visas (e.g. British, Canadian, American and Dutch.
Minimum stay: 3 months.
Wages/pocket money: A$150 per week for au pairs.
Qualifications: childcare experience needed. Driving licence essential.

Application procedure: interview required. 2-3 references which can be checked.
Fees: nil.
Contact: Nadine Broit, Owner/Manager.

DIAL-AN-ANGEL
78 Melbourne Street, North Adelaide, 5006 Australia.Tel: 61-8-8267-3700. Fax: 61-8-9267-3733.
In business since 1986.
Placements: 200 au pairs, nannies, mother's helps, demi pairs.
Jobs in: America and Europe.
Nationalities placed: those aged 18-26 to meet visa requirement.
Wages/pocket money: £150 for England, US$128 for America.
Qualifications: must speak the appropriate language for the country of placement.
Fees: average A$100.
Contact: Paul Evison, Owner.

DOGAN INTERNATIONAL ORGANIZATION
Sehitmuhtar Cad. 37/7, 80090 Taksim-Istanbul, Turkey. Tel: 212-235 1599/237 4291. Fax: 212-253 5706. Mobile: 0532-251 1716.
In business since 1988.
Placements: au pairs, nannies and mother's helps.
Jobs in: Turkey, England and Germany.
Nationalities placed: Turkish people sent abroad and Britons and Germans placed in Turkey.
Male applicants cannot be placed.
Qualifications: ages 18-40. Must be native speakers of English or German.
Application procedure: interested individuals should send 'dear family' letter, childcare and character references, photos, medical certificate and education certificates 1 or 2 months prior to their intended arrival.
Contact: Huseyin Dogan, Director.

DOMESTIC RECRUITMENTS INTERNATIONAL
'The Office', Unit 13, Anthony Road, Borehamwood, Herts. WD6 4NF. Tel: 0181-361 6662. Fax: 0181-207 6417.
In business since 1989. Incorporating the Canons Employment Agency, Charlotte Louise Au Pair Agency and the Busy Lizzie International Nanny Service. Member of FRES.
Placements: 300 nannies, au pairs, demi pairs and mother's helps.
Jobs in: UK mainly; occasionally Europe.
Nationalities placed: Europeans, in accordance with Home Office regulations; also Australians and others with working visas.
Male mother's help positions are occasionally available.
Minimum stay: 6 months. Summer stays for a minimum of 3 months.
Wages/pocket money: £35 per week for au pairs; £40-£50 for au pairs plus; £25 for demi-pairs, £80 for inexperienced mother's helps, £100 for those with experience; £120+ for nannies.
Application procedure: medical certificate needed, minimum 2 references and hand-written letter of introduction. Processing takes from 2 weeks.
Other services: advice on language schools given. Agency puts au pairs in touch with each other and tries to visit when problems arise.

Fees: nil; £40 or variable for overseas positions.
Contact: Michelle Bardon, Proprietor.

DUBLIN SCHOOL OF ENGLISH
10-12 Westmoreland Street, Dublin 2, Ireland. Tel: 1-677 3322. Fax: 1-679 5454/671 8451. E-mail: admin@dse.ie
In business since 1968.
Jobs in: Ireland plus France, Belgium, Germany, Spain and Italy.
Nationalities placed: no restrictions.
Minimum stay: 3 months. Summer placements available.
Wages/pocket money: IR£100 per month.
Qualifications: age limits 18-24 years. Basic knowledge of English required.
Other services: runs language classes which are compulsory for au pairs.
Fees: from IR£75 (for Irish girls going abroad).
Contact: Ernie Crossen, Principal and Margaret McAllister, Placement Officer.

EAST ANGLIAN NANNIES
140 Paddock Street, Soham, Ely, Cambs. CB7 5JA. Tel: 01353 624600. Fax: 01353 624670. Mobile: 0836 545270.
In business since August 1996.
Placements: nannies and mother's helps.
Jobs in: UK (East Anglian region).
Male positions are available.
Minimum stay: summer stays are available.
Wages/pocket money: £130-£160 per week net.
Qualifications: must have childcare experience.
Application procedure: placements generally take 10 days.
Fees: nil.
Contact: Sue Human, Proprietor.

EASY TRAVEL — GIOVANI IN EUROPA
Via Borgonuovo 9/b, 40125 Bologna, Italy. Tel/fax: 51-223983.
In business since 1994.
Placements: au pairs.
Jobs in: Italy for foreign girls, and Europe for Italians.
Minimum stay: 6-12 months. Summer stays of 2-3 months are sometimes available.
Wages/pocket money: 100,000 lire.
Qualifications: ages 17-30. Childcare experience preferred.
Contact: Milena Cerasi.

EDGWARE AU PAIR AGENCY
19 Manor Park Crescent, Edgware, Middlesex HA8 7NH. Tel: 0181-952 5522. Fax: 0181-951 5219/951 1005.
In business since 1963.
Placements: about 500-700 au pairs, nannies, mother's helps and demi pairs.
Jobs in: England (mainly the suburbs of London); also France, Spain, Italy, Germany, Austria, Switzerland, Belgium, Netherlands, Denmark, Greece, Hungary, USA and Australia.
Nationalities placed: Europeans in accordance with Home Office regulations.
Minimum stay: 6 months, preferably 1 year (1 year for USA). Summer stays: 3 months.

Wages/pocket money: £35-50 per week for au pairs; £10-15 for demi pairs.
Qualifications: minimum age 17/18 years; maximum 27 for UK, 26 for USA. Driving licence is a help, essential for USA. Childcare experience required for mother's helps and nannies; also for au pairs in the USA.
Application procedure: application form, CV if available, 2 references from teachers and/or previous employer, medical certificate and photos. Interview necessary for America (plus copy of driving licence and, if possible, life saving qualifications, first aid certificate or any evidence of childcare experience).
Other services: have 75 cooperating agents. Can place au pairs from country to country, e.g. Spain to Italy, France to Germany, etc. Agency advises on schools, helps with medical or dental problems and encourages meetings with other au pairs.
Fees: nil.
Contact: Lorraine Bass, Proprietor.

EF AU PAIR
Kensington Cloisters, 5 Kensington Church Street, London W8 4LD. Tel: 0171-795 6695. Fax: 0171-795 6635. E-mail: aupair.london@ef.com. Website: http://www.ef.com
In business since 1967 as an educational travel organisation. Member of IAPA.
Placements: au pairs.
Jobs in: USA.
Nationalities placed: Britons mainly by London office; EF has offices in 60 countries.
Male au pair positions are available.
Minimum stay: 12 months. Departures every month.
Wages/pocket money: $128 per week (due to rise) plus free return flights to family's address.
Qualifications: ages 18-26. Must have completed post GCSE studies, have a driving licence (or are learning to drive), have some childcare experience and no criminal record.
Application procedure: obtain brochure, apply for application package, attend Interview and Information Day in one of 15 cities in the United Kingdom. Suggested application deadline is at least 4 months prior to departure. 2 character and 2 work-related references needed.
Other services: free medical insurance. 4 day training course in New York. $500 given towards studies. 24 hour toll-free number to US office. EF Au Pair Handbook and Newsletter given out. Monthly meetings with other au pairs in area.
Fees: once placement is agreed, au pair pays £40 plus £350 refundable deposit.

EIL
287 Worcester Road, Malvern, Worcs. WR14 1AB. Tel: 01684 562577. Fax: 01684 562212. Brochure line: 0345 626984.
AuPair Homestay USA programme since 1986.
Placements: 300+ au pairs.
Jobs in: USA only.
Nationalities placed: British.
Males can be placed, though only if they have special childcare experience.
Minimum stay: 12 months.

Wages/pocket money: $128 per week plus maximum $500 towards educational studies. Au pairs also get 2 weeks paid holiday.
Qualifications: age limits 18-26 years. Childcare experience required. Must be non-smokers, English-speaking and have driving licence.
Application procedure: candidates submit detailed application dossier including 3 references and attend interview. Interviews last up to 2 hours. Choice of region and chance to select host family. When matched, family sends detailed information and photos. Telephone contact with family and one-day orientation with other programme participants arranged just prior to departure. Medical examination must be arranged at au pair's expense.
Other services: help with obtaining J-1 visa. Intensive 4-day orientation on arrival. Back-up provided by AuPair Homestay in US (Suite 750, 1015 15th St NW, Washington, DC 20005; 202-408-5380), plus network of local programme co-ordinators who meet au pairs and families once a month. Toll-free emergency phone number available. Free medical and accident insurance provided.
Fees: £350 refundable training fee.
Contact: Mr. Andrew Macleod.
Contact (in US): Program Director.

USA

Aupair Homestay offers AuPairs and nannies who drive and are between 18-26 – 1 legal year in the USA. As well as our 'Bring a friend' opportunity, there is a choice of region within the US – chance to select your own host family – Cash back incentive for qualified nannies – Free calls home each month – Toll free phone for emergencies – discounted travel passes as well as return air ticket – 4 days training on arrival in the US – $128+ per week pocket money – $500 allowance for study – Legal year in the USA – J1 visa – fully comprehensive insurance – fulltime local co-ordinator – constant programme support – monthly departures of UK – monthly get togethers in the USA – 2 weeks holiday allowance – 13th month visa concession to travel within the US.

Call for brochure on **0345 626984** *or write to*
EIL, 287 Worcester Road, Malvern WR14 1AB

ELIZABETH ELDER RECRUITMENT
Emberton House, 26 Shakespeare Road, Bedford MK40 2ED. Tel: 01234 352688. Fax: 01234 351070.
In business since 1984. Member of FRES.
Placements: nannies, au pairs, au pairs plus and mother's helps.
Jobs in: UK, Europe, USA and Australia (Work & Travel Programme).
Nationalities placed: Europeans in accordance with Home Office regulations.
Minimum stay: from 3 months in Europe (longer preferred). One year for USA.
Wages/pocket money: normally equivalent of £35-£40 per week, £36-£55 for au pairs plus. Nannies earn £150+ net per week.
Qualifications: minimum age 17 years for au pairs in Europe, 20 for nannies.
Other services: agency tries to help au pairs and nannies to meet others in the area.
Fees: £40 for au pairs; nil for nannies.
Contact: Elizabeth Elder, Proprietor.

ENGLISH-ITALIAN AGENCY
69 Woodside, Wimbledon, London SW19 7AP. Tel: 0181-946 5728.
In business since 1976.
Placements: nannies, au pairs, mother's helps, governesses and housekeepers.
Jobs in: Italy and worldwide.
Nationalities placed: all.
Minimum stay: 6-12 months from September. Summer stays: 1-3 months.
Wages/pocket money: 400,000 lire per month for au pairs.
Qualifications: minimum age 18. Childcare experience essential for nannies and mother's helps, babysitting for au pairs.
Application procedure: interviews not essential. Minimum 2 references, one related to childcare; also medical certificate, two passport-type (Polaroid) photos and s.a.e. Cooperates with TEA (The English Agency) in Turin — see entry.
Other services: agency puts nannies in touch with others in vicinity. Detailed job descriptions sent.
Fees: nil in UK; applicants from abroad pay 150,000 lire for placement in UK.
Contact: Agnes Coburn, Director; in Italy: Elaine Coburn, Director.

ENGLISH SOLUTIONS
Premier House, 11 Marlborough Place, Brighton BN1 1UB. Tel: 01273 608311. Fax: 01273 672288.
In business since 1995.
Placements: 150 au pairs.
Jobs in: Italy and England.
Male applicants cannot be placed.
Minimum stay: 3 months in the summer.
Wages/pocket money: £35-£50 per week.
Application procedure: interview not required. 2 references needed. Applications processed in 3-4 weeks.
Other services: support in England given by Italian-speaking representative. Wide range of language classes available in UK.
Fees: £50 (£35 cancellation fee).
Contact: Marco Piras, Proprietor.

EURO EMPLOYMENT CENTRE
14 Chadderton Drive, Bury, Lancashire BL9 8NL. Tel: 0161-796 8399. Fax: 0161-796 2249.
In business since 1979.
Placements: about 400 au pairs and mother's helps.
Jobs in: England, Germany, Austria, Switzerland, France, Italy, Spain, Greece and Israel.
Nationalities placed: girls from EU countries preferred.
Males are very rarely placed; applicants must have a good command of English.
Minimum stay: 1-3 months during summer.
Qualifications: age limits 17-27 years. Interest in children sufficient.
Application procedure: references with regard to childcare experience or character. Time taken to process application usually by return of post.
Other services: agency prepares written contract which includes 2 week trial period. All applicants are looked after by one of agency's 40 cooperating

agents, and are offered special insurance policy which provides £10,000 of health insurance and £200 of travel insurance for £12 a month.
Fees: £30 if going abroad.
Contact: Mrs. H. Verby.

EURO PAIR AGENCY
28 Derwent Avenue, Pinner, Middlesex HA5 4QJ. Tel: 0181-421 2100. Fax: 0181-428 6416. E-mail: christiane@europeanagy.demon.co.uk
In business since 1985.
Placements: 500 au pairs in UK and EU.
Jobs in: France, Spain, Italy and Germany, plus UK for European applicants.
Nationalities placed: Britons sent abroad and Europeans in accordance with Home Office regulations.
Minimum stay: 9-10 months from September; or 9 weeks (July-August).
Wages/pocket money: £40 per week in Britain; equivalent or more for working in EU countries.
Qualifications: ages 18-27 with basic skill in a foreign language. Must like children.
Application procedure: send SAE for application form 2 months in advance.
Fees: £40.
Contact: Mrs. Christiane Burt or Miss Nazlie Chan.

EURO PAIR SERVICES
13 rue Vavin, 75006 Paris, France. Tel: 1-43 29 80 01. Fax: 1-43 29 80 37.
In business since 1986.
Placements: 300 nannies, au pairs and mother's helps.
Jobs in: France; also England, Scotland, Ireland, Germany, Spain, Italy, Greece, Austria, Canada and the USA.
Nationalities placed: EU nationals, Eastern Europeans, South Africans, Canadians, etc.
Minimum stay: 6 months. Summer stays: 2-3 months.
Wages/pocket money: 1,600FF for au pairs in Paris (plus monthly transport ticket); 4,000FF for nannies.
Qualifications: childcare experience and some knowledge of language needed.
Other services: au pairs in Paris put in touch with each other. Back-up services from partner agents in south of France, Lyon, Brittany, the Southwest, etc. Advice on language courses given.
Fees: 350FF.
Contact: Mme. Davey.

EUROPEAN AU PAIR AGENCY
89 Valence Road, Lewes, East Sussex BN7 1SJ. Tel/fax: 01273 474738.
In business since 1990.
Placements: au pairs and mother's helps.
Jobs in: UK, France and Italy.
Nationalities placed: Europeans, according to Home Office list; specialise in Czech and Slovak applicants.
Minimum stay: 6 months. Summer stays 2-3 months.
Wages/pocket money: £35-£40 per week for au pairs; £50-£60 for mother's helps.

Qualifications: ages 18-27.
Application procedure: placement takes 2-4 weeks. Literature available in Czech and Slovak languages.
Other services: advice on language schools in Brighton area.
Fees: £35.
Contact: Mrs. Alena Stone, Proprietor.

EUROPEAN AU PAIRS — incorporated into Au Pairs of Surrey.

EUROPEAN CONNECTIONS
25 Eastgate House, High St, Guildford, Surrey GU1 3BY. Tel/fax: 01483 574035.
In business since 1991.
Placements: au pairs, nannies and mother's helps.
Jobs in: Italy only.
Male applicants can seldom be placed.
Minimum stay: 6 months. Summer stays are available.
Wages/pocket money: £250-£750/800 per month.
Qualifications: must have childcare experience and basic knowledge of Italian.
Application procedure: placement process normally takes 7-10 days.
Other services: cooperating agents in Italy help locate language schools and solve problems with the families.
Fees: £40.
Contact: Sabrina Caserta, Owner.

EURO PRACTICA e.V.
Hindenburgstrasse 8, PF 10 11 32, 45011 Essen, Germany. Tel: 201-82 05 20. Fax: 201-820 52 52.
In business since 1989. Member of AWO.
Placements: 500 au pairs and demi pairs.
Jobs in: Germany, Europe and USA.
Male au pair positions are available in some countries.
Minimum stay: 6 months. Summer stays (June-September) are available.
Wages/pocket money: DM100 per week.
Qualifications: minimum age 18. Basic knowledge of language required.
Application procedure: application processing time normally 8 weeks.
Other services: au pairs from outside EU are insured by the family.
Fees: nil for incoming au pairs; DM300 for outgoing (covers one year's service).
Contact: Mr. John A. Rainer, Programme Manager.

EUROYOUTH
301 Westborough Road, Westcliff, Southend-on-Sea, Essex. Tel: 01702 341434. Fax: 01702 330104.
In business since 1961.
Placements: about 300 au pairs, demi pairs and mother's helps.
Jobs in: Great Britain only.
Nationalities placed: Europeans in accordance with Home Office regulations.
Minimum stay: 6 months, sometimes shorter. Summer stays possible for those available for 10 weeks starting not later than the middle of May.
Wages/pocket money: varies from area to area, outside London about £35-£40 per week.

Qualifications: age limits 18-27 years. Driving licence and good knowledge of English are assets. Some experience with children preferred.
Application procedure: 2 references, a medical certificate and photographs.
Fees: nil.
Contact: Mrs. Rosa Hancock, Principal.

EXIS ApS
Rebslagergade 3, PO Box 291, 6400 Sonderborg, Denmark. Tel: +45 74 42 97 49. Fax: +45 74 42 97 47. E-mail: exis@po.ia.dk
In business since 1982. Member of IAPA.
Placements: au pairs, au pairs plus and mother's helps.
Jobs in: Denmark; Danish young people placed worldwide (Argentina, Australia, Belgium, Canada, England and Scotland, Finland, France, Germany, Greece, Hungary, Iceland, Ireland, Italy, Luxembourg, Netherlands, Norway, Portugal, South Africa, Spain, Sweden, Switzerland and USA).
Nationalities placed: Europeans in Scandinavia (with knowledge of English); Danes sent abroad.
Wages/pocket money: minimum 550 kroner per week plus free Danish language course and health insurance. 600 kroner for au pairs plus (35 hours a week) and 600-700 kroner for mother's helps (40 hours a week). One week's paid holiday given after six months.
Qualifications: minimum age 18.
Application procedure: 2 written references (in English or German), medical certificate and photo-collage needed.
Fees: nil for applicants for Denmark.
Contact: Lone Villadsen, Coordinator.

EXPERIMENT IN INTERNATIONAL LIVING — see EIL.

FAMILY FIRST INTERNATITONAL
Piccards Farmhouse, Sandy Lane, Guildford, Surrey GU3 1HD. Tel/fax: 01483 301729.
In business since 1991.
Placements: nannies and mother's helps.
Jobs in: UK, plus a few in France.
Nationalities placed: specialise in placing Australians, but others can be placed also.
Male applicants can rarely be placed.
Minimum stay: 6-24 months. Summer stays of 2-3 months can be made.
Wages/pocket money: £100-£150 per week for mother's helps; £120-£200 for nannies (in London).
Qualifications: ages 18-35. Must have impeccable references, medical certificate and solid childcare experience.
Application procedure: all applicants are interviewed, references are checked. Police certificate required by foreign nationals. All applicants must submit medical certificate, photos, 2 references and life story. If within the UK, interviews are essential; telephone and letter contact otherwise. Applications processed within one week.
Other services: maintain contact and offer advice.
Fees: nil.
Contact: Mrs. Angela Mayer and Mrs. Diana Chadwick, Partners.

AU-PAIRS, NANNIES & MOTHERS' HELPS
★ 18 - 27?
★ Experience with children?
★ Learning a European Language?
★ Jobs in UK and Europe

For advice and information, call
0181 874 1000 and 01962 855799

Head office: 12 Southgate Street, Winchester, SO23 9EF — FRES & IAPA Member
e-mail: info@family-match.co.uk   http://www.family-match.co.uk

FAMILY MATCH LTD
12 Southgate St, Winchester SO23 9EF. Tel: 01962 855799 and 0181-874 1000. Fax: 01962 840246. E-mail: info@family-match.co.uk
In business since 1993. Member of FRES and IAPA.
Placements: 350 au pairs, and 150-200 nannies, mother's helps and maternity nurses.
Jobs in: France, Spain, Germany, Austria, Italy and Belgium.
Nationalities placed: all that are legal.
Male applicants can occasionally be placed.
Minimum stay: 3 months in summer.
Wages/pocket money: £35-£40 per week for au pairs; £100-£200 for nannies.
Qualifications: minimum age 17. Reasonable English and some experience of childcare needed.
Application procedure: au pairs are interviewed when possible and references are checked. Au pair applications can be processed within a week or two. All nannies are interviewed and references checked before careful match is made.
Other services: Au Pair Club, excursions organised and first aid course offered.
Fees: £40 for au pairs; no charge for nanny placements.
Contact: Jenny Warner, Director.

FIOLA AGENCY
89 Fulford Grove, Watford, Herts. WD1 6QJ. Tel: 0181-428 5883. Fax: 0181-428 5883.
In business since 1962.
Placements: au pairs and demi pairs.
Jobs in: England only.
Minimum stay: 2 months in summer.
Wages/pocket money: £35 per week.
Qualifications: some English normally required.
Other services: all families organise local English course.
Fees: nil.
Contact: Judi Bayly, Owner.

FRANCE AU PAIR
Sud Ouest 'Au Pair', B.P. 29, 6 allée des Saules, 17420 Saint-Palais-sur-Mer, France. Tel: 5-46 23 99 88. Fax: 5-46 38 75 11.
In business since 1996. Member of CIDJ (Centre d'Information et de Documentation Jeunesse).
Placements: au pairs, demi pairs and au pairs plus.
Jobs in: France, also UK, Ireland, Germany, Italy, Spain, Greece, Canada and USA for French applicants.
Nationalities placed: Europeans in accordance with immigration regulations. Male applicants can occasionally be placed.
Minimum stay: 6 months. Summer stays are available.
Wages/pocket money: 1,600FF per month.
Qualifications: ages 18-28. Childcare experience and basic knowledge of target language needed. Driving licence useful.
Application procedure: 2 babysitting references required.
Other services: agency puts au pairs in touch with other au pairs via its 21 agents abroad. Asks families to arrange local language classes.
Fees: £40 upon acceptance.
Contact: Dany Chambard de Monti, Manager.

FREUNDINNEN JUNGER MADCHEN (FJM)
Placement Office, Zähringerstrasse 36, 8001 Zürich, Switzerland. Tel: 1-252 38 40. Fax: 1-261 18 07. See entry for Amies de la Jeune Fille for au pair placement in French-speaking cantons.
Office hours: mornings Tuesday to Friday.
In operation (on a non-profit basis) since 1887.
Placements: about 200 au pairs.
Jobs in: Switzerland. Swiss applicants can be placed in UK, France, Italy, Spain and Canada.
Nationalities placed: Western Europeans, Americans and Canadians.
Minimum stay: 1 year. Maximum stay 18 months.
Wages/pocket money: varies among cantons. In Zürich it is SFr600-700 per month, for working 30 h.p.w. 4 weeks paid holiday (5 weeks for au pairs under 20).
Qualifications: age limits 17-29 years. Should have some knowledge of a Swiss language, usually German. Childcare experience needed for some families.
Other services: back-up service plus meeting held annually for all au pairs.
Fees: SFr55 registration fee, plus SFr120 placement fee.
Contact: Frau Ursula Kappeler, Manager/Director.

GALENTINA'S EUROPEAN CHILDCARE CONSULTANCY
PO Box 51181, Kifissia, Athens, GR-145 10, Greece. Tel/fax: 1-808 1005.
E-mail: mskiniti@groovy.gr
In business since 1990.
Placements: 380 nannies, au pairs, mother's helps, maternity nurses and domestic couples.
Jobs in: Greece. Foreign agents in most European countries including Cyprus, Scandinavia and Portugal. Also Canada, USA and Australia.
Nationalities placed: EU nationals, Canadians, Americans, Australians and South Africans.
Minimum stay: 12-18 months preferred. Summer stays: 12th June-11th September preferred; 1, 2 and 3 month stays are possible.
Wages/pocket money: 90,000-130,000 drachmas per month for full-time au

pairs; 140,000-160,000 drachmas for mother's helps; 180,000-250,000+ drachmas for nannies. Families pay return airfare to nannies who complete contract and also medical insurance.
Qualifications: minimum age 20 years. Ability to swim is important.
Application procedure: in depth 10 page family biography and questionnaire. Letter of introduction written by prospective au pair accounts for two-thirds of decision.
Other services: 3 hour orientation given to new arrivals in Greece. Introductions arranged with other au pairs. Those who want to learn Greek can be referred to reasonably priced courses. 24 hour agency support and counselling. Airport pick-up for all candidates.
Fees: nil for incoming. 100,000 drachmas for outgoing.
Contact: Maritsa Skinitis, Owner.

GERMAN CATHOLIC SOCIAL CENTRE
Lioba House, 40 Exeter Road, London NW2 4SB. Tel: 0181-452 8566. Fax: 0181-452 4114.
In operation since 1952; as an agency/charity since 1976. The UK branch of In Via (see entry).
Placements: over 400 au pairs.
Jobs in: England mainly but also Germany and France.
Nationalities placed: German-speaking nationals preferred.
Minimum stay: 6 months; stays beginning August/September should be for 9 months. Summer stays are possible.
Wages/pocket money: £45 per week.
Qualifications: age limits 18-27 years. Childcare experience, basic knowledge of housework and basic knowledge of the language of the host country required.
Application procedure: applicants arrange placement by correspondence (including questionnaire, curriculum vitae, 2 references and health certificate). After arrival in Britain, they visit the host family (who has enrolled personally with the agency beforehand).
Other services: agency organises social activities, sends out newsletters in German with calendar of events in London, introduces au pairs to one another, advises on language courses, etc. Lioba House operates as a hostel.
Fees: nil.
Contact: Adelheid von Oy.

G.I.C. AU PAIRS
Pintor Sorolla Apart. 1080, 46901 Monte Vedat, Valencia, Spain. Tel: 6-156 7216. Tel/fax: 6-156 5837. E-mail: gic@redestb.es
In business since 1991. Member of IAPA.
Placements: 400 au pairs.
Jobs in: Spain; Europe and USA for Spanish au pairs. Male applicants can sometimes be placed.
Minimum stay: 1 month in summer for au pairs in Spain, 6 months from January, July or September. 6 months for Spaniards in Europe, 12 months in USA.
Wages/pocket money: 6,000-7,000 pesetas per week.
Qualifications: should have some childcare experience e.g. babysitting. Must be non-smoker.
Application procedure: if foreign applicants apply directly to agency, must submit an interview report as well as full application form. Otherwise all

documents submitted by partner agency, e.g. in UK: Ms. Sandrine Picquart, Au Pair International, 144 Cromwell Road, London SW7 4EF; 0171-370 3798/fax: 0171-370 4718. Average processing time is 2-3 months. Applicants should supply fax number to speed up exchange of information. Agency receives phone calls between 10am and 1pm.
Other services: can arrange ISIS insurance policy. Welcome packet sent on arrival with information on language classes. Problems can be discussed at regular gatherings at university coffee shop in Valencia.
Fees: nil to foreign applicants. 30,000 pesetas to Spanish applicants, which covers up to three placements in different countries.
Contact: Pilar Garreta de Nombela-Cesari, Director.

GIRLS ABOUT TOWN AU PAIR AGENCY
15 Maxim Road, Grange Park, London N21 1EY. Tel: 0181-364 0034. Fax: 0181-364 0354.
In business since 1978.
Placements: au pairs, demi pairs and mother's helps.
Jobs in: England, France, Spain, Italy and Netherlands.
Nationalities placed: Europeans in accordance with Home Office regulations.
Minimum stay: 6 months.
Wages/pocket money: £25 for demi pairs, £35-£40 for au pairs, £45-£50 for au pairs plus.
Qualifications: age limits 18-27 years. Childcare experience useful.
Application procedure: applicants fill in usual form and must supply 2 references, a medical certificate, 4 photographs and a letter stating why they want to come to England. Once details are received a suitable family will be found.
Fees: £40 if going abroad.
Contact: Barbara Feller.

Global Au Pairs and Nannies
Need Help? Need an Au Pair Nanny or Mother's help? Why not contact Global Au Pairs ?
0181-650 4860
A Division of
Paymaster Systems Limited
St Brides House,
32 High Street,
Beckenham, Kent BR3 1AY

Au Pairs available immediately throughout London and Southern England

GLOBAL AU PAIRS & NANNIES
St. Brides House, 32 High St, Beckenham, Kent BR3 1AY. Tel: 0181-650 4860. Fax: 0181-658 4020. E-mail: aupairs@dial.pipex.com. Web-site: http://www.au-pairs.co.uk
In business since 1986 (incorporating Swan Au Pairs, Au Pair Aide and Aaron Employment Agency). Member of FRES.

Placements: 4,000 au pairs, nannies and mother's helps.
Jobs in: UK, mainly London and Southeast England.
Nationalities placed: all that are legal.
A few male applicants can be placed.
Minimum stay: 3 months. Summer stays can be arranged via overseas agents.
Wages/pocket money: £40 per week.
Qualifications: minimum age 18. Some childcare experience for au pairs; experience essential for nannies/mother's helps.
Application procedure: medical certificate and 2 references needed. Nannies/mother's helps are interviewed where possible and all references checked. Au pairs from Europe normally placed within a week.
Other services: welcome packs for all au pairs including names and addresses of other au pairs in area. Regular coach trips organised.
Fees: nil.

GLOGOVIC d.o.o.
Nova Cesta 86, 10000 Zagreb, Croatia. Tel/fax: 1-327 664.
In business since 1994.
Placements: au pairs and au pairs plus.
Jobs in: UK (especially Home Counties); Spain (around Madrid), Italy (northern), France and Germany.
Nationalities placed: mainly Croatian, Bosnian and Slovenian.
Male applicants can rarely be placed.
Minimum stay: 3 months in summer. Early application needed for summer placements.
Wages/pocket money: from £40 per week in UK, DM90 in Germany, 90,000 lire in Italy.
Qualifications: ages 17-30 (17-27 for England). Must like children and have some knowledge of English (or a very keen desire to learn it).
Application procedure: applicants are interviewed in Zagreb if possible. Placement takes anything from a week.
Other services: au pairs given personal support and attention while collecting necessary documents. In case of a mismatch, au pair will be introduced to another family. Agency maintains contact with au pairs' parents if girl changes family. Contact numbers of other au pairs in area given. Advice on language classes available.
Fees: 500 kunas (circa £50).
Contact: Jasminka Glogovic (Director) and Martina Skaric (Assistant).

GLOGOVICH AU-PAIR AGENCY
Gransden Cottage, Tydcombe Road, Upper Warlingham, Surrey CR6 9LU. Tel/fax: 01883 624662. Tel: 01883 624842. Mobile: 0956 147 308.
In business since 1995.
Placements: au pairs and au pairs plus.
Jobs in: UK (especially Home Counties); plus British au pairs sent to Spain (Madrid).
Nationalities placed: specialise in placing Croatian au pairs but all nationalities.
Male applicants cannot be placed.
Minimum stay: 3 months. Summer stays are available if candidates speak good English, have good references and apply early (by April/May).
Wages/pocket money: £45 per week for au pairs working 25 hours; £50-£55 for au pairs plus working 35 or 40 hours.

Qualifications: minimum age 17. Must like children and want to learn English.
Application procedure: all documents can be faxed directly. Interested host family will then phone candidate and, if agreed, au pair can travel 7-14 days later.
Other services: telephone numbers of other au pairs in vicinity given. Advice on language classes available.
Fees: nil.
Contact: Mrs. Laura Rainbow, Owner.

GOELANGUES
33 rue de Trévise, 75009 Paris, France. Tel: 1-45 23 39 39. Fax: 1-45 23 39 23. E-mail: goelangues@aol.com
In business since 1982. Member of IAPA and ESS.
Placements: au pairs and demi pairs.
Jobs in: France; also England, Ireland, Germany, Spain, Italy and USA.
Male applicants can sometimes be placed in England.
Minimum stay: 6 months during academic year, 2 months in summer.
Wages/pocket money: 1,700FF per month in France; £35 per week in England, $128.25 in USA.
Qualifications: ages 18-27. Childcare experience needed and some knowledge of the language.
Other services: help given in finding a travel agency and language classes; advice given on insurance.
Fees: nil for foreign au pairs in France; French au pairs to Europe pay 920FF, to USA free.
Contact: Danielle Dumas, Director.

GOOD MORNING EUROPE
38 rue Traversière, 75012 Paris, France. Tel: 1-44 87 01 22. Fax: 1-44 87 01 42.
In business since 1992. Member of IAPA (via affiliation with Au Pair in America).
Placements: 180 au pairs, au pairs plus, demi pairs, mother's helps and nannies.
Jobs in: France; also Spain, UK, Italy, Germany and USA.
Nationalities placed: EU nationals.
Male au pairs can be placed but special requirements apply (i.e. good language skills, 4 childcare references, minimum stay 8 months).
Minimum stay: 6 months. Summer stays are available (May to end of September).
Wages/pocket money: 400FF per week for au pairs (plus transport pass); 4,000FF per month for mother's helps; 6,000FF per month for nannies.
Qualifications: ages 18-26. Must provide 2 childcare references.
Application procedure: processing takes about 3 weeks.
Other services: in Paris, agency organises language classes and au pair club. Weekly meetings on Friday evenings. Support given in case of problems.
Fees: 250FF.
Contact: DeBeaucorps, Director's Assistant.

HELI GRANDJEAN PLACEMENTS AU PAIR
Chemin de Relion 1E, 1245 Collonge-Bellerive, Switzerland. Tel/fax: 22-752 38 23. E-mail: h.grandjean@bluewin.ch

In business since 1992.
Placements: 60-100 au pairs.
Jobs in: Switzerland (both French and German-speaking parts), France (around Geneva) and England for Swiss au pairs.
Nationalities placed: Western European, Canadian and American.
Male applicants can sometimes be placed.
Minimum stay: 1 year normally; 6 months from January to June. 5-10 summer placements lasting 3-4 months are available.
Wages/pocket money: SFr500-710 per month.
Qualifications: ages 17-30.
Application procedure: application form, reference from teacher and/or previous employer, photos and 'dear family' letter needed.
Other services: written agreement setting out duties is sent to au pairs before they leave home. Assistance/advice with work permit and insurance given. All au pairs are contacted by agent after first fortnight to make sure all is well. New family is found if arrangement is unsatisfactory. Agency provides list of addresses of other au pairs.
Fees: SFr30 registration fee plus SFr75 placement fee.
Contact: Heli Grandjean, Proprietor.

THE HELPING HAND EMPLOYMENT AGENCY
24 Stourvale Gardens, Chandlers Ford, Hants. SO53 3NE. Tel: 01703 254287. Fax: 01703 570441. E-mail: helphand@tcp.co.uk
In business since 1992.
Placements: 130 au pairs, au pairs plus, nannies and mother's helps.
Jobs in: UK, Spain, France, Germany, Sweden, Italy and Turkey.
Nationalities placed: all that are legal.
Very few male applicants can be placed.
Minimum stay: 6-24 months. Summer stays of 2-3 months are possible.
Wages/pocket money: from £35 per week for au pairs; £45 for au pairs plus; £70-£100 for mother's helps; £120-180 for nannies.
Qualifications: ages 17-27 for most countries. Knowledge of language and childcare experience are advantages.
Application procedure: medical certificate, photo, 2 references and letter to potential family must be submitted by au pairs. Nannies and mother's helps should send CV or ask for application form (s.a.e. appreciated). References are checked.
Other services: applicants put in touch with one another. Advice given on schools. Agency tries to find different family or temporary accommodation if insoluable problems arise.
Fees: £40 for placements outside UK.
Contact: Irena Poje-Oxenham, Proprietor.

HELPING HANDS AU PAIR & DOMESTIC AGENCY
39 Rutland Avenue, Thorpe Bay, Essex SS1 2XJ. Tel: 01702 602067.
In business since 1981.
Placements: au pairs, au pairs plus, demi pairs, demi pairs plus and mother's helps.
Jobs in: England, France, Switzerland, Spain, Italy, Belgium, Germany, Austria and Denmark.
Nationalities placed: Europeans in accordance with Home Office regulations, and Canadians, Australians and New Zealanders with permission to work.
Minimum stay: 6 months. No summer stays.

Wages/pocket money: £25 for demi pairs; £30 for demi pairs plus; £35 + for au pairs; £40 + for au pairs plus; £60 + for mother's helps.
Qualifications: basic knowledge of relevant language as well as childcare experience necessary.
Application procedure: interviews where possible, otherwise 2 references required. Placements are normally immediate.
Fees: charged only once an English girl accepts overseas family.

HELPING HANDS LTD.
Heathcroft, Brockenhurst Road, Ascot, Berkshire SL5 9HA. Tel/fax: 01344 24144. Mobile: 0589 042485.
In business since 1995.
Placements: nannies, mother's helps, companions and housekeepers.
Jobs in: throughout UK.
Nationalities placed: all that are legal.
Male applicants can sometimes be placed.
Minimum stay: normally one year. No summer stays.
Wages/pocket money: £130-£200 per week for nannies; £120-£150 for mother's helps.
Qualifications: must have verifiable experience in field. Not too young.
Application procedure: interviews arranged by agent (or cooperating agents abroad). Candidates are personally vetted and references checked.
Other services: keeps tabs on all nannies, though families expected to offer support service.
Fees: nil.
Contact: Mary Kennedy, Director and Owner.

HILMA'S AU PAIR INTERMEDIARY
PO Box 91, (Street address: 5 Mohliver St), 75100 Rishon le Zion, Israel. Tel: 3-96 59 937. Fax: 3-95 00 577. Mobile: 052-684 906. E-mail: hilma§.netvision.net.il. Also have office in Jerusalem.
In business since 1982.
Placements: several hundred mother's helps (mainly).
Jobs in: Israel mainly, but have placed au pairs in the Netherlands, Germany, Australia, South Africa and Portugal.
Nationalities placed: all (especially Dutch and South African). Most demand for English-speaking and German-speaking candidates.
Male applicants can almost never be placed.
Minimum stay: 6 months.
Wages/pocket money: US$650 per month minimum, $900 maximum. Average is $700-$750. Good chance of rise during year. Family pays airfare home (within Europe) after a year.
Qualifications: ages 18-40. Must be willing to help the family, have a pleasant character and a smile in the morning. Should be prepared to undertake housework.
Application procedure: girls can usually be placed at short notice. Character reference needed, though childcare reference preferred. Medical check-up required including HIV-test.
Other services: strong support given to au pairs with regular contact with agent who sends out information about Israeli festivals and other relevant information. (She even reminds host families when it is their au pair's birthday). Up-to-date advice can be given to au pairs who want to study a language and detailed information is given about compulsory insurance.

Fees: nil. No penalty for asking to be placed with another family if problems arise.
Contact: Mrs. Hilma Shmoshkovitz, Director.

JILL HOLLIDAY
15 Boxgrove Avenue, Guildford, Surrey GU1 1XG. Tel: 01483 563447. Fax: 01483 570976.
In business since 1977.
Placements: 300-400 au pairs and demi pairs.
Jobs in: UK and France.
Nationalities placed: as permitted by Home Office.
Minimum stay: 6 months; September/October-June/July preferred. Summer stays available, minimum 2 months preferred.
Wages/pocket money: minimum £36 per week.
Qualifications: ages 17-27. Regular babysitting shows interest and liking for children.
Application procedure: direct applications encouraged; immediate placements always available.
Other services: contact continued with au pairs through letters, advice, help with courses, etc.
Fees: nil.
Contact: Jill Holliday.

HOMECARE PERSONNEL
39 Common Road, Chandlers Ford, Hampshire SO53 1HJ. Tel: 01703 273333.
In business since 1985.
Placements: every kind of domestic position (mainly residential) except au pairs. Agency specialises in care of the elderly.
Jobs available: UK mainly; Europe sometimes.
Nationalities placed: any except those for whom it is difficult to obtain work permits.
Male applicants can sometimes be placed.
Minimum stay: variable. Summer placements available.
Qualifications: driving licence is preferable, languages are a bonus. Impeccable references needed. Mother's helps and nannies should have childcare experience.
Application procedure: 2 references are required and checked, full details of background, training and job specification. All enquiries are dealt with on day of receipt. Interviews sometimes required by agency and invariably by families.
Fees: nil.
Contact: Miss Sheila Bladon.

HOME CONCERN
105 Leighton Gardens, London NW10 3PS. Tel/fax: 0181-968 6871.
In business since 1991.
Placements: au pairs, mother's helps and demi pairs.
Jobs in: Spain (all regions).
Nationalities placed: British mainly.
Male applicants can be placed with difficulty but are welcome to apply.
Minimum stay: summer placements are available.

Directory of Agencies 243

Wages/pocket money: equivalent of £35 per week.
Qualifications: minimum age 19. Must speak some Spanish. Knowledge of English is an advantage.
Application procedure: interviews are difficult since applicants are widely scattered. Must have solid references. Processing time normally 4-10 days after dossier submitted. Spanish agent is R.C.I. in Madrid (see entry).
Other services: advice given on language classes, etc.
Fees: £40 (£15 cancellation charge).
Contact: E. Cleary, Owner.

HOME FROM HOME AU PAIRS
Tel. 01844 208561
Walnut Orchard, Chearsley, Aylesbury. Bucks HP18 0DA   (Emp. Agy)

Cheerful and reliable girls required for UK and Europe, especially September for 10 months or more. Competent drivers and non-smokers preferred. Limited summer placements available (sae please)

HOME FROM HOME AU PAIR AGENCY
Walnut Orchard, Chearsley, Aylesbury, Bucks. HP18 0DA. Tel/fax: 01844 208561.
In business since 1977.
Placements: 350 au pairs per year.
Jobs in: throughout UK (especially Oxford area), France, Italy, Spain, Germany, Switzerland and Austria.
Nationalities placed: Europeans in accordance with Home Office regulations.
Minimum stay: 6 months minimum, school year preferred. Summer stays for minimum of 2 months.
Wages/pocket money: from £35 per week.
Qualifications: childcare experience usually required. Ages 18-27. Basic English required, sometimes driving licence. Positive attitude helpful.
Application procedure: 2 character references, medical certificate, photos and letter to host family required; interview is arranged when au pair and host are in the same country. Applications are processed immediately.
Other services: agency puts au pairs in touch with each other. General support given and advice on language courses.
Fees: nil for incoming au pairs; £40 if placed overseas.
Contact: Mrs. Carolyn Taylor, Proprietor.

HOMELIFE EMPLOYMENT AGENCY
Ty Rhosyn, Llangeitho, Tregaron, Ceredigion SY25 6TW. Tel: 01974 821347. Fax: 01974 821547. E-mail: HOMELIFEAG@aol.com. Web site: http://member.aolcom/HOMELIFEAG/homepage/file.html. Also Cardiff office: 4 Oakridge, Thornhill, Cardiff CF4 9BS. Tel/fax: 01222 752229. Branches due to open in London, Manchester and Birmingham areas.

In business since 1994. Member of ADM (Association of Domestic Management).
Placements: nannies, parent's helps, au pairs.
Jobs in: UK (especially London, Midlands and Wales), Europe (including Germany and Greece), and worldwide (including Israel). US programme interviewers.
Nationalities placed: all that are legal.
Male applicants with childcare experience can sometimes be placed.
Minimum stay: 6 months (1 year for USA). Some summer stays available.
Wages/pocket money: variable depending on applicant and country. £120-£250+ per week for nannies; £60-£100+ for mother's helps, £35-£60 for au pairs; $128.25 (unqualified) to $160 (qualified) for USA.
Qualifications: practical childcare experience and a love of children needed. Ages 18-27 for au pairs, no age limits for nannies. Non-smokers preferred. Driving licence advantageous (essential for USA). Nannies must be qualified or experienced.
Application procedure: at least 2 work/experience related references and qualifications, hand written introductory letter and (for overseas posts) medical certificate needed. Personal interviews are essential (only in exceptional circumstances will a telephone interview suffice). Immediate placements are available although applications are normally received at least 6 weeks before starting date.
Other services: agency can arrange contact with other au pairs and advise on language courses. Advice given on travel and insurance. 24 hour ansaphone.
Fees: nil for internal UK placements. Outgoing au pairs are charged £30 (except for USA), incoming £40.
Contact: Mrs. Karla Giles, Proprietor.

HUTCHINSON'S STAFF CONSULTANCY
33 Princes Gate Mews, Knightsbridge, London SW7 2RP. Tel: 0171-581 0010. Fax: 0171-581 1011.
In business since 1987.
Placements: 200+ professional nannies.
Jobs in: UK (London and country), Europe, Far East and Middle East.
Male positions are sometimes available.
Minimum stay: 1 year.
Wages/pocket money: from £160 net per week.

Qualifications: minimum 2 years live-in experience.
Application procedure: interviews held. All previous references are checked.
Fees: nil.
Contact: Mrs. Frances Hutchinson-Price, Proprietor.

HYDE PARK INTERNATIONAL
Permanent Division: 85 High St, Winchester, Hants. SO23 9AP. Tel: 01962 841234. Fax: 01962 867062. Temporary Division: 31 Huggins Place, London SW2 3UQ. Tel: 0181-561 1399.
In business since 1982.
Placements: nannies, nanny/housekeepers and maternity nurses.
Jobs in: Europe (France, Spain, Italy, Germany, Belgium, Scandinavia), Middle East, Turkey, America, etc.
Nationalities placed: all, provided they are experienced or qualified.
Male positions are rarely available, though agency is prepared to try.
Minimum stay: normally 1 year, though some temporary placements are available.
Wages/pocket money: £140-£250/350 depending on age and experience.
Qualifications: must have formal qualification or recent relevant experience. Driving licence almost always essential.
Application procedure: interview compulsory. References are checked. Nanny meets prospective family beforehand in most cases.
Other services: can arrange medical insurance and advise on supplementary policies.
Fees: nil.
Contact: Jennifer Harrison, Managing Director; Samantha Scott (Permanent) and Pamela Holmes (Temporary).

IANDA AU PAIR AGENCY (LONDON)
3 Greenacres Drive, Stanmore, Middx HA7 3QU
Tel: 0181 954 9900
Fax: 0181 954 5338

We are looking for girls who wish to be Au Pairs in England. We mainly have families all over London and surrounding areas and country wide. Families are carefully selected and as we have been in business for 15 years, we have many regular clients.

For a friendly and personal service contact **Suzanne Aarons**

IANDA AU PAIR AGENCY (LONDON)
3 Greenacres Drive, Stanmore, Middlesex HA7 3QU. Tel: 0181-954 9900. Fax: 0181-954 5338.
In business since 1982.
Placements: 170 au pairs, demi pairs and mother's helps.
Jobs in: UK.
Minimum stay: 6 months or longer during academic year. Minimum 3 months in the summer.

Wages/pocket money: from £35 per week for au pairs; £20 for demi pairs; £80 + for mother's helps.
Qualifications: must have some childcare experience and knowledge of language.
Application procedure: processing takes 1-4 weeks after all documents have been submitted.
Other services: advice on language schools given. Ongoing support provided.
Fees: nil.
Contact: Mrs. Suzanne Aarons, Proprietor.

INSTITUT D'ECHANGES FRANCO-EUROPEENS
11 Chemin de la Butte au Diable, 91570 Bièvres, France. Tel: 1-69 41 04 39. 9km south of Paris.
In business since 1958.
Placements: 600 au pairs and demi pairs.
Jobs in: UK, Ireland, Germany, Italy, Spain and Austria; not France.
Nationalities placed: EU nationals.
Male positions are available in some countries.
Minimum stay: 1/2 months in summer.
Qualifications: ages 18-24 years. Must have some knowledge of destination language.
Other services: complementary insurance policy available.
Fees: 320FF.
Contact: Mme. Lavergne, Director.

INTERCAMBIO 66
Fernández de Los Rios 80, 28015 Madrid, Spain. Tel: 1-549 33 68. Fax: 1-544 79 62. E-mail: EXPERIMENT-INTER66@MAD.SERVICOM.ES
In business since 1966.
Placements: au pairs and demi pairs.
Jobs in: USA, Ireland, England, Australia, Germany, France and Italy.
Nationalities placed: mostly Spanish.
Male applicants are occasionally placed.
Minimum stay: 6 months, or 3 months in summer.
Wages/pocket money: 7,000 pesetas per week.
Qualifications: minimum age 18. Must have knowledge of language and experience of childcare.
Application procedure: preferable for applications to arrive at least 6 weeks before proposed starting date. Childcare references compulsory and language certificate required.
Other services: can advise on insurance (which is compulsory).
Fees: 10,000 pesetas.
Contact: Pilar Mascaraque, Outbound Department Assistant.

INTERCLASS
c/ Bori i Fontestá, 14, 6° 4°, 08021 Barcelona, Spain. Tel: 93-414 29 21/414 29 81. Fax: 93-414 29 31.
In business since 1987.
Placements: au pairs, demi pairs and mother's helps. Also work study programmes, hotel and business training, workcamps, etc.
Jobs in: Spain; also England, Ireland, Austria, Belgium, France, Germany, USA, Australia and New Zealand.

Nationalities placed: European.
Male positions are not generally available.
Minimum stay: 6 months. Summer stays: 2-3 months.
Wages/pocket money: 6,000-7,000 pesetas per week for au pairs; 3,000-4,000 pesetas for demi pairs; 10,000 pesetas for mother's helps.
Application procedure: references from teachers and families needed.
Other services: can recommend language schools. Insurance can be arranged.
Fees: variable.
Contact: Fanny Tarré, Programme Director.

INTER EXCHANGE
161 Sixth Avenue, New York, NY 10013, USA. Tel: 212-924-0446. Fax: 212-924-0575. E-mail: interex@earthlink.net
In business since 1987.
Placements: 500 au pairs.
Jobs in: USA; also Americans sent to Europe (Austria, Finland, Netherlands, Italy, Norway and Spain).
Nationalities placed: Western Europeans in USA.
Male positions are available in Spain and the Netherlands.
Minimum stay: 12 months.
Wages/pocket money: $128 per week in USA.
Qualifications: childcare experience needed. Ages 18-25. Some knowledge of the language needed for Austria, Italy and Spain.
Application procedure: 6-12 weeks to process applications. One childcare reference must be included. Interviews carried out in Britain by UK agency Tinies International (see entry).
Other services: free round-trip flights, up to $500 for tuition fees and health insurance provided.
Fees: $500 returnable bond.
Contact: U. Christianson, Executive Director.

INTERMEDIATE
Via Bramante 13, 00153 Rome 13, Italy. Tel/fax: 6-57 47 444.
In business since 1990.
Placements: about 100 au pairs, au pairs plus, mother's helps and nannies.
Nationalities placed: mainly EU nationals.
Jobs in: Italy, and Europe for Italians (England, France, Germany and Netherlands).
Male au pairs can be placed.
Minimum stay: 6 months. Summer stays of minimum 2 months are available.
Qualifications: minimum age 18. Experience of childcare not essential.
Other services: Intermediate has its own language school in the central Aventino district of Rome and links with the Centre for Language and Culture in Naples as well.
Fees: 200,000 lire (150,000 lire for summer stay).
Contact: Eveline Hermans.

INTERNATIONAL AU PAIR INTERCAMBIO
P° de Gracia 86, 6°-7°, 08008 Barcelona, Spain. Tel: 93-215 48 95.
In business since 1973.
Placements: au pairs, au pairs plus, mother's helps and paying guests.

Jobs in: Spain; also other European countries.
Nationalities placed: all nationalities placed in Spain. Some male positions available.
Minimum stay: 6 months. Summer stays: 2-3 months.
Wages/pocket money: 27,000 pesetas per month.
Qualifications: a little childcare experience if possible. Age limits 18-35 years. Should speak basic Spanish or English for Spain.
Application procedure: for placements in Spain, 2 photos, 2 references (child-related, work/school) and medical certificate are needed. For other countries, all the above plus 4 photos and a handwritten curriculum vitae.
Other services: agency can advise on language courses.
Fees: nil for placements in Spain.
Contact: Michele Piguet(Manager) and Vicky Vicente (Au Pair Coordinator).

INTERNATIONAL CATHOLIC SOCIETY FOR GIRLS (ACISJF)
St. Patrick's International Centre, 24 Great Chapel Street, London W1V 3AF. Tel: 0171-734 2156/439 0116. Fax: 0171-287 6282. E-mail: info@stpatricks.org.uk
Office hours: 10am-4pm Monday-Friday (plus Sundays for visits).
In operation since 1929. English branch of the Association Catholique Internationale des Services de la Jeunesse Feminine with counterparts throughout Europe (e.g. In Via in Germany and Auslands Sozialdienst in Austria).
Placements: about 180 au pairs per year.
Jobs in: UK, France (mainly), also Germany, Austria, Spain and Belgium.
Nationalities placed: Europeans (in accordance with Home Office regulations).
Minimum stay: 9 months (September-June/July); sometimes 6 months (January-July). Summer stays are available in France.
Wages/pocket money: £40-£45 per week.
Qualifications: minimum age 17/18 years, though most families prefer 19+. Childcare experience required, driving licence an asset. Good basic knowledge of the language in question is essential.
Application procedure: 2 references (character and childcare experience) required, plus up-to-date medical certificate and interview if possible. Time to process application is about 2-3 weeks.
Other services: St. Patrick's is an international welfare organisation with about 800 members from 85 countries, providing a range of social activities which are publicised in a monthly leaflet. In London, ACISJF advises on state language schools and runs its own English language school.
Fees: nil for UK, £20 for abroad.
Contact: Sister Sheelah Clarke, Director of Social Welfare.

INTERNATIONAL NANNIES SERVICES & MOTHER'S LITTLE HELPER
59 Canterbury Road, Canterbury, VIC 3126, Australia. Tel: 3-9888 6066. Fax: 3-9888 6144.
In business since 1982. Member of AANA (Australian Association of Nanny Agencies).
Placements: nannies, mother's helps and limited number of au pairs.
Jobs in: Australia, England and America.
Male applicants can be placed if they are suitably qualified as nannies.
Minimum stay: 3 months. Summer stays are available.

Wages/pocket money: A$10-$13 per hour in Australia, or $260 per week live-in, $360 live-out.
Qualifications: minimum age 20 (19 for au pairs). Nannies must have 2 years childcare experience; au pairs must have extensive childcare experience.
Application procedure: initial screening by telephone. 6 page application form and 45-minute interview covering hypothetical situations. 3 childcare references and police clearance certificate needed. All nannies are given more informal second interview.
Other services: advice given to local candidates travelling to America or England. Professional development activities, e.g. first aid, self defence, cookery and interview dressing.
Fees: A$30 for Australia; A$100 for Au Pair in America; A$150-$300 for UK (discounts for nannies already working for agency).
Contact: Louise Dunham, Managing Director.

INTER-SEJOURS
179 rue de Courcelles, 75017 Paris, France. Tel: 1-47 63 06 81. Fax: 1-40 54 89 41.
Placements: 600 au pairs, demi pairs and au pairs plus per year.
Jobs in: France; plus UK, Ireland, Denmark, Germany, Austria, Spain, Italy and Canada.
Nationalities placed: EU nationals.
Minimum stay: 6 months, preferably a school year. Summer stays: 2 months minimum.
Wages/pocket money: from 1,600FF per month in France.
Qualifications: age limits 18-27 years. Childcare experience helpful.
Application procedure: questionnaire, 6 photos, medical certificate, 2 references (character, school) and an introductory letter are needed. Birth certificate must be translated into French and certified. The waiting period is usually 1-3 months, though sometimes families can be found within a fortnight.
Other services: agency can advise on language schools; au pairs must attend language classes in France.
Fees: 750FF.
Contact: Marie-Helene Pierrot, Director.

IN VIA
Katholische Mädchensozialarbeit, Deutscher Verband e.V., Ludwigstr. 36, D-79104 Freiburg, Germany. Tel: 761-200206. Fax: 761-200638.
In operation since 1905. Affiliated to international Catholic organisation ACISJF.
Placements: about 2,200 au pairs.
Jobs in: Germany; plus UK, Ireland, France, Italy, Spain, Belgium and Switzerland.
Nationalities placed: all.
Male positions are available.
Minimum stay: 6 months; 1 year preferred. Summer stays are not possible.
Wages/pocket money: DM400 per month.
Qualifications: childcare experience required. Age limits 18-25 years. Basic knowledge of language in question indispensable.
Application procedure: at least 1 reference is required; interviews if possible. Average time to process application is 3 months.
Other services: agency (which has 27 regional offices in Germany) has au pair

clubs in several cities in Germany, for example Munich, Stuttgart and Aachen. Host families assume responsibility for insurance.
Fees: nil.
Contact: Marianne Schmidle, Referee for au pair placements. Foreign branches of IN VIA are: German Catholic Social Centre (see entry) and Foyer Porta, 14 rue Pierre Demours, 75017 Paris, France (tel: 1-45 72 18 66).

IRCA INTERNATIONAL/SPRAKCENTER
Box 293, 291 23 Kristianstad, Sweden. Tel/fax: 44-12 22 63.
In business since 1979.
Placements: about 1,500 au pairs (plus a few housekeepers and nannies to some countries).
Jobs in: Sweden (very few); Scandinavian au pairs to USA, Canada, France, Switzerland, Austria, Italy, Spain and Mallorca, Netherlands, Belgium, UK and Ireland.
Nationalities placed: Western Europeans.
Male positions are available in some countries.
Minimum stay: 1 year in Sweden and occasional 3-month summer positions available.
Wages/pocket money: 2,000-2,5000 Swedish kroner per month for 25 hours a week plus babysitting.
Qualifications: babysitting experience sufficient for some jobs. Swedish language course compulsory in Sweden (for which family pays).
Application procedure: 3 photos, references and school certificates needed.
Other services: help given with visas and work permits if needed. 35 cooperating agents advise on social activities.
Fees: about £50.
Contact: Anitha Jacquemot, Manager.

IRISH NANNY SERVICES
81 Ailesbury Road, Ballsbridge, Dublin 4, Ireland. Tel: 1-269 3371. Fax: 1-269 8280. E-mail: AIRD@IOL.IE
In business since 1984.
Placements: 250 nannies and mother's helps.
Jobs in: Germany and Switzerland; also Ireland, UK, Italy and Belgium.
Nationalities placed: all that are legal.
Minimum stay: 1 year.
Wages/pocket money: £100+ per week.
Qualifications: childcare experience required. Should be non-smokers. Driving licence a distinct advantage.
Application procedure: interviews not required. Agency arranges contact between families and prospective nannies.
Fees: £50 payble after job has been assigned.
Contact: Jonathan Aird, Owner.

JANET WHITE AGENCY (CHILD AND FAMILY CARE)
67 Jackson Avenue, Leeds LS8 1NS. Tel: 0113 266 6507. Fax: 0113 268 3077.
In business since 1978, FRES member.
Placements: several hundred au pairs, nannies and mother's helps.
Jobs in: Canada (qualified experienced nannies only), USA ('Au Pair in America' Regional Organiser for Yorkshire, Lancashire and Greater Manchester) Europe and UK (especially the North of England).

Nationalities placed: British girls sent abroad; Europeans (in accordance with Home Office regulations) plus Australians, New Zealanders and Canadians with working holiday visas can be placed in the UK.
Minimum stay: from 6 months for au pairs, 1 year for nannies.
Wages/pocket money: £35-£45 per week for au pairs; £70-£100 for mother's helps; £120-£200 for nannies; $139 for Au Pair in America.
Qualifications: minimum age 18 years (Au Pair in America 18-26). Nannies need training and/or previous experience; au pairs and mother's helps must be confident with children and household tasks. Driving licence is a big advantage (essential for USA). Non-smoking almost essential.
Application procedure: appropriate form must be completed and references which can be checked supplied. Outbound applicants are interviewed, except au pairs in out-of-the-way places. Placement usually made within weeks (except Canada where it takes a few months).
Other services: advice on visas, travel arrangements, insurance and social introductions wherever possible.
Fees: nil for nannies. £40 plus VAT for au pairs placed through continental agency.
Contact: Janet White (BA, MECI), Principal.

JENNY'S AU PAIR AGENCY
27 Willows Avenue, Morden, Surrey SM4 5SG. Tel: 0181-687 2620. Fax: 0181-241 5542.
In business since 1994.
Placements: approximately 200 au pairs and commencing mother's helps, nannies 1997.
Jobs in: UK (London and suburbs).
Nationalities placed: in accordance with Home Office regulations.
Occasional male placements are available.
Minimum stay: 6+ months. Summer stays of 2-3 months are available.
Wages/pocket money: £40+ per week.
Qualifications: ages 18-27. Childcare experience and reasonable English preferred.
Application procedure: au pairs abroad apply through foreign agents; au pairs in the UK are interviewed.
Other services: regular coffee mornings for au pairs, to meet and exchange details.

Fees: nil.
Contact: Jenny Berrow, Proprietor.

JOB OPTIONS BUREAU
Tourist House, 40-41 Grand Parade, Cork, Ireland. Tel: 21-275369. Fax: 21-274829. Mobile: 087-641646.
In business since 1988. Founder member of IAPA.
Placements: au pairs and nannies.
Jobs in: throughout Ireland including Dublin area; also Austria, Belgium, France, Italy, Spain, England, Germany, Switzerland, USA and Canada.
Nationalities placed: EU nationals.
Very few male positions are available.
Minimum stay: 6-12 months. Summer stays: minimum 12 weeks.
Wages/pocket money: £40 per week for au pairs in Ireland.
Qualifications: minimum age 18. Practical childcare experience is essential and must be verified by referees.
Application procedure: must submit strip of passport photos, at least 2 references (which are checked) doctor's certificate and a copy of birth certificate. All outbound au pairs are interviewed in various locations around Ireland.
Other services: assistance given in preparing to travel, obtain insurance, etc. Foreign au pairs in Ireland are given orientation and chance to join training days and social events. 24 hour back-up support.
Fees: on request.
Contact: Kathy O'Dwyer, Owner/Manager.

JOHNSON'S AU PAIRS
211 Rectory Park Avenue, Northolt, Middlesex UB5 6SD. Tel/fax: 0181-845 6824.
In business since 1994.
Placements: au pairs, demi pairs and mother's helps.
Jobs in: Italy, Germany and England (London area).
Nationalities placed: all that are approved.
Male applicants can sometimes be placed if requested by family.
Minimum stay: 3 months. Summer stays are available.
Wages/pocket money: from £35 per week for au pairs.
Qualifications: ages 17-27. Some childcare experience needed.
Application procedure: personal interview carried out if applicant is in same country as family, otherwise telephone interview. Average processing time is 7-10 days.
Fees: vary with destination.
Contact: Gladys Johnson, Company Manager.

JOLAINE AGENCY
18 Escot Way, Barnet, Herts. EN5 3AN. Tel: 0181-449 1334. Fax: 0181-449 9183.
In business since 1975.
Placements: 500-800 au pairs, demi pairs, mother's helps and paying guests (groups and individuals).
Jobs in: UK, France, Italy, Spain, Germany, Austria, Greece and Belgium. Paying guest stays arranged in France, Belgium and Spain.
Nationalities placed: according to Home Office list.

Males can sometimes be placed.
Minimum stay: mostly long term stays. Summer, Easter and Christmas stays occasionally possible, though not as often as previously.
Wages/pocket money: from £35 per week for au pairs; £50 for au pairs plus; from £80 for mother's helps; £20 for demi plus (in UK only).
Qualifications: age limits 17-27 years. Some knowledge of destination language and childcare experience are needed in most cases.
Fees: £40 for placements abroad.
Contact: Mrs. Irene Rendlick, Principal.

JUST THE JOB (Nottingham) — incorporated in Mum's Army (see entry).

KENSINGTON NANNIES
49-53 Kensington High Street, London W8 5ED. Tel: 0171-937 2333. Fax: 0171-937 1027. E-mail: nannies@easynet.co.uk
In business since 1967. Member of FRES.
Placements: nannies and mother's helps (with minimum 2 years experience).
Jobs in: worldwide (except USA).
Male applicants with training and minimum 2 years experience can be placed.
Minimum stay: 1 year.
Wages/pocket money: varies according to experience.
Qualifications: minimum age 20. Must have perfect English. 2 years nannying experience.
Application procedure: personal interviews absolutely essential. 3 references are taken up. Placement takes 7-21 days depending on country requested.
Other services: insurance and travel can be arranged if client requests it.
Fees: nil.
Contact: Louise Taylor, Overseas Consultant.

KNIGHTSBRIDGE NANNIES LTD.
PO Box 7772, London SW6 2YN. Tel: 0171-610 9232. Fax: 0171-731 5792.
In business since 1958.
Placements: 1,000 nannies, mother's helps, cooks and housekeepers.
Jobs available: all over the world.
Nationalities placed: no restrictions, provided work permits can be obtained.
Minimum stay: variable.
Qualifications: one year live-in childcare experience and minimum age 20 required for all overseas posts. Minimum age 18 for UK.
Application procedure: interview with agency essential, with family whenever possible. All references are checked.
Fees: nil.
Contact: Julie Bremner, Director.

LANGTRAIN INTERNATIONAL
Torquay Road, Foxrock, Dublin 18, Ireland. Tel: 1-289 3876. Fax: 1-289 2586.
In business since 1961 (originally as Interlingua).
Placements: au pairs and nannies.
Jobs in: Ireland, UK, France, Germany, Spain, Italy, Belgium, Austria, Switzerland (both French and German parts), Denmark, Netherlands, Israel, USA, Canada and Australia.

Nationalities placed: all.
Minimum stay: 6 months in Europe including Ireland, 1 year in Canada. Summer stays: July-August or June-August.
Wages/pocket money: £45-£50 per week in Europe, from C$500 per month after deductions in Canada.
Qualifications: age limits 18-30 years (no upper age limit for Canada). Childcare experience essential, driving licence preferred for Canada. Knowledge of language necessary for France and Germany.
Application procedure: 2 recent references, 6 coloured passport photos, medical certificate, letter introducing yourself and $50 placement fee must be submitted.
Other services: network of agents will provide advice and assistance. Agents can also advise on language courses. Langtrain runs language classes for foreign au pairs in Dublin at a cost of £100 per term.
Contact: Mrs. Maura Gallagher, Director.

LANGUAGE CENTRE OF IRELAND
45 Kildare St, Dublin 2, Ireland. Tel: 1-671 6266. Fax: 1-671 6430. E-mail: langcntr@indigo.ie
In business since 1966.
Placements: 60/80 au pairs per year.
Jobs in: Ireland only (Dublin area).
Nationalities placed: Europeans only.
Minimum stay: 6 months. Summer stays: 3 months.
Wages/pocket money: IR£40-£45 per week.
Qualifications: some childcare experience needed. Age limits 18-23 years. Basic knowledge of the language and experience of housework needed.
Other services: all families are interviewed by agency. Social activities for au pairs, such as excursions and discos. All applicants are obliged to attend courses at the Language Centre twice a week for at least 12 weeks and are encouraged to take public examinations in EFL, Pitman, First Certificate, Advanced or Proficiency. Classes held Tuesday and Thursday 2.30-5pm year round or 7.30-10pm from late September to mid-June. The current fee is IR£231.
Fees: IR£50 plus registration fee of IR£35.
Contact: Elizabeth Murphy, Au Pair Placement Officer.

LEARN & TRAVEL (Giovani nel Mondo)
Via Borgonuovo 3/B, 40125 Bologna, Italy. Tel: 51-223983. Fax: 51-236394. E-mail: assltgm@iperbole.bologna.it
In business since 1994. Applying for membership in IAPA.
Placements: 150 au pairs, demi pairs and nannies.
Jobs in: Italy; also England, Ireland, Germany, France, Spain, Switzerland and USA.
Male au pair positions are sometimes available.
Minimum stay: 3 months. Summer stays are available.
Wages/pocket money: 100,000-120,000 lire.
Qualifications: ages 18-30. Childcare experience is needed. Driving licence a help; non-smokers preferred.
Application procedure: minimum 2 references needed, one related to childcare plus medical certificate, 2 photos and 'dear family' letter.
Fees: nil for incoming; 400,000-480,000 lire for outgoing.
Contact: Milena Cerasi (President) and Valeria Zacchini (Vice President).

LINDEN BUREAU — incorporated into Au Pairs of Surrey (see entry).

THE LINGUAVIVA CENTRE
45 Lower Leeson Street, Dublin 2, Ireland. Tel: 1-678 9384/661 2106. Fax: 1-676 5687. E-mail: enquiries@Linguaviva.com
In business since 1977.
Placements: 400-500 au pairs and demi pairs.
Jobs in: Ireland.
Nationalities placed: EU nationals.
Males are very difficult to place, but it is sometimes possible.
Minimum stay: 6 months. Summer stays: 3 months (available occasionally).
Wages/pocket money: IR£35 per week.
Qualifications: age limits 18-25 years, with some flexibility.
Application procedure: 2-3 references required. Processing time usually about 2 months.
Other services: in Dublin, language classes available at Linguaviva Centre. Also organises sports and social activities and runs programme of films, lectures and outings. Open-door policy for dealing with all problems.
Fees: IR£70.
Contact: Grainne Barton, Director.

LIV-IN LANGUAGES AU PAIRS
57A Beechfield, Kings Langley, Herts. WD4 8EE. Tel: 01923 267310. Fax: 01923 400063. E-mail: liv-in.languages@virgin.net.
In business since 1992. Member of IAPA.
Placements: 150 au pairs.
Jobs in: UK only.
Nationalities placed: Western Europe and Czech Republic.
Minimum stay: 6 months (occasional 3-month placements are available).
Wages/pocket money: £40-£50 per week.
Qualifications: minumum age 19. Must have enough English to sustain simple conversion.
Application procedure: 2 references, 4 photos and medical certificate needed.
Other services: agency acts as intermediary in cases of dispute and offers advice on almost anything.
Fees: nil.
Contact: Bernadette Murphy, Proprietor.

LLOYD'S
32 Kensington Place, Newport, South Wales NP9 8GP. Tel: 01633 216710. Fax: 01633 841230.
In business since 1989.
Placements: nannies, au pairs, parent's helps and all types of employment in private families..
Jobs in: Wales, UK and international (for example Switzerland, Germany, France and Egypt).
Nationalities placed: Europeans in accordance with Home Office regulations. Male positions are available; agency is committed to equal opportunities. Summer stays are available.
Wages/pocket money: £40 per week for au pairs.

Qualifications: childcare experience usually required.
Application procedure: interview arranged wherever possible.
Other services: agency helps to arrange social activities, outings and weekly meetings. 24 hour telephone line available. Contracts can be issued. Most families registered with Lloyd's pay some or all of the language course fees. Advice given on insurance.
Fees: £32 for placements abroad.
Contact: Mrs. Gaynor Lloyd, Proprietor.

THE LONDON AU PAIR AND NANNY AGENCY
4 Sunnyside, Childs Hill, London NW2 2QN. Tel: 0171-435 3891. Fax: 0171-794 2700.
In business since 1979.
Placements: about 400 nannies, mother's helps, au pairs, au pairs plus and nanny/housekeepers per year.
Jobs in: UK, France, Austria, Germany, Italy and Spain.
Nationalities placed: any nationality with a working visa.
Minimum stay: 10 months preferred (September-July). Long-term placements possible at other times of the year.
Wages/pocket money: £40+ per week for au pairs; £45-55 for au pairs plus; £80-£100 for mother's helps; £90-150 for nannies; £90-130 for nanny/housekeepers.
Qualifications: Childcare experience preferred. Driving is an asset; some knowledge of the language is essential. Smokers difficult to place.
Application procedure: all candidates submit application form, at least 2 references, 5 passport photos and medical certificate.
Other services: agency can advise on language schools, insurance and can provide contact lists of other au pairs in area.
Fees: £40 if placed through an agency abroad. £15 cancellation penalty requested.
Contact: Mrs. Maggie Dyer, Proprietor.

Nannies: UK, Europe & Australia
Mother's Help: UK, Europe & Australia
Au Pairs: UK, Europe & Australia
Chambermaids: UK *only*

Lucy Locketts & Vanessa Bancroft Nanny & Domestic Agency
Hillview Farm, Flecknoe, Nr. Rugby, Warks CV23 8AU
Tel/Fax: 01788 891626: *Eves/weekends:* 01788 891363   Licence No. M4516

LUCY LOCKETTS & VANESSA BANCROFT NANNY & DOMESTIC AGENCY
Hillview Farm, Flecknoe, Nr. Rugby, Warwickshire CV23 8AU. Tel/fax: 01788 891626; evenings and weekends: 01788 891363.

In business since 1984.
Placements: 300-350 nannies, mother's helps, housekeepers, chambermaids and au pairs.
Jobs in: UK and all European countries including Greece. Also Australia.
Nationalities placed: Europeans.
Minimum stay: 6-12 months.
Wages/pocket money: £35-£40 per week for au pairs, £60-£80 for mother's helps and £100 upwards for nannies.
Qualifications: childcare experience needed. Drivers and non-smokers preferred.
Application procedure: interviews where possible. After childcare references are received, placements can be made within 10 days.
Other services: agency can advise on schools in the UK and arrange for au pairs to meet each other.
Fees: nil.
Contact: Lucy Holland, Owner.

MAR'S AU PAIR AGENCY
16 Spencer Road, Chiswick, London W4. Tel: 0181-995 6594.
In business since 1986.
Placements: 200 au pairs and au pairs plus.
Jobs in: London only.
Nationalities placed: Europeans in accordance with Home Office regulations. A few positions for male caretakers available each year.
Minimum stay: 6 months from January. Summer stays: June/July- August.
Wages/pocket money: £35 per week for au pairs; £40 for au pairs plus.
Qualifications: some childcare experience needed.
Other services: au pair gatherings in London organised in September, January and July. Information on language courses at West London College given.
Fees: nil.
Contact: Mrs. Marianne Walsh, Managing Director.

MARY POPPINS NANNIES
132 Caulder Drive, Oakville, Ontario L6J 4T3, Canada. Tel: 905-849-9584. Fax: 905-338-1894.
In business since 1987. Licensed by the Ministry of Labour.
Placements: nannies only.
Jobs in: Canada.
Nationalities placed: mainly British, Irish and European.
Minimum stay: 1 year.
Wages/pocket money: C$185-C$220 per week after all deductions.
Qualifications: must have 6 months full-time professional nanny training or 12 months experience working full-time in paid employment. NNEB or equivalent preferred. Should be fluent in English and have 'O' levels or equivalent. Ability to drive and swim very helpful. Non-smokers preferred.
Application procedure: occasionally recruit nannies directly and check references by telephone. Visa requirements take 12-16 weeks.
Fees: nil.
Contact: Doroty-Anne Mills, Proprietor.

MIDSHIRES
MOTHERS HELP & AU PAIR BUREAU

- Finding it hard coping with home and work?
- Worried about meeting children after school?
- Too tired to do the ironing after a hard days work?
- Keen to pursue new interests outside home?

HOME HELP
£40
PER WEEK

SOLUTION:

Midshires au pairs specialise in finding work places for girls and boys from Eastern European countries who wish to improve their english and work as Mother's Helps/Au Pairs (Live-in).

You will have help 5 hours per day, 5 days a week, including 2–3 nights babysitting, which is flexible to your own requirements.

All our au pairs are interviewed and referenced and are between 17 and 27 years old.

FOR DETAILS AND INFORMATION PACK CONTACT MRS. DOUGHTY ON

Tel: 01455 285503   Fax: 01455 286676
Au Pairs of all nationalities always required.

For application form, please write to:
Midshires Au Pair Bureau, Willowbrook House, Cosby Road, Broughton Astley, Leicestershire, England LE9 6PA

MIDSHIRES AU PAIR & MOTHERS HELP BUREAU
Willowbrook House, Cosby Road, Broughton Astley, Leicestershire LE9 6PA. Tel: 01455 285503. Fax: 01455 286676.
In business since 1995. Member of IFAA.
Placements: 250-300 au pairs and mother's helps.
Jobs in: primarily UK. Also Europe
Nationalities placed: according to Home Office list. Specialise in placing au pairs from Czech and Slovak Republics and Turkey in the UK. Other nationalities welcome.
Male applicants can occasionally be placed.
Minimum stay: 3 months - 2 years. Lots of summer placements available.
Wages/pocket money: £40-£60 per week.
Qualifications: ages 17-27. Applicants need 2 references, medical report and previous experience.
Application procedure: processing time as little as a week if applicant can provide fax number.
Other services: full agency back-up. Replacement families available.
Fees: nil.
Contact: Mrs. Lindsay Doughty, Proprietor.

MILLRACE NANNIES
5 Victoria Road, Sevenoaks, Kent TN13 1YD. Tel: 01732 742987 (24 hours). Fax: 01732 742453.

In business since 1989.
Placements: 200 nannies and mother's helps.
Jobs in: UK only.
Nationalities placed: British nannies.
Minimum stay: temporary and permanent.
Wages/pocket money: £80+ for mother's helps; £120+ for nannies.
Fees: nil.
Contact: Mrs. Karen Smart, Partner.
Other services: help with employment contract and provide full back-up service after placement. Staff put in touch with one another.
Contact: Mrs. Karen Smart, Partner.

MONDIAL AU PAIR AGENCY
32 Links Road, West Wickham, Kent BR4 0QW. Tel: 0181-777 6271/0510. Fax: 0181-777 6765.
In business since 1949.
Placements: 500 au pairs.
Jobs in: UK, France, Austria and Spain.
Nationalities placed: all Europeans, especially French, Austrian, Yugoslav and Spanish girls to UK.
Minimum stay: 6 months. Summer placements: 3 months.
Wages/pocket money: minimum £38 per week.
Qualifications: 18-27 years. Love of children and babysitting experience necessary. Must be willing to help with light housework (hoovering, dusting, tidying, ironing, washing up). Health certificate and some knowledge of the language necessary; driving licence an asset.
Application procedure: interview with agency arranged for local applicants. 2 references and CV in form of a personal letter.
Fees: £40 for placements abroad.
Contact: Mrs. J. K. Talbot, Principal.

MONROE NANNIES
International Staff Consultants, 34 Brook St, Mayfair, London W1Y 1YA. Tel: 0171-499 8867. Fax: 0171-629 4165.
In business since 1984.
Placements: 250-350 permanent placements; 150-200 temporary placements of nannies, governesses, maternity nurses and mother's helps.
Jobs in: London and Home Counties; also worldwide, including Italy, Switzerland, Germany, France, Greece, Austria, Sweden, Netherlands, Belgium, Spain, Turkey, Middle East and Far East.
Nationalities placed: British, EU nationals, Australians and New Zealanders.
Minimum stay: permanent positions are for at least one year; temporary posts are from 2 weeks.
Wages/pocket money: approximately £150-£250 per week (net) for nannies under 23; £200-£400 over 23, depending on qualifications and experience.
Qualifications: nannies must have minimum 1 year experience or have formal training; mother's helps must have at least 1 year live-in experience.
Application procedure: interviews preferred. References are required and are checked. No job lists available; individual posts are discussed with each applicant.
Contact: Miss Jane Street, Principal.

MUM'S ARMY
10 Hither Green Lane, Abbey Park, Redditch, Worcestershire B98 9BW. Tel: 01527 61661. Fax: 01527 596056.
In business since 1983. Incorporating Just the Job agency (Nottingham).
Placements: 400 au pairs.
Jobs in: England, Scotland and Wales; also France, Germany and Spain.
Minimum stay: 6 months. Summer stays: 3 months June-August.
Wages/pocket money: minimum £35 per week.
Fees: nil for incoming au pairs; £40 outgoing.
Contact: Marion Farr, Owner.

MUM'S THE WORD
51a The Broadway, Ealing, London W5 5JN. Tel: 0181-810 0344. Fax: 0181-810 0355.
In business since 1994. Member of FRES.
Placements: 200 nannies, mother's helps, au pairs and demi pairs.
Jobs in: Belgium; also UK (London area).
Male applicants cannot easily be placed.
Minimum stay: 6 months.
Wages/pocket money: from £45 per week.
Qualifications: must speak reasonable English. Minimum age 18. 2 childcare references and medical certificate essential.
Application procedure: interviews arranged where possible. References can be taken verbally if there is an immediate vacancy.
Other services: monthly au pair club meeting held at agency office. Welcome pack sent on arrival with names of four other au pairs and details of local language school.
Fees: £40 for outgoing au pairs; nil for incoming.
Contact: K. Emmitt, Negotiator.

NANNIES INCORPORATED
317 The Linen Hall, 162-168 Regent St, London W1R 5TB. Tel: 0171-437 1312. Fax: 0171-437 1226. Also: 8 rue Dubropol, 75017 Paris, France (tel: 1-45 74 62 74/fax: 1-45 74 69 71) and Avenue de la Floride 105, 1180 Brussels; tel: 2-374 31 81.
In business since 1989.
Placements: qualified nannies, maternity nurses, midwives and health visitors.
Jobs in: London, Paris, Brussels and worldwide.
Nationalities placed: British, Irish, Australian, New Zealand, French.
Male positions are rarely available.
Minimum stay: temporary and permanent.
Wages/pocket money: £150-£500 per week.
Qualifications: must have training and/or experience.
Application procedure: initial telephone screening followed by a detailed application form. All candidates are personally interviewed in London or at agency's Brussels or Paris office.
Other services: English and French spoken at the agency. Nanny clubs operate in Paris and Brussels.
Fees: nil.
Contact: Annie Martin, Director.

NANNIES NOW
Avondale House, 63 Sydney Road, Haywards Heath, West Sussex RH16 1QD. Tel: 01444 453566. Fax: 01444 440445.
In business since 1989.
Placements: nannies, au pairs, mother's helps, housekeepers and carers.
Jobs in: UK, Europe including Finland, France, Germany and Sweden, USA and Australia.
Nationalities placed: any that are legal.
Minimum stay: from one day. Summer stays: from 2 months.
Wages/pocket money: from £35 per week for au pairs; from £100 for nannies.
Application procedure: most UK applicants are interviewed.
Other services: au pairs receive 'welcome pack' with details of other au pairs in the area, local language schools, etc.
Fees: £40.
Contact: Lesley Hanmore, Proprietor.

THE NANNY AGENCY
Suites 21-23, Kent House, 87 Regent St, London W1R 7HF (1 min from Piccadilly Circus). Tel: 0171-494 2929 (5 lines). Fax: 0171-494 2922. Also trades as UK & Overseas Nanny/Au Pair Agency and Central London Bureau/CLB. Office hours: Monday-Friday 9am-5pm.
In business for more than 25 years. Originally opened in 1969.
Placements: several thousand live-in-staff: nannies, maternity nurses, mother's helps, au pairs and housekeepers.
Jobs in: UK and Worldwide including USA and unusual places but excluding Canada, Australia and New Zealand. Specialise in UK and Germany. Jobs also in France, Switzerland, Spain, Italy, Belgium, Luxembourg, Netherlands, Sweden, Denmark, Norway, Greece, Hugary, Austria, USA and occasionally South America, etc.
Nationalities placed: any that can work legally.
Male au pairs can be placed if they have childcare experience supported by references and stay for a minimum of 12 months.
Minimum stay: usual stay 12 months plus. Some temp jobs including summer stays available for a minimum of 3 months (no less).
Wages/pocket money: depends on age, qualification, experience and country. Approximately £50 per week for au pairs; £100-£150 for mother's helps; £150-£250 for nannies and £250-£400 for maternity nurses.
Qualifications: au pairs need good written references only. Mother's helps need to be experienced or/and have good references. Nannies must have NNEB or similar qualification and have good references.
Application procedure: early application encouraged. Interested individuals should send SAE for introduction pack and application form or visit agency (no appointment necessary).

NANNY & AU PAIR CONNECTION
44 Albert Road West, Heaton, Bolton BL1 5HG. Tel: 01204 495000. Fax: 01204 496007.
Placements: nannies, mother's helps, au pairs and domestic staff.
Jobs in: UK, France, Spain, Austria, Belgium, Switzerland, Greece, Italy, Netherlands and Turkey.
Nationalities placed: any legal UK residents including students who have had childcare experience.

Males are accepted.
Minimum stay: 6, 9 or 12 month placements for au pairs in college terms. 3 month summer stays are available.
Wages/pocket money: £120 + for qualified nannies in UK and abroad; £35 per week for au pairs in Europe plus extra for babysitting and working on holidays.
Qualifications: au pairs require knowledge of childcare and a willingness to learn the lanugage. Nannies should have either an NNEB or B Tec equivalent in childcare and be able to speak the language.
Application procedure: references, medical certificate and family letter required. Send s.a.e. to agency for relevant application forms.
Other services: full back-up service; contracts of employment provided. Contact numbers given of other au pairs in area. Help given with travel arrangements and visas.
Fees: nil for nannies, mother's helps and incoming au pairs. £40 for British au pairs going to Europe.
Contact: Carole Payne, Proprietor.

NANNY CONNECTION
Stern House, 85 Gloucester Road, London SW7 4SS. Tel: 0171-835 2277. Fax: 0171-835 0888.
In business since 1987.
Placements: nannies only.
Jobs in: London, England.
Nationalities placed: all that are legal and speak English as their first language.
Male applicants are placed with great difficulty.
Minimum stay: 1 year.
Wages/pocket money: £130-£200 per week live-in.
Qualifications: minimum age 20. Must be qualified and/or experienced. Must be able to drive and a non-smoker.
Application procedure: must have at least 2 checkable references and good childcare background.
Other services: nannies can be put in touch with one another.
Fees: nil.
Contact: Sally-Anne Lloyd, Proprietor.

THE NANNY SERVICE
6 Nottingham St, London W1M 3RB. Tel: 0171-935 3515. Fax: 0171-224 0305.
In business since 1975.
Placements: live-in nannies and mother's helps.
Jobs in: London (mostly) and rural England.
Nationalities placed: EU passport holders, Australians and New Zealanders and all those eligible for working holiday visa.
Minimum stay: 1 year.
Wages: £100-170 per week according to age and experience.
Qualifications: minimum age 19 years; experience, references and driving licence essential.
Fees: nil.
Contact: Corrina Slater, Manager.

THE NORFOLK CARE SEARCH AGENCY
19 London Road, Downham Market, Norfolk PE38 9BJ. Tel: 01366 384448. Fax: 01366 385226.
In business since 1984.
Placements: temporary and permanent nannies, mother's helps, au pairs, companion/housekeepers and auxiliary nurses.
Jobs in: France (Nice and sometimes Corsica); also UK.
Nationalities placed: Europeans (in accordance with Home Office au pair regulations).
Some male placements are made.
Minimum stay: 6 months in the UK (except temporary nannies).
Summer placements: France only (minimum 6 weeks).
Wages/pocket money: £35-£55 per week for au pairs; £100-£200 for nannies; £100-£120 for mother's helps. 1,650FF in France (paid in arrears).
Qualifications: childcare experience essential for nannies, desirable for au pairs. Age limits 18 to 27 years for au pairs, 18-70 for nannies, minimum 22 years for a care/companion or nursing auxiliary.
Application procedure: enquiries should always enclose s.a.e.
Fees: fees on application.
Contact: Mrs. V. A. Parker, Proprietor.

NORTH LONDON NANNIES
92 Creighton Avenue, London, N10 1NT. Tel: 0181-444 4911.
Placements: about 1,000 nannies, mother's helps, au pairs, demi pairs and maternity nurses.
Jobs in: Europe mostly, some worldwide.
Minimum stay: 1 year preferred. No short-term stays.
Wages/pocket money: variable.
Qualifications: minimum age 18 years. Childcare experience and driving licence preferred. Clean bill of health required.
Application procedure: applicants must be in UK and attend interviews with family. Interviews with agency by appointment only. Childcare and character references with telephone numbers essential. Placement takes about 1 week.
Other services: can possibly advise on language schools. Friendship service.
Fees: nil.
Contact: Jacqueline Lewis, Owner.

NORTH SOUTH AGENCY
28 Wellington Road, Hastings, East Sussex TN34 3RN. Tel: 01424 422364. Fax: 01424 715120.
In business since 1984.
Placements: au pairs, au pairs plus, mother's helps, nannies and housekeepers.
Jobs in: Europe (mainly Germany, Switzerland, Spain, Sweden and Italy), USA and Turkey; also UK (majority in Greater London and Southeast England).
Nationalities placed: Europeans (in accordance with Home Office regulations); no restrictions on nannies provided they can get work permit.
Minimum stay: 9-12 months preferred; shorter stays possible depending on demand and starting date. No summer only placements.
Wages/pocket money: £35+ per week for au pairs; £45+ for au pairs plus; variable for nannies according to experience, qualifications and commitment.
Qualifications: childcare experience necessary for mother's helps and nannies. Qualifications (NNEB or similar) also preferred for nannies. Au pairs should

have a genuine liking for children and have some experience, if possible, and also experience with simple household duties. Driving licence and experience always an advantage.
Application procedure: enquiries should enclose s.a.e. (or international reply coupon if from abroad) plus letter of introduction, 2 written references, some friendly photos and health certificate.
Fees: nil in most cases.
Contact: Hanna Matthews and Susan Parlain.

OCCASIONAL & PERMANENT NANNIES
2 Cromwell Place, London SW7 2JE. Tel: 0171-225 1555. Fax: 0171-589 4966.
In business since 1962.
Placements: nannies, mother's helps, governesses and maternity nurses.
Jobs in: UK and all over the world (Europe, Americas, Australia, Africa and the Far East).
Nationalities placed: British, Australian, New Zealand, Canadian and European, provided they can obtain work permits. Agency has an agent in Hong Kong and contacts in Australia plus a sister company in the UK for all positions in private service.
Minimum stay: variable but overseas contracts mainly 1 year. Summer stays are possible.
Wages/pocket money: £130-£450 per week (depending on age and experience).
Qualifications: ages from 18 upwards. Childcare/nursing or teaching experience strongly preferred.
Application procedure: references for all work since leaving school required; all applicants are personally interviewed and references checked.
Other services: agency helps with contract details, medical insurance and travel arrangements. Also provides addresses of other nannies in the area.
Fees: nil.
Contact: Angela Hovey, Managing Director.

OKISTA
Austrian Committee for International Educational Exchange, Türkenstr. 8/11, 1090 Vienna, Austria. Tel: 1-401 48 8827. Fax: 1-401 48 8800. E-mail: rosi.weinmann@oekista.co.at
Branch offices in Salzburg, Graz, Linz and Innsbruck.
In business since 1950. Member of FIYTO (Federation of Youth Travel Organisations).
Placements: 250-300 au pairs a year in Austria, plus 700 Austrians sent abroad. Also arrange paying guest stays.
Jobs in: Austria; also France, Spain, UK, Italy, USA and Canada.
Nationalities placed: EU, American, Japanese, Australian, New Zealand and Canadian. Also Slovenian and Croatian au pairs sent to Norway, Iceland, etc.
Male positions very seldom available.
Minimum stay: 3 months, normally 6 months. Summer stays: 2-3 months.
Wages/pocket money: 800 schillings per week.
Qualifications: age limits 18-26 years. Basic knowledge of German useful though not essential. Must love children and be willing to work.
Application procedure: 2 application forms in German, 2 character references,

medical certificate, 2 photos and a curriculum vitae needed. Time to process application is about 3 weeks.
Other services: agency organises social activities, helps with visas and language classes, and advises on cheap travel.
Fees: 800 schillings.
Contact: Rosi Weinmann, Au Pair Department.

O'NEILL SCHOOL OF ENGLISH
Iberluce 20, 48960 Galdakao, Vizcaya, Spain. Tel:, 4-456 49 17. Fax: 4-443 2945.
In business since 1990.
Placements: about 50 au pairs.
Jobs in: Spain (mostly in the north).
Nationalities placed: all that are legal.
Male applicants can sometimes be placed in families looking for a live-in English tutor.
Minimum stay: 2-3 months in summer; very occasionally for just the month of August. Otherwise September/October to end of June.
Wages/pocket money: 8,000 pesetas per week. Extra money paid for extra duties.
Qualifications: native English speakers. Minimum age 18 (though families prefer older au pairs). Basic knowledge of Spanish and some experience of childminding preferred.
Application procedure: applications should be sent at least 2 months in advance, though summer placements tend to be made at the last minute.
Fees: one week's pocket money payable once au pair is installed.
Contact: Cristina Tejada, Manager.

OXFORD NANNIES
Blue House, 34 Union Street, Oxford OX4 1JP. Tel: 01865 721511.
In business since 1989.
Placements: nannies.
Jobs in: UK (most in Oxford area) and very occasionally Europe.
Nationalities placed: British, Australians and Americans.
Wages/pocket money: £120-150 net for daily nannies; £110-130 for residential nannies.
Qualifications: must have childcare experience, driving licence and no police convictions.
Application procedure: interview compulsory. 3 written references needed.
Contact: K. A. Wilder, Proprietor.

PARAGON PERSONNEL LTD
1-4529A Hastings St, Burnaby, British Columbia V5C 2K3, Canada. Tel: (604) 298-6633. Fax: (604) 298-6655. E-mail: paragon@smartt.com
In business since 1980.
Placements: 250 nannies, mother's helps and au pairs.
Jobs in: Canada (especially BC and Alberta); also UK, New Zealand and Switzerland.
Male applicants cannot be placed.
Minimum stay: 1 year.
Wages/pocket money: C$160 per week.
Qualifications: minimum secondary school education, and able to speak English. Must have one year's childcare experience.

Other services: advice given on insurance, travel, etc.
Fees: nil.
Contact: Ed Carmona, Manager.

PARK LANE NANNIES
22 Upper Maudlin Street, Bristol BS2 8DJ. Tel: 0117-949 2222. Fax: 0117-949 2333.
In business since 1987. Member of FRES.
Placements: 250-350 nannies, mother's helps and housekeepers.
Jobs in: worldwide (Europe, Canada, Middle East).
Nationalities placed: any that is legal.
Male positions are very occasionally available.
Minimum stay: 6 months.
Wages/pocket money: £100-£350 net per week for nannies.
Application procedure: average process time 2 weeks. Interviews whenever possible. Minimum 2 references required which are checked.
Fees: nil.
Contact: Ron or Shirley Hodges, Partners.

PAT-A-CAKE
10 Athena Close, Kingston upon Thames, Surrey KT1 3GA. Tel: 0181-541 0062. Fax: 0181-541 0062
In business since 1993.
Placements: 240 au pairs, nannies and mother's helps.
Jobs in: Germany and Australia.
Male applicants can sometimes be placed.
Minimum stay: 6 months. Summer stays are available.
Wages/pocket money: £40 per week for au pairs; £100-£150 for mother's helps and nannies.
Qualifications: must have childcare references and some knowledge of German for Germany.
Application procedure: interviews essential. References are checked. Processing takes around 3 weeks.
Other services: offer short intensive training course which includes first aid course leading to childcare certificate.
Fees: nil.
Contact: Bianca Effemey, Director.

PEC AU PAIRS
2 Spring Hill, Kilnbank, Market Drayton, Shropshire TF9 1LE. Tel: 01630 652985. Fax: 01630 654147. E-mail: 106226.2343@compuserve.com
In business since 1984. Member of FRES and FSB.
Placements: au pairs, mother's helps, nannies.
Jobs in: UK, France, Italy, Belgium, Spain and USA.
Nationalities placed: EC countries, plus Scandinavians, Czechs, Slovaks, Hungarians, Australians and New Zealanders.
Minimum stay: 6 months (nannies/mother's helps 1 year). Summer stays: 3 months.
Wages/pocket money: £35 per week for au pairs; £60-80+ for mother's helps; £100+ for nannies.
Qualifications: childcare experience needed, if only regular babysitting. Age limits 17-27 years. Must have reasonable standard of language of destination country. Driving licence useful. Non-smokers only.

Application procedure: references needed, preferably childcare-related. Interviews arranged when possible. Average processing time 1 month.
Fees: British going to Europe £40, Europeans coming to England nil.
Contact: Heather Nicholls, Partner.

PEC AU PAIRS

Recruiting European au pairs for England
British au pairs for Europe. Age 17–27
Member of FRES and FSB. Established 1984
e-mail: 106226.2343@compuserve.com

Tel: 01630 652985 / Fax: 01630 654147

PEOPLE & PLACES (P & P)
Trewornan, Wadebridge, Cornwall PL27 6EX. Tel: 01208 812652. Fax: 01208 816121.
In business since 1990.
Placements: 250 au pairs and 50 nannies per year.
Jobs in: au pairs placed in England, France, Germany, Austria, Italy, Netherlands and Spain. Nannies placed in England and Europe.
Minimum stay: 6 weeks in summer.
Wages/pocket money: minimum £40 per week for au pairs; hours in excess of 25 per week should be paid at £1 per hour. £100-£300 per week for nannies.
Qualifications: babysitting experience preferred.
Other services: will give phone numbers of other au pairs in the country, on request. Agency tries to contact family after au pair's arrival to make sure all is well.
Fees: £40.
Contact: Lester Tucker, Proprietor.

THE PERSONAL AU PAIR SERVICE
273 Eversholt Street, Camden, London NW1 1BA. Tel: 0171-383 5581. Fax: 0171-387 9086.
In business since 1985.
Placements: about 400 au pairs per year.
Jobs in: UK only, mainly Central London.
Nationalities placed: nationalities approved by Home Office.
Minimum stay: 6 months. Summer stays: minimum 2 months.
Wages/pocket money: £40+ per week.
Qualifications: childcare experience preferred. Age limits 17-27 years. Some command of English needed.
Application procedure: 2 references and 2 photos needed in first instance. Interviews required if applicant is already in the country. Time taken to process applications 2-14 days.

Other services: agency helps with visas, language schools and provides list of addresses of other au pairs.
Fees: nil.
Contact: Ms. Teresa Godbold, Director.

PORTLAND PLACEMENTS
The Priory, Cherry Orton Road, Orton Waterville, Peterborough PE2 5EQ.
Tel: 01733 703303. Fax: 01733 703305.
In business since 1994.
Placements: nannies, au pairs, mother's helps and maternity nurses.
Jobs in: France, Spain, USA.
Nationalities placed: mainly UK passports. Male au pair positions are occasionally available.
Minimum stay: 6 months (12 months for USA). Summer stays of at least 2 months are available.
Wages/pocket money: £35-£45 per week in Europe; US$118 in USA.
Qualifications: ages 18-26. Must have experience of childcare. Drivers preferred (essential for USA). Basic spoken language needed.
Application procedure: initial telephone interview, application form, and further telephone or personal interview. References are checked, forms despatched to agents, then telephone interview with family. Placement in Europe takes 2 days to 2 months. Placement in USA (via AuPairCare) takes 3 months (including police check, medical certificate, etc.).
Other services: USA programme provides insurance, travel, education and local counsellor support.
Fees: £45 for au pairs to Europe; £75 for au pairs to USA plus $500 refundable deposit.
Contact: Clare Cracknell, Proprietor.

PROBLEMS UNLIMITED AGENCY
AU PAIR INTRODUCTION SERVICE

Established in 1980 placing Au Pairs in UK and in Europe and Mother's Helps in the UK. We offer a friendly back-up service during the whole of the stay. Many families in Europe needing Au Pairs – support always given from agencies abroad.

French, Italian and some German spoken. No fee for placement in UK. £40 for placement in Europe. Minimum stay six months. Some for summer 2/3 months. Age 18–27. Non-smokers. Pocket money £35–£40 per week. Au Pair pays own travel and college fees.

For more information contact us at:
24 St Lukes Road, Old Windsor, Berks SL4 2QQ
Tel: 01753 830101   Fax: 01753 831194

PROBLEMS UNLIMITED AGENCY
24 St. Luke's Road, Old Windsor, Berks. SL4 2QQ. Tel: 01753 830101. Fax: 01753 831194.
Established in 1980. Member of FRES.
Placements: au pairs and mother's helps.
Families in: United Kingdom, France, Italy, Spain and Belgium.
Nationalities placed: EU, German, Scandinavian, Czech, Slovak and Hungarian.

Minimum stay: 6 months for au pairs; 12 months for mother's helps. Some summer stays of 2/3 months available.
Wages/pocket money: £35-£40 per 5-day week. £100 per week for mother's helps.
Qualifications: reasonable ability to converse in target language is important. Driving licence useful. Non-smokers.
Application procedure: 2 childcare related references required (regular babysitting is acceptable). Photographs, preferably taken with family and children. 'Dear family' letter to be written in the language of the country of choice.
Other services: special au pair insurance policy available. Contact number of foreign agency given in case of emergency.
Fees: £40 outgoing; nil incoming.
Contact: Hilli Matthews.

PRO FILIA
Nationalsekretariat, Beckenhofstr. 16, Postfach, 8035 Zürich, Switzerland. Tel/fax: 1-361 53 31.
In operation since 1896, with 6 branch offices.
Placements: 300-350 au pairs in Europe.
Jobs in: Switzerland; plus UK, Ireland, France, Italy, Germany, Austria and Spain.
Nationalities placed: Western Europeans, Canadians and Americans to Switzerland, Swiss girls abroad.
Minimum stay: 1 year normally, 6 months (January to June) occasionally.
Wages/pocket money: SFr600-700 net per month depending on age, plus board and lodging which is valued at SFr810. Deductions for insurance and contributions amount to about SFr100 per month.
Qualifications: age limits 17-30 years (18 in Geneva). Basic childcare experience and knowledge of household duties needed. Should have some knowledge of the relevant language and be prepared to study it seriously.
Application procedure: personal or telephone interviews if possible after written application. The three branch offices which deal with placements in Switzerland are: Pro Filia Bureau de Placement, 51 rue de Carouge, 1205 Geneva (22-329 84 62) and 32 Av. de Rumine, 1005 Lausanne (21-323 77 66) for families in French-speaking western Switzerland; and Pro Filia Zürich, Beckenhofstrasse 16, 8035 Zürich (1-363 55 01) for German-speaking families. Other addresses primarily of interest to Swiss candidates are Weierweg 22, 4054 Basel; Pilatusstrasse 70, 6003 Lucerne; Jugendamt Olten, Hammerallee 19, 4600 Olten; Herrengasse 20, 6430 Schwyz. Opening hours may be limited, for example the Geneva office is open 8.30-11am weekdays plus Wednesday afternoon 2.30-5pm.
Fees: application fee SFr30 plus SFr150 placement fee.
Contacts: Mme. Annelise Bossard (Geneva), Mme. Lili Pitteloud (Lausanne), Frau Theres Plüss (Zürich).

PROGRAMME 'AU PAIR IN ENGLAND' & 'AU PAIR IN SPAIN'
c/o Miss Laurence Chérifat, 16 Avenue Gambetta, 94700 Maisons-Alfort, France. Tel/fax: 1-43 75 72 02. Office hours: 8-9pm plus Wednesdays 5-9pm and Saturdays 12-2pm.
In business since 1994.
Placements: 120 au pairs and a few au pairs plus.
Jobs in: England (Greater London and surrounding counties) and Spain.

Nationalities placed: mainly French but all Western Europeans.
Male applicants cannot be placed.
Minimum stay: 6 months but many families prefer longer stays. A few summer stays are available.
Wages/pocket money: £40 per week for au pairs; £45-£50 for au pairs plus. 7,000-8,000 pesetas per week.
Qualifications: ages 18-27 for UK, 18-30 for Spain. Basic knowledge of English essential for England, but not Spanish for Spain. Some babysitting experience.
Application procedure: 2 references including 1 childcare (which are checked), medical certificate, 4 photos and 1 'dear family' letter of introduction. Information meeting can be organised for applicants living in Greater Paris. Processing time is 4-8 weeks.
Other services: programme run by former au pair in England and nanny in Paris. For UK, dossier given containing maps of London, list of useful hints, emergency addresses, local English schools and advice on travel. Social programmes arranged in both countries.
Fees: 195FF (non-refundable).
Contact: Laurence Chérifat, Director.

QC PERSONNEL
21 King St, Suite 108, London, Ontario N6A 5H3, Canada. Tel: 519-679-2805. Fax: 519-645-0698.
In business since 1974.
Placements: small number of nannies, mother's helps, nanny/housekeepers and carers for elderly and disabled people.
Jobs in: Canada only.
Nationalities placed: no restrictions.
Male positions rarely available.
Minimum stay: 12 month contracts.
Qualifications: as according to government regulations. Must speak English. Should be non-smokers, able to swim and drive.
Wages/pocket money: from C$6.85 per hour up to 44 hours per week. Higher salary paid to nannies with NNEB qualification.
Application procedure: contact agency direct for application form. If applicant is already in Canada, a personal interview/screening is arranged.
Other services: agency can advise on evening classes in London Ontario and provide names and numbers to new arrivals for purposes of socialising.
Fees: nil.
Contact: Viviane E. Logan, Owner/Manager.

QUICK HELP AGENCY
307A Finchley Road, London NW3 6EH Tel: 0171-794 8666. Fax: 0171-433 1993.
In business since 1972. Member of IAPA.
Placements: 2,000 nannies, au pairs, mother's helps and carers for the elderly.
Jobs in: France, Spain, Germany, Italy, Austria, Netherlands, Norway, Australia, New Zealand and UK.
Nationalities placed: any that are legal.
Male positions are sometimes available in Holland and France.
Minimum stay: 6-9 months. Summer stays are available.
Wages/pocket money: from £35 per week or equivalent for au pairs; £85-£120

for mother's helps and nannies. Mother's helps and nannies in New Zealand earn NZ$290-$310 per week, while in Australia A$190-$210.
Qualifications: nannies must have training, mother's helps and au pairs must have experience. Must have working knowledge of chosen language.
Other services: advice given on learning a language.
Fees: £47 (including VAT) for outgoing au pairs, otherwise nil.
Contact: Mrs. Norma Cutner, Owner.

R.C.I. (Madrid) — see Relaciones Culturales Internacionales, below.

REGENCY NANNIES OVERSEAS
50 Hans Crescent, Knightsbridge, London SW1X 0NA. Tel: 0171-225 1055. Fax: 0171-584 7265.
In business since 1983.
Placements: 100-150 nannies, mother's helps, governesses and maternity nurses.
Jobs: worldwide (placements include Moscow, Beijing, United Arab Emirates and many countries as well as Europe.
Nationalities placed: any with permission to work in UK.
Minimum stay: 6 months to 1 year. Maternity nurses are often placed on 1-3 month contracts.
Wages/pocket money: from £120 per week for mother's helps; £200-£350 for experienced nannies.
Qualifications: experience essential. Driving licence and second language helpful.
Application procedure: interviews essential. Childcare references required. Processing averages 1 week.
Other services: employers can purchase insurance for nannies from agency.
Fees: nil.
Contact: Lorna K. Bell, Manager (UK Division).

RELACIONES CULTURALES INTERNACIONALES (RCI)
Ferraz 82, 28008 Madrid, Spain. Tel: 91-541 71 03. Fax: 1-559 11 81.
In operation as a non-profit club since 1978. Member of IAPA.
Placements: 1,300 au pairs, mother's helps, nannies and demi pairs. Also arrange home stays and youth exchanges.
Jobs in: Spain, plus most countries for Spanish applicants.
Nationalities placed: no restrictions.
Males can be placed.
Minimum stay: 6-9 months preferred. Summer stays of 4-12 weeks very easy to arrange.
Wages/pocket money: 7,000-8,000 pesetas per week.
Qualifications: age limits 18-28/30 years. Interest in and caring attitude towards children required. Knowledge of language helpful but not required.
Application procedure: application form, 2 references, medical certificate and telephone contact needed. Offer of host family often made within 24 hours, since so many Spanish families are waiting for an au pair. One of RCI's UK partners is Home Concern (see entry).
Other services: Club RCI runs social programmes, Spanish courses at its own language centre and other summer courses in conjunction with Spanish universities. Also offers specially designed insurance policy, professional advisory service in the event of problems (including legal ones) and a travel service.

Fees: annual membership in Club RCI.
Contact: Leire Amburu.

RELATIONS INTERNATIONALES
20 rue de l'Exposition, 75007 Paris, France. Tel: (1) 45 50 23 23.
Métro: Ecole Militaire. In business since 1955.
Placements: 200 au pairs in Europe and USA.
Jobs in: France; also French girls sent to UK, Spain, Italy, Greece, Ireland, Germany and USA.
Nationalities placed: no restrictions.
Minimum stay: minimum 6 months during the year. Minimum 2 months in summer.
Wages/pocket money: 1,700FF per month and transport between family and school in Paris area.
Qualifications: age limits 18-27 years. Babysitting references required.
Application procedure: 2 references, medical certificate and personal letter to the family required. Telephone contact with host family.
Fees: 950FF.
Contact: Geneviève Bottet.

RICHMOND & TWICKENHAM AU PAIRS & NANNIES
The Old Coach House, Kineton Road, Southam, Leamington Spa, Warwickshire CV33 0HZ. Tel: 01926 812877. Fax: 01926 813811.
In business since 1992.
Placements: 500+ au pairs.
Jobs in: France, Italy and Spain; also UK.
Nationalities placed: in accordance with Home Office regulations.
Minimum stay: minimum 6 months preferred. 6+ weeks in summer. Maximum 2 years.
Qualifications: ages 17-27. Language ability of chosen country. Childcare experience.
Application procedure: application form, 2 references, 'dear family' letter, photos and medical certificate needed.
Other services: contact given between girls.
Contact: Vicki Whitwell.

RIVERSIDE NANNIES & MOTHER'S HELPS
29 Milligan St, London E14 8AT. Tel: 0171-536 9566. Fax/back-up ansaphone: 0171-374 6363.
In business since 1989.
Placements: nannies, mother's helps, maternity nurses and nursery staff.
Jobs in: worldwide (provided work permits can be obtained for nannies).
Nationalities placed: all that are legal including Americans on 6 month CIEE visas.
Agency is prepared to try to place male applicants.
Minimum stay: no minimum though normally 6-12 months.
Qualifications: childcare experience almost always essential.
Application procedure: interviews at agency are compulsory. References meticulously checked including verbal references from past employers overseas.
Fees: nil.
Contact: Gaby or Jill.

RODATA GMBH — AU PAIR VERMITTLUNG
Giessenbachstr. 16, D-83022 Rosenheim, Germany. Tel: + + 8031-381362. Fax: + + 8031-33369.
In business since 1995.
Placements: 120 + au pairs, nannies and mother's helps for EU nationals; au pairs for non-EU nationals.
Jobs in: Germany; also UK, Ireland, France, New Zealand, South Africa, Norway, Spain, Italy, Greece and Switzerland.
Nationalities placed: no restrictions. Nanny positions for EU applicants only. Male positions are available, but they take some time.
Minimum stay: preferably 6-12 months. Limited number of summer placements available (2 months minimum).
Wages/pocket money: about DM400 per month. Host families also pay for transport to language classes.
Qualifications: minimum age 17, maximum for non-EU nationals is 24. Should have basic knowledge of German, though sometimes English or French will suffice. Driver's licence and some childcare experience might be useful.
Application procedure: usual dossier including 4 passport photos and 2 snapshots, 2 references (babysitting family, teacher, recent work report, etc.) which should be translated into the language of the chosen country (or English in some cases), medical report and a 'dear family' letter. Placement normally takes a few weeks (except where visa must be applied for).
Other services: careful vetting of family. Comprehensive insurance package is offered to host family in addition to the compulsory health and accident insurance. Travel arranged and advice given on language classes. Monthly au pair meetings are held in Rosenheim (near Munich); phone number of other au pairs can be provided.
Fees: DM100 incoming; DM250 outgoing. Cancellation penalty of 50%.
Contact: Mrs. Annelore Sperk, Director.

S&C ASOCIADOS
Avda. Cruz del Campo 17A, 1°D, 41005 Seville, Spain. Tel/fax: 5-458 15 83.
In business since 1994.
Placements: 80/90 au pairs and au pairs plus.
Jobs in: EU, especially England for Spanish au pairs.
Nationalities placed: EU and Scandinavian. Male applicants can very occasionally be placed.
Minimum stay: 6 months. Very few summer stays are available.
Wages/pocket money: 7,000 pesetas per week for au pairs. 10,000 pesetas for au pairs plus.
Qualifications: ages 18-28. Should have some babysitting experience. Knowledge of Spanish not essential.
Application procedure: processing time normally 2-6 weeks depending on dossier. Minimum 2 references including 1 childcare. No interviews required if travelling to Spain.
Other services: discount flights can be arranged. Spanish classes available (10% discount for au pairs). Agency contacts au pairs after they have settled in. Tourist information on Spain is available.
Fees: incoming fee is nil (enquirers should send 3 international reply coupons). Spanish au pairs going abroad pay fee of 20,880 pesetas (7,000 peseta penalty for cancellation).
Contact: Cándido Guerrero del Castillo, Director.

SAPA (SLOVAKIAN AU PAIR AGENCY)
Sancová 43, 831 04 Bratislava, Slovakia. Tel: 7-566 23 12. Fax: 7-214 457. E-mail: sapa@sapa.sanet.sk
In business since 1993. Member of IFAA.
Placements: up to 1,000 au pairs.
Jobs in: Great Britain and Germany.
Nationalities placed: Slovak, Czech, Hungarian and EU.
Male applicants can be placed.
Minimum stay: 10 months for Germany; 2 months for UK (in summer).
Wages/pocket money: £35-£40 per week.
Qualifications: childcare experience required. Must have basic knowledge of English or German.
Application procedure: medical certificates, 4 photos and 2 references required. Interview necessary (though by phone is possible). Processing time takes 2-4 weeks; for Germany it takes 3-6 months.
Other services: SAPA sells insurance, coach tickets and young person card (Euro-26). Agency arranges for au pair to be met by family. Help given with problems. Distribute free 'Au Pair Handbook.'
Fees: equivalent of £40-£60.
Contact: Zuzana Cechvalova, Proprietor.

SAPPHIRE AU PAIR/NANNY AGENCY
4 Brookmans Avenue, Brookmans Park, Hatfield, Herts. AL9 7QJ. Tel: 01707 652182/7. Fax: 01707 652187.
In business since 1987.
Placements: 250 au pairs, au pairs plus, demi pairs, nannies and mother's helps.
Jobs in: Europe.
A few male applicants can be placed.
Minimum stay: 6 months. Summer stays (minimum 3 months) are available. Temporary placements of 1-2 months sometimes offered.
Wages/pocket money: £40 per week for au pairs, £20 for demi pairs, £50 for au pairs plus; £70 for mother's helps; £110+ for nannies.
Qualifications: au pairs must have some knowledge of chosen language. Previous childcare/domestic experience needed. Agency looking for good references and responsible and reliable attitude.
Application procedure: interviews where possible. If documents are satisfactory, compatible positions are offered. Fax number required if applicant is overseas to facilitate fast placement. Friendly and efficient after-care service.
Other services: information sheet provided.
Fees: £40 outgoing; nil inbound.
Contact: Mrs. Sapphire Ford, Proprietor/Director.

SCANAUPAIRS
28 Woodberry Close, Chiddingfold, Surrey GU8 4SF. Tel: 01428 685305.
In business since 1985.
Placements: 300-500 au pairs.
Jobs in: UK.
Nationalities placed: all Scandinavians.
Minimum stay: 6-12 months. Summer stays: 10-12 weeks.
Wages/pocket money: from £35.
Qualifications: knowledge of English needed; childcare experience useful.

Application procedure: processing time is 2-6 weeks.
Other services: information evenings organised in London and area.
Fees: nil.
Contact: Riitta-Liisa Baldwin, Owner.

SERVICES DE LA JEUNESSE FEMININE
29 rue Faider, 1050 Brussels, Belgium. Tel/fax: 2-539 35 14 (Monday and Friday 9.30am-2pm); 81-30 91 35 (Tuesday and Thursdsay 9-11am).
Affiliated to the international Catholic organisation ACISJF.
Placements: au pairs mainly.
Jobs in: Belgium (French and Dutch speaking regions); also UK, Germany, Austria, Canada, Spain, Netherlands and Switzerland.
Minimum stay: 6-12 months. Summer stays of 2-3 months are available.
Wages/pocket money: £35-£40 per week.
Qualifications: ages 18-27. Must have experience of childcare.
Other services: au pairs are introduced to others in their region. Advice given on insurance and travel.
Fees: BF1,000 registration fee plus BF2,000 placement fee on acceptance of a post.
Contact: Mme. Marie-Jeanne Benoit.

SILC
(Séjours Internationaux Linguistiques et Culturels), 32 Rempart de l'Est, 16022 Angoulême Cedex, France. Tel: 5-45 97 841 00. Fax: 5-45 94 20 63. E-mail: nadine.g@silc.asso.fr
In business since 1965. Member of IAPA and FIYTO (Federation of International Youth Travel Organizations.
Placements: 400 au pairs and au pairs plus. (Some catering jobs in UK).
Jobs in: France, UK, Ireland, Germany, Spain and USA.
Nationalities placed: immigration restrictions vary among countries. Males can be placed only in au pair positions in the USA.
Minimum stay: 6 months (Europe), 12 months (USA). Summer stays: 2-3 months.
Wages/pocket money: 350FF per week (Europe).
Qualifications: age limits 18-25 years. Childcare experience preferred; also non-smoking and with driving licence. Must have some knowledge of the relevant language and be in excellent health.
Other services: agency can advise on local schools in France and on necessary documentation.
Fees: 900FF (in France).
Contact: Morag Anderson.

SIMPLY DOMESTICS & HOMELINE
65 Colney Hatch Lane, London N10 1LR. Tel: 0181-444 4305 (5 lines). Fax: 0181-444 4791. Mobile: 04100 23238.
In business since 1989. Member of FRES.
Placements: nannies, mother's helps, domestics, housekeepers and au pairs.
Jobs in: Europe (France, Italy, Spain, etc.).
Nationalities placed: all that are legal.
Male candidates are occasionally placed.
Minimum stay: 3 months especially in summer.
Wages/pocket money: from £40 per week.

Application procedure: all written and verbal references are checked. Interviews given where possible.
Other services: 24 hour answerphone for problems. Friendship circle organised.
Fees: £30 plus VAT.
Contact: Judith Ivers, Proprietor.

SINCLAIRS NANNY & CARE AGENCY
Forest House, 3 Seaview Road, Highcliffe, Dorset BH23 5QJ. Tel/fax: 01425 279390.
In business since 1987.
Placements: nannies, mother's helps, maternity nurses, help for the elderly, au pairs, etc.
Jobs in: UK and worldwide (including Canada).
Nationalities placed: any that can arrange work permit, especially Australians and New Zealanders.
Male positions are sometimes available.
Minimum stay: short contracts and holiday placements may be available.
Wages/pocket money: from £35 per week.
Qualifications: experience not essential for mother's help positions in families where the mother does not work. Minimum age 18 years; no maximum age. Foreign applicants must be able to speak English.
Application procedure: initial approaches should be legible and should indicate dates of availability. Foreign applicants should enclose international reply coupons. Work-related and character references required. Processing begins the day the application arrives. Interviews carried out whenever possible. Trial day or week can sometimes be arranged.
Other services: advice may be given on language courses in UK. Contact encouraged with other au pairs and nannies in vicinity.
Contact: Shirley McMaster, Owner.

SOAMES INTERNATIONAL/PARIS NANNIES
B.P. 28, 77302 Fontainebleau, France. Tel: 1-64 78 37 98. Fax: 1-64 45 91 75.
In business since 1988. Member of IAPA.
Placements: 120 nannies, au pairs and mother's helps.
Jobs in: France (especially Paris and environs); also England, Ireland, Germany, Italy, Spain and USA.
Nationalities placed: EU.
Male au pair positions are available.
Minimum stay: 10 months for au pairs, 1 year for nannies and mother's helps. Summer au pair stays of 2-3 months are available.
Wages/pocket money: 400FF per week for au pairs; from 5,000FF per month net for nannies.
Qualifications: ages 18-29 for Europe. Must have good childcare experience.
Application procedure: interviews necessary for nannies. References are checked.
Other services: private health insurance can be arranged for au pairs. List of language classes given.
Fees: nil for incoming; 900FF for outgoing.
Contact: Marie Charti, Proprietor/Manager.

SOLIHULL AU PAIR & NANNY AGENCY

1565 Stratford Road, Hall Green,
Birmingham B28 9JA
Tel: 0121 733 6444
Fax: 0121 733 6555

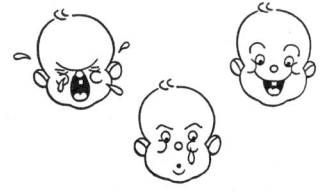

We place au pairs, nannies and mother's helps in France, Switzerland, Greece, Italy, Germany, Spain and all other major European countries. We are in communication with over 100 European agencies. We need 18–27-year-olds for 6 months — 1 year with child care experience.

U.S.A. We need 18–26-year-olds who can drive and have practical child care experience to spend 1 year/fare paid, au pairing with an American family. $128.25 per week/ legal visa/study opportunity. Programme open to most nationalities.

EDGWARE AU PAIR AGENCY

19 Manor Park Crescent,
Edgware,
Middlesex HA8 7NH
Tel: 0181 952 5522
Fax: 0181 951 5219/1005

We also offer nanny/ mother's helps positions in the UK. Excellent opportunities available. Placements throughout the UK, many families in London, Birmingham and other large cities/towns. Drivers preferred but not always essential.

We can help you make the right career move and are here to help assist you. For details phone/fax/write to one of our agencies.

ISLINGTON AU PAIR AGENCY

PO Box 358, Edgware,
Middlesex HA8 8JA
Tel: 0181 905 3355
Fax: 0181 905 3300

SOGGIORNI ALL'ESTERO PER LA GIOVENTU'
Via Fatebenefratelli 16, 20121 Milan, Italy. Tel: 2-753 00 61/290 00 631. Fax (daytime only): 2-753 00 61.
In business since 1957.
Placements: 400 au pairs, demi pairs, work/study, language students, homestays and holiday guests.
Jobs in: UK, Ireland, France, Germany, Austria and Spain. (No placement in Italy except on holiday guest basis.)
Nationalities placed: Italians (mainly).
Minimum stay: 2-3 months (6 months in Germany).
Qualifications: must have some babysitting experience and moderate competence in chosen language.
Fees: 300,000 lire.
Contact: Nicoletta Casalini.

SOLIHULL AU PAIR & NANNY AGENCY
1565 Stratford Road, Hall Green, Birmingham B28 9JA. Tel: 0121-733 6444. Fax: 0121-733 6555.
In business since 1990.
Placements: 500 nannies, mother's helps, au pairs and demi pairs.
Jobs in: Europe (France, Italy, Spain, Germany, Belgium, Sweden, Norway, Denmark, Netherlands, Austria, Greece, Switzerland and Turkey), UK (including Scotland, Wales and Northern Ireland) and America.
Nationalities placed: Europeans in accordance with Home Office regulations to UK.
Male positions are occasionally available for applicants with top-class childcare background.
Minimum stay: 6-12 months preferred. 1 year for USA. Summer stays: minimum 2½-3 months; applications must be in by mid-May. Possibility of Christmas and Easter positions.
Wages/pocket money: £100-£150 per week for nannies; £70-£90 for mother's helps; £30-£50 for au pairs, depending on country.
Qualifications: practical childcare experience (such as babysitting for au pairs) and love of children essential. Certificates in swimming or First Aid are useful.
Application procedure: application processing takes 2-6 weeks. Interviews given whenever possible.
Other services: details of local language school always given. Advice on insurance given. Sister agency is Edgware Au Pair Agency (see entry).
Fees: £40 for European placements (not UK). Fee for America is nil.
Contact: Raymond Bushell, Proprietor.

SONIA BROOKE PLACEMENT AGENCY
Rose Cottage, 11B Marlborough Place, Banbury, Oxfordshire OX16 8DA. Tel/fax: 01295 270024. Mobile: 0976 673891.
In business since 1995.
Placements: nannies, mother's helps, maternity nurses, au pairs and babysitters.
Jobs in: EU countries and Australia. Also UK.
Agency attempts to place males but difficult.
Minimum stay: 9-12 months or 2-3 months in summer.
Wages/pocket money: £35-£40 per week.

Qualifications: minimum age 18. Childcare requirements depend on job.
Application procedure: for nannies at least 3 references are needed which are checked verbally. Interview essential.
Other services: give outgoing au pairs information and telephone numbers for insurance. Incoming au pairs to Oxfordshire are given information on classes, busses, flights, etc. Gives advice on contracts, tax and a general listening ear.
Fees: £10 (au pairs only).
Contact: Sonia Brooke, Proprietor.

SONIA BROOKE PLACEMENT AGENCY

NANNIES, MOTHER'S HELPS, MATERNITY NURSES, LONG & SHORT-TERM AU-PAIRS

JOBS IN THE U.K. AND ABROAD (inc. AUS)

CALL Sonia Brooke NOW on 01295 270024
OR SEND CV TO
ROSE COTTAGE, 11B MARLBOROUGH PLACE, BANBURY OXON OX16 8DA

IRMHILD SPITZER, AGENTUR FUR AU PAIR
Sparkassenplatz 1, 7th Floor, 4040 Linz, Austria. Tel: 732-737 814. Fax: 732-711 060.
In business since 1986.
Placements: 150-200 au pairs, au pairs plus, holiday demi pairs and paying guests.
Jobs in: Austria; also UK, France, Italy, Spain, Canada and USA.
About 4-6 male positions are available each year.
Minimum stay: 3/6/9 months. Summer stays: 2 months.
Wages/pocket money: 800-1,000 Austrian schillings per week for au pairs; 1,000 schillings for au pairs plus; demi pairs receive only free room and board.
Qualifications: childcare experience usually needed.
Application procedure: interview preferred.
Other services: advises families on how to obtain work permit for au pairs. Also advises uninsured au pairs to take out special insurance (which costs about 4,000 schillings a year). Can recommend local language schools.
Fees: 1,800 schillings for long term au pairs; 1,080 schillings for summer au pairs, including tax.
Contact: Irmhild Spitzer, Owner.

STABLEMATE STAFF AGENCY
156 Pitt Town Road, Kenthurst, NSW 2156, Australia. Tel: 2-9654 9733. Fax: 2-9654 9643. Office hours 8am-4pm and 7.30-8.30pm Monday to Friday.
In business since 1990.
Placements: nannies and au pairs who have had experience with horses.
Jobs in: Australia; occasionally New Zealand and USA for equine placements.

Nationalities placed: Australian, British, Irish, Dutch, New Zealand, American and Canadian. Candidates with working holiday visas are welcome.
Male positions are occasionally available.
Minimum stay: 3 months.
Wages/pocket money: from A$100 per week.
Qualifications: childcare experience not always needed. Must have horse-related skills.
Application procedure: can sometimes be processed in 4 weeks. Must submit details of height and weight (for riding purposes) as well as usual information about ability to drive, non-smoking, etc.
Other services: can advise on Australian Medicare and worker's compensation.
Fees: nil.
Contact: Brenda McDonough, Managing Director.

STUDENT AGENCY
Basty 2, 657 91 Brno, Czech Republic. Tel: +420-5-42 21 67 54. Fax: +420-5-42 21 67 56. Also branch in Prague: Mikovcova 8, 120 00 Prague, Czech Republic; tel: +420-2-24 23 94 19/fax: +420-2-24 23 74 07.
In business since 1993.
Placements: 1,500 au pairs per year.
Jobs in: UK, USA, Germany, France, Belgium, Italy, Spain, Netherlands, Denmark; also starting to place girls in Czech and Slovak Republics.
Nationalities placed: Czech and Slovak.
Minimum stay: varies from country to country. Summer stays are available in England, Belgium, Italy and Spain.
Wages/pocket money: £35-£50 per week in Europe.
Qualifications: minimum age 17/18; maximum age 27 in UK, 26 in USA. Driving licence is useful, and is essential for USA. Placements in Czech and Slovak families involve childcare only, no housework.
Fees: from £26; nil for USA.
Contact: Mr. Radim Jancura, Owner.

STUDENTS ABROAD/GLOBAL NANNIES
3 Kneller Road, New Malden, Surrey KT3 5ND. Tel: 0181-330 0777. Fax: 0181-330 0345.
In business since 1976.
Placements: hundreds of au pairs, mother's helps and nannies.
Jobs in: France, Belgium, Germany, Greece (including housekeeper posts), Italy, Austria, Spain, Netherlands, Turkey, Israel, Canada, USA, Australia and UK; occasionally au pair posts in South Africa and Scandinavia.
Nationalities placed: any, provided it is legal.
Minimum stay: 6-12 months preferred for au pairs; 6-12 months for mother's helps and 12 months for nannies (and also US au pairs). Summer and winter ski resort placements: 5 months December to end of April (in great demand so early application necessary). Summer posts mainly in France, Italy and Spain.
Wages/pocket money: £35-£40 per week for au pairs; variable for other positions.
Qualifications: minimum age 18 years. Maximum age 27 years (though some leniency within the EU); maximum for US 25 years. Childcare experience preferred for au pairs; otherwise essential. Basic language skills preferred but

not essential. Non-smokers greatly preferred. Driving licence essential for USA and Canada, useful elsewhere.
Application procedure: send s.a.e. for registration form and details of dossier requirements. Every applicant is placed in contact with family prior to acceptance of a post. Personal interviews required for all nanny and US placements, others by arrangement.
Other services: optional information pack about travel, insurance, health cover and the host country available for £10.
Fees: nil to applicants placed in UK. £40 to au pairs going abroad.

STUFAM V.Z.W.
Vierwindenlaan 7, 1780 Wemmel, Belgium. Tel: 2-460 33 95. Fax: 2-460 00 71.
Office hours: Monday, Wednesday and Friday: 5.30-8pm; Tuesday and Thursday: 3-6pm.
In business since 1985.
Placements: 100-120 au pairs and demi pairs.
Jobs in: Belgium; also UK, Ireland, Netherlands, France, Spain, Italy, Norway, Denmark, Germany, Austria and Switzerland.
Nationalities placed: EU nationals; others must apply for visas.
Minimum stay: 6 months. Summer placements: 2-3 months.
Wages/pocket money: £45-£55 per week.
Qualifications: childcare references needed. Must have basic knowledge of the language. Ages 18-28.
Other services: assistance in case of problems. Assist au pairs who need visas. Agency puts au pairs in touch with one another.
Fees: £20 registration fee to be submitted with file.
Contact: Lieve Deschuymere, Manager.

SUNSHINE AGENCY
Viale Principessa Mafalda 14, 90149 Palermo, Italy. Tel/fax: 91-454870. Tel: 91-322650.
In business since 1989.
Placements: up to 100 au pairs.
Jobs in: Italy only.
Nationalities placed: EU nationals.
Male positions as drivers, gardeners and waiters are available.
Minimum stay: 6 months, though 1 year preferred. Many summer stays are available (minimum 2 months), especially in Sicilian seaside resorts.
Wages/pocket money: 100,000 lire per week for au pairs; 130,000-150,000 lire for au pairs plus.
Qualifications: ages 18-30. Au pairs need to have some experience if only with children in the family.
Application procedure: 2 references from teachers or previous employers needed as well as medical clearance, 2 photos, CV and introductory letter. Agency sends applicant a photo of the prospective employer and a letter from them describing the daily working routine.
Other services: agency provides a map and a list of addresses of other foreign au pairs. Can advise on affordable Italian language courses. If 1-week trial does not work out, agency will arrange another family or help au pair to book return ticket.
Fees: nil.
Contact: Silvana Verace and Nina Mangoni, Owners.

SWAN TRAINING INSTITUTE
AU PAIRS / AU PAIRS PLUS placed in ...

Ireland	Italy	Spain
France	Germany	Belgium

Minimum length of placement 3 months in
the summer or 6 months year round

For details and an application form contact:

Swan Training Institute Ltd
110 Grafton Street, Dublin 2, Ireland
Tel: 01-6775252   Fax: 01-6775254

SWAN TRAINING INSTITUTE LTD
110 Grafton Street, Dublin 2, Ireland. Tel: 1-677 5252. Fax: 1-677 5254.
E-mail: swann@indigo.ie
In business since 1988.
Placements: 150 au pairs and au pairs plus.
Jobs in: Ireland, Italy, Spain, France, Germany and Belgium.
Nationalities placed: no restrictions.
Minimum stay: 6 months (3 months in summer).
Wages/pocket money: £40-£55 per week.
Qualifications: ages 18-25. Must be able to speak English at an intermediate level. Some childcare and housework experience needed.
Application procedure: Application form should be submitted 3 months before intended departure.
Other services: language classes compulsory for au pairs in Dublin.
Fees: £100 per placement.
Contact: Oliver Lyons (Director) or Begona Camaano (Placement Officer).

SWISS-O-PAIR/ETTIE MOESKER BUREAU DE PLACEMENT
Case Postale 295, 1233 Bernex (GE), Switzerland. Tel: 22-757 43 62. Fax: 22-757 59 14. Mobile: 77 87 53 24.
In business since 1989.
Placements: 120 au pairs.
Jobs in: Switzerland (especially Geneva basin), France and Germany.

Nationalities placed: Western Europeans, Canadians and Americans. Approximately 2 males are placed per year.
Minimum stay: 6 months from January; most are for school year (10 months). About 4 summer placements are made each year.
Wages/pocket money: SFr710 per month.
Qualifications: at least babysitting and some housework experience needed. Must have basic knowledge of French. Ages 18-27.
Other services: provide brochures on language schools such as Ecole Migros in Geneva. Organise a meeting/party once a year.
Fees: nil for incoming; SFr50 registration plus SFr250 placement fee for outgoing (the legal maximum).
Contact: Ettie Moesker, Managing Director.

TAROOKI AU PAIR & CATERING AGENCY
1 Turnpike Close, Darlington, Co. Durham DL1 3SH. Tel/fax: 01325 483342.
In business since 1993.
Placements: au pairs and hotel staff (UK only).
Jobs in: UK, Belgium, Italy, Spain (including Tenerife), France, Germany and Turkey.
Nationalities placed: any that are from qualifying countries. Male au pair positions are available in some countries.
Minimum stay: 3 months. Summer stays are available, including one month stays.
Wages/pocket money: £35 per week.
Qualifications: ages 17-27. Must have at least babysitting experience.
Application procedure: processing time normally 2-3 weeks.
Other services: agents abroad help sort out problems.
Fees: £35 for outgoing au pairs.
Contact: Audrey Ameen-Ali, Director.

THE ENGLISH AGENCY (TEA)
Via Pigafetta 48, 10129 Turin, Italy. Tel/fax: 11-597458.
In business since 1976.
Placements: nannies, au pairs, mother's helps, governesses and housekeepers.
Jobs in: Italy, also UK and worldwide.
Nationalities placed: all.
Minimum stay: 6-12 months. A few summer stays of 1-4 months are available.
Wages/pocket money: 500,000 lire per month for au pairs, 800,000-140,000 lire for mother's helps and 1,500,000-2,400,000 lire for nannies. Air fare home sometimes paid on completion of contract.
Qualifications: must have childcare experience.
Application procedure: 2 photos (passport type), medical certificate and minimum 2 references, one related to childcare.
Other services: information pack on area. Contact with other au pairs and social evenings with other nannies arranged. Emergency accommodation arranged if necessary.
Fees: nil for Italy; 150,000 lire plus VAT for outgoing placements.
Contacts: Agnes Coburn and Elaine Coburn (Directors), Harry Blosier (Post Placement Coordinator).

TINIES U.K. LTD
79 London St, Reading RG1 4QA. Tel: 0118 957 6699/950 0455. Fax: 0118 951 1600.
In business since 1975. Incorporating Tinies International. Sole UK agent for InterExchange in New York (see entry).
Placements: nannies, mother's helps, maternity nurse/nanny.
Jobs in: Europe, worldwide, UK and USA.
Minimum stay: short temporary contracts and permanent posts. Minimum 12 months in USA.
Qualifications: nannies must be qualified and experienced. Mother's helps must have some childcare experience and references. For USA, applicants must have at least 6 months babysitting experience.
Application procedure: interviews arranged if possible. Childcare references checked verbally.
Other services: details given of contracts, nanny insurance and contact numbers of other nannies in the area.
Fees: nil.
Contact: Susan Boothroyd, Melanie Cardy and Jenny O'Neill, Partners.

TOP NOTCH NANNIES
22A Campden Grove, Kensington, London W8 4JG. Tel: 0171-938 2006. Fax: 0171-938 4742.
In business since 1992. Member of FRES. Affiliated with New Zealand agency: Top Notch Nannies NZ, 2/57 McFaddens Road, St. Albans, Christchurch 8005, New Zealand.
Placements: nannies, mother's helps, maternity nurses and babysitters.
Jobs in: Italy, France, Switzerland, Netherlands, Germany, UK and worldwide (excluding USA).
Good male nannies can be placed.
Male au pair positions are available in some countries.
Minimum stay: temporary and permanent positions available.
Wages/pocket money: live-in nannies earn £150-£200 per week, live-out nannies £200-£250.
Application procedure: interview essential. Must give 3 references with phone numbers.
Fees: nil for UK.
Contact: Jean Birtles, Director.

TRAVEL ACTIVE PROGRAMMES
PO Box 107, 5800 AC Venray (Albionstraat 30A, 5809 AE Venray), Netherlands. Tel: 478-551 900. Fax: 478 551 911. E-mail: info@travelactive.nl
In business since 1989. Member of IAPA and FIYTO. From 1995, incorporating Dutch agency Exis KLIX.
Placements: 500 au pairs sent abroad.
Jobs in: USA, Canada, Australia and Europe.
Nationalities placed: Dutch and Belgian.
Limited number of male positions are available in Europe only.
Minimum stay: 6-12 months in Europe, 1 year in USA and Canada. Summer stays available in Europe only. Maximum stay with one family in Australia (under terms of working holiday visa) is 3 months.
Qualifications: childcare experience necessary. Au pairs in Australia must participate in Work and Travel Program for Australia

Other services: offer Dutch au pairs special insurance cover.
Fees: 100 guilders (non-refundable) plus 200 guilders (USA), 375 guilders (Canada and Europe); 275 guilders (summer au pair in Europe).
Contact: Ellen Vola.

ENGLAND & OVERSEAS AU PAIR BUREAU
Also Nannies, Mother's Helps and Domestics
World's Largest Au Pair Bureau
With 28 Overseas Agency Representatives

Suite 21-23 (Kent House)
87 Regent Street, Piccadilly, London W1R 7HF
Tel: 0171 494 2929 (5 lines)   Fax: 0171 494 2922

Emp. Agy

UK & OVERSEAS NANNY/AU PAIR AGENCY LTD.
Suites 21-23, Kent House, 87 Regent St, London W1R 7HF. (1 min from Piccadilly Circus). Tel: 0171-494 2929 (5 lines). Fax: 0171-494 2922 (day or night). Also trades as The Nanny Agency and Central London Bureau/CLB. Office hours: Monday-Friday 9am-5pm.
In business for more than 25 years. Originally opened in 1969.
Placements: several thousand live-in-staff: nannies, maternity nurses, mother's helps, au pairs and housekeepers.
Jobs in: UK and Worldwide including USA and unusual places but excluding Canada, Australia and New Zealand. Specialise in UK and Germany. Jobs also in France, Switzerland, Spain, Italy, Belgium, Luxembourg, Netherlands, Sweden, Denmark, Norway, Greece, Hungary, Austria, USA and occasionally South America, etc.
Nationalities placed: any that can work legally.
Male au pairs can be placed if they have childcare experience supported by references and stay for a minimum of 12 months.
Minimum stay: usual stay 12 months plus. Some temp jobs including summer stays available for a minimum of 3 months (no less).
Wages/pocket money: depends on age, qualification, experience and country. Approximately £50 per week for au pairs; £100-£150 for mother's helps; £150-£250 for nannies and £250-£400 for maternity nurses.
Qualifications: au pairs need good written references only. Mother's helps need to be experienced or/and have good references. Nannies must have NNEB or similar qualification and have good references.
Application procedure: early application encouraged. Interested individuals should send SAE for introduction pack and application form or visit agency (no appointment necessary).

UNIVERSAL AUNTS
PO Box 304, London SW4 0NN. Tel: 0171-738 8937. Fax: 0171-622 1914.

In business since 1921.
Placements: nannies and mother's helps.
Jobs in: UK and Europe.
Agency cannot place male candidates.
Nationalities placed: any, provided they are legal.
Minimum stay: variable. Summer placements possible, but in great demand.
Wages/pocket money: approximately £130 per week for mother's helps.
Qualifications: childcare experience needed. Driving licence useful.
Application procedure: after childcare references received and interviews held, placement can usually be made within 10 days. Interviews by appointment only. Family and applicant always put in direct contact.
Fees: no registration fee.

UNIVERSAL CARE
Chester House, 9 Windsor End, Beaconsfield, Bucks. HP9 2JJ. Tel: 01494 678811. Fax: 01494 671259.
In business since 1965 (incorporating Baxter's Agency).
Placements: 350 au pairs, mother's helps and nannies.
Jobs in: Belgium, France, Germany, Italy, Spain and UK.
Nationalities placed: West Europeans.
Male placements occasionally possible. (Agency encourages males and at one time estimated that 10% of applicants were male.)
Minimum stay: 6 months.
Wages/pocket money: £35+ per week for au pairs; £80-£200 per week for mother's helps and nannies.
Qualifications: age limits for au pairs 17-27 years; no restrictions for nannies and mother's helps. Childcare experience an advantage but not necessary.
Application procedure: 4 photos, medical clearance and 2 references necessary. Placement normally takes 4 weeks.
Other services: advice on travel, documentation and language courses provided. Can arrange special insurance policy.
Fees: £47 if going abroad; maximum cancellation fee of $5.
Contact: Miss Katie Jones.

VEREIN FUR INTERNATIONALE JUGENDARBEIT (VIJ)
39 Craven Road, London W2 3BX. Tel: 0171-723 0216. Fax: 0171-262 0147.
UK branch of the German YWCA; affiliated to the Evangelical-Lutheran Synod. Office hours: Monday-Wednesday and Friday 9-12am; Thursday 2-4pm.
In operation since 1882.
Placements: 2,000 au pairs.
Jobs in: Germany and UK.
Nationalities placed: all.
Males can be placed if experienced in childcare.
Minimum stay: 6 months; school year preferred. Shorter summer placements possible in Germany for university students if they speak good German.
Wages/pocket money: DM400 per month plus season ticket for public transport (for travelling to language classes): £40 minimum in London, less elsewhere.
Qualifications: minimum age 18; maximum 24 in Germany, 27 in UK. Childcare experience desirable. Should have good knowledge of German (or English if coming to UK). Preferably non-smoker.
Application procedure: 3 application forms, 3 signed photos, 2 references,

medical certificate and CV (preferably in German) required. Personal interview for British girls desirable but not essential; interviews essential for German girls coming to UK.
Other services: social programme, meetings, counselling service and advice on language classes given by one of about 25 local VIJ branches in Germany and by London office in UK.
Fees: nil in UK; varies in Germany.

WALLEROO NANNIES
3 Adam & Eve Mews, Kensington, London W8 6UG. Tel: 0171-937 7075. Fax: 0171-937 3419.
In business since 1992.
Placements: nannies, mother's helps, maternity nurses and babysitters.
Jobs in: England and Europe.
Nationalities placed: any that can work legally, especially New Zealanders. Affiliated with agent in New Zealand: Jane Hulme, Walleroo New Zealand, PO Box 9194, Newmarket, New Zealand (tel 09-520 1349).
Male placements can be made.
Minimum stay: temporary and permanent. Summer positions available.
Wages/pocket money: £140-£200 per week for nannies, £120-£140 for mother's helps (both live-in). £200-£250 per week for live-out nannies and £300-£400 for maternity nurses.
Qualifications: minimum age 21. Childcare experience preferred. Must be English-speaking.
Application procedure: all applicants are interviewed and references checked.
Other services: can arrange travel and provide back-up. Nanny get-togethers are held once a month to introduce new nannies. Excursions are arranged.
Fees: nil.
Contact: Mrs. Clare Williams, Owner/Recruitment Consultant.

WEALDEN NANNIES

We specialist in placing Nannies & Mother's Helps in Kent & Sussex
Some child care experience & Driving licence preferred

Contact Mrs. R. Broadbent, Ringle Crouch, Sandhurst, Kent, U.K.
Tel/Fax: 01580 850585

WEALDEN NANNIES
Ringle Crouch, Sandhurst, Kent TN18 5PA. Tel/fax: 01580 850585.
In business since 1984.
Placements: nannies and mother's helps.
Jobs in: UK, mainly Kent and Sussex; Italy and Switzerland occasionally.

Agency is willing to try to place males candidates.
Minimum stay: 1 year. Summer stays are possible for staff resident in UK.
Wages/pocket money: £120-£200 per week net.
Qualifications: minimum age 18. Driving licence, childcare experience and/or qualification preferred.
Application procedure: compulsory interviews. 2 written references are checked by phone.
Other services: contract of employment supplied and back-up advice.
Fees: nil.
Contact: Mrs. R. Broadbent, Owner.

WESTMINSTER NANNIES INTERNATIONAL

LONDON – NATIONWIDE – WORLDWIDE

Specialists in the placement and recruitment of:
NANNIES, MOTHER'S HELPS & GOVERNESSES

TEL: 01275 876082   FAX: 01275 340152

16 The Croft, Clevedon BS21 6AT, U.K.

WESTMINSTER NANNIES INTERNATIONAL
16 The Croft, Clevedon, Bristol BS21 6AT. Tel: 01275 876082. Fax: 01275 340152.
In business since 1988.
Placements: nannies, mother's helps, governesses, maternity nurses and housekeepers.
Jobs in: UK and worldwide.
Minimum stay: permanent (1 year) and temporary (variable).
Qualifications: must have training and/or experience.
Application procedure: initial telephone screening followed by an application form. Interviews by appointment.
Fees: nil.
Contact: Gill Bassett, Proprietor.

WINDROSE
Av. Paul Dejaer 21a, 1060 Brussels, Belgium. Tel: 2-534 71 91. Fax: 2-534 71 92. Tel/fax (for emergencies): 15-52 96 53.
In business since 1982. Member of IAPA.
Placements: 200 au pairs, demi pairs and mother's helps.
Jobs in: Belgium, Europe and USA.
Nationalities placed: all nationalities in Belgium. EU nationals sent abroad.
Minimum stay: 5/6 months in Belgium minimum, 10 months preferred. Summer placements are made if applications received early.
Wages/pocket money: BF10,000-BF15,000 per month.
Qualifications: ages 18-29. Non-smokers. Must be flexible, independent, enthusiastic, creative and like children.

Application procedure: 4 photos, medical certificate, letter of motivation, 2 childcare references needed. Telephone contact with family arranged.
Other services: meetings with other au pairs arranged. Social activities and advice on language courses.
Fees: BF2,000 for placement in Belgium.
Contact: Nadine Fierens-Wackens.

WISE (Worldwide Internships & Service Education)
303 South Craig Street, Suite 202, Pittsburgh, PA 15213, USA. Tel: 412-681-8120. Fax: 412-681-8187. E-mail: wise+@pitt.edu. Web-site: http://www.pitt.edu/-wise
In business since 1993.
Placements: about 50 au pairs.
Jobs in: France, Germany, Netherlands, Norway, Iceland and Austria.
Nationalities placed: Americans and Canadians.
Male au pair positions are available.
Minimum stay: varying minimums, e.g. 10 months for Germany. Summer stays are arranged in France and Austria.
Wages/pocket money: equivalent of $300-$350 per month.
Qualifications: minimum age 18, maximum 24-26 depending on country. Should have some experience of childcare and competence in language (for France and Austria).
Other services: cooperating agencies abroad provide back-up.
Fees: from US$725.
Contact: Linda Greenberg, Executive Director.

WORLD LEARNING INC. — see AuPair Homestay Programme.

XTRA-PAIR
The Poplars, Down Hatherley Lane, Down Hatherley, Gloucestershire GL2 9QB. Tel/fax: 01242 570795 and 01542 731154.
Placements: au pairs.
Jobs in: UK and Europe.
Minimum stay: 3-12 months. Summer stays are arranged.
Wages/pocket money: £35-£40 per week.
Qualifications: childcare experience preferred.

YORKSHIRE NANNIES & NURSES
26-27 High Street, Doncaster, South Yorkshire DN1 1DW. Tel: 01302 349393 (6 lines).
In business since 1970.
Placements: nannies, maternity nurses, mother's helps, carers, couples, butlers, cooks and chauffeurs.
Jobs in: throughout UK and worldwide.
Minimum stay: temporary and permanent positions.
Qualifications: childcare experience and driving licence normally needed.
Application procedure: all applicants are interviewed on premises. Must bring full CV. References are checked. High standards expected.
Fees: nil.

PART IV

Appendices

Safety in the Home
Childhood Ailments
Cooking for Children
Fun and Games
Embassies/Consulates
Currency Conversion Chart

Appendix 1

Safety in the Home

Be sure that telephone numbers of the local doctors, hospital and ambulance service are kept in a prominent position by the telephone.

Prevention is better than cure, so let us first examine the potential dangers to children in the home, and how they may be avoided.

Most young children have little or no experience of danger so they are unable to anticipate the consequences of their actions. It is impossible to guard a child all the time, and continually restricting him is bad for developing self-confidence. But making sure the home is a safe place to play can help alleviate the problem. If you are caring for young children and the house has not already been child-proofed, this should be discussed with the employers. Safety catches can be fixed to the doors of cupboards containing dangerous items, and sharp corners on tables and work surfaces may be covered by buffers to help prevent the children hurting their heads. You can also buy slot-in plastic covers for open plug sockets in some countries.

Try to remember that when dealing with a serious first-aid situation, it is imperative that you keep calm. The child will be frightened as well as hurt and will look to you for reassurance. If the wound isn't serious, don't dismiss the child for making a fuss. They will genuinely require your sympathy, but once the initial fear has passed, they should be encouraged to carry on as normal. Absorbing the child in a game or reading a story is a good way of diverting attention from any mild injuries.

Suffocation and Choking

Suffocation of babies can be avoided by removing certain objects from their reach. This includes plastic bibs, pillows, garments with draw-strings or loose buttons and fluffy toys with loose eyes. Don't forget to mend or dispose of any torn blankets. Sharon once looked after a baby who got his head stuck through a hole in his cot-cover in the early hours of the morning. Luckily, she heard him crying and was able to remove it before he strangled himself. If a baby is left outside in a pram, be vigilant of cats in the area. They can sit on a child's face and suffocate him, so use a pram net if this is a problem. Remember, too, that once a baby can sit up by himself, he becomes more active so a safety harness is advisable, especially if the pram is untended at any time.

All objects smaller than a ten pence piece should not be allowed infants and toddlers who are not past the stage of putting everything in their mouths. Peanuts are a common cause of choking in infants and should not be given.

Poisoning

Potential poisons should be made inaccessible to children by placing them firmly out of reach or, even better, locking them away. This includes medicines, household cleaners, shampoo and garden chemicals in the shed. Warn the children not to pick berries or fungi which may also be harmful. If in doubt yourself, find out which ones are hazardous.

Burns

Children are fascinated by fire and, once again, do not appreciate the danger involved. Make sure open fires have guards and beware of clothes that are highly inflammable. Pyjamas are less dangerous for little girls than nightgowns because they fit more closely and there is therefore less danger of the clothing coming into contact with the fire. Keep matches out of sight. Children should never be left alone in the kitchen when the stove is alight. Remember that electric stoves remain hot even after they have been switched off. Handles of pans that are cooking should be turned inwards to avoid accidents. Kettles should point to the wall to prevent the jet of steam pouring towards the child. Never leave buckets of hot water on the floor untended. When running baths, put the cold water in before the hot and then test the temperature with your elbow because it is more sensitive to heat than your hands. Electrical appliances are not safe unless unplugged; just switching items off is not enough.

Table cloths which overhang the edges are dangerous because the child can pull on them, spilling hot food or drinks. Plastic table cloths which can be taped down are best (and are also easier to clean). Place teapots, casserole dishes, etc., in the centre of the table and out of reach, and avoid drinking hot beverages while holding a baby, since their movements are unpredictable.

Other Dangers

It goes without saying that children should never be left in or near a pool unsupervised, no matter how proficient they are at swimming. Garden fish ponds can prove an irresistible attraction to young children who can drown in them in minutes. Ideally they should be covered with strong wire mesh.

The same applies to children in the bath. Even if the water level is low, a child can still drown.

All sharp implements should be kept out of reach, including garden equipment. A gate for the stairs is advisable to prevent falls, and children should not be left alone near open upstairs windows. Either fix the window handle so a child can't open it more than a few inches, or air the room via windows that are well out of reach.

Make sure repairs are kept up on outdoor play equipment such as swings, slides and climbing frames. Do not allow children to play near the road. Quiet streets that are devoid of heavy traffic are just as risky because the children aren't expecting the cars and don't keep alert for them. Teach them road drills as soon as they are old enough to understand. When travelling in cars, children should always be in the back seat, and small children placed in car seats. Keep doors locked.

Above all, keep your eyes and ears open and your wits about you.

FIRST AID

First Aid Disasters are unlikely to befall you during your days as an au pair or nanny, but it is unrealistic to assume that the children in your care will never have accidents or health problems. Therefore you should be prepared. Registering in an official first-aid course is a very good idea and the advice below is no substitute. Here is an alphabetical list of the first-aid situations most common to children and instructions on how to cope.

Asthma

Asthma is directly caused by the muscles in the air passage going into spasm, which makes breathing difficult. This is distressing for anyone but is particularly frightening for children. Attacks can sometimes be triggered by an allergy or by nervous tension, and they can also occur at night. Whenever the child suffers from an asthma attack you should aim to calm him down. It is vital that you display confidence and reassurance even though such attacks can be alarming to witness. Place the child into a sitting position with his elbows resting on a solid support (a table, for example) and loosen all restricting clothing. This will aid him in his breathing. If possible, provide a source of fresh air. If the attack is prolonged or repeated, or you are in doubt about the child's condition, seek medical aid.

Bites

For superficial animal bites, wash the wound thoroughly with soapy water. Dry it and cover with a sterile, unmedicated dressing and then take the child to a doctor. Severe dog bites should be reported to the police.

If the bite is serious, control any bleeding by applying direct pressure to the wound and elevating the damaged limb. Bandage securely and remove to hospital. Check whether the child is immunised against tetanus.

Burns and Scalds

A burn is caused by dry heat, for example a fire or oven, while a scald is caused by damp heat, for example hot liquid or steam from a kettle.

For serious burns, lay the child down, protecting the burnt area from contact with the ground if possible. Remove any constricting clothing from the injured area before swelling begins, but do not remove anything that is sticking to the burn or apply any lotions or ointments. Cover the burn with a sterile, unmedicated dressing and secure with a bandage. The child will probably be in shock, so you should keep him warm and immobilised. Moisten his lips with water if he complains of thirst. Don't give him anything to drink or eat because it will interfere with the administration of an anaesthetic later on. If breathing and heart-beat stops, begin resuscitation immediately. Remove to hospital.

If the burns are superficial, immerse injury in cold water for as long as the pain persists. If no water is available, improvise with any cold harmless liquid (milk, for example). Remove any jewellery or constricting material and place a sterile dressing on the wound. Once again, do not apply any lotions or use adhesive dressings. In all cases, blisters and loose skin should be left intact.

Choking

Hook your fingers inside the child's mouth to dislodge any debris. If dealing with an older child, bend his head over so it is lower than the lungs. Slap him between the shoulder blades four times with the heel of your hand, hard enough to remove the obstruction. Check the mouth again and hook out any visible debris.

For infants, hold them upside down with their body along your forearm and tap them on the back. Small children should be lain over your knee with their head down, while back slaps are applied.

If this method fails, perform *Abdominal Thrust*. This involves standing the child in front of you, or, if small, sitting him on your knee. Place one of your arms around his abdomen, making a clenched fist with your hand. Support his back with your other hand. Press your fist into his abdomen with quick upward and outward strokes, but with less pressure for young children. The thrust must still be hard enough to dislodge the obstruction.

Infants should be placed on a firm surface with their head in the open airway position (see *Emergency Procedures*) below. Apply abdominal thrust but with two fingers only.

Concussion

This can result when a blow is received to the head. A child does not necessarily have to be unconscious to suffer from a concussion and it should be taken seriously in case compression develops. Compression means there is pressure on the brain caused by blood or a depressed fracture, and it may develop up to forty-eight hours later. Therefore, if a child has a bad knock on the head, it would be wise to see a doctor, especially if he or she seems unusually drowsy. Should the casualty be unconscious for any length of time, arrange removal to hospital.

Cuts and Bruises

With small wounds, a kiss, a wash and a plaster is all that is necessary. For larger wounds, apply a sterile unmedicated dressing and then bandage it. If your charge has a morbid fear of blood (not uncommon in small children), all you can do is remain calm and reassuring and deal with the wound as gently (but quickly) as possible.

If bleeding is serious, it can be controlled by applying direct pressure to the wound and elevating the injury. For a badly cut arm, for example, apply pressure, bandage and elevate into a sling. Do not bandage so tightly that the circulation is cut-off. Remove to hospital.

For bruises, apply a cold compress to reduce swelling and then dab with witch-hazel.

If you think a cut may be infected you should consult a doctor.

Dislocation

If a child has injured a joint so badly that it appears deformed, he may have dislocated it. This is very painful so you should treat the injury particularly gently. Try to immobilise the affected part with bandages or slings and then remove to hospital immediately.

Drowning

Clear air passages and apply artificial ventilation as soon as possible. When the child is on dry land, check breathing and heart-beat and continue resuscitation if necessary. As soon as the casualty is breathing normally, place in the Recovery Position (see below). Keep him warm and horizontal while removing to hospital.

Emergency Procedures/Resuscitation

There may be a time when a child in your care is knocked unconscious and it will be necessary to administer emergency first-aid procedures while you are waiting for medical aid to arrive. Whatever you do, don't forget to call an ambulance before applying the three techniques for resuscitation. If possible, anyone planning to work with children should have some training in First Aid.

To detect whether or not a child is breathing, place your ear above his mouth and look along his chest and abdomen. If you cannot feel or hear any breaths and there is no movement along his torso, apply artificial ventilation. You should first make sure the airway is open by supporting the neck while tilting the head gently backwards. Sweep your fingers around the inside of his mouth to make sure there is nothing obstructing the airway. In children and infants, seal your lips around both the nose and mouth with the head still in the open airway position, and breathe gently into his lungs at a rate of twenty breaths per minute. Check for heart-beat after the first four inflations by feeling for a pulse in the neck. This should be a little off to one side from his Adam's apple.

If there is no pulse you will need to circulate the oxygen around his body via external chest compressions. Lie him on his back on a firm surface and find his breast-bone by tracing the inside edge of his ribs until you find the point where the two sets of ribs join together. Place two of your fingers horizontally side-by-side on this point and then place the heel of your hand just above the mark you have located. For children you should use just one hand, pressing lightly but firmly. After every fifteen compressions, apply two ventilations so you can continue to pump sufficient oxygen around his body. As soon as a pulse returns you should stop the external chest compressions but continue artificial ventilation until natural breathing is restored. The same applies to infants except the chest compressions should be applied with just two fingers. Abdominal thrust and cardiac massage can be dangerous if done by someone untrained.

Once breathing and pulse have returned, place the child in the *Recovery Position*. To do this, you should kneel alongside him and turn his head towards you. Straighten the casualty's arm nearest you, down by his side and tuck his hand under his buttock, palm upwards. Place the other arm over the front of his chest as though supported in a sling. Hold the far leg under the ankle and bring it towards you, crossing it over the nearest leg. Support the head with one hand, while grasping the clothing at the hip furthest away and pull the child towards you. Support the casualty in this position with your knees while adjusting his head (which should be resting on one side on the floor) back into the open airway position, i.e. tilted upwards. Bend the casualty's uppermost arm into a position which will support his upper body. Bend the uppermost leg at the knee to support the lower body. Gently pull the other arm out from underneath the child and leave it lying parallel to his body to prevent him rolling back.

Fits

Sometimes infants between the ages of one and four suffer convulsions (sometimes called fever fits) caused by a high temperature during illness. The eyes may roll up, the breathing stop briefly and the body go stiff and then twitchy. Clear a space around the baby, and ensure a good supply of fresh air.

Loosen any clothing around the child's neck and cool him down with a sponge soaked in tepid water. Call a doctor.

If a child in your care suffers from epilepsy, he may experience convulsions from time to time. The most important thing is to prevent the child from hurting himself. You can do this by protecting the head with cushions or clothing and removing anything that is portable and in the way. Do not attempt to open his mouth or restrain him, but once the convulsion has ceased, place him in the recovery position. Advise the child's doctor about this latest attack.

Foreign bodies

If the child has something imbedded in his ear, don't attempt to dislodge it in case you perforate the eardrum. Take the child to hospital.

Should the foreign body be in the child's eye, try to restrain him from rubbing it. Take him into a good light and open the eye wide with your index finger and thumb so you can inspect it. If you can see the cause of the trouble, try to remove it by pouring water into the eye to flush it out. If it is the right eye that is damaged, incline the head also to the right so that the water will not run into the good eye and vice versa. If you cannot remove the foreign body, cover the eye with an eye-pad and remove to hospital.

Fractures

If you suspect that the child has a fractured limb, do not move the injured part unless absolutely necessary. Make him as comfortable as possible by padding him around with blankets and cushions, etc. and phone for an ambulance.

Hysteria

Sometimes children throw such terrible tantrums that they become hysterical. Do not slap the child since this will only make matters worse, but escort him firmly to a quiet place and keep an eye on him until he recovers. If this sort of reaction happens frequently, you should seek medical advice.

Insect Stings

If the sting has been left in the skin, try to remove it with tweezers. Don't attempt to squeeze it out or you will force the rest of the poison into the skin. To help deaden the pain and control swelling, apply a cold compress or a paste of water mixed with baking soda. If the swelling persists or is worse by the next day, consult a doctor.

Nose Bleeds

Sit the child down and lean him over a bowl while you persuade him to pinch his nostrils together and breathe through his mouth. Tell him to spit out any blood which accumulates in his mouth. The pressure should be released after ten minutes, but if the bleeding hasn't stopped, repeat the treatment. If it hasn't cleared up in half an hour, seek medical aid.

Poisoning

The first thing you should do is try to establish what the child has swallowed. Then call medical help immediately. If the casualty has swallowed acid, give him something alkaline to drink in the meantime, such as milk of magnesia. If it is something alkaline (ammonia, for instance) give him something acidic to drink, such as vinegar or lemon juice. Should the child have drunk phenol, which is contained in many disinfectants, give him plenty of water to drink. If you are not sure what the substance was, do not give him anything.

Only attempt to make a child vomit if you know he has swallowed a non-corrosive poison such as tablets, insecticides or poisonous plants. The symptoms are nausea and lethargy. Save any remains of the poison or vomit, especially if you are unsure of what he took in the first place. The hospital will need to identify the substance before treatment can be given.

Splinters

Cleanse around the splinter if the area is dirty. Sterilise a pair of tweezers or a sewing needle by passing them through a flame, and gently try to remove the splinter. Don't probe the area or you could make it worse. Seek medical aid.

Sprains

Apply a cold compress to help reduce swelling and then bandage. Only seek medical aid if the symptoms persist or you are concerned that it might actually be a fracture.

Suffocation

Remove any obstruction which may be cutting off the air supply, such as a pillow if the baby lies face down. If the child is unconscious but breathing normally, place in the recovery position. If unable to breathe, begin artificial ventilation as soon as an ambulance has been called.

Appendix 2

Childhood Ailments

The moment you become suspicious that a child in your care may be sick, you should inform the parents. If an emergency arises during their absence, always contact them as soon as the crisis is under control, i.e. the doctor has been called and the child has been made as comfortable as possible. If you have to collect a sick child from school, phone the mother immediately after the teacher has alerted you. Should the parents be absent for a period of days and you are worried about the child's health, consult a relative of the family or a close family friend. Ultimately, however, the child is your responsibility so, when in doubt, seek medical advice. One of the most important symptoms to recognise in a child is fever. If the child's temperature is raised for an extended period, always consult a doctor. It might be an indication of a serious illness like pneumonia.

Immunisation programmes against measles, mumps, rubella (i.e. German measles) and whooping cough are now well established in Britain and in most developed countries, so these childhood diseases have been greatly reduced. The only infectious disease against which there is no immunisation to date is chicken pox.

Chicken Pox

There is no immunisation against chicken pox. With chicken pox, the child may feel generally unwell for a day or two and there will be a slight rise in temperature. He will develop small round spots of a blistery appearance on his body and this will spread to his face, causing itchiness. Scabs will form and these will drop off after a few days, but new crops develop every four or five days, so there are always some spots present. It takes a couple of weeks for all the scabs to clear. The child will feel fine for most of this so there is no reason to keep him at home. However if you go to a park or anywhere where there are other children playing, you should warn the parents (who might even welcome the prospect of their child catching the disease and getting it over with).

Calamine lotion and frequent tepid baths will help relieve itching and nails should be kept short and clean to reduce the risk of infection. It's a good idea to put cotton gloves on the child's hands at night to avoid scratching. If the spots do become infected, they will require special ointment from the doctor.

Colds

The common cold is caused by a virus, not by cold air or wet clothing (though both of those can increase the likelihood of infection), and it takes about ten days for the body to fight it. Keep the child indoors in a well ventilated, sunny room for a couple of days and encourage plenty of fluids. It has not been scientifically proven that vitamin C fights the virus, but it certainly can't hurt and many people swear by it, so give plenty of fruit juices and citrus fruit.

It is unnecessary to contact a doctor unless the child develops a fever and/or other symptoms such as a bad cough, sore throat or earache. Nose drops will help a blocked nose but they shouldn't be used frequently over long periods because they can damage the lining of the nose.

Constipation

It is wise to remember that each child is an individual and frequency of bowel movements vary. It is not so much the regularity which is a problem, but whether or not the stools are hard enough to cause the child discomfort. Constipation is also frequently accompanied by headaches, stomach pains, furred tongue and listlessness.

If you have reason to believe your charge is constipated, an increase of roughage in his diet will usually help. Give him plenty of whole-wheat food, vegetables, fruits and fruit juices. Jacket potatoes, popcorn and baked beans are also a good source of roughage and plenty of fluids will encourage softer motions. Make sure the child is getting enough exercise. Remember, too, that most children reach an age where they prefer privacy when opening their bowels and your presence in the bathroom may be inhibiting them.

Never give a child laxatives as a routine means of regulating their bowels. Laxatives are addictive in the sense that the bowel can become lazy and unable to work efficiently without them. Administer them only on a doctor's advice.

Coughs and Sore Throats

If the cough is a loose one (that is to say, one that helps the child to clear mucus from his chest), do not administer cough medicine because this will inhibit its function. If the cough is a dry one and/or the child complains of a sore throat, a mixture of lemon juice and honey in equal parts should help sooth it. Encourage them to gargle with antiseptic mouth-wash if they are old enough to understand not to swallow it.

An older child might like an extra pillow or two to help ease a troublesome night cough, but do not do the same with a baby because of the risk of suffocation. Put the pillows underneath the head of the mattress instead, so it is raised slightly. Turning the child on his front or side at night may also reduce spates of coughing.

If the child becomes breathless at all, has pains in the chest, fever or vomiting, call a doctor straightaway.

Croup

This is a particularly nasty cough which is more common among two to four year olds than other age groups. The main symptom is a barking cough. If the child is having difficulty in breathing, a doctor should be called immediately. Sit your charge up and stay with him to give reassurance since a serious bout of croup is a frightening experience for a child. Boiling a kettle in the room or leaving a wet sheet over the radiator may offer relief because of the moisture created in the air. Normally croup disappears in a day or two.

Diarrhoea

This can be serious in small babies because of the risk of dehydration, so call a doctor. Stop milk foods and fruit but encourage all other fluids. In older children it may be due to a digestive upset, so stick to a bland diet for the rest of the day and keep the child warm in a well ventilated room. If the diarrhoea persists, or is accompanied by vomiting or fever, seek medical advice.

Earache

Pain from the ear usually warrants a visit to the doctor because it indicates an infection, which may require antibiotics. In the meantime, some relief can be brought by holding a covered hot water bottle or heated pad against the affected ear. One traditional remedy for the pain is to chop up an onion, wrap it in a clean handkerchief and hold it to the ear. Propping up the head-end of the mattress will also help fluid to drain from the ear.

Eczema

This condition is usually inherited but can be aggravated by allergy and/or nervous strain. The symptoms are an inflamed, itchy rash most commonly found on the face, inner sides of the arms and behind the knees, and a dry, flaky scalp. It will flare up for a limited time and then fade again, so the condition comes and goes. It is not an infectious ailment.

Prevent your charge from becoming over-heated as much as possible and use cotton fabrics next to the skin to avoid irritation. Keep him out of strong sunlight or winds because this will aggravate the rash, and try to distract the child from scratching. Consult a doctor because he will probably prescribe a special ointment (e.g. hydrocortisone cream), but in the meantime calamine lotion may be helpful.

Head-lice

Head-lice are not the result of dirty hair or unhygienic living conditions, as widely believed. Most children acquire head lice at school since young children often brush heads over their work or at play, allowing lice to jump from one scalp to the next.

The lice lay their eggs in the hair quite close to the scalp and are similar to flakes of dandruff except they are hard. Once the colony is well established, the child will keep scratching the scalp and behind the ears. Any chemist should be able to recommend a medicated shampoo treatment; alternatively schools will probably have an information sheet. Wash the child's hair thoroughly with this, being careful not to get any of it in the eyes. Afterwards, you should go through the hair with a fine comb to remove the nits (lice eggs). This is time consuming and tedious for a child so provide something to amuse him while you are doing it. A new book, or favourite TV programme should encourage him to sit still. It is usually a wise precaution to treat all the members of the family whose heads have been in close contact with the child. Headlice cannot live for very long away from the human scalp, so it is not necessary to wash everything that has come into contact with the child's hair, though of course the comb should be thoroughly rinsed in hot water.

Stomach Pains

The main worry with stomach pains is that they might possibly be an indication of appendicitis. If in any doubt call a doctor.

If the condition doesn't appear to be serious, encourage the child to lie down for an hour or so. If the pain persists for longer then two hours, however, or your charge begins vomiting, seek medical advice. In the meantime, it may help the doctor if you manage to obtain a specimen of the child's urine.

Teething or Toothache

Take the child to a dentist if the problem is toothache. In the meantime you can help deaden the pain by dabbing the affected tooth with oil of cloves. Alternatively, holding a heated pad or covered hot water bottle against the affected side of the face may also help.

If the pain is caused by teething, giving the baby something to chew on will help. Children often find frozen bananas or something hard like a tooth-brush, just as soothing as a teething ring. Various solutions are also available from chemists specially formulated for painful gums.

Don't blame any other symptoms of illness on teething. For example, diarrhoea. This should be dealt with as a separate problem and not left untreated because it is masked by the teething troubles.

Vomiting

A doctor should always be called if vomiting persists or is accompanied by diarrhoea and/or stomach pain. If the vomiting is just a short bout, stop giving solid food for twenty-four hours and concentrate instead on fluids. A glass of orange juice with one level teaspoon of bicarbonate of soda and a pinch of salt may also help settle the stomach. Avoid fats for forty-eight hours after vomiting has stopped, because these are difficult to digest.

Babies often eject milk after feeds and this is rarely serious. It may be due to swallowing too much air while feeding because they are drinking too quickly. Giving a couple of spoonfuls of water that has been boiled and left to cool prior to feeding times may take the edge off their appetite and encourage them to drink more slowly.

GENERAL CARE DURING SICKNESS

Caring for a sick child will take even more patience than usual, especially once your charge starts to recover and becomes more irritable and demanding. Things can be particularly difficult if there are other children to care for as well, and you still have household chores to attend to. If you have sole charge, try to come to some arrangement with the mother about any additional tasks you usually perform. It is much better for you to concentrate on the sick child rather than the house, and any reasonable family will understand this. Don't try to do too much, but organise yourself and set priorities. Otherwise you, yourself, can become run-down and if you fall ill, the whole family suffers even more.

Taking Temperatures

In cases of high fever, it is obvious by touch that the child has a high temperature. Kissing the child's forehead is a good way of detecting this because your lips are sensitive to heat.

If a precise measure is necessary, you will need to use a thermometer. Children under the age of two usually have their temperature taken rectally. Lay the child over your knee in a position that is as comfortable as possible, and swab the skin surrounding the anus with petroleum jelly or similar lubricant so you can insert it more easily about an inch into his anus. Most contemporary thermometers will give an accurate reading after thirty seconds.

Older children can have their temperature taken by placing a thermometer under the tongue or under the arm-pit. If you are taking it orally, remember not to do so immediately after a hot or cold drink or you will have an inaccurate reading. Clean all thermometers after each use by submersion in diluted disinfectant (one teaspoon to five fluid ounces of water) and leave it there if needed again later on.

Administering Medicines

When giving liquid medicine with an unpleasant taste rub ice over the child's tongue first to inhibit his taste-buds. If the child refuses to take it, gently pinch his nostrils and slip it in when he opens his mouth to breathe. Put your hand over his lips to prevent him from spitting it out and then give him a sweet as a reward for swallowing it. This is one situation in which bribery is well justified! Use a thoroughly cleaned eye-dropper to feed liquid medicines to babies.

In the case of tablets, crush between two spoons and bury the medication in a spoonful of jam, or whatever the child prefers. The same can be done with capsules, by emptying their contents onto a spoon. Note any bad reactions, since some children are allergic to certain kinds of medication. Keep all medicines well out of reach of the children.

Diet

Give sick children plenty of fluids and small, frequent meals if and when they want to eat. Fruit juices provide vitamins and sugar for energy, and soups and milk are very nutritious. Encourage light food such as toast, poached or boiled eggs, poached fish, jellies, milk puddings, fruit purees and sponge cake. Gradually return to a more normal diet as they progress.

Amusing a Sick Child

Try to spend as much time with your charge as possible, and as soon as he is no longer infectious, encourage visitors. If your charge is in bed, reading to him or arranging for him to watch a portable television set in his room should occupy him for a while. Let him draw and colour with crayons, and supply him with jigsaw puzzles on a tray.

If your charge has been seriously ill, assist in a gradual return to normality. Sit him up in bed for longer and longer periods and then gradually increase the time he is permitted to be up. He will require plenty of rest at first, but in the meantime permit him to play with anything which doesn't require too much exertion or excitement.

Imaginary Illness

Sometimes children complain of headaches, pains in their stomach or develop bowel problems with no apparent physical cause. These often occur prior to a stressful event such as returning to school after a holiday. If you suspect that a child's illness is an excuse or delaying tactic for something they prefer to avoid, don't dismiss the pain as imaginary. Even children worry, and anxiety can create genuine physical symptoms. Be sympathetic while applying a common sense approach to the problem.

Appendix 3

Cooking for Children

When cooking for children it is important to provide a balanced diet. Even if children will only eat one or two bites of some foods, it is still worth giving them the chance to eat healthy foods. A healthy diet will not only encourage good health by increasing resistance to disease, but also promote growth, regulate the body's processes and provide heat and energy. A balanced diet means one which provides a selection of food which includes protein, carbohydrate, fats, vitamins, minerals and roughage in the right proportions. The chart below gives the sources of the most important nutrients.

NUTRIENT	FUNCTION	SOURCE
PROTEIN	To build	Fish, meat, eggs, milk, cheese, cereals, nuts, beans, lentils, peas
FATS	To provide fuel	Butter, margarine, oils, meat, milk, cheese, fat, ice-cream
CARBOHYDRATES	To provide energy & warmth	Bread, cakes, cereals and biscuits, sugar, potatoes, root vegetables
VITAMIN A	Aids growth & vision	Dairy products, eggs, fruit, carrots
VITAMIN B	Promotes general good health and helps body utilise other nutrients	Wholewheat, oats, yeast, liver, eggs, meat
VITAMIN C	Helps heal wounds & resist infection	Fruit and vegetables
VITAMIN D	For healthy teeth & bones	Oily fish, offal, egg yolk, margarine, butter & sunshine
CALCIUM	For strong bones	Milk, cheese, nuts
IRON	For healthy blood	Eggs, cocoa, meat, offal, green vegetables
HIGH FIBRE	Aids the body's processes & prevents constipation	Bran, beans, brown rice, wholemeal bread, jacket potato

By encouraging your charge to eat a wide selection of food, you reduce the chance of his developing food sensitivity, which can lead to allergies. Having said that, however, all children go through phases when they are faddish about what they eat. Therefore, the meals that you cook should be interesting and served attractively so as to encourage them to try new and varied foods.

Baby's First Solids

When babies have few teeth, it is important to provide smooth textured food until more teeth develop and they can enjoy chunkier meals. There are many commercial brands of baby-food on the market but these often contain sugar, thickeners and modified starch which provide empty calories and can be damaging to teeth already formed in the gum. They are also highly processed so tend to be less nutritious than fresh food. Reserve their use for travelling and make the baby's food yourself. It really doesn't take much extra time since you can cook it along with your own meals, and just pop it in the blender or mash it by hand.

If there is one particular day when you have less to do than usual, it will save time on your busier days if you prepare food in bulk in advance, and then freeze it in the ice-cube trays, remembering to label all frozen food and date it. Not only do they thaw quickly, it is also easy to select just the right quantity. Most fruit and vegetables puree easily and as the baby develops more teeth, you can add ground pieces of meat or carefully boned fish that has been mashed into flakes. Meat tastes good and moist if pureed with a little natural yoghurt. Do not add salt or sugar to the food you prepare since neither is good for babies and they are quite happy to eat bland food. Any puréed left-overs can be mixed with egg, and baked on cake trays or utilised later as sandwich spreads.

COOKING FOR TODDLERS

Young children prefer food that is not very spicy and it should be served in small portions, cut into little pieces. For this reason, ground beef is usually a success with tiny tots. Try providing finger-food at lunch time such as cheese cubes, strips of cold meat, wholewheat crackers and raw vegetables or fruit. Do not serve food straight from the oven, but let it stand until it is cool enough for a toddler to eat comfortably. Liquid meals such as soups can be cooled quickly by dropping an ice-cube into the dish before serving.

Here are enough suggestions and recipes to get you through one week.

Breakfast

Encourage children to eat some protein during breakfast, especially if they are about to go off to school and may not have an opportunity to eat anything else until lunch time. Eggs or cereals with milk provide a good source of protein and the former can be cooked in a variety of ways: boiled, poached, fried or scrambled.

Egg in the Basket (serves one)
1 slice of wholemeal bread, 1 egg, 1 knob of butter.
1. Cut a round hole from the centre of the slice of bread and melt the butter in a frying pan over a moderate-to-high heat.
2. When the butter is bubbling, fry the slice of bread and the round piece in the pan, crack the egg and deposit it into the centre of the hole.
3. When the underneath side is cooked, serve the toasted bread with the egg in the middle, topping it with the round lid that has also been fried.

French Toast (serves one)
1 thick slice of bread with the crusts removed, 1 lge egg, drop of milk and knob of butter.
1. Beat the egg and add a little milk as though making scrambled egg.
2. Soak the bread in the batter on both sides for a few minutes or until it has absorbed most of the liquid without becoming too soggy.
3. Heat the butter in a frying-pan and fry the bread on both sides until golden-brown.

Kids love this served with jam or syrup, but honey would be more nutritious and is just as delicious.

Pancakes (serves two)
2 tbsp oil, 1 lge beaten egg, 2 tbsp sugar, 1 cup flour, 2 tsp baking-powder, ½ tsp salt, approx ½ pint of milk.
1. Beat all the ingredients together in a bowl, adding just enough milk to form a thick batter (about the consistency of a fairly thick milk-shake).
2. Melt the butter in a frying pan and when bubbling, ladle in some of the batter.
3. Turn when underside is cooked to brown and serve while warm.

May be served topped with syrup, honey, lemon juice or brown sugar or with yoghurt and chopped fruit.

Quick Bran Muffins (Makes one dozen)
These store well in the freezer, so they may be baked in advance and stored until required.
25g (1oz) soft marge or butter, 25g (1oz) soft brown sugar, 75g (3oz) wholemeal flour, 50g (2oz) bran, 1 medium egg, 1 level tsp baking powder,½ level tsp bicarbonate of soda, 125ml (5oz) milk and water mixture, pinch of salt.
1. Set the oven to 200°C/400°F/Gas reg 6
2. Cream the fat and sugar, and beat in the egg and milk mixture.
3. Stir in the bran and add the combined dry ingredients.
4. Divide the mixture among 12 well-greased cookie-moulds and bake for approx. 20 mins or until firm to the touch.

Lunch

These suggestions will also travel easily to school if transported via containers in lunch boxes.

Sandwiches (may be cut into interesting shapes with cookie-cutters and the surplus bread used as bread-crumbs); creamy dip and sliced, raw vegetables; home-made soups (carried to school in flasks); celery sticks stuffed with cottage-cheese or cream cheese (celery keeps longer if stored in the fridge in paper bags instead of plastic, while cottage cheese keeps twice as long stored upside-down.)

Tuna Fish Spread
1 small tin of tuna fish, 1 celery stalk, 1 small onion (if liked), few slices of cucumber, 1 medium hard-boiled egg, mayonnaise, lemon juice and seasoning.
1. Drain the liquid from the tin of tuna and mash up the fish into small flakes.
2. Finely chop the celery, cucumber and onion.
3. Mash the hard-boiled egg.
4. Mix everything together with a few drops of lemon juice and enough mayonnaise to make the mixture moist enough to spread on bread.
5. Season to taste, and use as a sandwich filler or serve with salads.

Chicken Liver Paté (stores well in the freezer)
100g (4oz) chicken livers, 50g (2oz) soft marge/butter, 50g (2oz) cream cheese, 1 tbsp single cream, squeeze of lemon juice, seasoning.
1. Fry the chicken livers gently in a little oil.
2. When cooked, put all the ingredients in a blender and blend to form a paste.

May be used as sandwich filler, or served with hot pieces of toast.

Peanut butter
    This can easily be bought in many countries, but it can just as easily be homemade and tastes more delicious than commercial brands. Just melt some butter in a pan and liquidise with equal weight of peanuts. The longer you liquidise, the smoother it will be. Season to taste with salt and store in an air-tight jar. It can be used for sandwiches, but it is a novelty to serve an ice-cream scoop of it in an ice-cream cone instead.

Creamy Cheese dip for Crudités
100g (4oz) cream cheese, ½ tbsp soured cream, 1 tbsp chopped chives, seasoning and a little milk.
Mix the ingredients together well, adding just enough milk to bring the dip to the required consistency.

Plain Omelette (serves one — may be cut in half to serve two toddlers)
2 eggs, 1tbsp cold water, ½ oz butter, seasoning.
Use a small frying pan, approx. 6in/15cm in diameter.
1. Beat the contents of the two eggs in a bowl, adding the seasoning and water.
2. Melt the butter in the pan, making sure the bottom and sides are coated. When bubbling, pour in the egg mixture.
3. Scrape the mixture slowly, using a wooden spoon, so that all the liquid has a chance to cook.
4. Remove the omelette by folding in half with a palette knife, and slide onto plate.
N.B. Finely chopped vegetables or grated cheese may be added to the mixture. This is also a good way of using up small pieces of meat such as diced ham.

Homemade Soups

    All the following recipes are enough for two servings, plus a little extra.
Leek and Potato
1 lge leek, 2 lge potatoes, 290ml (½pt) chicken stock, dash of single cream.
1. Chop the leek and peeled potatoes into bite-sized pieces.
2. Simmer in the stock until soft.
3. Pour into blender and blend to form a smooth soup.
4. Re-heat in pan, add seasoning to taste and stir in a dash of cream before serving.

Tomato
1 medium can of peeled tomatoes, 1 small onion, 1 lge carrot, 300ml (½pt) chicken stock, dash of Worcester sauce (optional), knob of butter.
1. Heat the butter in a pan, finely chop the carrot and onion and sauté together until the carrot is soft.
2. Add the tomatoes and juice, stock and Worcester sauce.
3. Simmer for half an hour.
4. Blend in blender and season to taste.

Cream of Mushroom
100g (4oz) mushrooms, 300ml (½pt) chicken stock, 150ml (quarter pt) milk, 50g (2oz) butter, 50g (2oz) flour, seasoning.
1. Chop the mushrooms and sauté in the butter.
2. Stir in the flour and cook for three mins.

3. Remove the pan from the heat and gradually add stock and milk.
4. Bring to the boil and cook until soup thickens. Season to taste.

Main Meals

Beef and Spinach Cake

Any mention of 'cake' in the recipe usually inspires children at least to try something. This is also a good way of feeding them spinach if it is not their favourite food since the taste is disguised somewhat by the other ingredients. The following recipe should be enough for two school aged children with room for second helpings.

1 pack frozen spinach, 225g (8oz) minced beef, 1 lge egg (lightly beaten), 1 beef stock-cube, ½ dozen button mushrooms, 1 small onion.

1. Heat oven to 200°C/400°F/Gas reg.6
2. Put the frozen spinach in a saucepan and thaw over low heat.
3. Meanwhile, finely chop the onion and mushrooms and sauté in a knob of butter.
4. Turn the heat higher and add the minced beef, stirring all the time so it is evenly browned.
5. Crumble the beef stock cube into the pan and add the thawed spinach, stirring all ingredients together. Add a little boiling water to moisten if ingredients seem too dry and start to stick to pan.
6. Remove pan from heat and stir in the egg.
7. Pour mixture into oven-proof dish and bake uncovered for approx. 20 mins or until firm to the touch. Cut into cake slices and serve.

Homemade Beef Burgers (Recipe will make 2 hamburger patties)
110g (4oz) minced beef, 1 cup of puréed vegetable of your choice, 1 small onion (finely chopped), sprinkling of fine wholewheat breadcrumbs, finely chopped parsley.
1. Mix all the ingredients together.
2. Divide the mixture to form hamburger patties.
3. Grill or fry in a little oil.

These can easily be turned into cheese burgers by topping with a thin slice of cheese and melting it under the grill. Serve in a wholemeal roll with a side dish of cooked vegetable or salad.

Fish Pie (serves 2)
170g (6oz) cooked white fish, deboned; 3 lge potatoes, peeled; 50g (2oz) butter, 570m (1pt) milk, 50g (2oz) flour, chopped parsley, 1 bay leaf and seasoning.
1. Turn the oven to 200°C/400°F/gas reg 6
2. Peel and cut the potatoes into chunks and boil until soft enough to mash.
3. In the meantime, prepare the sauce by melting the butter, adding the bay leaf and flour and stirring while cooking for 1 min.
4. Draw off heat and add milk, stirring all the time.
5. Return to heat and bring slowly to the boil, stirring until you have a thick, creamy sauce, the consistency of custard.
6. Remove the bay leaf and set the sauce aside.
7. Chop the cooked fish into small chunks and place in an oven-proof dish.
8. Pour the sauce on top and spinkle with parsley.
9. Drain potatoes when cooked, and mash.
10. Spread evenly on top of the fish/sauce mixture and run the back of a fork's prongs along it to create a pattern. If you have the time (and the inclination) you can pipe the potato on instead.

11. Bake in the oven for 15 mins, and then slip under the grill for a few minutes to brown it.

Serve with a lemon wedge and some brightly coloured vegetables, such as broccoli or grilled tomatoes. If you really want to catch your charge's interest, you could always put some food colouring in the mashed potato.

Fish cakes (4 servings)
450g (1lb) potatoes, 225g (½lb) cooked, canned fish (drained), 1 lge beaten egg, some dried breadcrumbs, a little milk and some finely chopped parsley.
1. Boil the potatoes, drain and mash.
2. Flake the fish and add to the mash. Sprinkle in the parsley.
3. Season to taste and bind with a little milk.
4. Shape into patties, similar to hamburgers.
5. Dip each patty into the egg and then the breadcrumbs.
6. Store in the fridge for about 1 hr to help the breadcrumbs adhere to the cakes.
7. Heat some oil in a large frying-pan and fry the cakes until crisp and golden.

Serve with chips and peas.

Chicken Baked In Sauce
You can make your own soup for this first but it's much quicker to use a commercial brand, although not as nutritious. The chicken absorbs the flavour but leaves enough liquid to use as a sauce.

Simply put one chicken portion per child in a casserole dish (or substitute chops if you prefer) and pour over a can of soup, for instance onion, mushroom, etc. Cover the dish and bake in the oven at 190°C/375°F/gas reg. 5, for 1½ hrs or until tender. Serve with rice and one or two vegetables.

Risotto (enough for 2 small children)
quarter cup wholegrain rice, 1 cup of water, 1 chicken stock cube, finely chopped vegetables, small pieces of meat such as chicken or pork (optional).
1. Boil the water and add stock cube. When dissolved, and with water still boiling, add rice.
2. Turn to a simmer and cook until soft (approx. 20-30 mins).
3. Lightly fry the vegetables and add the cooked meat, if desired. Mix in the cooked rice. Serve as a complete meal.

Stuffed Jacket Potatoes
1 potato per child, finely sliced onion, bacon, mushrooms, ham (in fact, anything which your charge enjoys), knob of butter, dash of milk and a sprinkling of cheese (optional).
1. Scrub the potato skins, prick them with a fork and place the potatoes in a hot oven for 1 hr or until soft to the touch (inserting a skewer or nail into each potato will reduce the baking time by 15 mins)
2. Stir-fry the other ingredients, except the cheese, butter and milk, until tender.
3. When potatoes are baked, slice in half and remove the potato flesh. Add a little butter and milk to create a mash.
4. Mix in the other ingredients and re-stuff each skin half.
5. Sprinkle a little cheese on top, if desired, and return to the oven for 10 mins, or place under grill to melt the cheese.

Serve with a crisp salad or cooked vegetables.

Tomato Sauce (serves 4)
1 small onion and 1 clove of garlic, finely chopped, 1 medium tin tomatoes, 2 rashers streaky bacon and a little oil.
1. Sauté the finely chopped onion and garlic in the oil in a saucepan.
2. Add the bacon, chopped, and cook for 5 mins.
3. Add the tomatoes, but not the juice (may be added later if sauce needs thinning).
4. Simmer, covered, for 20 mins.
5. Blend in blender.
Serve with spaghetti on a slice of wholewheat toast.

Desserts

Homemade Vanilla Ice-cream
70g (2½oz) caster sugar, 425ml (3/4pt) double cream, 3 egg yolks, 8 tbsp water, 1 tsp vanilla essence.
1. Dissolve the sugar in the water over a gentle heat.
2. Beat the egg yolks well.
3. Half whip the cream.
4. When the sugar has dissolved, bring the syrup to boiling point. Keep boiling until the mixture is ready. (You can test it by dipping your finger into cold water and then into a little of the syrup. Rub between your finger and thumb and then, when you draw them apart threads should form similar to sticky chewing-gum).
5. Whisk the egg yolks and gradually pour in the sugar-syrup. Whisk until the mixture is thick and mousse-like.
6. Cool, whisking occasionally. Fold in the cream and freeze.
7. When the ice-cream is half frozen, whisk again and return to freezer.
Serve with fresh chopped fruit or chocolate sauce.

Chocolate Sauce
170g (6oz) plain chocolate, 15g (1oz) butter, 2 tbsp water.
1. Melt the chocolate slowly with the water, stirring frequently.
2. Add the butter and heat (don't boil) until the butter is melted and the sauce is blended and shiny.
May be used as a topping for ice-cream, or give the children a dish of it and some chunks of fruit or sponge cake to dip into it.

Strawberry Mousse
This can be made one day ahead, and is enough for 4 servings.
2 egg whites (at room temperature), 1 quarter cup icing sugar, 2 cups strawberries (finely sliced), 2 cups whipping cream, pinch of salt.
1. Whisk egg whites and salt in a small bowl until glossy and stiff.
2. Whip the cream with the sugar in the bowl.
3. Gently fold in the egg whites and fruit, blending well.
4. Spoon the mixture into individual containers and refrigerate at least one hour before serving.

Apple Crumble (serves 4)
450g (1lb) cooking apples, 1½ tbsp brown sugar, pinch of cinnamon, 50g (2oz) butter, straight from the fridge so it is hard, 85g (3oz) plain flour, 30g (1oz) caster sugar and a pinch of salt.
1. Set the oven to 200°C/400°F/gas reg 6.

2. Peel and core the apples. Cut into chunks and place in a saucepan with the brown sugar and cinnamon.
3. Add just enough water to keep the bottom of the pan moist while the apples are stewing.
4. When the apples are soft, allow to cool and then drain any excess juice.
5. Rub the fat into the flour, add salt and when the mixture resembles breadcrumbs, mix in the caster sugar.
6. Pour the stewed apples into an ovenproof dish and sprinkle over the crumble mixture.
7. Bake for 1½ hrs and if the top still isn't brown, place it under the grill until golden.

May be served with cream or custard.

Custard Fruit
Place some chopped fruit in the bottom of a heat-proof container. Make some instant custard and pour over the fruit. Leave to cool and then chill in the fridge so it can be served cold.

Bananas In Caramel Sauce
1 banana per child, 170g (6oz) granulated sugar, 425ml (3/4 pt) water.
1. Melt two-thirds of the sugar slowly in a saucepan.
2. When it is bubbling and brown, pour on the water. (It will fizz dangerously so make sure the children stand well clear if they are watching you make this.)
3. Add the rest of the sugar and reboil, stirring, and then boil until the sauce is of syrupy consistency.

Pour over the banana and leave to cool off a little before serving to your charge.

Other dessert suggestions: fruit salad, jelly or yoghurt.

Snacks and Beverages

It is much more nutritious to serve raw vegetables, fruit, nuts, yoghurt or a few small slices of cheese if the children are hungry between meals. However, there will be times when a special treat may be appropriate.

Boiled Cake (very nutritious)
1 cup cold water, 1 cup sultanas, 1 cup raisins, 1 cup currants, 1 cup brown sugar, 2 cups wholewheat flour, peel, cherries and nuts (optional), 1 tsp baking soda, ½ tsp mixed spice, 2 lge beaten eggs, 170g (6oz) marge.
1. Set oven to 190°C/375°F/gas reg 5.
2. Put water, fruit, sugar and margarine in a saucepan and bring to the boil.
3. Boil 5-10 mins.
4. Meanwhile, sieve flour, baking soda and mixed spice into a bowl.
5. Pour in the boiling mixture and beat well.
6. Add beaten eggs and blend well.
7. Pour into prepared 20cm (8in) cake tin and bake for 1-1½ hrs.

Fairy Cakes (makes 18)
100g (4oz) margarine (at room temperature), 100g (4oz) caster sugar, 100g (4oz) self-raising flour, 2 medium eggs.
Icing: 50g (2oz) icing sugar, 75g (3oz) margarine, ½ tsp vanilla essence, 1 tsp milk.
1. Preheat oven to 190°C/375°F/gas reg 5.

2. Place 18 paper cases on a baking sheet.
3. Mix cake ingredients in a bowl and beat until smooth.
4. Deposit a dessert spoonful of the mixture into each paper cup.
5. Bake for ½ an hour or until golden-brown and firm to the touch.
6. Cool on a wire rack while preparing the icing.
7. To make icing, sift icing sugar into a bowl and beat together with the margarine, flavouring and milk until light and fluffy.
8. Deposit a little icing on the top of each cake and decorate with grated pieces of chocolate, chopped nuts or commercial cake decorations.

Chocolate Rice Crispies/Corn Flakes
100g (4oz) plain chocolate, 25g (1oz) butter, 2 tbsp golden syrup, rice crispies/corn flakes.
1. Slowly melt the chocolate and butter in a saucepan.
2. Add the golden syrup.
3. Sprinkle the cereal into the mixture and then form individual chocolate covered heaps on a baking sheet.
4. Chill in the fridge until firm but still gooey.

Chocolate Cake
225g (8oz) margerine or butter, 225g (8oz) self-raising flour. 225g (8oz) caster sugar, 50g (2oz) cocoa, 4 medium eggs.
Filling: 225g (8oz) icing sugar, 30g (1oz) cocoa, 110g (4oz) margarine or butter, 2 tbsp boiling water.
1. Heat oven to 190°C/375°F/gas reg 5.
2. Cream margarine and sugar. Add well beaten eggs and mix.
3. Sieve flour and cocoa and beat into the mixture a little at a time.
4. If mixuture is a little dry, add a small quantity of milk.
5. Place mixture in a 20cm (8in) baking tin.
6. Bake for approx 20 mins. Test to make sure it's cooked by gently pressing the surface with your finger. If the indentation springs back and disappears, it's cooked.
7. While it is baking, prepare the icing by mixing together all the icing ingredients.
8. When the cake has cooled, slice in half horizontally and sandwich together with the icing. Dust the top of the cake with a sprinkling of icing sugar.

Banana Cake (great for using up over-ripe bananas).
2 lge eggs (beaten well), 250g (9oz) self-raising flour, 110g (4oz) margarine, 2 ripe bananas, 170g (6oz) caster sugar.
1. Set oven to 180°C/350°F/gas reg 4.
2. Mash bananas until runny.
3. Beat the marge and the icing sugar together.
4. Add the flour and eggs and bananas.
5. Bake for 1½ hrs or until cooked (using finger test).

Homemade Yoghurt Ice-Lollies (makes 8)
150ml (quarter pt) natural yoghurt, 175ml (6oz) concentrated unsweetened orange juice, 2 drops vanilla essence.
1. Mix all the ingredients together and pour into ice-cube trays.
2. When mixture is half frozen and slushy, insert wooden lolly stick in each individual section.
3. Freeze until firm and serve with a circle of foil around the bottom of the stick to catch any drips.

Homemade Lemonade
Juice and rind of 3 lemons, 2 tbsp clear honey, 1-2 litres (approx. 2 pts) mineral water, ice-cubes.
1. Put lemon juice and rind in a large jug with honey.
2. Pour in water and stir well.
3. Leave to stand for at least 1 hr.
4. Strain out the rind and serve with ice-cubes.

Sparkling Juice
Add two thirds sparkling mineral water to one third orange or pineapple juice to make a fizzy drink. Add a slice of lemon or orange and ice-cubes before serving.

Milk-Shake (serves 1)
1 portion of fruit, 300ml (½pt) milk, 1 scoop of ice-cream. Put all the ingredients into a blender and pour over ice-cubes.

Carrot Cake
225gm (½lb) wholemeal flour, pinch of salt, quarter tsp bicarbonate of soda, 225g (½lb) grated carrots, 1 egg (beaten), 50g (2oz) melted butter, 50g (2oz) runny honey, 50g (2oz) brown sugar, quarter tsp nutmeg, 2 tsp cinnamon.
1. Set oven to 190°C/375°F/gas reg.5. Lightly grease a small loaf tin.
2. Sift flour with salt and bicarbonate of soda. Stir in all remaining ingredients.
3. Spoon mixture into loaf tin and bake for approx. 1 hour. Top should be brown and firm to the touch. Allow to cool before serving.

Appendix 4

Fun and Games

It is essential to appreciate the significance of play in children's lives because it is the main medium through which they learn. Creative play such as drawing or painting will expand their imagination and encourage them to implement ideas. Playing with others will teach them the art of socialising and the importance of co-operation and compromise. By providing stimulating play and encouraging experimentation, the au pair/nanny is making an important contribution to a child's development.

Amusing children doesn't have to be expensive; in fact it is often the simple things which occupy them the longest. Odds and ends that are bought can add up, though, so do ask the parents for extra cash if you find it necessary. Dipping into your own wages can prove expensive, especially if you want to plan plenty of outings. Be sensitive to the family budget, however, by keeping expenses in line with what they can afford. Equip yourself with a little notebook so you can record expenses and obtain receipts whenever possible. That way, if any discrepancies arise over finances, you can show the parents exactly how the money has been spent.

Here are some ideas for entertaining children which may provide some inspiration. Each child is an individual and some are more advanced than others so select those examples which appear to be most suitable or relevant to your own particular situation.

PLAYING IN THE HOME

At the start of a day when the children need to be kept inside, you will want them to occupy themselves while you get the morning's chores out of the way. Jigsaws, books, cards and board games don't necessarily require your participation but the younger the child, the more likely he is to require your attention. Try to save the more difficult chores which demand a high degree of concentration for when the younger children take a nap, or the older ones are watching television. Chores such as ironing, however, can be done while supervising their play, providing you set them up with everything they need so they don't keep interrupting you except, perhaps, to admire something they have made.

Craft Work

Saving empty packages which have not contained substances harmful to children can come in very handy when it comes to organising craft work. A special box can be set aside to store odds and ends such as empty cotton-reels, egg boxes, bits of silver foil, etc.

Make sure children are supplied with crayons, washable felt tips, paints, brushes, scissors, in fact, anything that is not dangerous and which will help them produce art work. A sticky paste can be made for gluing by simply mixing water and flour together in a small container. If it starts to dry out as the day progresses, just add a little more liquid. A plastic table-cloth to protect the furniture or carpet is a must, as is a plastic apron for the child. Remember to tie back long hair so it doesn't dip into anything.

Children go through reams of paper in no time at all, but a cheap supply can be obtained from office scraps. If one of the parents has access to a computer or telex machine, ask him/her to save the waste print-out material. The reverse side is blank and can be put to good use in the nursery. Alternatively, use the back of an old roll of wallpaper or buy a cheap roll of low-quality paper.

Instead of using paint brushes, you can encourage children to experiment with printing. Put different coloured paints in flat, separate containers (old saucers are ideal) and demonstrate how patterns can be made by dipping different objects in paint and transferring their outlines onto paper. A potato cut in half with a design chipped out of it can create a variety of prints, as can hands and thumbs. Try cotton reels or different types of uncooked pasta.

If you have large sheets of paper, ask your charge to lie down on it and keep still. Draw around the outline of the body and then let him colour himself in. Give him some strands of wool or cotton-wool for the hair, and remnants of material for the clothes.

Modelling clay and plasticine from shops can be expensive but an economic version is homemade play-dough. Combine four cups of flour with one cup of salt and add enough water to form a dough. Too little liquid will make it too crumbly to handle, but too much will make it sticky, so if this happens just add a little more flour/salt. The salt will help prevent it drying out and discourages toddlers from eating it! To provide colour, add powder paint to the flour before mixing, or use food colouring in the water. Provide children with cookie-cutters and a rolling-pin. The play-dough may be stored in the fridge, wrapped in a plastic bag.

Don't forget to praise the art work that is produced and always display it if possible. Blu-tac works well for mounting pictures because it doesn't harm walls, unlike sticky tape or drawing-pins. If cellotape has been used on painted walls, the sticky residue can be removed with methylated spirits. Magnets can be used to pin up pictures on metallic surfaces such as fridge doors. Drawings may be preserved by spraying with hair-lacquer upon completion.

Dressing up

All children enjoy the imaginative play involved in dressing up. Get a large cardboard box from the supermarket where old cast-offs from yourself or other adult members of the family can be discarded and saved for the children to use on rainy days. All kinds of interesting clothing and accessories can be obtained from jumble-sales or basement bargains including hats, colourful scarves, jewellery, etc. Little girls should probably be discouraged from wearing high-heeled shoes since they are dangerous to walk in. If they must wear dress-up shoes, buy a cheap pair of ballet slippers or let them wear men's shoes which tend to be flat.

A shoe box filled with cosmetics will keep them occupied for hours, but beware of sensitive skins. The hypo-allergic kind is best. Have plenty of cold-cream in store for removing afterwards.

The Magic Box

No play-room is complete without a magic box, and the nicest thing about one of these is that it is invisible! Not only does it cost nothing and save on space, it entertains the children for longer and expands their imagination.

It is basically a miming game. You can introduce it by explaining about the invisible box in the corner which is full of magic, and make a great show of opening the heavy (invisible) lid. Roll up the sleeve of one arm and pretend to feel about inside it, drawing out an invisible object. You then have to mime in such a way that the children will guess what you've found. For example, licking an ice-cream cone, pretending to use a bow and arrow or playing a game of catch with an invisible ball. Stick to simple mimes at first until they get the hang of it and make them more complicated as the game progresses, depending on the ability of the child. Encourage your charge to take a turn. You'll be amazed at how resourceful they can be at dreaming up ideas and then communicating them.

Indoor Games

The *Strand Game* can only be played with more than one child because it is competitive. Scatter strands of wool or elastic-bands around the room and then when you are finished the children run around collecting as many of them as they can find. When they have all been gathered, the child who has collected the most wins.

Match-the-Picture requires that the children cut out large pictures from magazines and then cut each picture in half. (Old post-cards will do just as well). Take one half of each picture and distribute them around the room. Divide the other halves evenly among the children and then ask them to search for each of the pieces missing from their individual bundles. The first child to match all the halves together wins.

For *The Memory Game* (also known as Pelmonism or 'Kim's Game' after the novel by Rudyard Kipling), place a variety of objects on a tray (no more than ten) and give the children a chance to study the arrangement. After a few minutes, blind-fold them and remove one of the objects. Then let him study the tray again so he can try to remember which object is missing. If it seems too difficult, try playing it with fewer articles. This game works well as a party game when chidren have to remember everything that was on the tray after studying it for a minute or so.

In *Smells and Tastes* you put a variety of objects on a tray — salt, sugar, flour, marmite, jam, etc. — blindfold the children and see if they can identify the substances by taste and smell. Also a good team game and usually gets plenty of laughs.

Are you there, Moriarty? is excellent for older boys and girls. Two contestants are blindfolded and lie face down on the floor supporting head and shoulders on their elbows and holding each other's hands. One has a rolled up newspaper as a weapon and calls 'Are you there Moriarty?' When the other says 'Yes' the attacker tries to hit his head with the rolled up newspaper. Each player gets say five shots and the one to score the most hits is the winner.

Other good party games include the old favourites *Blind Man's Buff, Hunt the Thimble, Musical Chairs, Pass the Parcel* and *Pass the Orange,* where the children divide into teams and have to pass an orange down the line by tucking it under their chins. *Chinese Whispers* is excellent for quite young children. They sit in a circle and the first child whispers something silly like a tongue twister to his next door neighbour who repeats it to his next door neighbour until it gets to the last child who calls it out loud. By this time the original has been turned into complete nonsense which for some reason children find hugely amusing.

Treasure Hunts with rhyming clues can be played indoors or out as can *Sardines* in which you join the hider in the hiding place once you locate him.

PLAYING IN THE GARDEN

On warm days it is nicer to arrange for the children to paint outside in the garden. One of the advantages of this is that you needn't worry so much about mess and spillage because you can hose your charges down if things become serious. Let them collect items such as flowers, leaves and grass to use for making pictures or for floating in a bowl of water to mix their fragrances.

If the weather is especially hot, try to provide something to paddle in. It doesn't have to be a proper pool; any large container will do. Careful supervision is necessary, however, because children can drown even in shallow water. Provide them with plastic cups and a sieve so they can experiment with pouring water, and also a variety of things which will sink and float: a pebble and a cork, for instance. A container of liquid for making bubbles will provide a great deal of entertainment. When the mixture is running low, you can pad it out by adding washing-up liquid and a little water.

Show them how to build a make-shift tent. All you need is a couple of chairs placed back to back with a large space in the middle and a blanket or sheet over the top. Providing a picnic lunch under it can complete the fun.

If you have a garden path, let the children decorate it with coloured chalk. Warn them in advance that they may have to wipe it away at the end of the day, depending on what the parents say. You could appease the children by offering to take a photograph of their handiwork if they still object to it being removed when the time comes.

OUTINGS

Keep in touch with children's activities and forthcoming events in your local area by regularly visiting libraries, community centres, museums or tourist bureaux. As well as play-schools for pre-school children, there may be special gym classes or a regular story-time at the local library where you can safely leave them for half an hour while you browse through the adult section in peace. Children are never too young to learn how to swim, so take your charge to the swimming-baths.

Get together with other au pairs or nannies you know and arrange picnics or visits to the zoo, fun-fairs, adventure playgrounds or the circus. Organise a few unusual outings that would appeal to children such as a visit to a toy factory or the local fire-brigade.

Take advantage of what the particular country you're living in has on offer, whether it be sunshine and beaches, or snow and ice for skating parties and toboggan rides. Remember, the more effort you are prepared to invest in play-time, the more job satisfaction you will reap in return.

Amusements While Travelling

Always take some snacks and cans of juice on long journeys with children since it's not always possible to eat meals at the usual time. A damp facecloth, some tissues and a spare carrier bag for containing any rubbish that is accumulated along the way, also come in handy.

Provide them with story books, puzzle books, children's tapes and board games designed for travel such as 'Travel Scrabble' which has a smaller board and magnetic pieces.

Here are some ideas for word games to keep them amused on boring car or

Amusements While Travelling

train journeys which are educational as well as fun. Take along some paper and pencils for scoring.

(1) Give each child a word to spell backwards. Each correct answer gets a point, and the first to earn ten points, wins. (Young children can spell the words in the usual way.)

(2) When travelling by car, call out a colour and the first child to point to another car of that shade wins a point.

(3) Each child starts out with ten points. During the next ten minutes or so, normal conversation takes place; only none of the children are allowed to say 'yes' or 'no', and if they do, they lose a point. The winner is the one who still has some points left after the others have lost theirs.

(4) Name a category (for example, animal, flower, fruit) and choose a letter from the alphabet. The children have to give the name of something in that category beginning with the appropriate letter.

(5) In the *Silence Game*, no one is supposed to speak and if they do, they lose a point. You can't expect children to play this for long, though, as they'll soon get bored, but it could give you five minutes peace and a chance to think of something else to play.

(6) *Twenty Questions.* Think of someone the children know well and then let them try to guess who it is by asking no more than twenty questions to which you can only answer yes or no. A more difficult variation on this is *Animal, Vegetable, Mineral,* where someone thinks of an object and tells the others whether it is animal, vegetable, mineral or abstract; as above, they have 20 questions to find out what it is.

(7) Give each child a sheet of paper, a pencil and a long word, for example, understanding'. They must then write down as many shorter words as they can from those letters. After five minutes the child with the most correct words wins.

(8) *I Spy With My Little Eye, something beginning with* ... Most nannies will remember this from their own childhood but in case you were deprived, here's how you play it. Think of an object within view of the child, but just give him the first letter. (The North American version uses colour, e.g. 'I spy with my little eye something that is yellow'.) He has to look around him and guess what the object could be.

(9) The *Geography Game* consists of naming any place in the world (continent, river, city, etc.) The children take it in turns to think of another place beginning with the last letter of the one that was named. Usually the one to win is the one who thinks up a place like Essex or Bordeaux.

(10) In the *Alphabet Game* everyone says a letter in turn and the first one to complete a word loses a life. (Three letter words don't count). If you add a letter and, when challenged, you cannot say what word the letters will spell when completed, you lose a life. In the more complicated version, you can add letters at the front as well as at the end.

(11) A fairly rowdy game which everyone in a car enjoys except the driver is *Bus Stop*. It is very simple and you just score one point for spotting a bus stop, two for a letter box and three for a telephone box. Whoever calls out 'bus stop!' etc. gets the points. If you call out the wrong one you lose points to the value of the wrong call. For some reason this game can be relied on to lead to some fearsome arguments.

Appendix 5

Embassies/Consulates

AUSTRALIA: Australia House, The Strand, London WC2B 4LA (0171-379 4334/0891 600333).
1601 Massachusetts Ave NW, Washington DC 20036-2273 (202-797-3000/3145).
AUSTRIA: 18 Belgrave Mews West, London SW1X 8HU (0171-235 3731).
3524 International Court NW, Washington DC 20008 (202-895-6767).
BELGIUM: 103 Eaton Square, London SW1W 9AB (0171-470 3700).
3330 Garfield St NW, Washington DC 20008 (202-333-6900).
CANADA: 38 Grosvenor St, London W1X 0AA (0171-258 6601).
501 Pennsylvania Ave, Washington DC 20001 (202-682-1740).
DENMARK: 55 Sloane St, London SW1X 9SR (0171-333 0200).
3200 White Haven St NW, Washington DC 20008 (202-234-4300).
FINLAND: 38 Chesham Place, London SW1X 8HW (0171-235 9531).
3216 New Mexico Ave NW, Washington DC 20016 (202-363-2430).
FRANCE: 21 Cromwell Road, London SW7 2DQ (0171-838 2000).
4101 Reservoir Road NW, Washington DC 20007 (202-944-6200/6215).
GERMANY: 23 Belgrave Square, London SW1X 8PZ (0171-824 1300).
4645 Reservoir Road NW, Washington DC 20007 (202-298-4000).
GREECE: 1A Holland Park, London W11 3TP (0171-221 6467).
2221 Massachusetts Ave NW, Washington DC 20008 (202-232-8222).
HUNGARY: 35b Eaton Place, London SW1X 8BY (0171-235 2664).
3910 Shoemaker St NW, Washington DC 20008 (202-362-6730).
ICELAND: 1 Eaton Terrace, London SW1W 8EY (0171-730 5131/2).
2022 Connecticut Ave NW, Washington DC 20008-6194 (202-265 6653).
IRELAND: 17 Grosvenor Place, London SW1X 7HR (0171-235 2171).
2234 Massachusetts Ave NW, Washington DC 20008 (202-462-3939).
ISRAEL: 15a Old Court Place, London W8 4QB (0171-957 9500).
3514 International Dr NW, Washington DC 20008-3099 (202-364-5500).
ITALY: 14 Three Kings Yard, Davies St, London W1Y 2EH (0171-629 8200).
1601 Fuller St NW, Washington DC 20009 (202-328-5500).
NETHERLANDS: 38 Hyde Park Gate, London SW7 5DP (0171-584 5040).
4200 Linnean Ave NW, Washington DC 20008 (202-244-5300).
NEW ZEALAND: New Zealand House, Haymarket, London SW1Y 4TE (0171-973 0366/0891 200288).
37 Observatory Circle NW, Washington DC 20008 (202-328-4848).
NORWAY: 25 Belgrave Square, London SW1X 8QD (0171-235 7151).
2820 34th St NW, Washington DC 20008-2799 (202-333-6000).
PORTUGAL: Silver City House, 62 Brompton Road, London SW3 1BJ (0171-581 8722/4).
2125 Kalorama Road NW, Washington DC 20008 (202-332-3307).
SOUTH AFRICA: South Africa House, Trafalgar Square, London WC2N 5DP (0171-839 2211).
3201 New Mexico Ave, Washington DC 20016 (202-966-1650).
SPAIN: 20 Draycott Place, London SW3 2SB (0171-581 5921).
2700 15th St NW, Washington DC 20009 (202-265-0190/1).
SWEDEN: 11 Montagu Place, London W1H 2AL (0171-914 6413).
Suite 1200, 600 New Hampshire Ave NW, Washington, DC 20037 (202-944-5600).
SWITZERLAND: 16/18 Montagu Place, London W1H 2BQ (0171-723 0701).
2900 Cathedral Ave NW, Washington DC 20008 (202-745-7900).
TURKEY: 43 Belgrave Square, London SW1X 8PA (0171-235 5252/3/4).
1714 Massachusetts Ave NW, Washington DC 20036 (202-659-0742).
UK: 19 Observatory Circle NW, Washington DC 20008 (202-986-0205).
USA: 5 Upper Grosvenor St, London W1A 2JB (0891 200290).

Appendix 6

Currency Conversion Chart

COUNTRY	£1	US$1
Australia	A$2.08	A$1.28
Austria	19.3 schillings	11.9 schillings
Belgium/Luxembourg	56 francs	35 francs
Canada	C$2.25	C$1.37
Czech Republic	49 koruna	30 koruna
Denmark	10 kroner	6 kroner
Finland	8.3 markka	5.1 markka
France	9.25 franc	5.7 franc
Germany	2.7 Deutsch Mark/DM	1.7 Deutsch Mark
Greece	436 drachma	270 drachma
Hong Kong	12.5 HK dollar	7.7 HK dollar
Hungary	291 forint	180 forint
Iceland	115 krona	71 krona
Ireland	1.06 punt	0.65 punt
Israel	5.5 shekel	3.4 shekel
Italy	2,700 lira	1,675 lira
Netherlands	3 guilder	1.9 guilder
New Zealand	NZ$2.39	NZ$1.41
Norway	11.4 krone	7 krone
Poland	5 zloty	3.1 zloty
Portugal	275 escudo	170 escudo
South Africa	7.2 rand	4.4 rand
Spain	232 peseta	143 peseta
Sweden	12.4 krona	7.6 krona
Switzerland	2.3 franc	1.43 franc
Turkey	221,000 lira	136,000 lira
United Kingdom	—	0.62 pound
USA	1.62 dollar	—

Vacation Work publish:

	Paperback	Hardback
The Directory of Summer Jobs Abroad	£7.99	£12.99
The Directory of Summer Jobs in Britain	£7.99	£12.99
Adventure Holidays	£6.99	£11.99
The Teenager's Vacation Guide to Work, Study & Adventure	£6.95	£9.95
Work Your Way Around the World	£10.99	£16.99
Working in Tourism — The UK, Europe & Beyond	£9.99	£15.99
Kibbutz Volunteer	£7.99	£12.99
Working on Cruise Ships	£8.99	£12.99
Teaching English Abroad	£10.99	£15.99
The Au Pair & Nanny's Guide to Working Abroad	£9.99	£14.99
Working in Ski Resorts — Europe & North America	£8.95	£14.95
Working with the Environment	£9.99	£15.99
Health Professionals Abroad	£9.99	£15.99
The Directory of Jobs and Careers Abroad	£10.99	£16.99
The International Directory of Voluntary Work	£9.99	£15.99
The Directory of Work & Study in Developing Countries	£8.99	£10.99
Live & Work in France	£8.95	£14.95
Live & Work in Australia & New Zealand	£8.95	£14.95
Live & Work in Scandinavia	£8.95	£14.95
Live & Work in USA & Canada	£8.95	£14.95
Live & Work in Spain & Portugal	£8.95	£11.95
Live & Work in Belgium, The Netherlands & Luxembourg	£8.95	–
Live & Work in Germany	£8.95	–
Live & Work in Italy	£7.95	–
Travellers Survival Kit: Lebanon	£9.99	–
Travellers Survival Kit: South Africa	£9.99	–
Travellers Survival Kit: India	£9.99	–
Travellers Survival Kit: Russia & the Republics	£9.95	–
Travellers Survival Kit: Western Europe	£8.95	–
Travellers Survival Kit: Eastern Europe	£9.95	–
Travellers Survival Kit: South America	£12.95	–
Travellers Survival Kit: Central America	£8.95	–
Travellers Survival Kit: Cuba	£9.99	–
Travellers Survival Kit: USA & Canada	£9.95	–
Travellers Survival Kit to the East	£6.95	–
Travellers Survival Kit: Australia & New Zealand	£9.99	–
Hitch-hikers' Manual Britain	£3.95	–
Europe — Manual for Hitch-hikers	£4.95	–

Distributors of:

Summer Jobs USA	£10.99	–
Internships (On-the-Job Training Opportunities in the USA)	£15.99	–
Sports Scholarships in the USA	£12.99	–
The Directory of College Accommodations USA	£5.95	–
Making it in Japan	£8.95	–

**Vacation Work Publications, 9 Park End Street, Oxford OX1 1HJ
(Tel 01865-241978. Fax 01865-790885)**